ISBN 978-0-266-17910-8
PIBN 10173497

LORD BACON'S WORKS,

VOLUME THE THIRTEENTH.

CONTAINING

LETTERS, MISCELLANIES, AND LAW TRACTS.

THE WORKS

OF

FRANCIS BACON,

Lord Chancellor of England.

A NEW EDITION:

BY

BASIL MONTAGU, ESQ.

VOL. XIII.

LONDON:
WILLIAM PICKERING.
MDCCCXXXI.

C. Whittingham, Tooks Court,
Chancery Lane.

LETTERS.

LETTER FROM THE LAMBETH LIBRARY CONTINUED.

Translation of the Latin Letter to Count Gondomar.*

EXCELLENT COUNT,

I DO first, as I ought, congratulate with you your new honour, which, though great in itself, it is much greater because it was given you upon so noble a ground. The repair of Mr. Matthew, my true friend as your lordship well knoweth, into these parts, makes me call to mind those great and singular favours, which upon your noble visits, which both in field and town, by his means and appointment, your Lordship vouchsafed me a little before your departure, and the great endeavours which your lordship used both with the King and the Marquis for my fortunes. At that time if one had whispered me in the ear and said, stay these things; England is a cold country; defer them till the Prince of Wales, and the Marquis of Buckingham, and the Count Gondomar meet in Spain, where fruits ripen faster, I should have smiled at it. But since your lordship hath had power to work these miracles in a public fortune, it is a much less matter for you to work a miracle† in the fortune of a private friend. And since your lordship hath power, and I have faith, a miracle is soon wrought if your lordship think it worth the stretching forth your noble hand. Having written so lately to your lordship, I shorten this letter, only desiring your lordship to give Mr. Matthew the same freedom to propound or advise with your lordship concerning my business, as heretofore you have vouchsafed; and resting

---

* MS. Gibson, Lambeth Lib. 936. fol. 184. d. See the original, vol. xii. 443.

† The remainder is in Lord Bacon's hand.

To his very loving Friends, the Parishioners and Feoffees for the Poor of the Parish of St. Alldats, in Oxford.

After my hearty commendations, I send ou here inclosed a copy of an order made by the late Lord Chancellor, my predecessor, in the cause depending in Chancery between Edmond Blyth, plaintiff, against John Phillips and others, defendants, and formerly directed by his lordship's letters unto you, to show cause why a decree made by commissioners for charitable purposes should not be confirmed by decree of the Chancery, which hitherto you have not done; and, therefore, it was desired that it might be decreed accordingly, which I have forborne to do, but have thought fit to recontinue the said order, and to renew the said letters unto you, requiring you to show good cause by the second return of the next term, why the commissioners' decree should not be confirmed, otherwise the plaintiff is to have his lease decreed as he hath desired. So wishing you due respect herein, I bid you farewell,

Your loving Friend,

From York House, this 13th of February, 1619.

FR. VERULAM.

LETTERS FROM MALLET.

To the Lord Viscount Villiers.

It may please your Lordship,

I pray let his majesty understand, that although my Lord Chancellor's answer, touching the dismission of the Farmer's cause, was full of respect and duty, yet I would be glad to avoid an express signification from his majesty, if his majesty may otherwise have his end. And therefore I have thought of a course, that a motion be made in open court, and that thereupon my lord move a compromise to some to be named on either part, with bond to stand to their award. And as I find this to be agreeable to my Lord Chancellor's disposition, so I do not find but the Farmers and the other party are willing enough towards it. And therefore his majesty may be pleased to forbear any other letter or message touching that business. God ever keep your lordship.

Your Lordship's true and most devoted Servant,

Jan. 23, 1616.

FR. BACON.

To the Earl of Buckingham.

My very good Lord,

I know your lordship hath a special care of any thing that concerneth the Queen. She was entered into dislike of her solicitor, this bearer Mr. Lowder, and resolute in it. To serve, and not to please, is no man's condition. Therefore upon knowledge of her pleasure he was willing to part with his place, upon hopes not to be destituted, but to be preferred to one of the Barons places in Ireland. I pray move the King for him, and let his majesty know from me that I think (howsoever he pleased not here) he is fit to do his majesty service in that place; he is grave and formal, which is somewhat there, and sufficient enough for that place. The Queen hath made Mr. Hackwell her solicitor, who hath for a long time taken much pains in her business, wherein she hath done well. He was an opposite in parliament, as Jones was, that the King hath made Chief Justice of Ireland. But I hold it no ill counsel to join, or to remove such men. God preserve and prosper you.

Your true and devoted Friend and Servant,

Whitehall, May 25, 1617. FR. BACON, C. S.

To the Lord Chancellor.

My most honourable Lord,

I acquainted his majesty with your letter, at the first opportunity after I received it, who was very well pleased with that account of your careful and speedy dispatch of businesses, &c.

Yours, &c.

Greenwich, May 13, 1619. G. BUCKINGHAM.

P.S. Your business had been done before this, but I knew not whether you would have the attorney or solicitor to draw it.

To my very loving friends Sir Thomas Leigh and Sir Thomas Puckering, Knights and Baronets.

After my hearty commendations, being informed by the petition of Mr. Thomas Porten, a poor Yorkshireman, of a heavy accident by fire, whereby his house, his wife, and a child, together with all his goods, were utterly burnt and consumed; which misfortune the petitioner suggests, with much eagerness, was occasioned by the wicked practices and conjurations of one John Clarkson of Knowington, in the county of Warwick, and his daughter, persons of a wandering condition; affirming, for instance, that one Mr. Hailes of Warwick did take from the said Clarkson certain books of conjuration and witchcraft. That the truth of the matter may be rightly known, and that Clarkson and his daughter, if there be ground for it, may answer the law according to the merit of so heinous a fact, I have thought good to wish and desire you to send for Clarkson, and his daughter; and as upon due examination you shall find cause, to take orders for their forthcoming, and answering of the matter at the next assize for the county of York; and also to confer with Mr. Hailes, whether he took from the said Clarkson any such book of conjuration, as the petitioner pretends he did, and to see them in safe custody. Whereupon I desire to be certified how you find the matter; and your doing thereupon. So not doubting of your special care and diligence herein, I bid you heartily farewell, and rest

Your very loving Friend,
York House, May 15, 1619. FR. VERULAM. Canc.

To the Marquis of Buckingham.

My very good Lord,

Your lordship I know, and the King both, might think me very unworthy of that I have been, or that I am, if I should not by all means desire to be freed from the restraint which debarreth my approach to his majesty's person, which I ever so much loved and admired; and severeth me likewise from all conference with your lordship, which is my second comfort. Nevertheless, if it be conceived that it may be matter of inconvenience, or envy, my particular respects must give place; only in regard of my present urgent occasions, to take some present order for the debts that press me most. I have petitioned his majesty to give me leave to stay at London till the last of July; and then I will dispose of my abode according to the sentence. I have sent to the Prince to join with you in it, for though the matter seem small, yet it importeth me much. God prosper you.

Your Lordship's true Servant,
June 20, 1621. FR. ST. ALBAN.

To the Marquis of Buckingham.

My very good Lord,

I thank God I am come very well to Gorhambury, whereof I thought your lordship would be glad to hear sometimes. My lord, I wish myself by you in this stirring world, not for any love to place or business, for that is almost gone with me, but for my love to yourself, which can never cease in

Your Lordship's most obliged Friend and true Servant,

FR. ST. ALBAN.

Being now out of use, and out of sight, I recommend myself to your lordship's love and favour, to maintain me in his majesty's grace and good intention.

To the Duke of Buckingham.

Excellent Lord,

I have received the warrant, not for land but for the money, which if it may be speedily served, is sure the better; for this I humbly kiss your grace's hands. But because the exchequer is thought to be somewhat barren, although I have good affiance of Mr. Chancellor, yet I hold it very essential, and therein I most humbly pray your grace's favour, that you would be pleased by your letter to recommend to Mr. Chancellor the speedy issuing of the money by this warrant, as a business whereof your grace hath an especial care; the rather for that I understand from him, there be some other warrants for money to private suitors at this time on foot. But your grace may be pleased to remember this difference, that the other are mere gifts; this of mine is a bargain, with an advance only.

I most humbly pray your grace likewise to present my most humble thanks to his majesty. God ever guide you by the hand. I always rest

Your faithful and more and more obliged Servant,

Gray's Inn, this 17th of November, 1624. FR. ST. ALBAN.

I most humbly thank your grace for your grace's favour to my honest deserving servant.

To the Lord St. Alban.

My noble Lord,

The hearty affection I have borne to your person and service, hath made me ambitious to be a messenger of good news to you, and an eschewer of ill; this hath been the true reason why I have been thus long in answering you, not any negligence in your discreet modest servant, you sent with your letter, nor his who now returns you this answer, ofttimes given me by your master and mine; who though by this may seem not to satisfy your desert and expectation, yet, take the word of a friend, who will never fail you, hath a tender care of you, full of a fresh memory of your by-past service. His majesty is but for the present, he says, able to yield unto the three years' advance, which if you please to accept, you are not hereafter the farther off from obtaining some better testimony of his favour, worthier both of him and you, though it can never be answerable to what my heart wishes you, as

Your Lordship's humble Servant,

G. BUCKINGHAM.

LETTERS FROM STEPHENS.

To the King.

It may please your most excellent Majesty,

According to your commandment, I send enclosed the Preface to the Patent of Creation of Sir George Villiers. I have not used any glaring terms, but drawn it according to your majesty's instructions, and the note which thereupon I framed, and your majesty allowed, with some additions, which I have inserted. But I hope your majesty will be pleased to correct and perfect it. Your majesty will be also pleased to remember, that if the creation shall be at Roughford, your pleasure and this draught be speedily returned; for it will ask a sending of the bill for your majesty's signature, and a sending back of the same to pass the seals, and a sending thereupon of the patent itself: so it must be twice sent up and down before the day. God evermore preserve your majesty.

Your Majesty's most devoted and most bounden Servant,

July 28, 1616. FR. BACON.

To Sir Francis Bacon, his Majesty's Attorney General.

Sir,

I have acquainted his majesty with your letter, and the other papers enclosed, who liketh very well of the course you purpose touching the manifest to be published of Bertram's fact, and will have you, according to your own motion, advise with my Lord Chancellor of the manner of it.

His majesty's pleasure likewise is, that according to the declaration he made before the lords of his council at Whitehall, touching the review of my Lord Coke's Reports, you draw a warrant ready for his signature, directed to those judges whom he then named to that effect, and send it speedily to him to be signed, that there may be a despatch of that business before the end of the term. And so I rest

Your faithful Friend at command,

Newmarket, Nov. 19, 1616. GEORGE VILLIERS.

To the Earl of Buckingham.

My singular good Lord,

When I heard here your lordship was dead, I thought I had lived too long. That was (to tell your lordship truly) the state of my mind upon that report. Since, I hear it was an idle mistaking of my Lord Evers for my Lord Villiers: God's name be blessed, that you are alive to do infinite good, and not so much as sick or ill disposed for any thing I now hear.

I have resigned the Prince's seal, and my Lord Hobart is placed. I made the Prince laugh, when I told him I resigned it with more comfort than I received it; he understanding me that I had changed for a better: but after I had given him that thought, I turned it upon this, that I left his state and business in good case, whereof I gave him a particular account.

The Queen calleth upon me for the matter of her house, wherein your lordship and my Lord Chamberlain and I dealt, and received his majesty's direction, so that I shall prepare a warrant first to my Lord Treasurer and Mr. Chancellor (for that is the right way) to advise how to settle it by assignment, in case she survive his majesty, which I hope in God she shall not.

Her desire was expressly and of herself, that when I had prepared a warrant to be sent to his majesty, I should send it by your lordship's hands.

We sit in council, that is all I can yet say. Sir John Denham is not come, upon whose coming the King shall have account of our consultations touching Ireland, which we cannot conclude, till we have spoken with him. God ever preserve and prosper you.

It grieveth me much that I cannot hear enough of his majesty's good disposition of health, and his pleasures, and other ordinary occurrences of his journey: I pray your Lordship will direct Mr. Packer to write to me sometime of matters of that kind. I have made the like request to Sir Edward Villiers, by whom I write this present, to whose good affection I think myself beholden, as I do also esteem him much for his good parts, besides his nearness to your lordship, which bindeth me above all.

Your Lordship's most faithful
and devoted Friend and Servant,
April 7, 1617. FR. BACON, C. S.

To the Earl of Buckingham.

My singular good Lord,

I pray your lordship to deliver to his majesty the inclosed.

I send your lordship also the warrant to my Lord Treasurer and Mr. Chancellor of the Exchequer for the Queen's House,* it is to come again to the King, when the bill is drawn for the letters patents; for this is only the warrant to be signed by his majesty.

I asked the Queen whether she would write to your lordship about it; her answer was very modest and discreet, that because it proceeded wholly from his majesty's kindness and goodness, who had referred it, it was not so fit for her to write to your lordship for the dispatch of it, but she desired me to thank your lordship for your former care of it, and to desire you to continue it: and withal she desireth your lordship not to press his majesty in it, but to take his best times. This answer (because I like it so well) I write to you at large, for other matters I will write by the next. God ever prosper you and preserve you.

Your Lordship's most faithful
and devoted Friend and Servant,
London, April 19, 1617. FR. BACON, C. S.

To the Lord Keeper.

My honoured Lord,

I have acquainted his majesty with your letter, and the papers that came inclosed, who is exceedingly well satisfied with that account you have given him therein, especially with the speech you made at the taking of your place in the Chancery. Whereby his majesty perceiveth that you have not only given proof how well you understand the place of a Chancellor, but done him much right also, in

* Somerset House.

giving notice unto those that were present, that you had received such instructions from his majesty; whose honour will be so much the greater, in that all men will acknowledge the sufficiency and worthiness of his majesty's choice, in preferring a man of such abilities to that place, which, besides, cannot but be a great advancement and furtherance to his service. And I can assure your lordship, that his majesty was never so well pleased as he is with this account you have given him of this passage. Thus, with the remembrance of my service, I rest

Your Lordship's ever at command,

Edinburgh, May 18, 1617. G. BUCKINGHAM.

To the Lord Keeper.

My honourable Lord,

His majesty commandeth me to write to your lordship, that he wonders your hand being at that letter of the lords of the council, which he saith is a very blunt one: you have not besides sent him some advice of your own, his majesty having only intrusted you to speak with Sir Lionel Cranfield about his estate.

Your Lordship's faithful Friend and Servant,

Newmarket, Nov. 19, 1617. G. BUCKINGHAM.

To the Earl of Buckingham.

My Lord,

How well I wish to Sir Gilbert Haughton, himself I dare say doth not doubt, partly out of mine own affection, and chiefly for your lordship's affection towards him, which to me is more than mine own. That the King should make bargains of hope, when his treasure sufficeth not for his own charge, I may not advise for my dearest friends; for I am nailed to the King's estate. But two things I shall assent unto; the one, that if the King can redeem his works without charge of officers, I shall be glad of it, both for the gentleman's sake, and because I perceive the uniting of the alum works in the King's hand is best; the other, that if his majesty be pleased to signify his pleasure to my Lord Treasurer and me, that there be no forfeiture taken by Banister till the King shall advise of this bargain, we will hold him to it. God preserve and prosper your lordship. Your lordship, I think, perceiveth both by scribbling and cursory inditing, that I write in straits of business.

Your Lordship's true Friend and devoted Servant,

York House, this 24th of Nov. 1617. FR. BACON, C. S.

To the King.

May it please your Majesty,

Being yesterday assembled in council to proceed in the course we had begun for retrenchment of your majesty's expenses; we received your princely letters, whereby we are directed to send to your majesty the names of the officers of the exchequer, custom-house, and auditors, out of which you purpose to make choice of some to be sub-committed to handle the mechanic and laborious part of that which your majesty had appointed to our care; we have according to our duty sent unto your majesty the names of the several officers of your majesty in those places, to be ordered as your wisdom shall think best to direct. But withal, we thought it appurtenant to our duties to inform your majesty how far we have proceeded in the several heads of retrenchments by your majesty at your departure committed unto us, that when you know in what estate our labours are, your judgment may the better direct any further course, as shall be meet.

The matter of the household, was by us, some days since, committed peremptorily to the officers of the house, as matter of commandment from your majesty, and of duty in them, to reduce the expense of your house to a limited charge of fifty thousand pounds by the year, besides the benefit of the compositions; and they have ever since painfully, as we are informed, travailed in it, and will be ready on Sunday next, which was the day given them, to present some models of retrenchments of divers kinds, all aiming at your majesty's service.

In the point of pensions we have made a beginning, by suspending some wholly for a time, and of others of a third part; in which course we are still going on, until we make it fit to be presented to your majesty; in like manner the Lord Chamberlain, and the Lord Hay, did yesterday report unto us, what their travail had ordered in the wardrobe; and, although some doubt did arise unto us, whether your majesty's letters intended a stay of our labours, until you had made choice of the sub-committee intended by you, yet, presuming that such a course by sub-committee was purposed rather for a furtherance than let to that work, we did resolve to go on still, till your majesty's further directions shall come unto us; and then, according to our duty, we will proceed as we shall be by your majesty commanded; in the mean time, we thought it our duty to inform your majesty of what we have done, that neither your majesty may conceive that we have been negligent in those things which were committed unto us, nor your directions by your late letters hinder or cast back that which is already so far proceeded in. And, so humbly kissing your royal hands, and praying to the Almighty for your long and happy reign over us, we rest

Your Majesty's most humble and obedient
Subjects and Servants,

G. Cant.	F. Bacon, C. S.	T. Suffolk,
E. Worcester,	Lennox,	Pembroke,
T. Arundel,	W. Wallingford,	L. Elie[n],
E. Wotton,	James Hay,	T. Edmondes,
T. Lake,	Jul. Cæsar,	Edw. Coke,
Dec. 5, 1617.		C. Edmondes.

To the Lord Chancellor.

My honourable Lord,

I have received your lordship's letters, wherein I see the continuance of your love and respect to me, in any thing I write to you of, for which I give your lordship many thanks, desiring nothing for any man but what you shall find just and convenient to pass. I am very glad to understand that there is so good hope of Sir Gilbert Houghton's business, which I must needs ascribe to your lordship's great favour toward him for my sake, which I will ever acknowledge. If his majesty at any time speak of the Lord Clifton's business, I will answer according to that your lordship hath written, &c.

Your Lordship's faithful Servant,
G. Buckingham.

Newmarket, the last of January, 1617.

To the Lord Chancellor.

My honourable Lord,

I have acquainted his majesty with your letter to me, and delivered likewise to him the letter and other things directed to his majesty, who hath commanded me to return this answer to them all.

First, for your memorial of your charge to the judges, he liketh it so well, that he findeth nothing either to be added or diminished; and was so well satisfied therewith, that he accounteth it needless to read the other papers, but sealed them up again, and sendeth them back to your lordship without reading them. Only in the point of recusants his majesty is of the quite contrary opinion to you; for though he would not by any means have a more severe course held than his laws appoint in that case, yet since the many reasons why, there should be no mitigation above that which his laws have enacted, and his own conscience telleth him to be fit. As first, the papists in his kingdom have taken such heart upon the commission given to Sir John Digby, touching the match with Spain, that they have sent copies thereof privately up and down, and are so lifted up in their hopes of what they desire, that his majesty cannot but take a more severe course, as far as by his laws he may, than hitherto he hath done. Besides, when they shall see a harder hand carried toward them than hath been accustomed, his majesty assureth himself they will employ all their means to further the match, in hope of mitigating of that severity when it shall be accomplished. And though these reasons were not, his majesty would account it a baseness in a prince to show such a desire of the match, as to slack any thing in his course of government, much more in propagation of the religion he professeth, for fear of giving hindrance to the match thereby. And so with many thanks for your favours to my brother in his business, I rest

Your Lordship's faithful Servant,

Newmarket, Feb. 8, 1617. G. BUCKINGHAM.

To the Marquis of Buckingham.

My very good Lord,

We have sat once upon the commission of treasure to no ill purpose, as may appear by the account inclosed; wherein his majesty will find no preposterous issue of treasure. Mr. Chancellor imagines well; Coke seeks, and beats over, as well where it is not, as where it is; Secretary Naunton forgets nothing. I will look to bow things to the true ends. God bless and prosper his majesty and yourself.

Your Lordship's most obliged Friend
and faithful Servant,

July 25, 1618. FR. VERULAM, Canc.

To the Marquis of Buckingham.

My very good Lord,

What passed in your lordship's presence your lordship can tell, touching the navy. The morrow following we concluded in approbation of the books, save in one point, touching the number convenient for manning the ships, wherein the number allowed by the commissioners had, in my judgment, a little of the merchant; for to measure by so many as were above dead pays, is no good argument. For the abuse of dead pays is to be amended, and not the necessary number abated. In this his majesty may fall upon a middle proportion between that of the commissioners and that of the officers.

It were good, now the three books which we have appointed to be ingrossed into one ledger book are affirmed, there were a short book of his majesty's royal directions, and orders thereupon, extracted.

For the commission of the treasury, I persuade myself, they are of the first hours that have been well spent in that kind. We have put those particulars whereof his majesty gave us charge into a way.

Bingley's information will be to good purpose, and we find another of like nature revealed to Mr. Secretary and myself. God ever prosper you.

Your Lordship's most obliged Friend
and faithful Servant,
October 9, 1618. FR. VERULAM, Canc.

To the Lord Chancellor.

My Lord,

I have acquainted his majesty with your letter, who giveth you thanks for your advice to communicate the business of the Dutchmen to the commissioners of the treasury, which his majesty was before purposed to refer to them, as it concerns his treasure, for the carriage of it; and to your lordship and the rest named in your letter, for the relation it hath to the law. For the proposers of the suit, his majesty intendeth only to reward their pains as may stand with his service and his princely disposition, but to preserve the main benefit himself: all that his majesty would have your lordship to do for the present, is to take order about the writ of *ne exeant Regnum*, to advise with his learned counsel what course is to be taken, and if by a warrant from his majesty, that your lordship send him a warrant to be signed, which shall be returned with all speed. Of other things his majesty thinketh it will be time enough to speak at his return to London. In the mean time I rest

Your Lordship's faithful Friend and Servant,
Hinchenbroke, Oct. 21, 1618. G. BUCKINGHAM.

To the Marquis of Buckingham.

My very good Lord,

I have this morning received the petty roll for the sheriffs. I received also the papers exhibited by Sir Miles Fleetwood, which I will use to his majesty's best service, and thereupon give account to his majesty when time serveth.

My care, which is not dormant, touching his majesty's service, specially that of treasure (which is now *summa summarum*), maketh me propound to his majesty a matter, which, God is my witness, I do without contemplation of friend or end, but *animo recto*.

If Sir Edward Coke continue sick, or keep in, I fear his majesty's service will languish too, in those things which touch upon law; as the calling in debts, recusants, alienations, defalcations, &c. And this is most certain, that in these new diligences, if the first beginning cool, all will go back to the old bias. Therefore it may please his majesty to think of it, whether there will not be a kind of necessity to add my Lord Chief Justice of England to the commissioners of treasure. This I move only to the King and your lordship, otherwise it is a thing *ex non entibus*. God preserve and prosper you.

Your Lordship's most faithful Servant,

From the Star Chamber, Nov. 25, 1618. FR. VERULAM, Canc.

I forget not Tufton's cause. All things stay, and precedents are in search.

To the King.*

May it please your most excellent Majesty,

According to your majesty's pleasure, signified to us by the Lord Marquis Buckingham, we have considered of the fitness and conveniency of the gold and silver thread business, as also the profit that may accrue unto your majesty.

We are all of opinion that it is convenient that the same should be settled, having been brought hither at the great charge of your majesty's now agents, and being a means to set many of your poor subjects on work; and to this purpose there was a former certificate to your majesty from some of us with others.

---

* October 4, 1618. The Marquis of Buckingham writes from Theobalds to the Lord Chancellor, that the King being desirous to be satisfied of the gold and silver thread business, would have his lordship consult the Lord Chief Justice, and the Attorney and Solicitor General therein.

And for the profit that will arise, we see no cause to doubt; but do conceive apparent likelihood, that it will redound much to your majesty's profit, which we esteem may be at the least ten thousand pounds by the year; and therefore, in a business of such benefit to your majesty, it were good it were settled with all convenient speed, by all lawful means that may be thought of; which, notwithstanding, we most humbly leave to your majesty's highest wisdom.

Your Majesty's most humble and faithful Servants,

FR. VERULAM, Canc.
H. MONTAGU,
HENRY YELVERTON.

To the Marquis of Buckingham.

My very good Lord,

If I should use the Count de Gondomar's action, I should first lay your last letter to my mouth, in token of thanks, and then to my heart in token of contentment, and then to my forehead in token of a perpetual remembrance.

I send now to know how his majesty doth after his remove, and to give you account, that yesterday was a day of motions in the Chancery. This day was a day of motions in the Star Chamber, and it was my hap to clear the bar, that no man was left to move any thing, which my lords were pleased to note they never saw before. To-morrow is a sealing day; Thursday is the funeral day; so that I pray your lordship to direct me whether I shall attend his majesty Friday or Saturday. Friday hath some relics of business, and the commissioners of treasure have appointed to meet; but to see his majesty is to me above all.

I have set down, *de bene esse*, Suffolk's cause, the third sitting next term; if the wind suffer the commission of Ireland to be sped. I ever more and more rest

Your Lordship's most obliged Friend
and faithful Servant,

This 11th of May, 1619. FR. VERULAM, Canc.

To the Lord Chancellor.

My honourable Lord,

Your lordship hath sent so good news to his majesty that I could have wished you had been the reporter of it yourself; but seeing you came not, I cannot but give you thanks for employing me in the delivering of that which pleased his majesty so well, whereof he will put your lordship in mind when he seeth you. I am glad we are come so near together, and hoping to see you at Windsor, I rest

Your Lordship's faithful Friend and Servant,

G. BUCKINGHAM.

August 29th, 1619.

To the Lord Chancellor.

My honourable Lord,

As I was reading your lordship's letter, his majesty came, and took it out of my hands, when he knew from whom it came, before I could read the paper inclosed, and told me that you had done like a wise counsellor; first setting down the state of the question, and then propounding the difficulties, the rest being to be done in its own time.

I am glad of this occasion of writing to your lordship, that I may now let your lordship understand his majesty's good conceit and acceptation of your service, upon your discourse with him at Windsor; which, though I heard not myself, yet I heard his majesty much commend it, both for the method and the affection you showed therein to his affairs, in such earnest manner, as if you made it your only study and care to advance his majesty's service. And so I rest

Your Lordship's faithful Friend and Servant,

G. BUCKINGHAM.

Wanstead, September 9th, 1619.

To the Lord Chancellor.

My honourable Lord,

I have received your letters by both your servants, and have acquainted his majesty with them, who is exceedingly pleased with the course you have held in the Earl of Suffolk's business, and holdeth himself so much the more beholden to you, because you sent the letter of your own motion, without order or consent of the lords, whereby his majesty is not tied to an answer. His majesty hath understood by many how worthily your lordship hath carried yourself both in this and the Dutch business; for which he hath commanded me to give you thanks in his name; and seeth your care to be so great in all things that concern his service, that he cannot but much rejoice in the trust of such a servant, which is no less comfort to

Your Lordship's faithful Friend and Servant,

G. BUCKINGHAM.

Royston, October 23d, 1619.

Indorsed—*On my Lord of Bucks, inclosing a Letter of Submission from my Lord of Suffolk.*

To the Lord Chancellor.

My honourable Lord,

The news of this victory hath so well pleased his majesty, that he giveth thanks to all; and I, among the rest, who had no other part but the delivering of your letter, had my part of his good acceptation, which he would have rewarded after the Roman fashion with every man a garland, if it had been now in use; but after the fashion of his gracious goodness, he giveth your lordship thanks; and would have you deliver the like, in his majesty's name, to Sir Edward Coke and the judges. Your news, which came the first, gave his majesty a very good breakfast, and I hope his health will be the better after it.

Your Lordship's faithful Friend and Servant,

G. BUCKINGHAM.

October 14th, 1619.

Indorsed—*Thanks on the Success in the* Ore Tenus *against the Dutch.*

To the Marquis of Buckingham.

My very good Lord,

I send the submission of Sir Thomas Laque, drawn in such form as, upon a meeting with me of the chief justices and the learned counsel, was conceived agreeable to his majesty's meaning and directions; yet, lest we should err, we thought good to send it to his majesty. It is to be returned with speed, or else there will be no day in court to make it. God bless and prosper you. I rest

Your Lordship's most obliged Friend
and faithful Servant,

November 28th, 1619. FR. VERULAM, Canc.

To the Lord Chancellor.

My honourable Lord,

I have acquainted his majesty with your lordship's letter, and with the submission you sent drawn for Sir Thomas Lake, which his majesty liketh well, and, because he served him in so honourable a place, is graciously pleased that he maketh submission in writing, so that my Lady of Exeter be contented and the lords, whom his majesty would have you acquaint therewith. And so I rest

Your Lordship's faithful Friend and Servant,

G. BUCKINGHAM.

Newmarket, 29th Nov. 1619.

To the Marquis of Buckingham.

My very good Lord,

We sentence to-morrow, but I write to-day, because I would not leave the King in suspense.

I shall write not so good news as I would, but better than I expected.

We met amongst ourselves to-day, which I find was necessary more than convenient. I gave aim that the meeting was not to give a privie verdict, or to determine what was a good proof or not a good proof, nor who was guilty or not guilty, but only to think of some fit proportion of the fines, that there might be less distraction in the sentence, in a cause so scattered; some would have entered into the matter itself, but I made it good and kept them from it.

I perceive the old defendants will be censured as well as the new (which was the goal), and I am persuaded the King will have a great deal of honour of the cause. Their fines will be moderate, but far from contemptible. The attorney did very well to-day; I perceive he is a better pleader than a director, and more eloquent than considerate.

Little thinks the King what ado I have here, but I am sure I acquit my trust. To-morrow I will write particularly. God ever preserve you.

Your Lordship's most obliged Friend
and faithful Servant,
FR. VERULAM, Canc.

Tuesday Afternoon,
this 7th December, 1619.

To the Lord Chancellor.

My Lord,

His majesty having seen in this great business your exceeding care and diligence in his service by the effect which hath followed thereupon, hath commanded me to give you many thanks in his name, and to tell you that he seeth you play the part of all in all, &c.

Yours, &c.
G. BUCKINGHAM.

Newmarket,
the 10th December, 1619.

Endorsed—*In the Dutch Cause.*

To the Marquis of Buckingham.

My very good Lord,

To keep form, I have written immediately to his majesty of Justice Croke's death, and send your lordship the letter open, wishing time were not lost. God preserve and prosper you.

Your Lordship's ever,
FR. VERULAM, Canc.

January 24th, 1619.

To the Marquis of Buckingham.

My very good Lord,

I doubt not but Sir Giles Montpesson advertiseth your lordship how our revenue business proceeds. I would his majesty had rested upon the first names; for the additionals, specially the exchequer man, doth not only weaken the matter, but weakeneth my forces in it, he being thought to have been brought in across. But I go on and hope good service will be done.

For the commissions to be published in the Star-Chamber, for which it pleaseth his majesty to give me special thanks, I will have special care of them in time. God ever prosper you.

Your Lordship's most obliged Friend
and faithful Servant,

February 10th, 1619. FR. VERULAM, Canc.

To the Marquis of Buckingham.

My very good Lord,

One gave me a very good precept for the stone; that I should think of it most when I feel it least. This I apply to the King's business, which surely I revolve most when I am least in action, whereof, at my attendance, I will give his majesty such account as can proceed from my poor and mean abilities, which as his majesty, out of grace, may think to be more than they are, so I, out of desire, may think sometime they can effect more than they can. But still it must be remembered, that the stringing of the harp, nor the tuning of it will not serve, except it be well played on from time to time.

If his majesty's business or commandments require it, I will attend him at Windsor, though I would be glad to be spared, because quick airs at this time of the year do affect me. At London, and so at Theobalds and Hampton Court, I will not fail, God willing, to wait upon his majesty. Meanwhile I am exceeding glad to hear his majesty hath been lusty and well this progress. Thus, much desiring to see your lordship, *cujus amor tantum mihi crescit in horas* (as the poet saith), I ever remain

Your Lordship's most obliged Friend
and faithful Servant,

Gorhambury,
this 30th August, 1620. FR. VERULAM, Canc.

To the Marquis of Buckingham.

My very good Lord,

The tobacco business is well settled in all points. For the coals, they that brought the offer to Secretary Calvert do very basely shrink from their words; but we are casting about to piece it and perfect it. The two goose quills, Maxwell and Alured, have been pulled, and they have made submissions in that kind which the board thought fit: for we would not do them the honour to require a recantation of their opinion, but an acknowledgment of their presumption.

His majesty doth very wisely (not showing much care or dreard to it) yet really to suppress this licentious course of talking and writing. My old Lord Burghley was wont to say, that the Frenchman when he hath talked he hath done; but the Englishman when he hath talked, he begins. It evaporateth malice and discontent in the one, and kindleth it in the other. And therefore upon some fit occasion I wish a more public example. The King's state, if I should now die and were opened, would be found at my heart, as Queen Mary said of Calais; we find additionals still, but the consumption goeth on. I pray God give his majesty resolution, passing by at once all impediments and less respects, to do that which may help it, before it be irremediable. God ever preserve and prosper your lordship.

Your Lordship's most obliged Friend
and faithful Servant,

July 23d, 1620. FR. VERULAM, Canc.

I have staid the thousand pounds set upon Englefield for his majesty, and given order for levying it.

To the Marquis of Buckingham.

My very good Lord,

I write now only a letter of thanks to his majesty, for that I hear, in my absence, he was pleased to express towards me (though unworthy) a great deal of grace and good opinion before his lords; which is much to my comfort, whereunto I must ever impute your lordship as accessary. I have also written to him what signification I received from Secretary Naunton of his majesty's will and pleasure, lest in so great a business there should be any mistaking.

The pain of my foot is gone, but the weakness doth a little remain, so as I hope, within a day or two, to have full use of it. I ever remain

Your Lordship's most obliged Friend
and faithful Servant,
October 2d, 1620. FR. VERULAM, Canc.

To the King.

It may please your Majesty,

I thought myself an unfortunate man that I could not attend you at Theobald's. But I hear that your majesty hath done, as God Almighty useth to do, which is to turn evil into good, in that your majesty hath been pleased upon that occasion to express, before your lords, your gracious opinion and favour towards me, which I most humbly thank your majesty for, and will aspire to deserve.

Secretary Naunton this day brought me your pleasure in certain notes: that I should advise with the two chief justices (old parliament men) and Sir Edward Coke (who is also their senior in that school) and Sir Randall Crewe, the last speaker, and such other judges as we should think fit, touching that which might in true policy, without packing or degenerate arts, prepare to a parliament, in case your majesty should resolve of one to be held; and withal he signified to me some particular points, which your majesty very wisely had deduced.

All your majesty's business is *super cor meum*, for I lay it to heart, but this is a business *secundum cor meum;* and yet, as I will do your majesty all possible good services in it, so I am far from seeking to impropriate to myself the thanks, but shall become *omnibus omnia* (as St. Paul saith) to attain your majesty's ends.

As soon as I have occasion, I will write to your majesty touching the same, and will have special care to communicate with my lords in some principal points, though all things are not at first fit for the whole table. I ever rest

Your Majesty's most bounden
and most devoted Servant,
October 2d, 1620. FR. VERULAM, Canc.

Your majesty needeth not to doubt but I shall carry the business with that secrecy which appertaineth.

To the Lord Chancellor.

My Lord,

I have acquainted his majesty with your letter, and labour in his service, for which he commandeth me to give you thanks, and to let your lordship know, that he liketh exceeding well your method held by the judges, which could not be amended, and concurreth with you in your opinions. First, touching the proclamation, that it should be monitory and persuasive rather than compulsive: and, secondly, that the point concerning the persons, who should be admitted and who avoided, is fit to be kept from the knowledge of the council table, and to be carried with all secrecy.

For the business of Ireland, his majesty had heard of it before, and gave commandment to the master of the wards, that it should be hastened and set in hand with all speed, which his majesty doubteth not but is done by this time. Touching your advice for a treasurer, his majesty is very mindful of it, and will let you know as much at his return, when he will speak further with your lordship of it: and so I rest

Yours, &c.

Royston, Oct. 9th, 1620. G. BUCKINGHAM.

To the Lord Chancellor.

My honourable Lord,

I have showed your letter and the proclamation to his majesty, who expecting only, according as his meaning was, directions therein for the well ordering of the elections of the burgesses, findeth a great deal more, containing matter of state, and the reasons of calling the parliament; whereof neither the people are capable, nor is it fit for his majesty to open unto them; but to reserve to the time of their assembling, according to the course of his predecessors, which his majesty intendeth to follow. The declaring whereof, in the proclamation, would cut off the ground of his majesty's and your lordship's speech at the proper time; his majesty hath, therefore, extracted somewhat of the latter part of the draught you have sent, purposing to take a few days' space to set down himself what he thinketh fit, and to make it ready against his return hither, or to Theobalds at the furthest, and then to communicate it to your lordship, and the rest of the lords. And so I rest

Yours, &c.

Royston, Oct. 19th, 1620. G. BUCKINGHAM.

To the Marquis of Buckingham.

Our very good Lord,

We thought it our duty to impart to his majesty, by your lordship, one particular of parliament business, which we hold it our part to relate, though it be too high for us to give our opinion of it.

The officers that make out the writs of parliament addressed themselves to me, the Chancellor, to know whether they should make such a writ of summons to the Prince, giving me to understand, that there were some precedents of it, which I, the Chancellor, communicated with the rest of the committees for parliament business, in whose assistance I find so much strength, that I am not willing to do any thing without them. Whereupon we (according to his majesty's prudent and constant rule, for observing in what reigns the precedents were) upon diligent search have found as followeth.

That King Edward I. called his eldest son, Prince Edward, to his parliament in the thirtieth year of his reign, the Prince then being about the age of eighteen years; and to another parliament in the four and thirtieth year of his reign.

Edward III. called the Black Prince, his eldest son, to his parliament in the five and twentieth, eight and twentieth, and two and fortieth years of his reign.

Henry IV. called Prince Henry to his parliaments in the first, third, eighth, and eleventh years of his reign, the Prince being under age in the three first parliaments: and we find in particular, that the eighth year, the Prince sat in the upper-house in days of business and recommended a bill to the lords.

King Edward IV. called Prince Edward, his son, to his parliament, in *anno* 22 of his reign, being within age.

King Henry VII. called Prince Arthur to his parliament in the seventh year of his reign, being within age.

Of King Edward VI. we find nothing; his years were tender, and he was not created Prince of Wales.

And for Prince Henry, he was created Prince of Wales during the last parliament at which he lived.

We have thought it our duty to relate to his majesty what we have found; and, withal, that the writs of sum mons to the Prince are not much differing from the writs to the peers; for they run in *fide et ligeanciâ*, and sometimes in *fide et homagio in quibus nobis tenemini*, and after *consilium nobis impensuri circa ardua regni.* Whereby it should seem that princes came to parliament, not only the days of solemnity, when they came without writ, but also on the days of sitting. And if it should be so, then the Prince may vote, and likewise may be of a committee of the upper-house, and consequently may be of a conference with the lower-house, and the like.

This might have been made more manifest as to the presence and acts of the Prince in days of sitting, if through the negligence of officers, the journal-books of the upper-house of parliament, before the reign of King Henry VIII. were not all missing.

All which we thought it appertained to our care to look through, and faithfully to represent to his majesty. And having agreed secrecy amongst ourselves, and enjoined it to the inferior officers, we humbly desire to know his majesty's pleasure, whether he will silence the question altogether, or make use of it for his service, or refer it to his council, or what other course he will be pleased to take according to his great wisdom and good pleasure.

This we have dispatched the sooner, because the writs of summons must have forty days distance from the first days of the parliament. And for the other parts of our accounts, his majesty shall hear from us, by the grace of God, within few days. Evermore praying for his majesty's prosperity, and wishing your lordship much happiness,

Your Lordship's to be commanded,
FR. VERULAM, Canc. HENRY HOBARTE,
H. MONTAGU, RAN. CREW.
EDW. COKE,

York House, Nov. 21st, 1620.

To the Marquis of Buckingham.

My very good Lord,

We have, these two days past, made report to the board of our parliament committee, upon relation whereof, for some things we provide, for some things we arm.

The King, by my Lord Treasurer's signification, did wisely put it upon a consult, whether the patents which we mentioned in our joint letters, were at this time to be removed, by act of council before parliament. I opined (but yet somewhat like Ovid's mistress that strove, but yet as one that would be overcome) that yes. My reasons:—

That men would go better and faster to the main errand.

That these things should not be staged, nor talked of, and so the less fuel to the fire.

That in things of this nature, wherein the council had done the like in former particulars (which I enumerated) before parliament, near parliament, during parliament, the council were to keep their wonted centinel, as if they thought not of a parliament, to destroy in other patents, as concealments.

The reasons on the other side were,

That it would be thought but a humouring of the parliament (being now in the calends of a parliament), and that after parliament they would come up again.

That offered graces, by reason and experience, lose their thanks.

They that are to be suffered to play upon something, since they can do nothing of themselves.

That the choosing out of some things, when perhaps their minds might be more upon other things, would do no great effect.

That former patents, taken away by act of council, were upon the complaints of particular persons; whereas now it should seem to be done *tanquam ex officio*.

To this I yielded, though I confess I am yet a little doubtful to the point of *suavibus modis*. But it is true that the speech of these, though in the lower-house, may be contemned; and if way be given to them (as I writ to your lordship of some of them in my last) it will sort to your honour. For other things, the lords have put them in a very good way, of which I will give express account when I see his majesty, as also of other observations concerning parliament. For if his majesty said well that when he knew the men and the elections, he would guess at the success; the prognostics are not so good as I expected, occasioned by the late occurrents abroad, and the general licentious speaking of state matters, of which I wrote in my last. God ever keep you.

Your Lordship's most obliged Friend
and faithful Servant,

Dec. 16, 1620. FR. VERULAM, Canc.

To the Lord Chancellor.

My honourable Lord,

As soon as his majesty's convenience would permit, I have acquainted him with the draught of the proclamation your lordship sent me by his majesty's direction. His majesty liketh it in every point so well, both in matter and form, that he findeth no cause to alter a word in it, and would have your lordship acquaint the lords of the council with it (though he assureth himself, no man can find any thing in it to be changed) and to take order for the speedy setting it forth. And so I rest

Yours, &c.

Theobalds, Dec. 21, 1620. G. BUCKINGHAM.

To the Lord Chancellor.

I have acquainted his majesty with your letter and the inclosed, the matter which his majesty hath been thinking upon for his speech, concerneth both the points of the institution of a parliament, and of the end for which this is called; yet his majesty thinketh it fit that some extract be made out of it which needeth to be but very short, as he will show you at his return.

Yours, &c.

Theobalds, Jan. 19, 1620. G. BUCKINGHAM.

To the Right Honourable his very good Lords, the Lords Spiritual and Temporal in the Upper House of Parliament assembled.

My very good Lords,

I humbly pray your lordships all to make a favourable and true construction of my absence. It is no feigning or fainting, but sickness both of my heart and of my back, though joined with that comfort of mind that persuadeth me that I am not far from Heaven, whereof I feel the first fruits.

And because, whether I live or die I would be glad to preserve my honour and fame, so far as I am worthy; hearing that some complaints of base bribery are coming before your lordships, my requests unto your lordships are:

First, That you will maintain me in your good opinion, without prejudice, until my cause be heard.

Secondly, That in regard I have sequestered my mind at this time in great part from worldly matters, thinking of my account and answers in a higher court, your lordships will give me convenient time, according to the course of other courts, to advise with my counsel, and to make my answer; wherein, nevertheless, my counsel's part will be the least: for I shall not, by the grace of God, trick up an innocency with cavillations, but plainly and ingenuously (as your lordships know my manner is) declare what I know or remember.

Thirdly, That according to the course of justice, I may be allowed to except to the witnesses brought against me; and to move questions to your lordships for their cross-examinations; and likewise to produce my own witnesses for the discovery of the truth.

And lastly, That if there be any more petitions of like nature, that your lordships would be pleased not to take any prejudice or apprehension of any number or muster of them, especially against a judge, that makes two thousand orders and decrees in a year (not to speak of the courses that have been taken for hunting out complaints against me) but that I may answer them according to the rules of justice, severally and respectively.

These requests I hope appear to your lordships no other than just. And so thinking myself happy to have so noble peers, and reverend prelates to discern of my cause; and desiring no privilege of greatness for subterfuge of guiltiness; but meaning, as I said, to deal fairly and plainly with your lordships, and to put myself upon your honours and favours; I pray God to bless your counsels and persons. And rest

Your Lordships' humble Servant,

March 19th, 1620. FR. ST. ALBAN, Canc.

To the King.

It may please your most excellent Majesty,

I think myself infinitely bounden to your majesty, for vouchsafing me access to your royal person, and to touch the hem of your garment. I see your majesty imitateth him that would not break the broken reed, nor quench the smoking flax; and as your majesty imitateth Christ, so I hope assuredly my lords of the upper-house will imitate you, and unto your majesty's grace and mercy, and next to my lords, I recommend myself. It is not possible, nor it were not safe, for me to answer particulars till I have my charge; which, when I shall receive, I shall, without fig-leaves or disguise, excuse what I can excuse, extenuate what I can extenuate, and ingenuously confess what I can neither clear nor extenuate. And if there be any thing which I might conceive to be no offence, and yet is, I desire to be informed, that I may be twice penitent, once for my fault, and the second time for my error, and so submitting all that I am to your majesty's grace, I rest

April 20, 1621.

To the King.

It may please your Majesty,

It hath pleased God for these three days past, to visit me with such extremity of headach upon the hinder part of my head, fixed in one place, that I thought verily it had been some imposthumation; and then the little physic that I have told me that either it must grow to a congelation, and so to a lethargy, or to break, and so to a mortal fever or sudden death; which apprehension, and chiefly the anguish of the pain, made me unable to think of any business. But now that the pain itself is assuaged to be tolerable, I resume the care of my business, and therein prostrate myself again, by my letter, at your majesty's feet.

Your majesty can bear me witness, that at my last so comfortable access, I did not so much as move your majesty by your absolute power of pardon, or otherwise, to take my cause into your hands, and to interpose between the sentence of the house. And according to my desire, your majesty left it to the sentence of the house by my Lord Treasurer's report.

But now if not *per omnipotentiam*, as the divines say, but *per potestatem suaviter disponentem*, your majesty will graciously save me from a sentence, with the good liking of the house, and that cup may pass from me, it is the utmost of my desires. This I move with the more belief, because I assure myself, that if it be reformation that is sought, the very taking away of the seal, upon my general submission, will be as much in example, for these four hundred years, as any further severity.

The means of this I most humbly leave unto your majesty, but surely I should conceive, that your majesty opening yourself in this kind to the Lords, Counsellors, and a motion of the Prince, after my submission, and my Lord Marquis using his interest with his friends in the house, may affect the sparing of the sentence; I making my humble suit to the house for that purpose, joined with the delivery up of the seal into your majesty's hands. This is my last suit that I shall make to your majesty in this business, prostrating myself at your mercy-seat, after fifteen years' service, wherein I have served your majesty in my poor endeavours, with an entire heart. And, as I presume to say unto your majesty, am still a virgin, for matters that concern your person or crown, and now only craving that after eight steps of honour, I be not precipitated altogether.

But because he that hath taken bribes is apt to give bribes, I will go further, and present your majesty with bribe; for if your majesty give me peace and leisure, and God give me life, I will present you with a good History of England, and a better Digest of your Laws. And so concluding with my prayers, I rest

Clay in your Majesty's hands,

May 2, 1621. FR. ST. ALBAN.

To the Prince of Wales.

It may please your Highness,

When I called to mind how infinitely I am bound to your highness, that stretched forth your arm to save me from a sentence, that took hold of me to keep me from being plunged deep in a sentence, that hath kept me alive in your gracious memory and mention since the sentence, pitying me, as I hope I deserve, and valuing me far above that I can deserve, I find my words almost as barren as my fortunes, to express unto your highness the thankfulness I owe. Therefore I can but resort to prayers to Almighty God to clothe you with his most rich and precious blessings, and likewise joyfully to meditate upon those he hath conferred upon you already; in that he hath made you to the King your father a principal part of his safety, contentment, and continuance; in yourself so judicious, accomplished, and graceful in all your doings, with more virtues in the buds, which are the sweetest that have been known in a young Prince of long time; with the realm so well beloved, so much honoured, as it is men's daily observation how nearly you approach to his majesty's perfections; how every day you exceed yourself; how compared with other Princes, which God hath ordained to be young at this time, you shine amongst them; they rather setting off your religious, moral, and natural excellencies, than matching them, though you be but a second person. These and such like meditations I feed upon, since I can yield your highness no other retribution. And for myself, I hope by the assistance of God above, of whose grace and favour I have had extraordinary signs and effects during my afflictions, to lead such a life in the last acts thereof, as whether his majesty employ me, or whether I live to myself, I shall make the world say that I was not unworthy such a patron.

I am much beholden to your highess's worthy servant, Sir John Vaughan, the sweet air and loving usage of whose house hath already much revived my languishing spirits, I beseech your highness, thank him for me. God ever preserve and prosper your highness.

Your Highness's most humble and
most bounden Servant,

June 1, 1621. FR. ST. ALBAN.

To the King.

It may please your most excellent Majesty,

I humbly thank your majesty for my liberty, without which timely grant, any farther grace would have come too late. But your majesty, that did shed tears in the beginning of my trouble, will, I hope, shed the dew of your grace and goodness upon me in the end. Let me live to serve you, else life is but the shadow of death to

Your Majesty's most devoted Servant,

June 4, 1621. FR. ST. ALBAN.

To the Marquis of Buckingham.

My very good Lord,

I heartily thank your lordship for getting me out of prison; and now my body is out, my mind nevertheless will be still in prison, till I may be on my feet to do his majesty and your lordship faithful service. Wherein your lordship, by the grace of God, shall find that my adversity hath neither spent, nor pent my spirits. God prosper you.

Your Lordship's most obliged Friend
and faithful Servant,

June 4, 1621. FR. ST. ALBAN.

To the King.

It may please your most excellent Majesty,

I perceive, by my noble and constant friend, the Marquis, that your majesty hath a gracious inclination towards me, and taketh care of me, for fifteen years the subject of your favour, now of your compassion, for which I most humbly thank your majesty. This same *Nova Creatura* is the work of God's pardon and the King's, and since I have the inward seal of the one, I hope well of the other.

Utar, saith Seneca to his master, *magnis exemplis; nec meæ fortunæ, sed tuæ.* Demosthenes was banished for bribery of the highest nature, yet was recalled with honour; Marcus Livius was condemned for exactions, yet afterwards made consul and censor. Seneca banished for divers corruptions, yet was afterwards restored, and an instrument of that memorable Quinquennium Neronis. Many more. This, if it please your majesty, I do not say for appetite of employment, but for hope that if I do by myself as is fit, your majesty will never suffer me to die in want or dishonour. I do now feed myself upon remembrance, how when your majesty used to go a progress, what loving and confident charges you were wont to give me touching your business. For, as Aristotle saith, young men may be happy by hope, so why should not old men, and sequestered men, by remembrance. God ever prosper and preserve your majesty.

Your Majesty's most bounden and devoted Servant,

FR. ST. ALBAN.

July 16, 1621.

To the Lord St. Alban.

My honourable Lord,

I have delivered your lordship's letter of thanks to his majesty, who accepted it very graciously, and will be glad to see your book, which you promised to send very shortly, as soon as it cometh. I send your lordship his majesty's warrant for your pardon, as you desired it; but am sorry, that in the current of my service to your lordship there should be the least stop of any thing; yet having moved his majesty, upon your servant's intimation, for your stay in London till Christmas, I found his majesty, who hath in all other occasions, and even in that particular already, to the dislike of many of your own friends, showed with great forwardness his gracious favour towards you, very unwilling to grant you any longer liberty to abide there; which, being but a small advantage to you, would be a great and general distaste, as you cannot but easily conceive, to the whole state. And I am the more sorry for this refusal of his majesty's falling in a time when I was a suitor to your lordship in a particular concerning myself, wherein though your servant insisted further than, I am sure, would ever enter into your thoughts, I cannot but take it as a part of a faithful servant in him. But if your lordship, or your lady, find it inconvenient for you to part with the house, I would rather provide myself otherwise than any way incommodate you, but will never slack any thing of my affection to do you service; whereof, if I have not yet given good proof, I will desire nothing more than the fittest occasion to show how much I am

Your Lordship's faithful Servant,

October, 1621. G. BUCKINGHAM.

To the Marquis of Buckingham.

My very good Lord,

An unexpected accident maketh me hasten this letter to your lordship, before I could dispatch Mr. Meautis; it is that my Lord Keeper hath staid my pardon at the seal. But it is with good respect; for he saith it shall be private, and then he would forthwith write to your lordship, and would pass it if he received your pleasure; and doth also show his reason of stay, which is, that he doubteth the exception of the sentence of parliament is not well drawn, nor strong enough, which if it be doubtful my lord hath great reason. But sure I am, both myself, and the King, and your lordship, and Mr. Attorney meant clearly, and I think Mr. Attorney's pen hath gone well. My humble request to your lordship is, that, for my Lord's satisfaction, Mr. Solicitor may be joined with Mr. Attorney, and if it be safe enough, it may go on; if not it may be amended. I ever rest

Your Lordship's most obliged Friend
and faithful Servant,
FR. ST. ALBAN.

October 18, 1621.

To the Lord St. Alban.

My honourable Lord,

I have brought your servant along to this place, in expectation of the letter from the Lord Keeper, which your lordship mentioneth in yours, but having not yet received it, I cannot make answer to the business you write of; and therefore thought fit not to detain your man here any longer, having nothing else to write, but that I always rest

Your Lordship's faithful Friend and Servant,
G. BUCKINGHAM.

Hinchenbrook.
Oct. 20, 1621.

To the Lord St. Alban.

My noble Lord,

Now that I am provided of a house I have thought it congruous to give your lordship notice thereof, that you may no longer hang upon the treaty, which hath been between your lordship and me, touching York House; in which I assure your lordship, I never desired to put you to the least inconvenience. So I rest

Your Lordship's Servant,
G. BUCKINGHAM.

To the Lord St. Alban.

My Lord,

I am glad your lordship understands me so rightly in my last letter. I continue still in the same mind, for I, thank God, I am settled to my contentment; and so I hope you shall enjoy yours with the more, because I am so well pleased in mine. And, my Lord, I shall be very far from taking it ill, if you part with it to any else, judging it alike unreasonableness to desire that which is another man's, and to bind him by promise or otherwise not to let it to another.

My Lord, I will move his majesty to take commiseration of your long imprisonment,* which, in some respects, both you and I have reason to think harder than the Tower; you for the help of physic, your parley with your creditors, your conference for your writings and studies, dealing with friends about your business; and I for this advantage, to be sometimes happy in visiting and conversing with your lordship, whose company I am much desirous to enjoy, as being tied by ancient acquaintance to rest

Your Lordship's faithful Friend and Servant,

G. BUCKINGHAM.

To the Marquis of Buckingham.

My very good Lord,

These main and real favours which I have lately received from your good lordship in procuring my liberty, and a reference of the consideration of my release, are such as I now find, that in building upon your lordship's noble nature and friendship, I have built upon the rock where neither winds or waves can cause overthrow. I humbly pray your lordship to accept from me such thanks as ought to come from him whom you have much comforted in fortune, and much more comforted in showing your love and affection to him, of which I have heard by my Lord of Faulkland, Sir Edward Sackville, Mr. Matthew, and otherwise.

I have written, as my duty was, to his majesty, thanks, touching the same, by the letter I here put into your noble hands.

I have made also, in that letter, an offer to his majesty, of my service, for bringing into better order and frame the Laws of England. The declaration whereof I have left

---

* Restraint from coming within the verge of the Court.

with Sir Edward Sackville, because it were no good manners to clog his majesty, at this time of triumph and recreation, with a business of this nature, so as your lordship may be pleased to call for it to Sir Edward Sackville, when you think the time reasonable.

I am bold likewise to present your lordship with a book of my History of King Henry VII. and now that, in summer was twelve months, I dedicated a book to his majesty, and this last summer, this book to the Prince, your lordship's turn is next; and this summer that cometh, if I live to it, shall be yours. I have desired his majesty to appoint me the task, otherwise I shall use my own choice, for this is the best retribution I can make to your lordship. God prosper you. I rest

Your Lordship's most obliged Friend,
and faithful Servant,
FR. ST. ALBAN.

Gorhambury, this 20th of March, 1621

Indorsed—*To the Right Honourable his very good Lord, the Lord Marquis of Buckingham, High Admiral of England.*

To the King.

May it please your Majesty,

I acknowledge myself in all humbleness infinitely bounden to your majesty's grace and goodness, for that, at the intercession of my noble and constant friend, my Lord Marquis, your majesty hath been pleased to grant me that which the civilians say, is *res inæstimabilis*, my liberty; so that now, whenever God calleth me, I shall not die a prisoner; nay, further, your majesty hath vouchsafed to rest a second and iterate aspect of your eye of compassion upon me, in the referring the consideration of my broken estate to my good lord, the Treasurer, which as it is a singular bounty in your majesty, so I have yet so much left of a late Commissioner of your Treasure, as I would be sorry to sue for any thing that might seem immodest. These your majesty's great benefits, in casting your bread upon the waters, as the Scripture saith, because my thanks cannot any ways be sufficient to attain, I have raised your progenitor of famous memory, and now I hope of more famous memory than before, King Henry VII. to give your majesty thanks for me; which work, most humbly kissing your majesty's hands, I do present. And because in the beginning of my trouble, when in the midst of the tempest I had a kenning of the harbour, which I hope now, by your majesty's favour,

I am entering into, I made a tender to your majesty of two works, a History of England, and a Digest of your Laws, as I have by a figure of *pars pro toto* performed the one, so I have herewith sent your majesty, by way of an epistle, a new offer of the other; but my desire is farther, if it stand with your majesty's good pleasure, since now my study is my exchange, and my pen my factor for the use of my talent, that your majesty, who is a great master in these things, would be pleased to appoint me some task to write, and that I should take for an oracle. And because my Instauration, which I esteem my great work, and do still go on with in silence, was dedicated to your majesty, and this History of King Henry VII. to your lively and excellent image the Prince, if now your majesty will be pleased to give me a theme to dedicate to my Lord of Buckingham, whom I have so much reason to honour, I should with more alacrity embrace your majesty's direction than my own choice. Your majesty will pardon me for troubling you thus long. God evermore preserve and prosper you.

Your Majesty's poor Beadsman most devoted,

Gorhambury, this 20th March, 1621. FR. ST. ALBAN.

To the Lord Digby.

My very good Lord,

I now only send my best wishes, to follow you at sea and land, with due thanks for your late great favours. God knows, whether the length of your voyage will not exceed the size of my hour-glass. But whilst I live, my affection to do you service shall remain quick under the ashes of my fortune.

To the Lord St. Alban.

My Lord,

I have despatched the business your lordship recommended to me, which I send your Lordship here inclosed, signed by his majesty, and have likewise moved him for your coming to kiss his hand, which he is pleased you shall do at Whitehall when he returneth next thither. In the mean time I rest

Your Lordship's faithful Friend and Servant,

Newmarket, Nov. 13th, 1622. G. BUCKINGHAM.

I will give order to my secretary to wait upon Sir John Suckling about your other business.

Indorsed—*My Lord of Bucks touching my warrant and access.*

To the Marquis of Buckingham.

Excellent Lord,

Though I have troubled your lordship with many letters, oftener than I think I should (save that affection keepeth no account), yet upon the repair of Mr. Matthew, a gentleman so much your lordship's servant, and to me another myself, as your lordship best knoweth, you would not have thought me a man alive, except I had put a letter into his hand, and withal, by so faithful and approved a man, commended my fortunes afresh unto your lordship.

My lord, to speak my heart to your lordship, I never felt my misfortunes so much as now: not for that part which may concern myself, who profit (I thank God for it) both in patience and in settling mine own courses; but when I look abroad and see the times so stirring, and so much dissimulation and falsehood, baseness and envy in the world, and so many idle clocks going in men's heads, then it grieveth me much, that I am not sometimes at your lordship's elbow, that I might give you some of the fruits of the careful advice, modest liberty, and true information of a friend that loveth your lordship as I do. For though your lordship's fortunes be above the thunder and storms of inferior regions, yet, nevertheless, to hear the wind, and not to feel it, will make one sleep the better.

My good lord, somewhat I have been, and much I have read; so that few things that concern states or greatness, are new cases unto me: and therefore I hope I may be no unprofitable servant to your lordship. I remember the King was wont to make a character of me, far above my worth, that I was not made for small matters: and your lordship would sometimes bring me from his majesty that Latin sentence *de minimis non curat lex;* and it hath so fallen out, that since my retiring, times have been fuller of great matters than before; wherein, perhaps, if I had continued near his majesty, he might have found more use of my service, if my gift lay that way: but that is but a vain imagination of mine. True it is, that as I do not aspire to use my talent in the King's great affairs; yet for that which may concern your lordship, and your fortune, no man living shall give you a better account of faith, industry, and affection than I shall. I must conclude with that which gave me occasion of this letter, which is Mr. Mathew's employment to your lordship in those parts, wherein I am verily persuaded your lordship shall find him a wise and able gentleman, and one that will bend his knowledge of the world (which is great) to serve his majesty, and the Prince, and in especial your lordship. So I rest

Your Lordship's most obliged and faithful Servant,

Gray's-Inn, this 18th April, 1623. FR. ST. ALBAN.

To the Duke of Buckingham.

Excellent Lord,

How much I rejoice in your grace's safe return you will easily believe, knowing how well I love you, and how much I need you. There be many things in this journey both in the felicity and in the carriage thereof, that I do not a little admire, and wish your grace may reap more and more fruits in continuance answerable to the beginnings: myself have ridden at anchor all your grace's absence, and my cables are now quite worn. I had from Sir Toby Mathew, out of Spain, a very comfortable message, that your grace had said, I should be the first that you would remember in any great favour after your return; and now coming from court, he telleth me he had commission from your lordship to confirm it: for which I humbly kiss your hands.

My lord, do some good work upon me, that I may end my days in comfort, which nevertheless cannot be complete except you put me in some way to do your noble self service, for I must ever rest

Your Grace's most obliged and faithful Servant,

October 12, 1623. FR. ST. ALBAN.

I have written to his highness, and had presented my duty to his highness to kiss his hands at York House, but that my health is scarce yet confirmed.

To the Lord St. Alban.

My Lord,

The assurance of your love makes me easily believe your joy at my return; and if I may be so happy as by the credit of my place, to supply the decay of your cables, I shall account it one of the special fruits thereof. What Sir Toby Matthew hath delivered on my behalf, I will be ready to make good, and omit no opportunity that may serve for the endeavours of

Your Lordship's faithful Friend and Servant,

G. BUCKINGHAM.

Royston, Oct. 14th, 1623.

To the Lord St. Alban.

My Honourable Lord,

I have delivered your lordship's letter and your book to his majesty, who hath promised to read it over: I wish I could promise as much for that which you sent me, that my understanding of that language might make me capable of those good fruits, which I assure myself, by an implicit faith, proceed from your pen; but I will tell you in good English, with my thanks for your book, that I ever rest

Your Lordship's faithful Friend and Servant,

G. Buckingham.

Hinchenbrook, October 29th, 1623.

To the Duke of Buckingham.

Excellent Lord,

I send your grace for a *parabien*, a book of mine, written first and dedicated to his majesty in English, and now translated into Latin, and enriched. After his majesty and his highness, your grace is ever to have the third turn with me. Vouchsafe, of your wonted favour, to present also the King's book to his majesty. The Prince's I have sent to Mr. Endimion Porter. I hope your grace (because you are wont to disable your Latin) will not send your book to the Conde d'Olivares, because he was a deacon, for I understand by one (that your grace may guess whom I mean) that the Conde is not rational, and I hold this book to be very rational. Your grace will pardon me to be merry however the world goeth with me. I ever rest,

Your Grace's most faithful and obliged Servant,

Fr. St. Alban.

Gray's Inn, this 22d October, 1623.

I have added a begging postscript in the King's letter; for, as I writ before, my cables are worn out, my hope of tackling is by your lordship's means. For me and mine, I pray command.

To the Lord St. Alban.

My Lord,

I give your lordship many thanks for the *parabien* you have sent me; which is so welcome unto me, both for the author's sake and for the worth of itself, that I cannot spare a work of so much pains to your lordship and value to me, unto a man of so little reason and less art; who if his skill in languages be no greater than I found it in argument, may, perhaps, have as much need of an interpreter (for all his deaconry) as myself; and whatsoever mine ignorance is in the tongue, yet this much I understand in the book, that it is a noble monument of your love, which I will entail to my posterity, who, I hope, will both reap the fruit of the work, and honour the memory of the author. The other book I delivered to his majesty, who is tied here by the feet longer than he purposed to stay.

For the business your lordship wrote of in your other letters, I am sorry I can do you no service, having engaged myself to Sir William Becher before my going into Spain, so that I cannot free myself, unless there were means to give him satisfaction. But I will ever continue

Your Lordship's assured Friend and Servant,

G. BUCKINGHAM.

Hinchenbrook, Oct. 27th, 1623.

To the Duke of Buckingham.

Excellent Lord,

I send Mr. Parker to have ready, according to the speech I had with your grace, my two suits to his majesty, the one for a full pardon, that I may die out of a cloud; the other for the translation of my honours after my decease. I hope his majesty will have compassion on me, as he promised me he would. My heart telleth me that no man hath loved his majesty and his service more entirely, and love is the law and the prophets. I ever rest

Your Grace's most obliged and faithful Servant,

FR. ST. ALBAN.

November 25th, 1623.

To the Lord St. Alban.

My Lord,

I have moved his majesty in your suit, and find him very gracious inclined to grant it; but he desireth first to know from my Lord Treasurer his opinion and the value of it, to whom I have written to that purpose this inclosed letter, and would wish your lordship to speak with him yourself for his favour and furtherance therein, and for my part I will omit nothing that appertaineth to

Your Lordship's faithful Friend and Servant,

G. BUCKINGHAM.

Newmarket,
28th of January, 1623.

To the Lord St. Alban,

Right honourable and my very noble Lord,

Mr. Doctor Rawley, by his modest choice, hath much obliged me to be careful of him, when God shall send any opportunity. And if his majesty shall remove me from this see, before any such occasion be offered, not to change my intentions with my bishoprick.

It is true that those ancients, Cicero, Demosthenes, and Plinius Secundus, have preserved their orations (the heads and effects of them at least) and their epistles; and I have ever been of opinion, that those two pieces, are the principal pieces of our antiquities. Those orations discovering the form of administering justice, and the letters the carriage of the affairs in those times. For our histories (or rather lives of men) borrow as much from the affections and phantasies of the writers, as from the truth itself, and are for the most of them built together upon unwritten relations and traditions. But letters written *è re nata*, and bearing a synchronism or equality of time *cum rebus gestis*, have no other fault, than that which was imputed unto Virgil, *nihil peccat nisi, quod nihil peccet*, they speak the truth too plainly, and cast too glaring a light for that age, wherein they were, or are written.

Your lordship doth most worthily, therefore, in preserving those two pieces, amongst the rest of those matchless monuments you shall leave behind you; considering that, as one age hath not bred your experience, so is it not fit it should be confined to one age, and not imparted to the times to come. For my part therein, I do embrace the honour with all thankfulness, and the trust imposed upon me, with all religion and devotion. For those two lectures in natural philosophy, and the sciences woven and involved with the same; it is a great and a noble foundation, both for the use and the salary, and a foot that will teach the age to come, to guess in part at the greatness of that herculean mind which gave them their existence. Only your lordship may be advised for the seats of this foundation. The two universities are the two eyes of this land, and fittest to contemplate the lustre of this bounty; these two lectures are as the two apples of these eyes. An apple when it is single is an ornament, when double a pearl, or a blemish in the eye. Your lordship may therefore inform yourself if one Sidley, of Kent, hath not already founded in Oxford a lecture of this nature and condition. But if Oxford in this kind be an Argus, I am sure poor Cambridge is a right Polyphemus, it hath but one eye, and that not so steadily or artificially placed, but *bonum est facile sui diffusivum;* your lordship being so full of goodness, will quickly find an object to pour it on. That which made me say thus much I will say in verse, that your lordship may remember it the better,

Sola ruinosis stat Cantabrigia pannis
Atque inopi linguâ disertas invocat Artes.

I will conclude with this vow: *Deus, qui animum istum tibi, animoisti tempus quam longissimum tribuat.* It is the most affectionate prayer of

Your Lordship's most humble Servant,
Jo. Lincoln.

Buckden,
the last of December, 1625.

LETTERS FROM MATHEWS,

NOT BEFORE PUBLISHED.

Sir Francis Bacon, desiring a Friend to do him a Service.

Sir,

The report of this act, which I hope will prove the last of this business, will probably, by the weight it carries, fall, and seize on me. And therefore, not now at will, but upon necessity, it will become me to call to mind what passed; and (my head being then wholly employed about invention) I may the worse put things upon the account of mine own memory. I shall take physic to-day, upon this change of weather, and vantage of leisure; and I pray you not to allow yourself so much business, but that you may have time to bring me your friendly aid before night, &c.

Sir Francis Bacon to a Friend, about Reading and giving Judgment upon his Writings.

Sir,

Because you shall not lose your labour this afternoon, which now I must needs spend with my Lord Chancellor, I send my desire to you in this letter, that you will take care not to leave the writing which I left with you last with any man so long as that he may be able to take a copy of it; because, first, it must be censured by you, and then considered again by me. The thing which I expect most from you is, that you would read it carefully over by yourself, and to make some little note in writing, where you think (to speak like a critic) that I do perhaps *indormiscere;* or where I do *indulgere genio;* or where, in fine, I give any manner of disadvantage to myself. This, *super totam materiam,* you must not fail to note, besides all such words and phrases as you cannot like; for you know in how high account I have your judgment.

Sir Francis Bacon to the same Person upon the like Subject; with an Addition of condoling the Death of a Friend.

Sir,

The reason of so much time taken before my answer to yours of the fourth of August, was chiefly my accompanying my letter with the paper which here I send you; and again, now lately (not to hold from you till the end of a letter, that which by grief may, for a time, efface all the former contents), the death of your good friend and mine, A. B.; to whom, because I used to send my letters for conveyance to you, it made me so much the more unready in the despatch of them. In the mean time, I think myself (howsoever it hath pleased God otherwise to bless me) a most unfortunate man, to be deprived of two (a great number in true friendship) of those friends whom I accounted as no stage friends, but private friends (and such as with whom I might both freely and safely communicate); him by death, and you by absence. As for the memorial of the late deceased Queen, I will not question whether you be to pass for a disinterested man or no; I freely confess myself am not, and so I leave it. As for my other writings you make me very glad of your approbation; the rather because you add a concurrence in opinion with others; for else I might have conceived that affection would, perhaps, have prevailed with you, beyond that which (if your judgment had been neat and free) you could have esteemed. And as for your caution touching the dignity of ecclesiastical persons, I shall not have cause to meet with them, any otherwise than in that some schoolmen have, with excess, advanced the authority of Aristotle. Other occasion I shall have none. But now I have sent you that only part of the whole writing which may perhaps have a little harshness and provocation in it, although I may almost secure myself that if the Preface passed so well this will not irritate more; being, indeed, to the Preface but as *palma ad pugnum*. Your own love expressed to me I heartily embrace; and hope that there will never be occasion of other than entireness between us, which nothing but *majores charitates* shall ever be able to break off.

Sir Francis Bacon to a Friend, in Reflection upon some Astrologers in Italy.

Sir,

I write to you chiefly now to the end that, by the continuance of my acquaintance with you, by letters, you may perceive how much I desire, and how much I do not despair of the recontinuance of our acquaintance by conversation. In the mean time, I wish you would desire the astronomers of Italy to amuse us less than they do with their fabulous and foolish traditions, and come nearer to the experiments of sense; and tell us that when all the planets, except the moon are beyond the line in the other hemisphere for six months together, we must needs have a cold winter, as we saw it was the last year. For, understanding that this was general over all these parts of the world, and finding that it was cold weather with all winds, and namely west wind, I imagined there was some higher cause of this effect; though yet, I confess, I thought not that ever I should have found that cause so palpable a one as it proved: which yet, when I came quickly afterwards to observe, I found also very clearly, that the summer must needs be cold too; though yet, it were generally thought that the year would make a shift to pay itself; and that we should be sure to have heats for our cold. You see that though I be full of business yet I can be glad rather to lay it all aside than to say nothing to you. But I long much more to be speaking often with you; and I hope I shall not long want my wish.

The Lord of St. Albans, Bacon, to an humble Servant, my Lord believing his own Danger to be much less than he found it.

Sir,

I say to you, upon the occasion which you give me in your last, *modicæ fiæi quare dubitasti?* I would not have my friends (though I know it to be out of love) too apprehensive, either of me, or for me. For I thank God, my ways are sound and good, and I hope God will bless me in them. When once my master, and afterwards myself, were both of us in extremity of sickness (which was no time to dissemble), I never had so great pledges and certainties of his love and favour: and that which I knew then, such as took a little poor advantage of these latter times, know since. As for the nobleman who passed that way by you, I think he is fallen out with me for his pleasure, or else, perhaps, to make good some of his own mistakings: for he cannot in his heart but think worthily of my affection and well deserving towards him; and as for me, I am very sure that I love his nature and parts.

My Lord of St. Albans, Bacon, to the same humble Servant employing him to do a good Office with another great Man.

Sir,

I have received your letter wherein you mention some passages at large concerning the lord you know of. You touched also that point in a letter which you wrote upon my lord's going over, which I answered; and am a little doubtful whether mine ever came to your hands. It is true that I wrote a little sullenly therein; how I conceived that my lord was a wise man in his own way, and perhaps thought it fit for him to be out with me; for, at least, I found no cause thereof in myself. As for the latter of these points, I am of the same judgment still; but for the former, I perceive, by what you write, that it is merely some misunderstanding of his. And I do a little marvel, at the instance which had relation to that other crabbed man; for I conceived that both in passing that book, and (as I remember) two more, immediately after my lord's going over, I had showed more readiness than many times I use in like cases. But to conclude, no man hath thought better of my lord than I have done. I know his virtues, and, namely, that he hath much greatness of mind, which is a thing almost lost amongst men; nor can any body be more sensible and remembering than I am of his former favours, so that I shall be most glad of his friendship; neither are the past occasions, in my opinion, such as need either reparation or declaration, but may well go under the title of nothing. Now, I had rather you dealt between us than any body else, because you are no way drenched in any man's humour. Of other things at another time; but this I was forward to write, in the midst of more business than ever I had.

The Lord of St. Albans to a most dear Friend, in whom he notes an Entireness and impatient Attention to do him Service.

Sir,

It is not for nothing that I have deferred my *Essay de Amicitia*, whereby it hath expected the proof of your great friendship towards me. Whatsoever the event be (wherein I depend upon God, who ordains the effect, the instrument, all) yet your incessant thinking of me, without loss of a moment of time, or a hint of occasion, or a circumstance of endeavour, or the stroke of a pulse in demonstration of your affection to me, doth infinitely tie me to you. Commend my service to my friend. The rest to-morrow, for I hope to lodge at London this night, &c.

Secrecy I need not recommend, otherwise than that you may recommend it over to our friend; both because it prevents opposition, and because it is both the King's and my Lord Marquis's nature to love to do things unexpected.

The Lord St. Albans to the Lord Treasurer Marlborough, expostulating about his Unkindness, and Injustice.

My Lord,

I humbly entreat your lordship, and (if I may use the word) advise you to make me a better answer. Your lordship is interested in honour, in the opinion of all them who hear how I am dealt with. If your lordship malice me for such a cause, surely it was one of the justest businesses that ever was in Chancery. I will avouch it; and how deeply I was tempted therein, your lordship knows best. Your Lordship may do well, in this great age of yours, to think of your grave, as I do of mine, and to beware of hardness of heart. And as for fair words, it is a wind, by which neither your lordship nor any man else can sail long. Howsoever, I am the man who will give all due respects and reverence to your great place, &c.

A Letter of Sir Francis Bacon to a Servant of his, in expression of great Acknowledgment and Kindness.

Sir,

I have been too long a debtor to you for a letter, and especially for such a letter, the words whereof were delivered by your hand, as if it had been in old gold; for it was not possible for entire affection to be more generously and effectually expressed. I can but return thanks to you; or rather, indeed, such an answer as may better be of thoughts than words. As for that which may concern myself, I hope God hath ordained me some small time whereby I may redeem the loss of much. Your company was ever of contentment to me, and your absence of grief; but now it is of grief upon grief. I beseech you, therefore, make haste hither, where you shall meet with as good a welcome as your own heart can wish.

MISCELLANEOUS LETTERS.

The Lord Bacon, his Letter to the most illustrious, and most excellent Prince Charles, Prince of Wales, Duke of Cornwall, Earl of Chester, &c.*

It may please your Highness,

In part of my acknowledgment to your highness, I have endeavoured to do honour to the memory of the last King of England, that was ancestor to the King your father and yourself, and was that King to whom both unions may in a sort refer, that of the roses being in him consummate, and that of the kingdoms by him begun: besides, his times deserve it, for he was a wise man and an excellent King; and yet the times very rough and full of mutations and rare accidents: and it is with times as it is with ways, some are more up hill and down hill, and some are more flat and plain, and the one is better for the liver, and the other for the writer. I have not flattered him, but took him to life as well as I could, sitting so far off, and having no better light; it is true your highness hath a living pattern, incomparable of the King your father, but is not amiss for you also to see it in one of these ancient pieces. God preserve your highness.

Your Highness's most humble and devoted Servant,

FRANCIS ST. ALBAN.

Mr. Francis Bacon to Mr. Robert Cecil.†

Sir,

I am very glad that the good affection and friendship, which conversation and familiarity did knit between us, is not by absence and intermission of society discontinued; which assureth me it had a farther root than ordinary acquaintance. The signification whereof, as it is very welcome to

* Third Edition of Resuscitatio.

† From the original draught in the Library of Queen's College, Oxford. *Arch. D.* 2. This letter seems to be of a very early date, and to have been written to Mr. Robert Cecil while he was upon his travels.

me, so it maketh me wish, that if you have accomplished yourself as well in the points of virtue and experience, which you sought by your travel, as you have won the perfection of the Italian tongue, I might have the contentment to see you again in England, that we may renew the fruit of our mutual good will; which, I may truly affirm, is, on my part, much increased towards you, both by your own demonstration of kind remembrance, and because I discern the like affection in your honourable and nearest friends.

Our news are all but in seed; for our navy is set forth with happy winds, in token of happy adventures, so as we do but expect and pray, as the husbandman when his corn is in the ground.

Thus commending me to your love, I commend you to God's preservation.

To the Right Honourable his very good Lord, the Lord Keeper of the Great Seal, &c.*

My very good Lord,

I was wished to be here ready in expectation of some good effect; and therefore I commend my fortune to your lordship's kind and honourable furtherance. My affection inclineth me to be much [your] lordship's, and my course and way, in all reason and policy for myself, leadeth me to the same dependence: hereunto if there shall be joined your lordship's obligation in dealing strongly for me as you have begun, no man can be more yours. A timorous man is every body's, and a covetous man is his own. But if your lordship consider my nature, my course, my friends, my opinion with her majesty, if this eclipse of her favour were past, I hope you will think, I am no unlikely piece of wood to shape you a true servant of. My present thankfulness shall be as much as I have said. I humbly take my leave.

Your Lordship's true humble servant,

From Greenwich,
this 5th of April, 1594.

FR. BACON.

To the Right Honourable my very good Lord, the Lord Keeper.†

My Lord,

I have, since I spake with your lordship, pleaded to the Queen against herself for the injury she doth Mr. Bacon in delaying him so long, and the unkindness she doth me in

* Harl MSS. vol. 6997, No. 20.

† Ibid. No. 87.

granting no better expedition in a suit which I have followed so long, and so affectionately. And though I find that she makes some difficulty, to have the more thanks, yet I do assure myself she is resolved to make him. I do write this not to solicit your lordship to stand firm in assisting me, because, I know, you hold yourself already tied by your affection to Mr. Bacon, and by your promise to me; but to acquaint your lordship of my resolution to set up my rest, and employ my uttermost strength to get him placed before the term: so as I beseech your lordship think of no temporising course, for I shall think the Queen deals unkindly with me, if she do not both give him the place, and give it with favour and some extraordinary advantage. I wish your lordship all honour and happiness, and rest

Your Lordship's very assured,

Greenwich, this 14th of January, [1594]. ESSEX.

Indorsed.—*My Lord of Essex for Mr. Fran. Bacon to be Solicitor.*

To the Right Honourable his very good Lord, the Lord Keeper of the Great Seal.*

My very good Lord,

Sir Thomas Egerton failing of your lordship, being newly gone, sent his letter to me to see conveyed unto you, which I send inclosed; desiring your lordship, according to your kind affection, to make the best use thereof for my furtherance. And I pray your lordship to call to remembrance my Lord Treasurer's kind course, who affirmed directly all the rest to be unfit. And because *vis unita fortior*, I pray your lordship to take a time with the Queen when my Lord Treasurer is present. Thus in hope to-morrow will bring forth some good effect, I rest

Your Lordship's, in all humble duty and service,

FR. BACON.

To the Right Honourable, &c. the Lord Keeper, &c.†

My very good Lord,

Because I understand your lordship remaineth at court till this day, and that my Lord of Essex writeth to me, that his lordship cometh to London, I thought good to remember

---

* Harl. MSS. vol. 6996, No. 52. † Ibid. No. 50.

your lordship, and to request you, as I touched in my last, that if my Lord Treasurer be absent, your lordship would forbear to fall into my business with her majesty, lest it might receive some foil before the time when it should be resolutely dealt in. And so commending myself to your good favour, I most humbly take my leave.

Your Lordship's, in all humble duty and service,

From Gray's Inn, this 8th of April, 1594. FR. BACON.

Earl of Essex to Lord Keeper Puckering.*

My Lord,

My short stay at the court made me fail of speaking with your lordship, therefore I must write that which myself had told you; that is, that your lordship will be pleased to forbear pressing for a solicitor, since there is no cause towards the end of a term to call for it; and because the absence of Mr. Bacon's friends may be much to his disadvantage. I wish your lordship all happiness, and rest

Your Lordship's very assured to be commanded,

Wanstead, this 4th of May, 1594. ESSEX.

To the Right Honourable the Lord Keeper, &c.

It may please your good Lordship,

I understand of some business like enough to detain the Queen to-morrow, which maketh me earnestly to pray your good lordship, as one that I have found to take my fortune to heart, to take some time to remember her majesty of a solicitor this present day.

Our Tower employment stayeth, and hath done these three days, because one of the principal offenders being brought to confess, and the other persisting in denial, her majesty, in her wisdom, thought best some time were given to him that is obstinate, to bethink himself; which indeed is singular good in such cases. Thus desiring your lordship's pardon, in haste I commend my fortune and duty to your favour.

Your Lordship's most humbly
to receive your commandments,

From Gray's Inn, this 13th of August, 1594. FR. BACON.

---

* Harl. MSS. vol. 6996, No. 72.

To the Right Honourable the Lord Keeper, &c.*

It may please your good Lordship,

As your lordship hath at divers times helped me to pass over contrary times, so I humbly pray you not to omit this favourable time. I cannot bear myself as I should till I be settled. And thus desiring pardon, I leave your lordship to God's preservation.

Your lordship's, most humbly at commandment,

From Gray's Inn, this 25th of August, 1594. FR. BACON.

To the Right Honourable his very good Lord, the Lord Keeper, &c.†

It may please your good Lordship,

I was minded, according to the place of employment, though not of office, wherein I serve, for my better direction and the advancement of the service, to have acquainted your lordship, now before the term, with such her majesty's causes as are in my hands. Which course, intended out of duty, I do now find by that I hear from my Lord of Essex, your lordship of your favour is willing to use for my good, upon that satisfaction you may find in my travels. And I now send to your lordship, together with my humble thanks, to understand of your lordship's being at leisure, what part of to-morrow, to the end I may attend your lordship, which this afternoon I cannot, in regard of some conference I have appointed with Mr. Attorney General. And so I commend your honourable lordship to God's good preservation.

Your good Lordship's,

Humbly at your honourable commandments,

From Gray's Inn, the 25th of September, Friday. FR. BACON.

To the Right Honourable the Lord Keeper, &c.‡

It may please your Lordship,

I thought good to step aside for nine days, which is the durance of a wonder, and not for any dislike in the world; for I think her majesty hath done me as great a favour in making an end of this matter, as if she had enlarged me

* Harl. MSS. vol. 6996, No. 103. † Ibid. No. 109.
‡ Ibid. vol. 6697. No 14.

from some restraint. And I humbly pray your lordship, if it so please you, to deliver to her majesty from me, that I would have been glad to have done her majesty service now in the best of my years, and the same mind remains in me still; and that it may be, when her majesty hath tried others, she will think of him that she hath cast aside. For I will take it upon that which her majesty hath often said, that she doth reserve me, and not reject me. And so I leave your good lordship to God's good preservation.

Your Lordship's much bounden

From Twickenham Park, this 20th of May, 1595. FR. BACON.

Indorsed—*Mr. Fr. Bacon, his Contentation to leave the Solicitorship.*

To Sir George Villiers.*

Sir,

I think I cannot do better service towards the good estate of the kingdom of Ireland than to procure the king to be well served in the eminent places of law and justice; I shall therefore name unto you for the attorney's place there, or for the solicitor's place if the new solicitor shall go up, a gentleman of mine own breeding and framing, Mr. Edward Wyrthington, of Gray's Inn: he is born to eight hundred pounds a year; he is the eldest son of a most severe justicer amongst the recusants of Lancashire, and a man most able for law and speech, and by me trained in the King's causes. My Lord Deputy, by my description, is much in love with the man. I hear my Lord of Canterbury and Sir Thomas Laque should name one Sir John Beare, and some other mean men. This man I commend upon my credit, for the good of his majesty's service. God ever preserve and prosper you. I rest

Your most devoted and most bounden Servant,

FR. BACON.

July 2, 1616.

To the Marquis of Buckingham.†

My very good Lord,

I write now only, rather in a kind of continuance and fresh suit, upon the King's business, than that the same is yet ripe either for advertisement or advice.

---

* Stephens's second collection p. 4. † Ibid.

The subcommissioners meet forenoon and afternoon with great diligence, and without distraction or running several ways; which if it be no more than necessary, what would less have done? that is, if there had been no subcommissioners, or they not well chosen.

I speak with Sir Lionel Cranfield as cause requireth either for account or direction, and as far as I can, by the taste I have from him, discern, probably their service will attain, and may exceed his majesty's expectation.

I do well like the course they take, which is, in every kind to set down, as in beer, in wine, in beef, in muttons, in corn, &c. what cometh to the King's use, and then what is spent, and lastly what may be saved. This way, though it be not so accusative, yet it is demonstrative. *Nam rectum est index sui et obliqui*, and the false manner of accounting, and where the gain cleaveth will appear after by consequence. I humbly pray his majesty to pardon me for troubling him with these imperfect glances, which I do, both because I know his majesty thinketh long to understand somewhat, and lest his majesty should conceive, that he multiplying honours and favours upon me, I should not also increase and redouble my endeavours and cares for his service. God ever bless, preserve, and prosper his majesty and your lordship, to whom I ever remain

Your true and most devoted Servant,

FR. BACON, C. S.

Jan. 16, 1617.

To the Right Honourable the Lord Keeper, &c.*

It may please your good Lordship,

Not able to attend your lordship myself before your going to the court, by reason of an ague, which offered me a fit on Wednesday morning, but since, by abstinence, I thank God, I have starved it, so as now he hath turned his back, I am chasing him away with a little physic, I thought good to write these few words to your lordship; partly to signify my excuse, if need be, that I assisted not Mr. Attorney on Thursday last in the Star Chamber, at which time, it is some comfort to me, that I hear by relation somewhat was generally taken hold of by the court which I formerly had opened and moved; and partly to express a little my con-

* Harl. MSS. vol. 6997. No. 18.

ceit touching the news which your lordship last told me from the queen, concerning a condition in law knit to an interest, which your lordship remembereth, and is supposed to be broken by misfeyance. Wherein surely my mind, as far as it appertaineth to me, is this, that as I never liked not so much as the coming in upon a lease by way of forfeiture, so I am so much enemy to myself as I take no contentment in any such hope of advantage. For as your lordship can give me best testimony, that I never in my life propounded any such like motion, though I have been incited thereto; so the world will hardly believe, but that it is underhand quickened and nourished from me. And truly, my lord, I would not be thought to supplant any man for great gain; and I humbly pray your lordship to continue your commendations and countenance to me in the course of the Queen's service that I am entered into: which when it shall please God to move the Queen to profit*, I hope I shall give cause for your lordship to obtain as many thanks as you have endured chidings. And so I commend your good lordship to God's good preservation.

Your Lordship's,

Most humbly at your honourable commandment,

From Gray's Inn, the 11th of June, 1595. FR. BACON.

To the Right Honourable the Lord Keeper, &c.†

It may please your Lordship,

There hath nothing happened to me in the course of my business more contrary to my expectation, than your lordship's failing me, and crossing me now in the conclusion, when friends are best tried. But now I desire no more favour of your lordship, than I would do if I were a suitor in the Chancery; which is this only, that you would do me right. And I for my part, though I have much to allege, yet, nevertheless, if I see her majesty settle her choice upon an able man, such a one as Mr. Serjeant Fleming, I will make no means to alter it. On the other side, if I perceive any insufficient, obscure,‡ idol man offered to her majesty, then I think myself double bound to use the best means I can for myself; which I humbly pray your lordship I may do with your favour, and that you will not disable me far-

* f. Perfect. † Harl MSS. vol. 6997, No. 37. ‡ Ita. MSS.

ther than is cause. And so I commend your lordship to God's preservation,

That beareth your Lordship all humble respect,

From Gray's Inn, the 28th of July, 1595. FR. BACON.

Indorsed, in Lord Keeper's hand—*Mr. Bacon wronging me.*

To the Right Honourable the Lord Keeper, &c.*

It may please your Lordship,

I thought it became me to write to your lordship, upon that which I have understood from my Lord of Essex, who vouchsafed, as I perceive, to deal with your lordship of himself to join with him in the concluding of my business, and findeth your lordship hath conceived offence, as well upon my manner when I saw your lordship at Temple last, as upon a letter, which I did write to your lordship some time before. Surely, my lord, for my behaviour, I am well assured, I omitted no point of duty or ceremony towards your lordship. But I know too much of the court to beg a countenance in public place, where I make account I shall not receive it. And for my letter, the principal point of it was, that which I hope God will give me grace to perform, which is, that if any idol may be offered to her majesty, since it is mixed with my particular, to inform her majesty truly, which I must do, as long as I have a tongue to speak, or a pen to write, or a friend to use. And farther I remember not of my letter, except it were that I writ, I hoped your lordship would do me no wrong, which hope I do still continue. For if it please your lordship but to call to mind from whom I am descended, and by whom, next to God, her majesty, and your own virtue, your lordship is ascended; I know you will have a compunction of mind to do me any wrong. And therefore, good my lord, when your lordship favoureth others before me, do not lay the separation of your love and favour upon myself. For I will give no cause, neither can I acknowledge any, where none is; but humbly pray your lordship to understand things as they are. Thus sorry to write to your lordship in an argument which is to me unpleasant, though necessary, I commend your Lordship to God's good preservation.

Your Lordship's, in all humble respect,

From Twickenham Park, this 19th of August, 1595. FR. BACON.

* Harl. MSS. vol. 6997, No. 44.

To the Right Honourable the Lord Keeper, &c.*

It may please your good Lordship,

I am sorry the opportunity permitteth me not to attend your lordship as I minded. But I hope your lordship will not be the less sparing in using the argument of my being studied and prepared in the Queen's causes, for my furtherance upon belief that I had imparted to your lordship my travels, which some time next week I mean to do. Neither have I been able to confer with Mr. Attorney, as I desired, because he was removing from one building to another. And besides, he alleged his note-book was in the country, at——, and so we respited it to some time next week. I think he will rather do me good offices than otherwise, except it be for the township your lordship remembereth by the verse. Thus I commend your honourable lordship to God's good preservation.

Your Lordship's most humble
at your honourable commandment,
FR. BACON.

From Gray's Inn,
this 25th of September, 1595.

To the Right Honourable my good Lord, the Lord Keeper of the Great Seal of England.†

It may please your good Lordship,

My not acquainting your lordship hath proceeded of my not knowing any thing, and of my not knowing of my absence at Byssam with my Lady Russel, upon some important cause of her son's. And as I have heard nothing, so I look for nothing, though my Lord of Essex sent me word, he would not write till his lordship had good news. But his lordship may go on in his affection, which nevertheless myself have desired him to limit. But I do assure your lordship, I can take no farther care for the matter. I am now at Twickenham Park, where I think to stay: for her majesty placing a solicitor, my travel shall not need in her causes, though whensoever her majesty shall like to employ me in any particular, I shall be ready to do her willing service. This I write lest your lordship might think my silence came of any conceit towards your lordship, which I do assure you, I have not. And this needed I not to do, if I

* Harl. MSS. vol. 6997, No. 59. † Ibid. No. 60.

thought not so: for my course will not give me any ordinary occasion to use your favour, whereof nevertheless I shall ever be glad. So I commend your good lordship to God's holy preservation.

Your Lordship's humble, &c.

FR. BACON.

This 11th of October, 1595.

To the Right Honourable the Lord Keeper, &c.*

It may please your good Lordship,

I conceive the end already made, which will, I trust, be to me a beginning of good fortune, or at least of content. Her majesty, by God's grace, shall live and reign long, she is not running away, I may trust her. Or whether she look towards me or no, I remain the same, not altered in my intention. If I had been an ambitious man, it would have overthrown me, but minded as I am, *Revertet benedictio mea in sinum meum.* If I had made any reckoning of any thing to be stirred, I would have waited on your lordship, and will be at any time ready to wait on you to do you service. So I commend your good lordship to God's holy preservation.

Your Lordship's most humble,
at your honourable commandment,

From Twickenham Park,
this 14th of October.

FR. BACON.

Indorsed.—14 *October*, 95.

To the Right Honourable the Lord Keeper, &c.†

My very good Lord,

I received a letter from a very friend of mine, requesting me to move your lordship, to put into the commission for the subsidy, Mr. Richard Kempe, a reader of Gray's Inn, and besides born to good estate, being also my friend and familiar acquaintance. And because I conceive the gentleman to be every way sortable with the service, I am bold to commend him to your lordship's good favour. And even so, with remembrance of my most humble duty, I rest,

Your Lordship's affectionate to do you humble service,

Twickenham Park,
July 3, 1595.

FR. BACON.

---

* Harl. MSS. vol. 6997, No. 61. † Ibid. No. 29.

To the Right Honourable the Lord Keeper, &c.*

My Lord,

In my last conference with your lordship, I did entreat you both to forbear hurting of Mr. Fr. Bacon's cause, and to suspend your judgment of his mind towards your lordship, till I had spoken with him. I went since that time to Twickenham Park to confer with him, and had signified the effect of our conference by letter ere this, if I had not hoped to have met with your lordship, and so to have delivered it by speech. I told your lordship when I last saw you, that this manner of his was only a natural freedom, and plainness, which he had used with me, and in my knowledge with some other of his best friends, than any want of reverence towards your lordship; and therefore I was more curious to look into the moving cause of his style, than into the form of it; which now I find to be only a diffidence of your lordship's favour and love towards him, and no alienation of that dutiful mind which he hath borne towards your lordship. And therefore I am fully persuaded, that if your lordship would please to send for him, there would grow so good satisfaction, as hereafter he should enjoy your lordship's honourable favour, in as great a measure as ever, and your lordship have the use of his service, who, I assure your Lordship, is as strong in his kindness, as you find him in his jealousy. I will use no argument to persuade your lordship, that I should be glad of his being restored to your lordship's wonted favour; since your lordship both knoweth how much my credit is engaged in his fortune, and may easily judge how sorry I should be, that a gentleman whom I love so much, should lack the favour of a person whom I honour so much. And thus commending your lordship to God's best protection, I rest

Your Lordship's very assured,

ESSEX.

Indorsed—31 *August*, 95. *My Lord of Essex to have me send for Mr. Bacon, for he will satisfy me.*
In my Lord Keeper's own hand.

To the Right Honourable the Lord Keeper, &c.†

My very good Lord,

The want of assistance from them which should be Mr. Fr. Bacon's friends, makes [me] the more industrious myself, and the more earnest in soliciting mine own friends.

---

* Harl. MSS. vol. 6997, No. 47.

† Ibid. No. 106.

Upon me the labour must lie of his establishment, and upon me the disgrace will light of his being refused. Therefore I pray your lordship, now account me not as a solicitor only of my friend's cause, but as a party interested in this; and employ all your lordship's favour to me, or strength for me, in procuring a short and speedy end. For though I know, it will never be carried any other way, yet I hold both my friend and myself disgraced by this protraction. More I would write, but that I know to so honourable and kind a friend, this which I have said is enough. And so I commend your lordship to God's best protection, resting,

At your Lordship's commandment,

[No date.] ESSEX.

A Letter to Dr. Morison,* a Scottish Physician, upon his Majesty's coming in.

Mr. Doctor Morison,

I have thought good by this my letter to renew this my ancient acquaintance which hath passed between us, signifying my good mind to you, to perform to you any good office, for your particular, and my expectation, and a firm assurance of the like on your part towards me: wherein I confess you may have the start of me, because occasion hath given you the precedency in investing you with opportunity to use my name well, and by your loving testimony to further a good opinion of me in his majesty, and the court.

But I hope my experience of matters here will, with the light of his majesty's favour, enable me speedily both to requite your kindness, and to acquit and make good your testimony and report. So not doubting to see you here with his majesty, considering that it belongeth to your art to feel pulses, and I assure you Galen doth not set down greater variety of pulses than do vent here in men's hearts, I wish you all prosperity, and remain

Yours, &c.

From my Chamber at Gray's Inn, &c. 1603.

---

* He had held a correspondence with Mr. Anthony Bacon, and was employed to find intelligence from Scotland to the Earl of Essex.—See *Memoirs of the Reign of Queen Elizabeth, from the year* 1581 *till her death*, vol i. p. 79, 109, 116.

A Letter to Mr. Murray, of the King's Bed Chamber.

Mr. Murray,

It is very true that his majesty most graciously, at my humble request, knighted the last Sunday my brother-in-law, a towardly young gentleman;* for which favour I think myself more bound to his majesty, than for the benefit of ten knights: and to tell you truly, my meaning was not that the suit of this other gentleman, Mr. Temple,† should have been moved in my name. For I should have been unwilling to have moved his majesty for more than one at once, though many times in his majesty's courts of justice, if we move once for our friends, we are allowed to move again for our fee.

But indeed my purpose was, that you might have been pleased to have moved it as for myself.

Nevertheless, since it is so far gone, and that the gentleman's friends are in some expectation of success, I leave it to your kind regard what is farther to be done, as willing to give satisfaction to those which have put me in trust, and loth on the other side to press above good manners. And so with my loving commendations I remain

Yours, &c.

1603.

To Mr. Matthew.‡

Sir,

I perceive you have some time when you can be content to think of your friends; from whom, since you have borrowed yourself, you do well, not paying the principal, to send the interest at six months' day. The relation, which here I send you enclosed, carries the truth of that which is public: and though my little leisure might have required a briefer, yet the matter would have endured and asked a larger.

I have now, at last, taught that child to go, at the swaddling whereof you were. My work touching the Proficiency and Advancement of Learning I have put into two

---

* To this Sir John Constable, Sir Francis Bacon dedicated the second edition of his Essays, published at London 1612, in octavo.

† Probably Mr. William Temple, who had been educated in King's College, Cambridge, then master of the free school at Lincoln, next successively secretary to Sir Philip Sidney, Secretary Davison, and the Earl of Essex, made provost of Dublin College in 1609, and at last knighted, and appointed one of the Masters in Chancery in Ireland. He died about 1626, at the age of 72.

‡ Sir Tobie Matthew's Collection of Letters, p. 11.

books; whereof the former, which you saw, I cannot but account as a page of the latter. I have now published them both; whereof I thought it a small adventure to send you a copy, who have more right to it than any man, except Bishop Andrews, who was my inquisitor.

The death of the late great judge concerned not me, because the other was not removed. I write this in answer to your good wishes, which I return not as flowers of Florence,* but as you mean them; whom I conceive place cannot alter, no more than time shall me, except it be for the better.

1605.

To my Lady Packington, in Answer to a Message by her sent.†

Madam,

You shall with right good will be made acquainted with any thing that concerneth your daughters, if you bear a mind of love and concord, otherwise you must be content to be a stranger unto us; for I may not be so unwise as to suffer you to be an author or occasion of dissension between your daughters and their husbands, having seen so much misery of that kind in yourself.

And above all things I will turn back your kindness, in which you say, you will receive my wife if she be cast off: for it is much more likely we have occasion to receive you being cast off, if you remember what is passed. But it is time to make an end of those follies, and you shall at this time pardon me this one fault of writing to you; for I mean to do it no more till you use me and respect me as you ought. So wishing you better than it seemeth you will draw upon yourself, I rest,

Yours,

Fr. Bacon.

To Sir Thomas Bodeley, after he had imparted to him a Writing, intitled, *Cogitata et Visa*.‡

Sir,

In respect of my going down to my house in the country, I shall have miss of my papers, which I pray you therefore to return unto me. You are, I bear you witness, slothful,

---

* Mr. Matthew wrote an Elegy on the Duke of Florence's felicity.
† From an old copy of Sir Francis Bacon's Letters.
‡ Rawley's Resuscitatio.

and you help me nothing: so as I am half in conceit that you affect not the argument, for myself, I know well, you love and affect. I can say no more to you, but *non canimus surdis, respondent omnia sylvæ.* If you be not of the lodgings chalked up, whereof I speak in my preface, I am but to pass by your door. But if I had you a fortnight at Gorhambury I would make you tell me another tale; or else I would add a cogitation against libraries, and be revenged on you that way. I pray you send me some good news of Sir Thomas Smith, and commend me very kindly to him. So I rest.

1607.

To the King.*

It may please your excellent Majesty,

Mr. St. John his day is past, and well past. I hold it to be Janus Bifrons; it hath a good aspect to that which is past, and to the future; and doth both satisfy and prepare. All did well; my Lord Chief Justice delivered the law for the benevolence strongly; I would he had done it timely. Mr. Chancellor of the Exchequer† spake finely, somewhat after the manner of my late Lord Privy Seal;‡ not all out so sharply, but as elegantly. Sir Thomas Lake, who is also new in that court, did very well, familiarly and counsellor-like.§ My Lord of Pembroke, who is likewise a stranger there, did extraordinary well, and became him-

---

* Rawley's Resuscitatio.

† The chancellor of the exchequer here meant was Sir Fulke Greville, who being early initiated into the court of Queen Elizabeth, became a polite and fine gentleman; and in the 18th of King James was created Lord Brooke. He erected a noble monument for himself on the north side of Warwick Church, which hath escaped the late desolation, with this well known inscription, "Fulke Greville, servant to Queen Elizabeth, counsellor to King James, and friend to Sir Philip Sidney." Nor is he less remembered by the monument he has left in his writings and poems, chiefly composed in his youth, and in familiar exercises with the gentleman I have before mentioned.—*Stephens.*

‡ Late Earl of Northampton.

§ Sir Thomas Lake was about this time made one of the principal secretaries of state, as he had been formerly Latin secretary to Queen Elizabeth, and before that time bred under Sir Francis Walsingham. But in the year 1618, falling into the king's displeasure, and being engaged in the quarrels of his wife and daughter the Lady Roos, with the Countess of Exeter, he was at first suspended from the execution of his place, and afterwards removed, and deeply censured and fined in the Star Chamber; although it is said the King then gave him in open court this public eulogy, that he was a minister of state fit to serve the greatest prince in Europe. Whilst this storm was hanging over his head, he writ many letters to the King and the Marquis of Buckingham, which I have seen, complaining of his misfortune, that his ruin was likely to proceed from the assistance he gave to his nearest relations.—*Stephens.*

self well, and had an evident applause.* I meant well also; and because my information was the ground; having spoken out of a few heads which I had gathered, for I seldom do more, I set down, as soon as I came home, cursorily, a frame of that I had said; though I persuade myself I spake it with more life. I have sent it to Mr. Murray sealed; if your majesty have so much idle time to look upon it, it may give some light of the day's work: but I most humbly pray your majesty to pardon the errors. God preserve you ever.

Your majesty's most humble Subject,
and devoted Servant,

April 29, 1615. FR. BACON.

Sir Francis Bacon to King James.†

It may please your most excellent Majesty,

It pleased your majesty to commit to my care and trust for Westminster Hall three particulars; that of the *rege inconsulto*, which concerneth Murray; that of the commendams, which concerneth the Bishop of Lincoln; and that of the *habeas corpus*, which concerneth the Chancery.

These causes, although I gave them private additions, yet they are merely, or at least chiefly, yours; and the die runneth upon your royal prerogatives diminution, or entire conservation. Of these it is my duty to give your majesty a short account.

For that of the *rege inconsulto*, I argued the same in the King's Bench on Thursday last. There argued on the other part Mr. George Crook, the judge's brother, an able book-man, and one that was manned forth with all the furniture that the bar could give him, I will not say the bench, and with the study of a long vacation. I was to

---

* William, Earl of Pembroke, son to Henry Herbert, Earl of Pembroke, Lord President of the Council in the marches of Wales, by Mary his wife, a lady in whom the muses and graces seemed to meet; whose very letters, in the judgment of one who saw many of them, declared her to be mistress of a pen not inferior to that of her brother, the admirable Sir Philip Sidney, and to whom he addressed his Arcadia. Nor did this gentleman degenerate from their wit and spirit, as his poems, his great patronage of learned men, and resolute opposition to the Spanish match, did, among other instances, fully prove. In the year 1616, he was made lord chamberlain, and chosen chancellor of the university of Oxford. He died suddenly on the 10th of April, 1630, having just completed fifty years. But his only son deceasing, a child, before him, his estate and honours descended upon his younger brother, Philip, Earl of Montgomery, the lineal ancestor of the present noble and learned earl.—*Stephens.*

† Sir David Dalrymple's Memorials and Letters, p. 46.

answer, which hath a mixture of the sudden; and of myself I will not, nor cannot say any thing, but that my voice served me well for two hours and a half; and that those that understood nothing could tell me that I lost not one auditor that was present in the beginning, but staid till the latter end. If I should say more, there were too many witnesses, for I never saw the court more full, that might disprove me.

My Lord Coke was pleased to say, that it was a famous argument; but withal, he asked me a politic and tempting question: for, taking occasion by a notable precedent I had cited, where, upon the like writ brought, all the judges in England assembled, and that privately, lest they should seem to dispute the King's commandment, and, upon conference, with one mind agreed, that the writ must be obeyed. Upon this hold, my lord asked me, whether I would have all the rest of the judges called to it. I was not caught; but knowing well that the judges of the Common Pleas were most of all others interested in respect of the prothonotaries, I answered, civilly, that I could advise of it; but that I did not distrust the court; and, besides, I thought the case so clear, as it needed not.

Sir, I do perceive, that I have not only stopped, but almost turned the stream; and I see how things cool by this, that the judges that were wont to call so hotly upon the business, when they had heard, of themselves, took a fortnight day to advise what they will do, by which time the term will be near at an end; and I know they little expected to have the matter so beaten down with book-law, upon which my argument wholly went; so that every mean student was satisfied. Yet, because the times are as they are, I could wish, in all humbleness, that your majesty would remember and renew your former commandment which you gave my Lord Chief Justice in Michaelmas term, which was, that after he had heard your attorney, which is now done, he should forbear further proceeding till he had spoke with your majesty.

It concerneth your majesty threefold. First, in this particular of Murray; next, in the consequence of fourteen several patents, part in Queen Elizabeth's time, some in your majesty's time, which depend upon the like question; but chiefly because this writ is a mean provided by the ancient law of England, to bring any case that may concern your majesty, in profit or power, from the ordinary benches, to be tried and judged before your Chancellor of

England, by the ordinary and legal part of his power: and your majesty knoweth your Chancellor is ever a principal counsellor, and instrument of monarchy, of immediate dependence upon the King: and therefore like to be a safe and tender guardian of the royal rights.

For the case of the commendams, a matter likewise of great consequence, though nothing near the first, this day I was prepared to have argued it before all the judges; but, by reason of the sickness of the serjeant which was provided to argue on the other side, although I pressed to have had some other day appointed this term; yet it pleased divers of the judges to do me the honour, as to say it was not fit any should argue against me, upon so small time of warning, it is adjourned to the first Saturday next term.

For the matter of the *habeas corpus*, I perceive this common employment of my Lord Chancellor, and my Lord Chief Justice, in these examinations, is such a *vinculum*, as they will not square while these matters are in hand, so that there is *altum silentium* of that matter. God ever preserve your majesty.

Your Majesty's most humble
and bounden Subject and Servant,

Jan. 27, 1615. FR. BACON.

To Sir George Villiers, on sending his Bill for Viscount.*

Sir,

I send you the bill for his majesty's signature, reformed according to his majesty's amendments, both in the two places, which, I assure you, were both altered with great judgment, and in the third place, which his majesty termed a question only. But he is an idle body that thinks his majesty asks an idle question; and therefore his majesty's questions are to be answered by taking away the cause of the question, and not by replying.

For the name, his majesty's will, is law in those things; and to speak truth, it is a well sounding and noble name, both here and abroad; and being your proper name, I will take it for a good sign that you shall give honour to your dignity, and not your dignity to you. Therefore I have made it Viscount Villiers: and for your barony, I will keep it for an earldom; for though the other had been more orderly, yet that is as usual, and both alike good in law.

* Stephens's second Collection, p. 10.

For Roper's place,* I would have it by all means despatched; and therefore I marvel it lingereth. It were no good manners to take the business out of my Lord Treasurer's hands; and therefore I purpose to write to his lordship, if I hear not from him first by Mr. Deccomb. But if I hear of any delay, you will give me leave, especially since the King named me, to deal with Sir John Roper myself; for neither I nor my Lord Treasurer can deserve any great thanks of you in this business, considering the King hath spoken to Sir John Roper, and he hath promised; and, besides, the thing itself is so reasonable as it ought to be as soon done as said. I am now gotten into the country to my house, where I have some little liberty to think of that I would think of, and not of that which other men hourly break my head withal, as it was at London. Upon this you may conclude, that most of my thoughts are of his majesty; and then you cannot be far off. God ever keep you, and prosper you. I rest always

Your true and most devoted Servant,

Aug. 5, one of the happiest days, 1616. FR. BACON.

† To Father Redempt. Baranzan.‡

Domine Baranzane,

Literas tuas legi libenter: cumque inter veritatis amatores ardor etiam candorem generet, ad ea, quæ ingenue petiisti, ingenue respondebo.

Non est meum abdicare in totum syllogismum. Res est

---

* Sir John Roper, who had for many years enjoyed the place of the chief clerk for enrolling of pleas in the court of King's Bench, esteemed to be worth about four thousand pounds per annum, being grown old, was prevailed with to surrender it upon being created Lord Teynham, with a reservation of the profits thereof to himself during life. Upon which surrender Sir George Villiers was to have the office granted to two of his trustees for their lives, as Carr, Earl of Somerset, was to have had before. But the Lord Chief Justice Coke not being very forward to accept of the surrender, or make a new grant of it upon those terms, he was, upon the 3d of October, 1616, commanded to desist from the service of this place, and at last removed from it upon the 15th of November following. His successor Sir Henry Montagu, third son of Sir Edward Montagu, of Boughton in Northamptonshire, recorder of London, and king's serjeant, being more complaisant, Sir John Roper resigned towards the latter end of the same month; and Mr. Shute, and Mr. Heath, who was afterwards the king's solicitor general, being the deputies and trustees of Sir George Villiers, were admitted.—*Stephens's Introduct.* p. 37.

† From Niceron, tom. iii. p. 45.

‡ He was a Barnabite monk at Annecy in Savoy, who in his Lectures on Philosophy, began to discard the authority of Aristotle. He died the 23d of December, 1622, at the age of 33.

syllogismus magis inhabilis ad præcipua, quam inutilis ad plurima.

Ad mathematica quidni adhibeatur? Cum fluxus materiæ et inconstantia corporis physici illud sit, quod inductionem desideret; ut per eam veluti figatur, atque inde eruantur notiones bene terminatæ.

De metaphysica ne sis sollicitus. Nulla enim erit post veram physicam inventam; ultra quam nihil præter divina.

In physica prudenter notas, et idem tecum sentio, pos notiones primæ classis, et axiomata super ipsas, per inductionem bene eruta et terminata, tuto adhiberi syllogismum, modo inhibeatur saltus ad generalissima, et fiat progressus per scalam convenientem.

De multitudine instantiarum, quæ homines deterrere possit, hæc respondeo:

Primo, quid opus est dissimulatione? Aut copia instantiarum comparanda, aut negotium deserendum. Aliæ omnes viæ, utcunque blandiantur, imperviæ.

Secundo (quod et ipse notas) prærogativæ instantiarum, et modus experimentandi circa experimenta lucifera (quem aliquando trademus) de multitudine ipsarum plurimum detrahent.

Tertio, quid magni foret, rogo, si in describendis instantiis impleantur volumina, quæ historiam C. Plinii sextuplicent? In qua tamen ipsa plurima philologica, fabulosa, antiquitatis, non naturæ. Etenim veram historiam naturalem nihil aliud ingreditur præter instantias, connexiones, observationes, canones. Cogita altera ex parte immensa volumina philosophica; facile perspicies maxime solida esse maxime finita.

Postremo, ex nostra philosophandi methodo excipietur in via plurimorum operum utilium messis, quæ ex speculationibus aut disputationibus sterilis aut nulla est.

Historiam naturalem ad condendam philosophiam (ut et tu mones) ante omnia præopto; neque huic rei deero, quantum in me est. Utinam habeam et adjutores idoneos. Neque in hac parte mihi quidpiam accidere poterit felicius, quam si tu, talis vir, primitias huic operi præbeas conscribendo historiam cœlestium, in qua ipsa tantum phænomena, atque una instrumenta astronomica, eorumque genera et usum; dein hypotheses præcipuas et maxime illustres, tam antiquas quam modernas, atque simul exactas restitutionum calculationes, et alia hujusmodi sincere proponas, absque omni dogmate et themate. Quod si huic cœlestium historiæ historiam cometarum adjeceris (de qua conficienda ecce tibi articulos quosdam et quasi topica particularia) magnificum prorsus frontispicium historiæ naturali extruxeris, et optime de scientiarum instauratione merueris, mihique gratissimum feceris.

Librum meum de progressu scientiarum traducendum commisi. Illa translatio, volente Deo, sub finem æstatis perficietur: eam ad te mittam.

Opera tua, quæ publici juris sunt, inspexi; magnæ certe subtilitatis et diligentiæ in via vestra. Novatores, quos nominas, Patricium, Telesium, etiam alios, quos prætermittis, legi. Possint esse tales innumeri velut etiam antiquis temporibus fuerunt Anaximenes, Anaxagoras, Democritus, Parmenides, et alii (nam Pythagoram ut superstitiosum omitto). Inter istos tam antiquos quam modernos differentiam facultatis agnosco maximam, veritatis preparvam. Summa rei est, si homines se rebus submittere velint, aliquid confiet; sin minus, ingenia ista redibunt in orbem.

Stabilita jam sit inter nos notitia; meque, ut cœpisti, maxime autem veritatem ama. Vale.

Tui amantissimus,

S. ALBANS.

Apud Ædes meas,
Londinii, Junii ultimo, 1622.

By King James.*

To our trusty and well beloved Thomas Coventry our Attorney General.

Trusty and well beloved, we greet you well:

Whereas our right trusty and right well beloved cousin, the Viscount of St. Alban, upon a sentence given in the upper house of parliament full three years since, and more, hath endured loss of his place, imprisonment, and confinement† also for a great time, which may suffice for the satisfaction of justice, and example to others: we being always graciously inclined to temper mercy with justice, and calling to mind his former good services, and how well and profitably he hath spent his time since his trouble, are pleased to remove from him that blot of ignominy which yet remaineth upon him, of incapacity and disablement; and to remit to him all penalties whatsoever inflicted by that sentence. Having therefore formerly pardoned his fine, and released his confinement, these are to will and require you to prepare, for our signature, a bill containing a pardon, in

* Cabala, 270. Edw. 1663.

† His sentence forbid his coming within the verge of the court. [In consequence of this letter, my Lord Bacon was summoned to parliament in the first year of King Charles].

due form of law, of the whole sentence; for which this shall be your sufficient warrant.

Mr. Francis Bacon to the Earl of Essex.*

My Lord,

I did almost conjecture, by your silence and countenance, a distaste in the course I imparted to your lordship touching mine own fortune; the care whereof in your lordship as it is no news to me, so nevertheless the main effects and demonstrations past are so far from dulling in me the sense of any new, as contrariwise every new refresheth the memory of many past. And for the free and loving advice your lordship hath given me, I cannot correspond to the same with greater duty, than by assuring your lordship, that I will not dispose of myself without your allowance, not only because it is the best wisdom in any man in his own matters, to rest in the wisdom of a friend (for who can by often looking in the glass discern and judge so well of his own favour as another with whom he converseth?) but also because my affection to your lordship hath made mine own contentment inseparable from your satisfaction. But, notwithstanding, I know it will be pleasing to your good lordship that I use my liberty of replying; and I do almost assure myself, that your lordship will rest persuaded by the answer of those reasons which your lordship vouchsafed to open. They were two, the one, that I should include * * *

April, 1593.

The rest of the letter is wanting.

The Earl of Essex to Mr. Francis Bacon.†

Mr. Bacon,

Your letter met me here yesterday. When I came, I found the Queen so wayward, as I thought it no fit time to deal with her in any sort, especially since her choler grew towards myself, which I have well satisfied this day, and will take the first opportunity I can to move your suit. And if you come hither, I pray you let me know still where you are. And so, being full of business, I must end, wishing you what you wish to yourself.

Your assured Friend,

Sept. 1593. ESSEX.

---

* Among the papers of Antony Bacon, Esq. vol. iii. fol. 74. in the Lambeth Library.

† Ibid. fol. 197.

Lord Treasurer Burghley to Mr. Francis Bacon.*

Nephew,

I have no leisure to write much; but for answer I have attempted to place you: but her majesty hath required the Lord Keeper† to give to her the names of divers lawyers to be preferred, wherewith he made me acquainted, and I did name you as a meet man, whom his lordship allowed in way of friendship, for your father's sake: but he made scruple to equal you with certain, whom he named, as Brograve‡ and Branthwayt, whom he specially commendeth. But I will continue the remembrance of you to her majesty, and implore my Lord of Essex's help.

Your loving Uncle,

Sept. 27, 1593. N. BURGHLEY.

Sir Robert Cecil to Mr. Francis Bacon.§

Cousin,

Assure yourself that the solicitor's|| coming gave no cause of speech; for it was concerning a book to be drawn, concerning the bargain of wines. If there had been you should have known, or when there shall. To satisfy your request of making my lord know, how recommended your desires are to me, I have spoken with his lordship, who answereth he hath done and will do his best. I think your absence longer than for my good aunt's comfort will do you no good: for, as I ever told you, it is not likely to find the Queen apt to give an office, when the scruple is not removed of her forbearance to speak with you. This being not yet perfected may stop good, when the hour comes of conclusion, though it be but a trifle, and questionless would be straight dispatched, if it were luckily handled. But herein do I, out of my desire to satisfy you, use this my opinion, leaving you to your own better knowledge what hath been done for you, or in what terms

---

* Among the papers of Antony Bacon, Esq. vol. iii. fol. 197, in the Lambeth Library.

† Puckering.

‡ John Brograve, attorney of the duchy of Lancaster, and afterwards knighted. He is mentioned by Mr Francis Bacon, in his letter to the Lord Treasurer of 7th June, 1595, from Gray's Inn, as having discharged his post of attorney of the duchy with great sufficiency. There is extant of his, in print, a reading upon the statute of 27 Henry VIII. concerning jointures.

§ Among the papers of Antony Bacon, Esq. vol. iii. fol. 197, *verso*, in the Lambeth Library.

|| Mr. Edward Coke.

that matter standeth. And thus, desirous to be recommended to my good aunt, to whom my wife heartily commends her, I leave you to the protection of Almighty God.

Your loving Cousin and Friend,

From the Court at Windsor, this 27th of September, 1593. ROBERT CECIL.

I have heard in these causes, *Facies hominis est tanquam leonis.*

Mr. Francis Bacon to the Queen.*

Madam,

Remembering that your majesty had been gracious to me both in countenancing me, and conferring upon me the reversion of a good place, and perceiving that your majesty had taken some displeasure towards me, both these were arguments to move me to offer unto your majesty my service, to the end to have means to deserve your favour, and to repair my error. Upon this ground, I affected myself to no great matter, but only a place of my profession, such as I do see divers younger in proceeding to myself, and men of no great note, do without blame aspire unto. But if any of my friends do press this matter, I do assure your majesty my spirit is not with them.

It sufficeth me that I have let your majesty know that I am ready to do that for the service, which I never would do for mine own gain. And if your majesty like others better, I shall, with the Lacedemonian, be glad that there is such choice of abler men than myself. Your majesty's favour indeed, and access to your royal person, I did ever, encouraged by your own speeches, seek and desire; and I would be very glad to be reintegrate in that. But I will not wrong mine own good mind so much as to stand upon that now, when your majesty may conceive I do it but to make my profit of it. But my mind turneth upon other wheels than those of profit. The conclusion shall be, that I wish your majesty served answerable to yourself. *Principis est virtus maxima nosse suos.* Thus I most humbly crave pardon of my boldness and plainness. God preserve your majesty.

Mr. Francis Bacon to Robert Kemp, of Gray's Inn, Esq.†

Good Robin,

There is no news you can write to me, which I take more pleasure to hear, than of your health, and of your loving

* Among the papers of Antony Bacon, Esq. vol. iii. fol. 315, in the Lambeth Library. † Ibid. fol. 281.

remembrance of me; the former whereof though you mention not in your letter, yet I straight presumed well of it, because your mention was so fresh to make such a flourish. And it was afterwards accordingly confirmed by your man, Roger, who made me a particular relation of the former negotiation between your ague and you. Of the latter, though you profess largely, yet I make more doubt, because your coming is turned into a sending; which when I thought would have been repaired by some promise or intention of yourself, your man Roger entered into a very subtle distinction to this purpose, that you could not come except you heard I was attorney; but I ascribe that to your man's invention, who had his reward in laughing; for I hope you are not so stately, but that I shall be one to you *stylo vetere* or *stylo novo.* For my fortune (to speak court) it is very slow, if any thing can be slow to him that is secure of the event. In short nothing is done in it; but I propose to remain here at Twickenham till Michaelmas term, then to St. Albans, and after the term to court. Advise you, whether you will play the honest man or no. In the mean time I think long to see you, and pray to be remembered to your father and mother.

Yours, in loving affection,

From Twickenham Park,
this 4th of Nov. 1593.

FR. BACON.

Mr. Francis Bacon to the Earl of Essex.*

My Lord,

I thought it not amiss to inform your lordship of that, which I gather partly by conjecture, and partly by advertisement of the late recovered man, that is so much at your devotion, of whom I have some cause to think, that he† worketh for the Huddler‡ underhand. And though it may seem strange, considering how much it importeth him to join straight with your lordship, in regard both of his enemies and of his ends; yet I do the less rest secure upon the conceit, because he is a man likely to trust so much to his art and finesse (as he, that is an excellent wherryman, who, you know, looketh towards the bridge, when he pulleth towards Westminster) that he will hope to serve his turn, and yet to preserve your lordship's good opinion. This I write

* Among the papers of Antony Bacon, Esq. vol. iii. fol. 283, in the Lambeth Library.
† Probably Lord Keeper Puckering.
‡ Mr. Edward Coke.

to the end, that if your lordship do see nothing to the contrary, you may assure him more, or trust him less; and chiefly, that your lordship be pleased to sound again, whether they have not, amongst them, drawn out the nail, which your lordship had driven in for the negative of the Huddler; which, if they have, it will be necessary for your lordship to iterate more forcibly your former reasons, whereof there is such *copia*, as I think you may use all the places of logic against his placing.

Thus, with my humble thanks for your lordship's honourable usage of Mr. Standen, I wish you all honour.

Your Lordship's, in most faithful duty,

Nov. 10, 1593. FR. BACON.

I pray, Sir, let not my jargon privilege my letter from burning; because it is not such, but the light showeth through.

Earl of Essex to Mr. Francis Bacon.*

Sir,

I have received your letter, and since I have had opportunity to deal freely with the Queen. I have dealt confidently with her as a matter, wherein I did more labour to overcome her delays, than that I did fear her denial. I told her how much you were thrown down with the correction she had already given you, that she might in that point hold herself already satisfied. And because I found, that Tanfield† had been most propounded to her, I did most disable him. I find the Queen very reserved, staying herself upon giving any kind of hope, yet not passionate against you, till I grew passionate for you. Then she said, that none thought you fit for the place but my Lord Treasurer and myself. Marry, the others must some of them say before us for fear or for flattery. I told her, the most and wisest of her council had delivered their opinions, and preferred you before all men for that place. And if it would please her majesty to think, that whatsoever they said contrary to their own words when they spake without witness, might be as factiously spoken, as the other way flatteringly, she would not be deceived. Yet if they had been never for you, but contrarily against you, I thought my credit, joined

---

* Among the papers of Antony Bacon, Esq. vol. iv. fol. 90, in the Lambeth Library.

† Probably Laurence Tanfield, made Lord Chief Baron of the Exchequer in June, 1607.

with the approbation and mediation of her greatest counsellors, might prevail in a greater matter than this; and urged her, that though she could not signify her mind to others, I might have a secret promise, wherein I should receive great comfort, as in the contrary great unkindness. She said she was neither persuaded nor would hear of it till Easter, when she might advise with her council, who were now all absent; and, therefore, in passion bid me go to bed, if I would talk of nothing else. Wherefore in passion I went away, saying, while I was with her, I could not but solicit for the cause and the man I so much affected; and therefore I would retire myself till I might be more graciously heard; and so we parted. To-morrow I will go hence of purpose, and on Thursday I will write an expostulating letter to her. That night or upon Friday morning I will be here again, and follow on the same course, stirring a discontentment in her, &c. And so wish you all happiness, and rest

Your most assured Friend,

ESSEX.

Indorsed—*March* 28, 1594.

The Earl of Essex to Mr. Francis Bacon.*

Sir,

I have now spoken with the Queen, and I see no stay from obtaining a full resolution of that we desire. But the passion she is in by reason of the tales that have been told her against Nicholas Clifford, with whom she is in such rage, for a matter, which I think you have heard of, doth put her infinitely out of quiet; and her passionate humour is nourished by some foolish women. Else I find nothing to distaste us, for she doth not contradict confidently; which they, that know the minds of women, say is a sign of yielding. I will to-morrow take more time to deal with her, and will sweeten her with all the art I have to make *benevolum auditorem.* I have already spoken with Mr. Vice-Chamberlain,† and will to-morrow speak with the rest. Of Mr. Vice-Chamberlain you may assure yourself; for so much he hath faithfully promised me. The exceptions against the competitors I will use to-morrow; for then I do resolve to have a full and large discourse, having pre-

---

* Among the papers of Antony Bacon, Esq. vol. iv. fol. 89, in the Lambeth Library.

† Sir Thomas Heneage.

pared the Queen to-night to assign me a time under colour of some such business, as I have pretended. In the mean time I must tell you, that I do not respect either my absence, or my showing a discontentment in going away, for I was received at my return, and I think I shall not be the worse. And for that I am oppressed with multitude of letters that are come, of which I must give the Queen some account to-morrow morning, I therefore desire to be excused for writing no more to-night: to-morrow you shall hear from me again. I wish you what you wish yourself in this and all things else, and rest

Your most affectionate Friend,

This Friday at night ESSEX.

Indorsed, March 29, 1594.

Mr. Francis Bacon to the Earl of Essex.*

My Lord,

I thank your lordship very much for your kind and comfortable letter, which I hope will be followed at hand with another of more assurance. And I must confess this very delay hath gone so near me, as it hath almost overthrown my health; for when I revolved the good memory of my father, the near degree of alliance I stand in to my Lord Treasurer, your lordship's so signalled and declared favour the honourable testimony of so many counsellors, the commendations unlaboured, and in sort offered by my lords the Judges and the Master of the Rolls elect;† that I was voiced with great expectation, and, though I say it myself, with the wishes of most men, to the higher place;‡ that I am a man, that the Queen hath already done for; and that princes, especially her majesty, love to make an end where they begin; and then add hereunto the obscureness and many exceptions to my competitors: when I say I revolve all this, I cannot but conclude with myself, that no man ever read a more exquisite disgrace; and therefore truly, my lord, I was determined, if her majesty reject me, this to do. My nature can take no evil ply; but I will, by God's assistance, with this disgrace of my fortune, and yet with that comfort of the good opinion of so many honourable and worthy persons, retire myself with a couple of men to Cambridge, and there spend my life in my studies and con-

---

* Among the papers of Antony Bacon, Esq. vol. iii. fol. 62, in the Lambeth Library.

† Sir Thomas Egerton.

‡ That of Attorney-General.

templations without looking back: I humbly pray your lordship to pardon me for troubling you with my melancholy. For the matter itself, I commend it to your love; only I pray you communicate afresh this day with my Lord Treasurer and Sir Robert Cecil; and if you esteem my fortune, remember the point of precedency. The objections to my competitors your lordship knoweth partly. I pray spare them not, not over the Queen, but to the great ones, to show your confidence, and to work their distrust. Thus longing exceedingly to exchange troubling your lordship with serving you, I rest

Your Lordship's,
in most intire and faithful service,
March 30, 1594. FANCIS BACON.

I humbly pray your lordship I may hear from you some time this day.

Mr. Francis Bacon to Sir Robert Cecil.*

My most honourable good Cousin,

Your honour in your wisdom doth well perceive, that my access at this time is grown desperate in regard of the hard terms, that as well the Earl of Essex as Mr. Vice-Chamberlain, who were to have been the means thereof, stand in with her majesty, according to their occasions. And therefore I am only to stay upon that point of delaying and preserving the matter intire till a better constellation; which, as it is not hard, as I conceive, considering the French business and the instant progress, &c. so I commend in special to you the care, who in sort assured me thereof, and upon whom now, in my Lord of Essex's absence, I have only to rely; and, if it be needful, I humbly pray you to move my lord your father to lay his hand to the same delay. And so I wish you all increase of honour.

Your Honour's poor kinsman,
in faithful service and duty,
From Gray's Inn, this 1st of May, 1594. FRANCIS BACON.

Sir Robert Cecil's Answer.*

Cousin,

I do think nothing cut the throat more of your present access than the earl's being somewhat troubled at this time.

---

* Among the papers of Antony Bacon, Esq. vol. iv. fol. 122, in the Lambeth Libiaiy.

† Ibid. fol. 122.

For the delaying I think it not hard, neither shall there want my best endeavour to make it easy, of which I hope you shall not need to doubt by the judgment, which I gather of divers circumstances confirming my opinion. I protest I suffer with you in mind, that you are thus gravelled; but time will founder all your competitors, and set you on your feet, or else I have little understanding.

Earl of Essex to Mr. Francis Bacon.*

Sir,

I wrote not to you till I had had a second conference with the Queen, because the first was spent only in compliments: she in the beginning excepted all business: this day she hath seen me again. After I had followed her humour in talking of those things, which she would entertain me with, I told her, in my absence I had written to Sir Robert Cecil, to solicit her to call you to that place, to which all the world had named you; and being now here, I must follow it myself; for I know what service I should do her in procuring you the place; and she knew not how great a comfort I should take in it. Her answer in playing just was, that she came not to me for that, I should talk of those things when I came to her, not when she came to me; the term was coming, and she would advise. I would have replied, but she stopped my mouth. To-morrow or the next day I will go to her, and then this excuse will be taken away. When I know more, you shall hear more; and so I end full of pain in my head, which makes me write thus confusedly.

Your most affectionate Friend.

Earl of Essex to Mr. Francis Bacon.†

Sir,

I went yesterday to the Queen through the galleries in the morning, afternoon, and at night. I had long speech with her of you, wherein I urged both the point of your extraordinary sufficiency proved to me not only by your last argument, but by the opinion of all men I spake withal, and the point of mine own satisfaction, which, I protested, should be exceeding great, if, for all her unkindness and discomforts past, she should do this one thing for my sake.

---

* Among the papers of Antony Bacon, Esq. vol. iv. fol. 122, in the Lambeth Library.

† Ibid. 123.

To the first she answered, that the greatness of your friends, as of my Lord Treasurer and myself, did make men give a more favourable testimony than else they would do, thinking thereby they pleased us. And that she did acknowledge you had a great wit, and an excellent gift of speech, and much other good learning. But in law she rather thought you could make show to the uttermost of your knowledge, than that you were deep. To the second she said, she showed her mislike to the suit, as well as I had done my affection in it; and that if there were a yielding, it was fitter to be of my side. I then added, that this was an answer, with which she might deny me all things, if she did not grant them at the first, which was not her manner to do. But her majesty had made me suffer and give way in many things else; which all I should bear, not only with patience, but with great contentment, if she would but grant my humble suit in this one. And for the pretence of the approbation given you upon partiality, that all the world, lawyers, judges, and all, could not be partial to you; for somewhat you were crossed for their own interest, and some for their friends; but yet all did yield to your merit. She did in this as she useth in all, went from a denial to a delay, and said, when the council were all here, she would think of it; and there was no haste in determining of the place. To which I answered, that my sad heart had need of hasty comfort; and therefore her majesty must pardon me, if I were hasty and importunate in it. When they come we shall see what will be done; and I wish you all happiness, and rest

Your most affectionate Friend,

ESSEX.

Indorsed—18*th of May*, 1594.

Foulke Grevill, Esq. to Mr. Francis Bacon.*

Mr. Francis Bacon,

Saturda was my first coming to the court, from whence I departedy again as soon as I had kissed her majesty's hands, because I had no lodging nearer than my uncle's, which is four miles off. This day I came thither to dinner, and waiting for to speak with the Queen, took occasion to tell how I met you, as I passed through London; and among other speeches, how you lamented your misfortune

* Among the papers of Antony Bacon, Esq. vol. iv. fol. 132, in the Lambeth Library.

to me, that remained as a withered branch of her roots, which she had cherished and made to flourish in her service. I added what I thought of your worth, and the expectation for all this, that the world had of her princely goodness towards you: which it pleased her majesty to confess, that indeed you began to frame very well, insomuch as she saw an amends in those little supposed errors, avowing the respect she carried to the dead, with very exceeding gracious inclination towards you. Some comparisons there fell out besides, which I leave till we meet, which I hope shall be this week. It pleased her withal to tell of the jewel you offered her by Mr. Vice-Chamberlain, which she had refused, yet with exceeding praise. I marvel, that as a prince she should refuse those havings of her poor subjects, because it did include a small sentence of despair; but either I deceive myself, or she was resolved to take it; and the conclusion was very kind and gracious. Sure as I will one hundred pounds to fifty pounds that you shall be her solicitor, and my friend; in which mind and for which mind I commend you to God. From the court this Monday in haste,

Your true Friend to be commanded by you,

FOULKE GREVILL.

We cannot tell whether she come to ——— or stay here. I am much absent for want of lodging; wherein my own man hath only been to blame.

Indorsed—17*th of June*, 1594.

Mr. Francis Bacon to the Queen.*

Most gracious and admirable Sovereign,

As I do acknowledge a providence of God towards me, that findeth it expedient for me *tolerare jugum in juventute meâ;* so this present arrest of mine by his divine majesty from your majesty's service is not the least affliction, that I have proved; and I hope your majesty doth conceive, that nothing under mere impossibility could have detained me from earning so gracious a vail, as it pleased your majesty to give me. But your majesty's service by the grace of God shall take no lack thereby; and, thanks to God, it hath lighted upon him that may be best spared. Only the

* Among the papers of Antony Bacon, Esq. vol. iv. fol. 141 and 156, in the Lambeth Library.

discomfort is mine, who nevertheless have the private comfort, that in the time I have been made acquainted with this service, it hath been my hap to stumble upon somewhat unseen, which may import the same, as I made my Lord Keeper acquainted before my going. So leaving it to God to make a good end of a hard beginning, and most humbly craving your majesty's pardon for presuming to trouble you, I recommend your sacred majesty to God's tenderest preservation.

Your sacred Majesty's,
in most humble obedience and devotion,
FR. BACON.

From Huntingdon,
this 20th of July, 1594.

Mr. Francis Bacon to his Brother Antony.*

My good Brother,

One day draweth on another; and I am well pleased in my being here; for methinks solitariness collecteth the mind, as shutting the eyes doth the sight. I pray you, therefore, advertise me what you find, by my Lord of Essex (who, I am sure, hath been with you), was done last Sunday; and what he conceiveth of the matter. I hold in one secret, and therefore you may trust your servant. I would be glad to receive my parsonage rent as soon as it cometh. So leave I you to God's good preservation.

Your ever loving Brother,
FR. BACON.

From Twickenham Park,
this Tuesday morning, 1594.

Indorsed—16 *Oct.* 1594.

Earl of Essex to Mr. Francis Bacon.†

Sir,

I will be to-morrow night at London. I purpose to hear your argument the next day. I pray you send me word by this bearer of the hour and place where it is. Of your own cause I shall give better account when I see you, than I can do now; for that which will be done, will be this afternoon or to-morrow.

I am fast unto you, as you can be to yourself,
ESSEX.

Indorsed—23 *Oct.* 1594.

---

* Among the papers of Antony Bacon, Esq. vol. iv. fol. 197, in the Lambeth Library.

† Ibid. fol. 195.

Mr. Francis Bacon to his Brother Antony.*

Good Brother,

Since I saw you this hath passed. Tuesday, though sent for, I saw not the Queen. Her majesty alledged she was then to resolve with the council upon her places of law. But this resolution was *ut supra;* and note the rest of the counsellors were persuaded she came rather forwards than otherwise; for against me she is never peremptory but to my lord of Essex. I missed a line of my Lord Keeper's; but thus much I hear otherwise. The Queen seemeth to apprehend my travel. Whereupon I was sent for by Sir Robert Cecil in sort as from her majesty; himself having of purpose immediately gone to London to speak with me; and not finding me there, he wrote to me. Whereupon I came to the court, and upon his relation to me of her majesty's speeches, I desired leave to answer it in writing; not, I said, that I mistrusted his report, but mine own wit; the copy of which answer I send. We parted in kindness *secundum exterius.* This copy you must needs return, for I have no other; and I wrote this by memory after the original was sent away. The Queen's speech is after this sort. *Why? I have made no solicitor. Hath any body carried a solicitor with him in his pocket? But he must have it in his own time* (as if it were but yesterday's nomination) *or else I must be thought to cast him away.* Then her majesty sweareth thus: "If I continue this manner, she will seek all England for a solicitor rather than take me. Yea, she will send for Heuston and Coventry† to-morrow next," as if she would swear them both. Again she entereth into it, that "she never deals so with any as with me *(in hoc erratum non est)* she hath pulled me over the bar *(note the words, for they cannot be her own)* she hath used me in her greatest causes. But this is Essex, and she is more angry with him than with me." And such like speeches, so strange, as I should lose myself in it, but that I have cast off the care of it. My conceit is, that I am the least part of mine own matter. But her majesty would have a delay, and yet would not bear it herself. Therefore she giveth no way to me, and she perceiveth her council giveth no way

---

* Among the papers of Antony Bacon, Esq. vol. iv. fol. 28, in the Lambeth Library.

† Thomas Coventry, afterwards one of the Justices of the Common Pleas, and father of the Lord Keeper Coventry.

to others; and so it sticketh as she would have it. But what the secret of it is *oculus aquilæ non penetravit.* My lord* continueth on kindly and wisely a course worthy to obtain a better effect than a delay, which to me is the most unwelcome condition.

Now to return to you the part of a brother, and to render you the like kindness, advise you, whether it were not a good time to set in strongly with the Queen to draw her to honour your travels. For in the course I am like to take, it will be a great and necessary stay to me, besides the natural comfort I shall receive. And if you will have me deal with my Lord of Essex, or otherwise break it by mean to the Queen, as that, which shall give me full contentment, I will do it as effectually, and with as much good discretion as I can. Wherein if you aid me with your direction, I shall observe it. This as I did ever account it sure and certain to be accomplished, in case myself had been placed, and therefore deferred it till then, as to the proper opportunity; so now that I see such delay in mine own placing, I wish *ex animo* it should not expect.

I pray you let me know what mine uncle Killigrew will do;† for I must be more careful of my credit than ever, since I receive so little thence where I deserved best. And, to be plain with you, I mean even to make the best of those small things I have with as much expedition, as may be without loss; and so sing a mass of *requiem*, I hope, abroad. For I know her majesty's nature, that she neither careth though the whole surname of Bacons travelled, nor of the Cecils neither.

I have here an idle pen or two, specially one, that was cozened, thinking to have got some money this term. I pray send me somewhat else for them to write out besides your Irish collection, which is almost done. There is a collection of King James, of foreign states, largeliest of Flanders; which, though it be no great matter, yet I would be glad to have it. Thus I commend you to God's good protection.

Your entire loving Brother,

From my lodging, at Twickenham Park,
this 25th of January, 1594.

FR. BACON.

---

* Essex.

† Mr. Antony Bacon had written to Sir Henry Killigrew on the 14th of January, 1594-5, to desire the loan of two hundred pounds for six months. Vol. iv. fol. 4.

Letter of Mr. Francis Bacon to Sir Robert Cecil;* a copy of which was sent with the preceding to Mr. Antony Bacon.

Sir,

Your honour may remember, that upon relation of her majesty's speech concerning my travel, I asked leave to make answer in writing; not but I knew then what was true, but because I was careful to express it without doing myself wrong. And it is true, I had then opinion to have written to her majesty: but, since weighing with myself, that her majesty gave no ear to the motion made by yourself, that I might answer by mine own attendance, I began to doubt the second degree, whether it might not be taken for presumption in me to write to her majesty; and so resolved, that it was best for me to follow her majesty's own way in committing it to your report.

It may please your honour to deliver to her majesty, first, that it is an exceeding grief to me, that any not motion (for it was not a motion) but mention, that should come from me, should offend her majesty, whom for these one and twenty years (for so long it is, that I kissed her majesty's hands upon my journey into France) I have used the best of my wits to please.

Next, mine answer standing upon two points, the one, that this mention of travel to my Lord of Essex was no present motion, suit, or request; but casting the worst of my fortune with an honourable friend, that had long used me privately, I told his lordship of this purpose of mine to travel, accompanying it with these very words, that upon her majesty's rejecting me with such circumstance, though my heart might be good, yet mine eyes would be sore, that I should take no pleasure to look upon my friends; for that I was not an impudent man, that could face out a disgrace; and that I hoped her majesty would not be offended, that, not able to endure the sun, I fled into the shade. The other, that it was more than this; for I did expressly and particularly (for so much wit God then lent me), by way of caveat, restrain my lord's good affection, that he should in no wise utter or mention this matter till her majesty had made a solicitor; wherewith (now since my looking upon your letter) I did in a dutiful manner challenge my lord, who very honourably acknow-

* Among the papers of Antony Bacon, Esq. vol. iv. fol. 31.

ledged it, seeing he did it for the best; and therefore I leave his lordship to answer for himself. All this my Lord of Essex can testify to be true: and I report me to yourself, whether at the first, when I desired deliberation to answer, yet nevertheless said, I would to you privately declare what had passed, I said not in effect so much. The conclusion shall be, that wheresoever God and her majesty shall appoint me to live, I shall truly pray for her majesty's preservation and felicity. And so I humbly commend me to you.

Your poor Kinsman to do you service,

FR. BACON.

Indorsed—*January*, 1594.

To Sir Thomas Egerton, Lord Keeper of the Great Seal.*

May it please your honourable good Lordship,

Of your lordship's honourable disposition, both generally and to me, I have that belief, as what I think, I am not afraid to speak; and what I would speak, I am not afraid to write. And therefore I have thought to commit to letter some matter, whereunto [which] I have been [conceived] led [into the same] by two motives: the one, the consideration of my own estate; the other, the appetite which I have to give your lordship some evidence of the thoughtful and voluntary desire, which is in me, to merit well of your most honourable lordship: which desire in me hath been bred chiefly by the consent I have to your great virtue come in good time to do this state pleasure; and next by your loving courses held towards me, especially in your nomination and inablement of me long since to the solicitor's place, as your lordship best knows. Which your two honourable friendships I esteem so much [in so great sort] as your countenance and favour in my practice, which are somewhat to my poverty; yet I count them not the best [greatest] part of the obligation wherein I stand bound to you.

And now, my lord, I pray you right humbly, that you will vouchsafe your honourable license and patience, that I may express to you, what in a doubtful liberty I have

* From the original draught in the library of Queen's College, Oxford, Arch. D. 2. the copy of which was communicated to me by Thomas Tyrwhitt, Esq. Clerk of the honourable House of Commons. Sir William Dugdale, in his Baronage of England, vol. ii, p. 438, has given two short passages of this letter transcribed by him from the unpublished original.

thought fit, partly by way of praying your help, and partly by way of offering my good will; partly again by way of preoccupating your conceit, lest you may in some things mistake.

My estate, to confess a truth to your lordship, is weak and indebted, and needeth comfort; for both my father, though I think I had greatest part in his love to all his children, yet in his wisdom served me in as a last comer; and myself, in mine own industry, have rather referred and aspired to virtue than to gain: whereof I am not yet wise enough to repent me. But the while, whereas Solomon speaketh that "want cometh first like a wayfaring man," and after like "an armed man," I must acknowledge to your lordship myself to [be] *in primo gradu;* for it stealeth upon me. But for the second, that it should not be able to be resisted, I hope in God I am not in that case; for the preventing whereof, as I do depend upon God's providence all in all, so in the same his providence I see opened unto me three not unlikely expectations of help: the one my practice, the other some proceeding in the Queen's service, the third [the] place I have in reversion; which, as it standeth now unto me, is but like another man's ground reaching upon my house, which may mend my prospect, but it doth not fill my barn.

For my practice, it presupposeth my health, which, if I should judge of as a man that judgeth of a fair morrow by a fair evening, I might have reason to value well. But myself having this error of mind, that I am apter to conclude in every thing of change from the present tense than of a continuance, do make no such appointment. Besides I am not so far deceived in myself but that I know very well, and I think your lordship is *major corde,* and in your wisdom you note it more deeply than I can in myself, that in practising the law, I play not all my best game, which maketh me accept it with a *nisi quod potius,* as the best of my fortune, and a thing agreeable to better gifts than mine, but not to mine.

For my placing, our lordship best knows, that when I was much dejected with her majesty's strange dealing towards me, it pleased you, of your singular favour, so far to comfort and encourage me, as to hold me worthy to be excited to think of succeeding your lordship in your second place;* signifying in your plainness, that no man should

* The masteıship of the ıolls; which office the Lord Keeper held till the Lord Bruce was advanced to it, May 18, 1603.

better content yourself: which your exceeding favour you have not since varied from, both in pleading the like signification into the hands of some of my best friends, and also in an honourable and answerable nomination and commendation of me to her majesty. Wherein I hope your lordship, if it please you to call to mind, did find me neither overweening in presuming too much upon it, nor much deceived in my opinion of the event for the continuing it still in yourself, nor sleepy in doing some good offices to the same purpose.

Now upon this matter I am to make your lordship three humble requests, which had need be very reasonable, coming so many together. First, that your lordship will hold and make good your wishes towards me in your own time, for no other I mean it, and in thankfulness thereof, I will present your lordship with the fairest flower of my estate, though it yet bear no fruit, and that is the poor reversion, which of her majesty's gift I hold; in the which I shall be no less willing Mr. John Egerton,* if it seem good to you, should succeed me in that, than I would be willing to succeed your lordship in the other place.

My next humble request is, that your lordship would believe a protestation, which is, that if there be now against the next term, or hereafter, for a little bought knowledge of the court teacheth me to foresee these things, any beaving or palting at that place upon my honesty and troth, my spirit is not in, nor with it; I for my part, being resolutely resolved not to proceed one pace or degree in this matter but with your lordship's foreknowledge and approbation. The truth of which protestation will best appear, if by any accident, which I look not for, I shall receive any further strength. For as I now am, your lordship may impute it only to policy alone in me, that being without present hope myself, I would be content the matter sleep.

My third humble petition to your lordship is, that you would believe an intelligence, and not take it for a fiction in court; of which manner I like Cicero's speech well, who, writing to Appius Claudius, saith; *Sin autem quæ tibi ipsi*

---

* Second son of the Lord Keeper, whose eldest son, Sir Thomas, knighted at Cadiz upon the taking it in 1596 by the Earl of Essex, died in Ireland, whither he attended that Earl in 1599, as Mr. John Egerton likewise did, and was knighted by his Lordship, and at the Coronation of King James was made Knight of the Bath. He succeeded his father in the titles of Baron of Ellesmere and Viscount Brackley, and on the 17th of May was created Earl of Bridgewater.

in mentem veniant, ea aliis tribuere soles, inducis genus sermonis in amicitiam minime liberale. But I do assure your lordship, it is both true and fresh, and from a person of that sort, as having some glimpse of it before, I now rest fully confirmed in it; and it is this, that there should be a plot laid of some strength between Mr. Attorney General,* and Mr. Attorney of the Wards,† for the one's remove to the rolls, and the other to be drawn to his place. Which, to be plain with your lordship, I do apprehend much. For first, I know Mr. Attorney General, whatsoever he pretendeth or protesteth to your lordship, or any other, doth seek it; and I perceive well by his dealing towards his best friends, to whom he oweth most, how perfectly he hath conned the adage of *proximus egomet mihi;* and then I see no man ripened for the place of the rolls in competition with Mr. Attorney General. And lastly, Mr. Attorney of the Wards being noted for a pregnant and stirring man, the objection of any hurt her majesty's business may receive in her causes by the drawing up of Mr. Attorney General will wax cold. And yet, nevertheless, if it may please your lordship to pardon me so to say, of the second of those placings I think with some scorn; only I commend the knowledge hereof to your lordship's wisdom, as a matter not to be neglected.

And now lastly, my honourable good lord, for my third poor help, I account [it] will do me small good, except there be a heave; and that is this place of the Star Chamber. I do confess ingenuously to your lordship, out of my love to the public, besides my particular, that I am of opinion, that rules without examples will do little good, at least not to continue; but that there is such a concordance between the time to come and the time passed, as there will be no reforming the one without informing of the other. And I will not, as the proverb is, spit against the wind, but yield so far to a general opinion, as there was never a more * * or particular example. But I submit it wholly to your honourable grave consideration; only I humbly pray you to conceive that it is not any money that I have borrowed of Mr. Mills, nor any gratification I receive for my aid, that makes me show myself any ways in it, but simply a desire to preserve the rights of the office, as far as it is meet and incorrupt; and secondly his importunity, who, neverthe-

* Coke.

† Probably Sir Thomas Heskett, who died 15th of October, 1605, and has a monument erected to his memory in Westminster Abbey.

less, as far as I see, taketh a course to bring this matter in question to his farther disadvantage, and to be principal in his own harm. But if it be true that I have heard of more than one or two, that besides this forerunning in taking of fees, there are other deep corruptions, which in an ordinary course are intended to be proved against him; surely, for my part, I am not superstitious, as I will not take any shadow of it, nor labour to stop it, since it is a thing medicineable for the office of the realm. And then if the place by such an occasion or otherwise should come in possession, the better to testify my affection to your lordship, I shall be glad, as I offered it to your lordship by way of [surrender], so in this case to offer it by way of joint-patency, in nature of a reversion, which, as it is now, there wanteth no good will in me to offer, but that both, in that condition it is not worth the offering; and besides, I know not whether my necessity may enforce me to sell it away; which, if it were locked in by any reversion or joint-patency, I were disabled to do for my relief.

Thus your lordship may perceive how assured a persuasion I have of your love towards me, and care of me; which hath made me so freely to communicate of my poor state with your lordship, as I could have done to my honourable father, if he had lived: which I most humbly pray your lordship may be private to yourself, to whom I commit it to be used to such purpose as, in your wisdom and honourable love and favour, should seem good. And so, humbly craving your pardon, I commend your lordship to the divine preservation.

At your Lordship's honourable commandment
humbly and particularly.

Mr. Francis Bacon to the Earl of Essex,* on his Lordship's going on the Expedition against Cadiz.

My singular good Lord,

I have no other argument to write on to your good lordship, but upon demonstration of my deepest and most bounden duty, in fulness whereof I mourn for your lordship's absence, though I mitigate it as much as I can with the hope of your happy success, the greatest part whereof, be it never so great, will be the safety of your most honourable person; for the which in the first place, and then for

* Among the papers of Antony Bacon, Esq. vol. xi. fol. 69, in the Lambeth Library.

the prosperity of your enterprise, I frequently pray. And as in so great discomfort it hath pleased God someways to regard my desolateness, by raising me so great and so worthy a friend in your absence, as the new placed Lord Keeper,* in whose placing as it hath pleased God to establish mightily one of the chief pillars of this estate, that is, the justice of the land, which began to shake and sink, and for that purpose no doubt gave her majesty strength of heart of herself to do that in six days, which the deepest judgment thought would be the work of many months; so for my particular, I do find in an extraordinary manner, that his lordship doth succeed my father almost in his fatherly care of me, and love towards me, as much as he professeth to follow him in his honourable and sound courses of justice and estate; of which so special favour the open and apparent reason I can ascribe to nothing more than the impression, which, upon many conferences of long time used between his lordship and me, he may have received both of your lordship's high love and good opinion towards his lordship, verified in many and singular offices, whereof now the realm, rather than himself, is like to reap the fruit; and also of your singular affection towards me, as a man chosen by you to set forth the excellency of your nature and mind, though with some error of your judgment. Hereof if it may please your lordship to take knowledge to my lord, according to the style of your wonted kindness, your lordship shall do me great contentment. My lord told me he had written to your lordship, and wished with great affection he had been so lucky as to have had two hours' talk with you upon those occasions, which have since fallen out. So wishing that God may conduct you by the hand pace by pace, I commend you and your actions to his divine providence.

Your Lordship's ever deepliest bounden,

May 10, 1596. FR. BACON.

The Earl of Essex to Mr. Francis Bacon.†

Sir,

I have thought the contemplation of the art military harder than the execution. But now I see where the number is great, compounded of sea and land forces, the

---

* Egerton.

† Among the papers of Antony Bacon, Esq. vol. xi. fol. 139, in the Lambeth Library.

most *tyrones*, and almost all voluntaries, the officers equal almost in age, quality, and standing in the wars, it is hard for any man to approve himself a good commander. So great is my zeal to omit nothing, and so short my sufficiency to perform all, as, besides my charge, myself doth afflict myself. For I cannot follow the precedents of our dissolute armies, and my helpers are a little amazed with me, when they are come from governing a little troop to a great; and from ——— to all the great spirits of our state. And sometimes I am as much troubled with them, as with all the troops. But though these be warrants for my seldom writing, yet they shall be no excuses for my fainting industry. I have written to my Lord Keeper and some other friends to have care of you in my absence. And so commending you to God's happy and heavenly protection, I rest

Your true Friend,
ESSEX.

Plymouth,
this 17th of May, 1596.

Mr. Francis Bacon to his Brother Antony.*

Good Brother,

Yesternight Sir John Fortescu† told me he had not many hours before imparted to the Queen your advertisements, and the gazette likewise; which the Queen caused Mr. John Stanhope‡ to read all over unto her; and her majesty conceiveth they be not vulgar. The advertisements her majesty made estimation of as concurring with other advertisements, and alike concurring also with her opinion of the affairs. So he willed me to return you the Queen's thanks. Other particular of any speech from her majesty of yourself he did not relate to me. For my Lord of Essex's and your letters, he said, he was ready and desirous to do his best. But I seemed to make it but a love-wish, and passed presently from it, the rather, because it was late in the night, and I mean to deal with him at some better leisure after another manner, as you shall hereafter understand from me. I do find in the speech of some ladies and the very face of the court some addition of reputation, as methinks to us both; and I doubt not but God hath an

* Among the papers of Antony Bacon, Esq. vol. xi. fol. 29, in the Lambeth Library.

† Chancellor of the Exchequer.

‡ Made Treasurer of the Chamber in July, 1596; and in May, 1605, created Lord Stanhope of Harrington, in Northamptonshire.

operation in it, that will not suffer good endeavours to perish.

The Queen saluted me to-day as she went to chapel. I had long speech with Sir Robert Cecil this morning, who seemed apt to discourse with me; yet of yourself, *ne verbum quidem,* not so much as a *quomodo valet?*

This I write to you in haste, *aliud ex alio,* I pray set in a course of acquainting my Lord Keeper what passeth, at first by me, and after from yourself. I am more and more bound to him.

Thus wishing you good health, I recommend you to God's happy preservation.

Your entire loving Brother,

From the Court, this 30th of May, [1596.]

FR. BACON.

The Substance of a Letter I* now wish your Lordship† should write to her Majesty.

That you desire her majesty to believe *id, quod res ipsa loquitur,* that it is not conscience to yourself of any advantage her majesty hath towards you, otherwise than the general and infinite advantage of a queen and a mistress; nor any drift or device to win her majesty to any point or particular, that moveth you to send her these lines of your own mind: but first, and principally, gratitude; next a natural desire of, you will not say, the tedious remembrance, for you can hold nothing tedious that hath been derived from her majesty, but the troubled and pensive remembrance of that which is past, of enjoying better times with her majesty, such as others have had, and that you have wanted. You cannot impute the difference to the continuance of time, which addeth nothing to her majesty but increase of virtue, but rather to your own misfortune or errors. Wherein, nevertheless, if it were only question of your own endurances, though any strength never so good may be oppressed, yet you think you should have suffocated them, as you had often done, to the impairing of your health, and weighing down of your mind. But that which indeed toucheth the quick is, that whereas you accounted it the choice fruit of yourself to be a contentment and entertainment to her majesty's mind, you found many times to the contrary, that you were rather a disquiet to her, and a distaste.

---

* Francis Bacon.

† Robert, Earl of Essex.

Again, whereas in the course of her service, though you confess the weakness of your own judgment, yet true zeal, not misled with any mercenary nor glorious respect, made you light sometimes upon the best and soundest counsels; you had reason to fear, that the distaste particular against yourself made her majesty farther off from accepting any of them from such a hand. So as you seemed, to your deep discomfort, to trouble her majesty's mind, and to foil her business; inconveniences, which, if you be minded as you ought, thankfulness should teach you to redeem, with stepping down, nay throwing yourself down, from your own fortune. In which intricate case, finding no end of this former course, and therefore desirous to find the beginning of a new, you have not whither to resort, but unto the oracle of her majesty's direction. For though the true introduction *ad tempora meliora* be by an *amnestia* of that which is past, except it be in the sense, that the verse speaketh, *Olim hæc meminisse juvabit*, when tempests past are remembered in the calm; and that you do not doubt of her majesty's goodness in pardoning and obliterating any of your errors and mistakings heretofore; refreshing the memory and contemplations of your poor services, or any thing that hath been grateful to her majesty from you; yea, and somewhat of your sufferings, so though that be, yet you may be to seek for the time to come. For as you have determined your hope in a good hour not willingly to offend her majesty, either in matter of court or state, but to depend absolutely upon her will and pleasure, so you do more doubt and mistrust your wit and insight in finding her majesty's mind, than your conformities and submission in obeying it; the rather because you cannot but nourish a doubt in your breast, that her majesty, as princes' hearts are inscrutable, hath many times towards you *aliud in ore, et aliud in corde*. So that you, that take her *secundum literam*, go many times farther out of your way.

Therefore your most humble suit to her majesty is, that she will vouchsafe you that approach to her heart and bosom, *et ad scrinium pectoris*, plainly, for as much as concerneth yourself, to open and expound her mind towards you, suffering you to see clear what may have bred any dislike in her majesty; and in what points she would have you reform yourself; and how she would be served by you. Which done, you do assure her majesty, she shall be both at the beginning and the ending of all, that you do, of that regard, as you may presume to impart to her majesty.

And so that hoping that this may be an occasion of some farther serenity from her majesty towards you, you refer the rest to your actions, which may verify what you have written; as that you have written may interpret your actions, and the course you shall hereafter take.

Indorsed by Mr. Francis Bacon—*A Letter framed for my Lord of Essex to the Queen.*

To Sir John Davis, his Majesty's Attorney General in Ireland.*

Mr. Attorney,

I thank you for your letter, and the discourse you sent of this new accident, as things then appeared. I see manifestly the beginning of better or worse: but me thinketh it is first a tender of the better, and worse followeth but upon refusal or default. I would have been glad to see you here; but I hope occasion reserveth our meeting for a vacation, when we may have more fruit of conference. To requite your proclamation, which, in my judgment, is wisely and seriously penned, I send you another with us, which happened to be in my hands when yours came. I would be glad to hear often from you, and to be advertised how things pass, whereby to have some occasion to think some good thoughts; though I can do little. At the least it will be a continuance in exercise of our friendship, which on my part remaineth increased by that I hear of your service, and the good respects I find towards myself. And so in Tormour's haste, I continue

Your very loving Friend,

FR. BACON.

From Gray's Inn,
this 23d of October, 1607.

To the Reverend University of Oxford.†

Amongst the gratulations I have received, none are more welcome and agreeable to me than your letters, wherein the less I acknowledge of those attributes you give me, the more I must acknowledge of your affection, which bindeth me no less to you, that are professors of learning, than my own dedication doth to learning itself. And therefore you have no need to doubt, but I will emulate, as much as in me is, towards you the merits of him that is gone, by how

* From the MS. collections of Robert Stephens, Esq. deceased.

† From the collections of the late Robert Stephens, Esq. Historiographer-Royal, and John Locker, Esq. now in possession of the Editor.

much the more I take myself to have more propriety in the principal motive thereof. And for the equality you write of, I shall, by the grace of God, far as may concern me, hold the balance as equally between the two universities, as I shall hold the balance of other justice between party and party. And yet in both cases I must meet with some inclinations of affection, which nevertheless shall not carry me aside. And so I commend you to God's goodness.

Your most loving and assured Friend,

FR. BACON.

Gorhambury, April 12, 1617.

Lord Keeper Bacon to Mr. Maxey, Fellow of Trinity College, Cambridge.*

After my hearty commendations, I having heard of you, as a man well deserving, and of able gifts to become profitable in the church, and there being fallen within my gift the rectory of Frome St. Quintin, with the chapel of Evershot, in Dorsetshire, which seems to be a thing of good value, eighteen pounds in the King's books, and in a good country, I have thought good to make offer of it to you; the rather for that you are of Trinity College, whereof myself was some time: and my purpose is to make choice of men rather by care and inquiry, than by their own suits and commendatory letters. So I bid you farewell.

From your loving Friend,

FR. BACON, C. S.

From Dorset House,
April 23, 1617.

To the Lord Keeper Bacon.†

My Lord,

If your man had been addressed only to me, I should have been careful to have procured him a more speedy dispatch: but now you have found another way of address, I am excused; and since you are grown weary of employing me, I can be no otherwise in being employed. In this business of my brother's, that you overtrouble yourself with, I understand from London, by some of my friends, that you have carried yourself with much scorn and neglect both toward myself and friends; which, if it prove true, I blame not you, but myself, who was ever

Your Lordship's assured Friend,

G. BUCKINGHAM.

[July, 1617.]

* From the collections of the late Robert Stephens, Esq. † Ibid.

The Earl of Buckingham to the Lord Keeper, Sir Francis Bacon.*

My Lord,

I have made his majesty acquainted with your note concerning that wicked fellow's speeches, which his majesty contemneth, as is usual to his great spirit in these cases. But, notwithstanding, his majesty is pleased, that it shall be exactly tried, whether this foul-mouthed fellow was taken either with drunkenness or madness, when he spake it. And as for your lordship's advice for setting up again the commissioners for suits, his majesty saith, there will be time enough for thinking upon that, at his coming to Hampton Court.

But his majesty's direction, in answer of your letter, hath given me occasion to join hereunto a discovery upon the discourse you had with me this day.† For I do freely confess, that your offer of submission unto me, and in writing, if so I would have it, battered so the unkindness that I had conceived in my heart for your behaviour towards me in my absence, as out of the sparks of my old affection towards you, I went to sound his majesty's intention towards you, specially in any public meeting; where I found, on the one part, his majesty so little satisfied with your late answer unto him, which he counted (for I protest I use his own terms) confused and childish, and his rigorous resolution, on the other part, so fixed, that he would put some public exemplary mark upon you; as I pro es the sight of his deep-conceived indignation quenchedt mty passion, making me upon the instant change from the person of a party into a peace-maker; so as I was forced upon my knees to beg of his majesty, that he would put no public act of disgrace upon you. And as, I dare say, no other person would have been patiently heard in this suit by his majesty but myself; so did I, though not without difficulty, obtain thus much, that he would not so far disable you from the merit of your future service, as to put any particular mark of disgrace upon your person. Only thus far his majesty protesteth, that upon the conscience of his office he cannot omit, though laying aside all passion, to give a kindly reprimand, at his first sitting in council, to so many of his counsellors as

* This seems to be the letter to which the Lord Keeper returned an answer, September 22, 1617, printed in his works.

† At Windsor, according to Sir Antony Weldon, who may perhaps be believed in such a circumstance as this. *See Court and Character of King James I.* p. 122.

were then here behind, and were actors in this business, for their ill behaviour in it. Some of the particular errors committed in this business he will name, but without accusing any particular persons by name.

Thus your lordship seeth the fruits of my natural inclination. I protest, all this time past it was no small grief unto me to hear the mouth of so many, upon this occasion, open to load you with innumerable malicious and detracting speeches, as if no music were more pleasing to my ear than to rail of you; which made me rather regret the ill nature of mankind, that, like dogs, love to set upon them that they see snatched at.

And, to conclude, my lord, you have hereby a fair occasion so to make good hereafter your reputation, by your sincere service to his majesty, as also by your firm and constant kindness to your friends, as I may, your lordship's old friend, participate of the comfort and honour that will thereby come to you. Thus I rest at last

Your Lordship's faithful Friend and Servant,

G. B.

The force of your old kindness hath made me set down this in writing unto you, which some, that have deserved ill of me in this action, would be glad to obtain by word of mouth, though they be far enough from it, for ought I yet see. But I beseech your lordship to reserve this secretly to yourself only, till our meeting at Hampton Court, lest his majesty should be highly offended, for a cause that I know.

Indorsed—*A Letter of reconciliation from Lord Buckingham, after his majesty's return from Scotland.*

To Henry Cary, Lord Viscount Falkland.*

My very good Lord,

Your lordship's letter was the best letter I received this good while, except the last kind letter from my Lord of Buckingham, which this confirmeth. It is the best accident, one of them, amongst men, when they hap to be obliged to those whom naturally and personally they love, as I ever did your lordship; in troth not many between my Lord Marquis and yourself; so that the sparks of my affection shall ever rest quick, under the ashes of my fortune, to do you service: and wishing to your fortune and family all good. Your Lordship's most affectionate,

and much obliged, &c.

* Appointed Lord Deputy of Ireland, September 8, 1622.

I pray your lordship to present my humble service and thanks to my Lord Marquis, to whom, when I have a little paused, I purpose to write; as likewise to his majesty, for whose health and happiness, as his true beadsman, I most frequently pray.

Indorsed, *March* 11—*Copy of my answer to Lord Falkland.*

Secretary Conway to the Lord Viscount St. Alban.*

Right Honourable,

I do so well remember the motives, why I presented you so with my humble service, and particular application of it to your particular use, as I neither forget nor repent the offer. And I must confess a greater quickening could not have been added to my resolution to serve you, than the challenge you lay to my duty, to follow, in his absence, the affection of your most noble and hearty friend the Marquis.

I lost no time to deliver your letter, and to contribute the most advantageous arguments I could. It seems your motion had been more than enough, if a former engagement to Sir William Becher upon the Marquis his score had not opposed it.

I will give you his majesty's answer, which was, That he could not value you so little, or conceive you would have humbled your desires and your worth so low. That it had been a great deal of ease to him to have had such a scantling of your mind, to which he could never have laid so unequal a measure. His majesty adding further, that since your intentions moved that way, he would study your accommodation. And it is not out of hope, but that he may give some other contentment to Sir William Becher in due time, to accommodate your lordship, of whom, to your comfort, it is my duty to tell you, his majesty declared a good opinion, and princely care and respect.

I will not fail to use time and opportunity to your advantage; and if you can think of any thing to instruct my affection and industry, your lordship may have the more quick and handsome proof of my sure and real intentions to serve you, being indeed

Your Lordship's affectionate Servant,

Royston,
March 27, 1623.

Ed. Conway.

---

* From the collections of Robert Stephens, Esq. deceased.

The five following letters, wanting both date and circumstances to determine such dates, are placed here together.

To the Lord Treasurer.*

It may please your honourable Lordship,

I account myself much bound to your lordship for your favour shown to Mr. Higgins upon my commendations about Pawlet's wardship; the effect of which your lordship's favour, though it hath been intercepted by my Lord Deputy's suit, yet the signification remains: and I must in all reason consent and acknowledge, that your lordship had as just and good cause to satisfy my Lord Deputy's request, as I did think it unlikely, that my lord would have been suitor for so mean a matter.

So this being to none other end but to give your lordship humble thanks for your intended favour, I commend your lordship to the preservation of the divine majesty.

From Gray's Inn.

To Sir Francis Vere.†

Sir,

I am to recommend to your favour one Mr. John Ashe, as to serve under you, as agent of your company: whose desire how much I do affect, you may perceive if it be but in this, that myself being no further interested in you, by acquaintance or deserving, yet have intruded myself into this commendation: which, if it shall take place, I shall by so much the more find cause to take it kindly, by how much I find less cause in myself to take upon me the part of a mover or commender towards you, whom nevertheless I will not so far estrange myself from, but that in a general or mutual respect, incident to persons of our qualities and service, and not without particular inducements of friendship, I might, without breaking decorum, offer to you a request of this nature, the rather honouring you so much for your virtues, I would gladly take occasion to be beholden to you; yet no more gladly than to have occasion to do you any good office. And so this being to no other end, I commend you to God's goodness.

From my chamber at the

---

* From the original draught in the library of Queen's College, Oxford. Arch. D. 2.

† Id. ib.

To Mr. Cawfeilde.*

Sir,

I made full account to have seen you here this reading, but your neither coming nor sending the interr. as you undertook, I may perceive† of a wonder. And you know *super mirari cœperunt philosophari.* The redemption of both these consisteth in the vouchsafing of your coming up now, as soon as you conveniently can; for now is the time of conference and counsel. Besides, if the course of the court be held *super interrogat. judicis,* then must the interr. be ready ere the commission be sealed; and if the commission proceed not forthwith, then will it be caught hold of for further delay. I will not, by way of admittance, desire you to send with all speed the interr. because I presume much of your coming, which I hold necessary; and accordingly, *pro more amicitiæ,* I desire you earnestly to have regard both of the matter itself, and my so conceiving. And so, &c. Your Friend particularly.

To Mr. Tobie Matthew.

Good Mr. Matthew,

The event of the business, whereof you write, is, it may be, for the best: for seeing my lord, of himself, beginneth to come about, *quorsum* as yet? I could not in my heart suffer my Lord Digby to go hence without my thanks and acknowledgments. I send my letter open, which I pray seal and deliver. Particulars I would not touch.

Your most affectionate and assured Friend,

FR. ST. ALBAN.

To my Lord Montjoye.‡

My very good Lord,

Finding by my last going to my lodge at Twickenham, and tossing over my papers, somewhat that I thought might like you, I had neither leisure to perfect them, nor the patience to expect leisure; so desirous I was to make demonstration of my honour and love towards you, and to increase your good love towards me. And I would not have your lordship conceive, though it be my manner and rule to keep state in contemplative matters, *si quis venerit nomine suo, eum recipietis,* that I think so well of the col-

* From the original draught in the library of Queen's College, Oxford. Arch. D. 2.

† Query whether perceive.

‡ From the original draught in the library of Queen's College, Oxford. Arch. D. 2.

lection as I seem to do: and yet I dare not take too much from it, because I have chosen to dedicate it to you. To be short, it is the honour I can do to you at this time. And so I commend me to your love and honourable friendship.

To the Lord Chancellor, and the Lord Mandeville, Lord Treasurer of England.*

My honourable Lords,

His majesty is pleased, according to your lordships' certificate, to rely upon your judgments, and hath made choice of Sir Robert Lloyd, knight, to be Patentee and Master of the Office of ingrossing the transcripts of all wills and inventories in the Prerogative Courts, during his highness's pleasure, and to be accountable unto his majesty for such profits as shall arise out of the same office. And his majesty's farther pleasure is, that your lordship forthwith proportion and set down, as well, a reasonable rate of fees for the subject to pay for ingrossing the said transcripts, as also such fees as your lordship shall conceive fit to be allowed to the said patentee for the charge of clerks and ministers for execution of the said office. And to this effect his majesty hath commanded me to signify his pleasure to his Solicitor General,† to prepare a book for his majesty's signature. And so I bid your lordship heartily well to fare, and remain

Your Lordship's very loving Friend,

Royston, December 17, 1620. G. BUCKINGHAM.

To the Reverend University of Oxford.‡

Amongst the gratulations I have received, none are more welcome and agreeable to me than your letters, wherein the less I acknowledge of those attributes you give me, the more I must acknowledge of your affection, which bindeth me no less to you, that are professors of learning, than mine own dedication doth to learning itself. And therefore you have no need to doubt, but I will emulate (as much as in me is) towards you the merits of him that is gone, by how much the more I take myself to have more propriety in the principal motive thereof. And for the equality you write of, I shall by the grace of God (far as may concern me) hold

* Harl. MSS. vol. 7000. † Sir Thomas Coventry.

‡ This and the following letter are from the collections of the late Robert Stephens, Esq. historiographer royal, and John Locker, Esq. deceased, now in possession of the Editor.

the balance as equally between the two Universities, as I shall hold the balance of other justice between party and party. And yet in both cases I must meet with some inclinations of affection, which nevertheless shall not carry me aside. And so I commend you to God's goodness.

Your most loving and assured Friend,

Gorhambury, April 12, 1617.

FR. BACON.

To the Lord Keeper Bacon.

My Lord,

If your man had been addressed only to me, I should have been careful to have procured him a more speedy dispatch; but now you have found another way of address, I am excused; and since you are grown weary of employing me, I can be no otherwise in being employed. In this business of my brother's, that you overtrouble yourself with, I understand from London, by some of my friends, that you have carried yourself with much scorn and neglect both toward myself and friends; which, if it prove true, I blame not you, but myself, who was ever

Your Lordship's assured Friend,

[July, 1617.]

G. BUCKINGHAM.

Sir Francis Bacon to Lord Norris, in answer to him.*

My Lord,

I am sorry of your misfortune, and for any thing that is within mine own command, your lordship may expect no other than the respects of him, that forgetteth not your lordship is to him a near ally, and an ancient acquaintance, client, and friend. For that, which may concern my place, which governeth me, and not I it; if any thing be demanded at my hands or directed, or that I am *ex officio* to do any thing; if, I say, it come to any of these three; for as yet I am a stranger to the business; yet saving my duties, which I will never live to violate, your lordship shall find, that I will observe those degrees and limitations of proceeding, which belongeth to him, that knoweth well he serveth a clement and merciful master, and that in his own nature shall ever incline to the more benign part; and that knoweth also what belongeth to nobility, and to a house of such merit and reputation as the Lord Norris is come from. And even so I remain,

Your Lordship's very loving Friend.

Sept. 20, 1615.

* From the collections of the late Robert Stephens, Esq.

Sir Francis Bacon to the King.*

It may please your excellent Majesty,

According to your majesty's reference signified by Sir Roger Wilbraham, I have considered of the petition of Sir Gilbert Houghton, your majesty's servant, for a license of sole transportation of tallow, butter, and hides, &c. out of your realm of Ireland; and have had conference with the Lord Chichester, late Lord Deputy of Ireland, and likewise with Sir John Davies, your majesty's attorney there. And this is that which I find.

First, that hides and skins may not be meddled withal, being a staple commodity of the kingdom, wherein the towns are principally interested.

That for tallow, butter, beef, not understanding it of live cattle, and pipe-staves, for upon these things we fell, although they were not all contained in the petition, but in respect hides were more worth than all the rest, they were thought of by way of some supply; these commodities are such as the kingdom may well spare, and in that respect fit to be transported; wherein nevertheless some consideration may be had of the profit, that shall be taken upon the license. Neither do I find, that the farmers of the customs there, of which some of them were before me, did much stand upon it, but seemed rather to give way to it.

I find, also, that at this time all these commodities are free to be transported by proclamation, so as no profit can be made of it, except there be first a restraint; which restraint I think fitter to be by some prohibition in the letters patents, than by any new proclamation; and the said letters patents to pass rather here than there, as it was in the license of wines granted to the Lady Arabella; but then those letters patents to be inrolled in the Chancery of Ireland, whereby exemplifications of them may be taken to be sent to the ports.

All which, nevertheless, I submit to your majesty's better judgment.

Your Majesty's most humble
bounden Subject and Servant,

June 5, 1616. FR. BACON.

---

* From the collections of the late Robert Stephens, Esq.

The Lord Chancellor and two Chief Justices* to the Marquis of Buckingham.

Our very good Lord,

It may please his majesty to call to mind, that when we gave his majesty our last account of parliament business in his presence, we went over the grievances of the last parliament in 7mo,† with our opinion by way of probable conjecture, which of them are like to fall off, and which may perchance stick and be renewed. And we did also then acquaint his majesty, that we thought it no less fit to take into consideration grievances of like nature, which have sprung up since the said last session, which are the more like to be called upon, by how much they are the more fresh, signifying withal, that they were of two kinds; some proclamations and commissions, and many patents; which, nevertheless, we did not trouble his majesty withal in particular; partly, for that we were not then fully prepared (as being a work of some length), and partly, for that we then desired and obtained leave of his majesty to communicate them with the council-table. But now since, I, the Chancellor, received his majesty's pleasure by Secretary Calvert, that we should first present them to his majesty with some advice thereupon provisionally, and as we are capable, and thereupon know his majesty's pleasure before they be brought to the table, which is the work of this dispatch.

And hereupon his majesty may be likewise pleased to call to mind, that we then said, and do now also humbly make remonstrance to his majesty, that in this we do not so much express the sense of our own minds or judgments upon the particulars, as we do personate the lower house, and cast with ourselves what is like to be stirred there. And therefore if there be any thing, either in respect of the matter, or the persons, that stands not so well with his majesty's good liking, that his majesty would be graciously pleased not to impute it unto us; and withal to consider, that it is to this good end, that his majesty may either remove such of them, as in his own princely judgment, or

---

* Sir Henry Montagu of the King's Bench, and Sir Henry Hobart of the Common Pleas.

† That which began February 9, 1609, and was prorogued July 23, 1610.

with the advice of his council, he shall think fit to be removed; or be the better provided to carry through such of them as he shall think fit to be maintained, in case they should be moved, and so the less surprised.

First, therefore, to begin with the patents, we find three sorts of patents, and those somewhat frequent, since the session of 7mo, which *in genere* we conceive may be most subject to exception of grievance; patents of old debts, patents of concealments, and patents of monopolies, and forfeitures for dispensations of penal laws, together with some other particulars, which fall not so properly under any one head.

In these three heads, we do humbly advise several courses to be taken; for the first two, of old debts and concealments, for that they are in a sort legal, though there may be found out some point in law to overthrow them; yet it would be a long business by course of law, and a matter unusual by act of council, to call them in. But that, that moves us chiefly, to avoid the questioning them at the council table is, because if they shall be taken away by the King's act, it may let in upon him a flood of suitors for recompense; whereas, if they be taken away at the suit of the parliament, and a law thereupon made, it frees the King, and leaves him to give recompense only where he shall be pleased to intend grace. Wherefore we conceive the most convenient way will be, if some grave and discreet gentlemen of the country, such as have lost relation to the court, make, at fit times, some modest motion touching the same; and that his majesty would be graciously pleased to permit some law to pass (for the time past only, no ways touching his majesty's regal power) to free the subjects from the same; and so his majesty, after due consultation, to give way unto it.

For the third, we do humbly advise, that such of them, as his majesty shall give way to have called in, may be questioned before the council-table, either as granted contrary to his majesty's book of bounty, or found since to have been abused in the execution, or otherwise by experience discovered to be burdensome to the country. But herein we shall add this farther humble advice, that it be not done as matter of preparation to a parliament; but that occasion be taken, partly upon revising of the book of bounty, and partly upon the fresh examples in Sir Henry Yelverton's case of abuse and surreption in obtaining of patents; and likewise, that it be but as a continuance in conformity of the council's former diligence and vigilancy, which hath already stayed and revoked divers patents of like nature, whereof we are ready to show the examples. Thus, we conceive, his majesty shall keep his greatness, and somewhat shall be done in parliament, and somewhat out of parliament, as the nature of the subject and business require.

We have sent his majesty herewith a schedule of the particulars of these three kinds; wherein, for the first two, we have set down all that we could at this time discover: but in the latter, we have chosen out but some, that are most in speech, and do most tend, either to the vexation of the common people, or the discountenancing of our gentlemen and justices, the one being the original, the other the representative of the commons.

There being many more of like nature, but not of like weight, nor so much rumoured, which, to take away now in a blaze, will give more scandal, that such things were granted, than thanks, that they be now revoked.

And because all things may appear to his majesty in the true light, we have set down, as well the suitors as the grants, and not only those in whose names the patents were taken, but those whom they concern, as far as comes to our knowledge.

For proclamations and commissions, they are tender things; and we are willing to meddle with them sparingly. For as for such as do but wait upon patents (wherein his majesty, as we conceived, gave some approbation to have them taken away), it is better they fall away, by taking away the patent itself, than otherwise; for a proclamation cannot be revoked but by proclamation, which we avoid.

For those commonwealth bills, which his majesty approved to be put in readiness, and some other things, there will be time enough hereafter to give his majesty account, and amongst them, of the extent of his majesty's pardon, which, if his subjects do their part, as we hope they will, we do wish may be more liberal than of later times, a pardon being the ancient remuneration in parliament.

Thus hoping his majesty, out of his gracious and accustomed benignity, will accept of our faithful endeavours, and supply the rest by his own princely wisdom and direction; and also humbly praying his majesty, that when he hath himself considered of our humble propositions, he will give us leave to impart them all, or as much as he shall think fit, to the Lords of his Council, for the better strength of his service, we conclude with our prayers for his majesty's happy preservation, and always rest, &c.

Indorsed—*The Lord Chancellor and the two Chief Justices to the King concerning parliament business.*

Sir Francis Bacon to King James.*

It may please your excellent Majesty,

I perceive by the Bishop of Bath and Wells, that although it seemeth he hath dealt in an effectual manner with Peacham, yet he prevaileth little hitherto; for he hath gotten of him no new names, neither doth Peacham alter in his tale touching Sir John Sydenham.

Peacham standeth off in two material points *de novo.*

The one, he will not yet discover into whose hands he did put his papers touching the consistory villanies. They were not found with the other bundles upon the search; neither did he ever say that he had burned or defaced them. Therefore it is like they are in some person's hands; and it is like again, that that person that he hath trusted with those papers, he likewise trusted with these others of the treasons, I mean with the sight of them.

The other, that he taketh time to answer, when he is asked, whether he heard not from Mr. Paulet some such words, as, he saith, he heard from Sir John Sydenham, or in some lighter manner.

I hold it fit, that myself, and my fellows, go to the Tower, and so I purpose to examine him upon these points, and some others; at the least, that the world may take notice that the business is followed as heretofore, and that the stay of the trial is upon farther discovery, according to that we give out.

I think also it were not amiss to make a false fire, as if all things were ready for his going down to his trial, and that he were upon the very point of being carried down, to see what that will work with him.

Lastly, I do think it most necessary, and a point princi-

* Sir David Dalrymple's Memorials and Letters, p. 29.

pally to be regarded, that because we live in an age wherein no counsel is kept, and that it is true there is some bruit abroad, that the judges of the King's Bench do doubt of the case, that it should not be treason; that it be given out constantly, and yet as it were a secret, and so a fame to slide, that the doubt was only upon the publication, in that it was never published, for that (if your majesty marketh it) taketh away, or least qualifies the danger of the example; for that will be no man's case.

This is all I can do to thridd your majesty's business with a continual and settled care, turning and returning, not with any thing in the world, save only the occasions themselves, and your majesty's good pleasure.

I had no time to report to your majesty, at your being here, the business referred, touching Mr. John Murray. I find a shrewd ground of a title against your majesty and the patentees of these lands, by the coheir of Thomas, Earl of Northumberland; for I see a fair deed, I find a reasonable consideration for the making the said deed, being for the advancement of his daughters; for that all the possessions of the earldom were entailed upon his brother; I find it was made four years before his rebellion; and I see some probable cause why it hath slept so long. But Mr. Murray's petition speaketh only of the moiety of one of the coheirs, whereunto if your majesty should give way, you might be prejudiced in the other moiety. Therefore if Mr. Murray can get power of the whole, then it may be safe for your majesty to give way to the trial of the right; when the whole shall be submitted to you.

Mr. Murray is my dear friend; but I must cut even in these things, and so I know he would himself wish no other. God preserve your majesty.

Your Majesty's most humble and
devoted Subject and Servant,
FR. BACON.

Feb. the 28, 1614.

it was never published, for that (if your majesty marketh it) taketh away, or at least qualifies the danger of the example; for that will be no man's case.

This is all I can do to furnish your majesty's business with a continual and a sealed care, turning and returning, not with any thing in the world, save only the occasions themselves, and your majesty's good pleasure.

I had no time to report to your majesty at your being here, the business referred touching Mr. John Murray. I find a shrewd ground of a title against your majesty and the patentees of these lands, by the attainder of the last Earl of Northumberland; for I see a fair deed. I find a reasonable consideration for the making the said deed, being for the advancement of his daughters; for that all the possessions of the earldom were entailed upon his brother; I find it was made four years before his rebellion; and I see some probable cause why it hath slept so long. But Mr. Murray's petition speaketh only of the moiety of one of the coheirs, whereunto if your majesty should give way, you might be prejudiced in the other moiety. Therefore if Mr. Murray can get power of the whole, then it may be safe for your majesty to give way to the trial of the right: when the whole shall be submitted to you.

Mr. Murray is my dear friend; but I must cut even in these things, and as I know he would himself wish no other. God preserve your majesty.

Your Majesty's most humble and
devoted Subject and Servant,

Fr. Bacon.

Feb. the 21 1616.

MISCELLANEOUS.

THE FIRST COPY OF MY DISCOURSE TOUCHING THE SAFETY OF THE QUEEN'S PERSON.

THESE be the principal remedies, I could think of, for extirping the principal cause of those conspiracies, by the breaking the nest of those fugitive traitors, and the filling them full of terror, despair, jealousy, and revolt. And it is true, I thought of some other remedies, which, because in mine own conceit I did not so well allow, I therefore do forbear to express. And so likewise I have thought, and thought again, of the means to stop and divert as well the attempts of violence, as poison, in the performance and execution. But not knowing how my travel may be accepted, being the unwarranted wishes of a private man, I leave; humbly praying her majesty's pardon, if in the zeal of my simplicity I have roved at things above my aim.

THE FIRST FRAGMENTS OF A DISCOURSE
TOUCHING INTELLIGENCE AND THE SAFETY OF THE QUEEN'S PERSON.

THE first remedy, in my poor opinion, is that against which, as I conceive, least exception can be taken, as a thing, without controversy, honourable and politic; and that is reputation of good intelligence. I say not only good intelligence, but the reputation and fame thereof. For I see, that where booths are set for watching thievish places, there is no more robbing: and though, no doubt, the watchmen many times are asleep or away; yet that is more than the thief knoweth; so as the empty booth is strength and safeguard enough. So likewise, if there be sown an opinion abroad, that her majesty hath much secret intelligence, and that all is full of spies and false brethren; the fugitives will grow into such a mutual jealousy and suspicion one of another, as they will not have the confidence to conspire together, not knowing whom to trust, and thinking all practice bootless, as that which is assured to be discovered. And to this purpose, to speak reverently, as becometh me, as I do not doubt but those honourable counsellors, to whom it doth appertain, do carefully and sufficiently provide and take order, that her majesty receive good intelligence; so yet, under correction, methinks it is not done with that glory and note of the world, which was in Mr. Secretary Walsingham's* time; and in this case, as was said, *opinio veritate major*.

The second remedy I deliver with less assurance, as that, which is more removed from the compass of mine understanding; and that is, to treat and negociate with the king of Spain, or Archduke Earnest,† who resides in the place, where these conspiracies are most forged, upon the point of the law of nations, upon which kind of points, princes' enemies may with honour negociate, *viz.* that, contrary to the same law of nations, and the sacred dignity of kings, and the honour of arms, certain of her majesty's subjects (if it be not thought meet to impeach any of his ministers) refuged in his dominions, have conspired and practised assassination against her majesty's person.

THE SPEECHES‡

DRAWN UP BY MR. FRANCIS BACON FOR THE EARL OF ESSEX, IN A DEVICE§ EXHIBITED BY HIS LORDSHIP BEFORE QUEEN ELIZABETH, ON THE ANNIVERSARY OF HER ACCESSION TO THE THRONE, NOVEMBER 17, 1595.

THE SQUIRE'S SPEECH.

MOST excellent and most glorious queen, give me leave, I beseech your majesty, to offer my master's complaint and petition; complaint that, coming hither to your majesty's most happy day, he is tormented with the importunity of

---

* Who died April 6, 1590. After his death the business of secretary of state appears to be chiefly done by Mr. Robert Cecil, who was knighted by Queen Elizabeth at Theobald's, about the beginning of June, 1591, and in August following sworn of the privy council; but not actually appointed secretary of state till July 5, 1596.

† Ernest, Archduke of Austria, son of the Emperor Maximilian II. and governor of the Low Countries, upon which government he entered in June, 1594; but held it only a short time, dying February 11, following. It was probably in pursuance of the advice of Mr. Francis Bacon in this paper, that Queen Elizabeth sent to the Archduke, in 1594, to complain of the designs which had been formed against her life by the Count de Fuentes, and Don Diego de Ibarra, and other Spanish ministers concerned in governing the Low Countries after the death of Alexander, Duke of Parma, in December, 1592, and by the English fugitives there; and to desire him to signify those facts to the King of Spain, in order that he might vindicate his own character, by punishing his ministers, and delivering up to her such fugitives as were parties in such designs. *Camdeni Annales Eliz. Reginæ*, p. 625. Edit. Lugduni Bat. 1625.

‡ Bishop Gibson's Papers, Vol. V. No. 118.

§ An account of this device, which was much applauded, is given by Mr. Rowland Whyte to Sir Robert Sydney, in a letter dated at London, Saturday, the 22d of November, 1595, and printed in the Letters and Memorials of State

a melancholy dreaming hermit, a mutinous brain-sick soldier, and a busy tedious secretary. His petition is, that he may be as free as the rest; and, at least, while he is here, troubled with nothing but with care how to please and honour you.

THE HERMIT'S SPEECH IN THE PRESENCE.

THOUGH our ends be diverse, and therefore may be one more just than another; yet the complaint of this squire is general, and therefore alike unjust against us all. Albeit he is angry, that we offer ourselves to his master uncalled, and forgets we come not of ourselves, but as the messengers of self-love, from whom all that comes should be well taken. He saith, when we come, we are importunate. If he mean, that we err in form, we have that of his master, who, being a lover, useth no other form of soliciting. If he will charge us to err in matter, I, for my part, will presently prove, that I persuade him to nothing but for his own good. For I wish him to leave turning over the book of fortune, which is but a play for children; when there be

of the Sydney Family, Vol. I. p. 362. According to this letter, the Earl of Essex, some considerable time before he came himself into the Tilt-yard, sent his page with some speech to the queen, who returned with her majesty's glove; and when his lordship came himself, he was met by an old hermit, a secretary of state, a brave soldier, and an esquire. The first presented him with a book of meditations; the second with political discourses; the third with orations of bravely fought battles; the fourth was his own follower, to whom the other three imparted much of their purpose before the earl came in.' "Another, adds Mr. Whyte, devised with him, persuading him to this and that course of life, according to their inclinations. Comes into the Tilt-yard unthought upon, the ordinary postboy of London, a ragged villain, all bemired, upon a poor lean jade, galloping and blowing for life, and delivered the secretary a pac et of letters, which he presently offered my Lord of Essex. And with this dumb show our eyes were fed for that time. In the after-supper, before the queen, they first delivered a well penned speech to move this worthy knight to leave his following of love, and to betake him to heavenly meditation; the secretaries all tending to have him follow matters of state; the soldiers persuading him to the war: but the squire answered them all, and concluded with an excellent, but too plain, English, that this knight would never forsake his mistress's love, whose virtue made all his thoughts divine; whose wisdom taught him all true policy; whose beauty and worth were at all times able to make him fit to command armies. He showed all the defects and imperfections of all their times; and therefore thought his course of life to be best in serving his mistress." Mr. Whyte then mentions, that the part of the old hermit was performed by him, who, at Cambridge, played that of Giraldi; that Morley acted the secretary; and that the soldier was represented by him who acted the pedant, and that Mr. Tobie Matthew was the squire. "The world," says Mr. Whyte, "makes many untrue constructions of these speeches, comparing the hermit and the secretary to two of the lords; and the soldier to Sir Roger Williams. But the queen said, 'that if she had thought there had been so much said of her, she would not have been there that night;' and so went to bed."

so many books of truth and knowledge, better worthy the revolving; and not fix his view only upon a picture in a little table, when there be so many tables of histories, yea, to life, excellent to behold and admire. Whether he believe me or no, there is no prison to the prison of the thoughts, which are free under the greatest tyrants. Shall any man make his conceit, as an anchor, mured up with the compass of one beauty or person, that may have the liberty of all contemplation? Shall he exchange the sweet travelling through the universal variety, for one wearisome and endless round or labyrinth? Let thy master, squire, offer his service to the muses. It is long since they received any into their court. They give alms continually at their gate, that many come to live upon; but few they have ever admitted into their palace. There shall he find secrets not dangerous to know; sides and parties not factious to hold; precepts and commandments not penal to disobey. The gardens of love, wherein he now placeth himself, are fresh to-day, and fading to-morrow, as the sun comforts them, or is turned from them. But the gardens of the muses keep the privilege of the golden age; they ever flourish, and are in league with time. The monuments of wit survive the monuments of power. The verses of a poet endure without a syllable lost, while states and empires pass many periods. Let him not think he shall descend; for he is now upon a hill, as a ship is mounted upon the ridge of a wave; but that hill of the muses is above tempests, always clear and calm; a hill of the goodliest discovery that man can have, being a prospect upon all the errors and wanderings of the present and former times. Yea, in some cliff it leadeth the eye beyond the horizon of time, and giveth no obscure divinations of times to come. So that if he will indeed lead *vitam vitalem*, a life, that unites safety and dignity, pleasure and merit; if he will win admiration without envy; if he will be in the feast, and not in the throng; in the light, and not in the heat; let him embrace the life of study and contemplation. And if he will accept of no other reason, yet because the gift of the muses will enworthy him in love, and where he now looks on his mistress's outside with the eyes of sense, which are dazzled and amazed, he shall then behold her high perfections and heavenly mind with the eyes of judgment, which grow stronger by more nearly and more directly viewing such an object.

SQUIRE, the good old man hath said well to you; but I dare say, thou wouldst be sorry to leave to carry thy master's shield, and to carry his books: and I am sure thy master had rather be a falcon, a bird of prey, than a singing bird in a cage. The muses are to serve martial man, to sing their famous actions; and not to be served by them. Then hearken to me.

It is the war that giveth all spirits of valour, not only honour, but contentment. For mark, whether ever you did see a man grown to any honourable commandment in the wars, but whensoever he gave it over, he was ready to die with melancholy? Such a sweet felicity is in that noble exercise, that he, that hath tasted it thoroughly, is distasted for all other. And no marvel; for if the hunter takes such solace in his chace; if the matches and wagers of sport pass away with such satisfaction and delight; if the looker on be affected with pleasure in the representation of a feigned tragedy; think what contentment a man receiveth, when they, that are equal to him in nature, from the height of insolency and fury are brought to the condition of a chaced prey; when a victory is obtained, whereof the victories of games are but counterfeits and shadows; and when, in a lively tragedy, a man's enemies are sacrificed before his eyes to his fortune.

Then for the dignity of military profession, is it not the truest and perfectest practice of all virtues? of wisdom, in disposing those things, which are most subject to confusion and accident; of justice, in continual distributing rewards; of temperance, in exercising of the straightest discipline; of fortitude, in toleration of all labours and abstinence from effeminate delights; of constancy, in bearing and digesting the greatest variety of fortune. So that when all other places and professions require but their several virtues, a brave leader in the wars must be accomplished with all. It is the wars, that are the tribunal seat, where the highest rights and possessions are decided; the occupation of kings, the root of nobility, the protection of all estates. And, lastly, lovers never thought their profession sufficiently graced, till they have compared it to a warfare. All that in any other profession can be wished for, is but to live happily: but to be a brave commander in the field, death itself doth crown the head with glory. Therefore, squire, let thy master go with me; and though he be resolved in the pursuit of his love, let him aspire to it by the noblest means. For ladies count it no honour to subdue them with their fairest eyes, which will be daunted with the fierce encounter of an enemy. And they will quickly discern a champion fit to wear their glove from a page not worthy to carry their pantofle. Therefore, I say again, let him seek his fortune in the field, where he may either lose his love, or find new argument to advance it.

THE STATESMAN'S SPEECH.

SQUIRE, my advice to thy master shall be as a token wrapped up in words; but then will it show itself fair, when it is unfolded in his actions. To wish him to change from one humour to another, were but as if, for the cure of a man in pain, one should advise him to lie upon the other side, but not enable him to stand on his feet. If from a sanguine delightful humour of love, he turn to a melancholy retired humour of contemplation, or a turbulent boiling humour of the wars; what doth he but change tyrants? Contemplation is a dream; love a trance; and the humour of war is raving. These be shifts of humour, but no reclaiming to reason. I debar him not studies nor books, to give him stay and variety of conceit, to refresh his mind, to cover sloth and indisposition, and to draw to him from those that are studious, respect and commendation. But let him beware, lest they possess not too much of his time; that they abstract not his judgment from present experience, nor make him presume upon knowing much, to apply the less. For the wars, I deny him no enterprise, that shall be worthy in greatness, likely in success, or necessary in duty; not mixed with any circumstance of jealousy, but duly laid upon him. But I would not have him take the alarm from his own humour, but from the occasion; and I would again he should know an employment from a discourting. And for his love, let it not disarm his heart within, as it make him too credulous to favours, nor too tender to unkindnesses, nor too apt to depend upon the heart he knows not. Nay, in his demonstration of love, let him not go too far; for these seely lovers, when they profess such infinite affection and obligation, they tax themselves at so high a rate, that they are ever under arrest. It makes their service seem nothing, and every cavil or imputation very great. But what, Squire, is thy master's end? If to make the prince happy he serves, let the instructions to employ men, the relations of ambassadors, the treaties between princes, and actions of the present time, be the books he reads; let the orations of wise princes, or experimented counsellors in council or parliament, and the final sentences of grave and learned judges in weighty aud doubtful causes, be the lecturers he frequents. Let the holding of affection with confederates without charge, the frustrating of the attempts of enemies without battles, the entitling of the crown to new possessions without show of wrong, the filling of the prince's coffers without violence, the keeping of men in appetite without impatience, be the inventions he seeks out. Let policy and matters of state be the chief, and almost the only thing, he intends. But if he will believe Philautia, and seek most his own happiness, he must not of them embrace all kinds, but make choice, and avoid all matter of peril, displeasure, and charge, and turn them over to some novices, that know not manacles from bracelets, nor burdens from robes. For himself, let him set for matters of commodity and strength, though they be joined with envy. Let him not trouble himself too laboriously to sound into any matter deeply, or to execute any thing exactly; but let himself make himself cunning rather in the humours and drifts of persons, than in the nature of business and affairs. Of that it sufficeth to know only so much, as may make him able to make use of other men's wits, and to make again a smooth and pleasing report. Let him entertain the proposition of others, and ever rather let him have an eye to the circumstances, than to the matter itself; for then shall he ever seem to add somewhat of his own; and, besides, when a man doth not forget so much as a circumstance, men do think his wit doth superabound for the substance. In his councils let him not be confident; for that will rather make him obnoxious to the success; but let him follow the wisdom of oracles, which uttered that which might ever be applied to the event. And ever rather let him take the side which is likeliest to be followed, than that which is soundest and best, that every thing may seem to be carried by his direction. To conclude, let him be true to himself, and avoid all tedious reaches of state, that are not merely pertinent to his particular. And if he will needs pursue his affection, and go on his course, what can so much advance him in his own way? The merit of war is too outwardly glorious to be inwardly grateful; and it is the exile of his eyes, which, looking with such affection upon the picture, cannot but with infinite contentment behold the life. But when his mistress shall perceive, that his endeavours are become a true support of her, a discharge of her care, a watchman of her person, a scholar of her wisdom, an instrument of her operation, and a conduit of her virtue; this, with his diligences, accesses, humility, and patience, may move him to give her further degrees and approaches to her favour. So that I conclude, I have traced him the way to that, which hath been granted to some few, *amare et sapere*, to love and be wise.

THE REPLY OF THE SQUIRE.

WANDERING Hermit, storming Soldier, and hollow Statesman, the enchanting orators of Philautia, which have attempted by your high charms to turn resolved Erophilus into a statue deprived of action, or into a vulture attending about dead bodies, or into a monster with a double heart; with infinite assurance, but with just indignation, and forced patience, I have suffered you to bring in play your whole forces. For I would not vouchsafe to combat you one by one, as if I trusted to the goodness of my breath, and not the goodness of my strength, which little needeth the advantage of your severing, and much less of your disagreeing. Therefore, first, I would know of you all what assurance you have of the fruit whereto you aspire.

You, father, that pretend to truth and knowledge, how are you assured that you adore not vain chimæras and imaginations? that in your high prospect, when you think men wander up and down, that they stand not indeed still in their place, and it is some smoke or cloud between you and them, which moveth, or else the dazzling of your own eyes? Have not many, which take themselves to be inward counsellors with nature, proved but idle believers, which told us tales, which were no such matter? And, soldier, what security have you for these victories and garlands, which you promise to yourself? Know you not of many, which have made provision of laurel for the victory, and have been fain to exchange it with cypress for the funeral? of many which have bespoken fame to sound their triumphs, and have been glad to pray her to say nothing of them, and not to discover them in their flights?

Corrupt statesman, you that think, by your engines and motions, to govern the wheel of fortune; do you not mark, that clocks cannot be long in temper? that jugglers are no longer in request when their tricks and slights are once perceived? Nay, do you not see, that never any man made his own cunning and practice (without religion and moral honesty) his foundation, but he overbuilt himself, and in the end made his house a windfall? But give ear now to the comparison of my master's condition, and acknowledge such a difference, as is betwixt the melting hailstone and the solid pearl. Indeed it seemeth to depend, as the globe of the earth seemeth to hang in the air; but yet it is firm and stable in itself. It is like a cube, or a die-form, which toss it or throw it any way, it ever lighteth upon a square. Is he denied the hopes of favours to come? He can resort to the remembrance of contentments past. Destiny cannot repeal that which is past. Doth he find the acknowledgment of his affection small? He may find the merit of his affection the greater. Fortune cannot have power over that which is within. Nay, his falls are like the falls of Antæus; they renew his strength. His clouds are like the clouds of harvest, which make the sun break forth with greater force. His wanes are changes like the moon's, whose globe is all light towards the sun, when it is all dark towards the world; such is the excellency of her nature, and of his estate. Attend, you beadsman of the muses, you take your pleasure in a wilderness of variety; but it is but of shadows. You are as a man rich in pictures, medals, and crystals. Your mind is of the water, which taketh all forms and impressions, but is weak of substance. Will you compare shadows with bodies, picture with life, variety of many beauties with the peerless excellency of one? the element of water with the element of fire? And such is the comparison between knowledge and love.

Come out, man of war; you must be ever in noise. You will give laws, and advance force, and trouble nations, and remove landmarks of kingdoms, and hunt men, and pen tragedies in blood; and that, which is worst of all, make all the virtues accessary to bloodshed. Hath the practice of force so deprived you of the use of reason, as that you will compare the interruption of society with the perfection of society? the conquest of bodies with the conquest of spirits? the terrestrial fire, which destroyeth and dissolveth, with the celestial fire, which quickeneth and giveth life? And such is the comparison between the soldier and the lover.

And as for you, untrue politique, but truest bondman to Philautia, you, that presume to bind occasion, and to overwork fortune, I would ask you but one question. Did ever any lady, hard to please, or disposed to exercise her lover, enjoin him so good tasks and commandments as Philautia exacteth of you? While your life is nothing but a continual acting upon a stage; and that your mind must serve your humour, and yet your outward person must serve your end; so as you carry in one person two several servitudes to contrary masters. But I will leave you to the scorn of that mistress whom you undertake to govern; that is, to fortune, to whom Philautia hath bound you. And yet, you commissioner of Philautia, I will proceed one degree farther: if I allowed both of your assurance, and of your values, as you have set them, may not my master enjoy his own felicity; and have all yours for advantage? I do not mean, that he should divide himself in both pursuits, as in your feigning tales towards the conclusion you did yield him; but because all these are in the hands of his mistress more fully to bestow, than they can be attained by your addresses, knowledge, fame, fortune. For the muses, they are tributary to her majesty for the great liberties they have enjoyed in her kingdom, during her most flourishing reign; in thankfulness whereof, they have adorned and accomplished her majesty with the gifts of all the sisters. What library can present such a story of great actions, as her majesty carrieth in her royal breast by the often return of this happy day? What worthy author, or favourite of the muses, is not familiar with her? Or what language, wherein the muses have used to speak, is unknown to her? Therefore, the hearing of her, the observing of her, the receiving instructions from her, may be to Erophilus a lecture exceeding all dead monuments of the muses. For fame, can all the exploits of the war win him such a title, as to have the name of favoured and selected servant of such a queen? For fortune, can any insolent politique promise to himself such a fortune, by making his own way, as the excellency of her nature cannot deny to a careful, obsequious, and dutiful servant? And if he could, were it equal honour to obtain it by a shop of cunning, as by the gift of such a hand?

Therefore Erophilus's resolution is fixed: he renounceth Philautia, and all her enchantments. For her recreation, he will confer with his muse; for her defence and honour he will sacrifice his life in the wars, hoping to be embalmed in the sweet odours of her remembrance. To her service will he consecrate all his watchful endeavours, and will ever bear in his heart the picture of her beauty; in his actions, of her will; and in his fortune, of her grace and favour.

REMEMBRANCES FOR THE KING BEFORE HIS GOING INTO SCOTLAND.

May it please your Majesty,

ALTHOUGH your journey be but as a long progress, and that your majesty shall be still within your own land, and therefore any extraordinary course neither needful, nor, in my opinion, fit; yet, nevertheless, I thought it agreeable to my duty and care of your service to put you in mind of those points of form, which have relation, not so much to a journey into Scotland, as to an absence from your city of London for six months, or to a distance from your said city near three hundred miles, and that in an ordinary course; wherein I lead myself by calling to consideration what things there are that require your signature, and may seem not so fit to expect sending to and fro; and therefore to be supplied by some precedent warrants.

First, your ordinary commissions of justice, of assize, and the peace need not your signature, but pass of course by your chancellor. And your commissions of lieutenancy, though they need your signature, yet if any of the lieutenants should die, your majesty's choice and pleasure may be very well attended. Only I should think fit, under your majesty's correction, that such of your lord lieutenants as do not attend your person were commanded to abide within their countries respectively.

For grants, if there were a longer cessation, I think your majesty will easily believe it will do no hurt. And yet if any be necessary, the continual dispatches will supply that turn.

That which is chiefly considerable is proclamations, which all do require your majesty's signature, except you leave some warrant under your great seal to your standing council here in London.

It is true I cannot foresee any such case of such sudden necessity, except it should be the apprehension of some great offenders, or the adjournment of the term upon sickness, or some riot in the city, such as hath been about the liberties of the Tower, or against strangers, &c. But your majesty, in your great wisdom, may perhaps think of many things that I cannot remember or foresee: and therefore it was fit to refer those things to your better judgment.

Also my lord chancellor's age and health is such as it doth not only admit, but require the accident of his death* to be thought of, which may fall in such a time as the very commissions of ordinary justice beforementioned, and writs, which require present dispatch, cannot well be put off. Therefore your majesty may be pleased to take into consideration, whether you will not have such a commission as was prepared about this time twelvemonth in my lord's extreme sickness, for the taking of the seal into custody,

* He died at the age of seventy, on the 15th of March, 1616-7, having resigned the great seal on the third of that month; which was given on the 7th to Sir Francis Bacon.

and for the seal of writs and commissions for ordinary justice, till you may advise of a chancellor or keeper of the great seal.

Your majesty will graciously pardon my care, which is assiduous; and it is good to err in caring even rather too much than too little. These things, for so much as concerneth forms, ought to proceed from my place, as attorney, unto which you have added some interest in matter, by making me of your privy council. But for the main they rest wholly in your princely judgment, being well informed; because miracles are ceased, though admiration will not cease while you live.

Indorsed—*February* 21, 1616.

ACCOUNT OF COUNCIL BUSINESS.

For remedy against the infestation of pirates, than which there is not a better work under heaven, and therefore worthy of the great care his majesty hath expressed concerning the same, this is done:

First, Sir Thomas Smith* hath certified in writing, on the behalf of the merchants of London, that there will be a contribution of twenty thousand pounds a year, during two years' space, towards the charge of repressing the pirates; wherein we do both conceive that this, being as the first offer, will be increased. And we consider, also, that the merchants of the west, who have sustained in proportion far greater damage than those of London, will come into the circle, and follow the example; and for that purpose letters are directed unto them.

Secondly for the consultation *de modo* of the arming and proceeding against them, in respect that my Lord Admiral† cometh not yet abroad, the table hath referred it to my Lord Treasurer,‡ the Lord Carew,§ and Mr. Chancellor of the Exchequer,‖ who heretofore hath served as treasurer

* Of Biborough in Kent, second son of Thomas Smith, of Ostenhanger, of that county, Esq. He had farmed the customs in the reign of Queen Elizabeth, and was sent by King James I. ambassador to the court of Russia in March, 1604; from whence returning, he was made governor of the society of merchants trading to the East Indies, Muscovy, the French and Summer Islands; and treasurer for the colony and company of Virginia. He built a magnificent house at Deptford, which was burnt on the 30th of January, 1618; and in April, 1619, he was removed from his employments of governor and treasurer, upon several complaints of frauds committed by him.

† Charles Howard, Earl of Nottingham.

‡ Thomas Howard, Earl of Suffolk.

§ George, Lord Carew, who had been president of Munster, in Ireland, and was now master of the ordnance. He was created Earl of Totness by King Charles I. in 1626.

‖ Sir Fulk Greville.

of the navy, to confer with the Lord Admiral, calling to that conference Sir Robert Mansell, and others expert in sea service, and so to make report unto the board. At which time some principal merchants shall likewise attend for the lords' better information.

So that, when this is done, his majesty shall be advertised from the table; whereupon his majesty may be pleased to take into his royal consideration, both the business in itself, and as it may have relation to Sir John Digby's embassage.

For safety and caution against tumults and disorders in and near the city, in respect of some idle flying papers, that were cast abroad of a May day, &c. the lords have wisely taken a course neither to nurse it or nourish it by too much apprehension, nor much less to neglect due provision to make all sure. And therefore order is given, that as well the trained bands as the military bands newly erected shall be in muster as well weekly, in the meantime, on every Thursday, which is the day upon which May day falleth, as in the May week itself, the Monday, Tuesday, Wednesday, and Thursday. Besides that the strength of the watch shall that day be increased.

For the buildings in and about London, order is given for four selected aldermen and four selected justices to have the care and charge thereof laid upon them; and they answerable for the observing of his majesty's proclamation, and for stop of all farther building; for which purposes the said Eslus are warned to be before the board, where they shall receive a strait charge, and be tied to a continual account.

For the provost's marshals there is already direction given for the city and the counties adjacent; and it shall be strengthened with farther commission if there be cause.

For the proclamation that lieutenants (not being counsellors), deputy lieutenants, justices of the peace, and gentlemen of quality should depart the city, and reside in their countries, we find the city so dead of company of that kind for the present as we account it out of season to command that which is already done. But after men have attended their business the two next terms, in the end of Trinity term, according to the custom, when the justices shall attend at the Star-chamber, I shall give a charge concerning the same; and that shall be corroborated by a proclamation, if cause be.

For the information given against the Witheringtons, that they should countenance and abet the spoils and disorders in the middle shires, we find the informers to faulter and fail in their accusation. Nevertheless, upon my motion, the table hath ordered, that the informer shall attend one of the clerks of the council, and set down articulately what he can speak, and how he can prove it, and against whom, either the Witheringtons or others.

For the causes of Ireland, and the late letters from the deputy,* we have but entered into them, and have appointed Tuesday for a farther consultation of the same; and, therefore of that subject I forbear to write more for this present.

Indorsed—*March* 30, 1617. *An account of Council Business.*

AN ACCOUNT OF COUNCIL BUSINESS, AND OF OTHER MATTERS COMMITTED TO ME BY HIS MAJESTY.

FIRST, for May day, at which time there was great apprehension of tumult by apprentices and loose people. There was never such a still. The remedies that did the effect were three.

First, the putting in muster of the trained bands and military bands in a brave fashion that way. Next the laying a strait charge upon the mayor and aldermen for the city, and justices of the peace for the suburbs, that the apprentices and others might go abroad with their flags and other gauderies, but without weapon of shot and pike, as they formerly took liberty to do; which charge was exceedingly well performed and obeyed. And the last was that we had, according to our warrant dormant, strengthened our commissions of the peace in London and Middlesex with new clauses of lieutenancy; which as soon as it was known abroad all was quiet by the terror it wrought. This I write because it maketh good my further assurance I gave his majesty at his first removes, that all should be quiet, for which I received his thanks.

For the Irish affairs, I received this day his majesty's letters to the lords, which we have not yet opened, but shall sit upon them this afternoon. I do not forget, besides the points of state, to put my lord treasurer in remembrance that his majesty laid upon him the care of the improvement of the revenue of Ireland by all good means, of which I find his lordship very careful, and I will help him the best I can.

The matter of the revenue of the recusants here in England I purpose to put forward by a conference with my

* Sir Oliver St. John, afterwards Viscount Grandison.

Lord of Canterbury, upon whom the king laid it, and upon Secretary Winwood; and because it is matter of the exchequer, with my lord treasurer and Mr. Chancellor, and after to take the assistance of Mr. Attorney and the learned counsel, and when we have put it in a frame to certify his majesty.

The business of the pirates is, I doubt not, by this time come to his majesty upon the letters of us the commissioners, whereof I took special care. And I must say I find Mr. Vice-Chamberlain a good able man with his pen. But to speak of the main business, which is the match with Spain, the king knows my mind by a former letter; that I would be glad it proceeded with a united counsel; not but that votes and thoughts are to be free. But yet, after a king hath resolved, all men ought to cooperate, and neither to be active nor much *loquutive* in *oppositum;* especially in a case where a few, dissenting from the rest, may hurt the business in *foro famæ.*

Yesterday, which was my weary day, I bid all the judges to dinner (which was not used to be), and entertained them in a private withdrawing chamber, with the learned counsel. When the feast was passed, I came amongst them, and set me down at the end of the table, and prayed them to think I was one of them, and but a foreman. I told them I was weary, and therefore must be short, and that I would now speak to them upon two points. Whereof the one was that I would tell them plainly, that I was firmly persuaded, that the former discords and differences between the Chancery and other courts were but flesh and blood; and that now the men were gone, the matter was gone; and that, for my part, as I would not suffer any the least diminution or derogation from the ancient and due power of the Chancery, so if any thing should be brought to them at any time, touching the proceedings of the Chancery, which did seem to them exorbitant or inordinate; that they should freely and friendly acquaint me with it, and we should soon agree; or if not, we had a master that could easily both discern and rule. At which speech of mine, besides a great deal of thanks and acknowledgment, I did see cheer and comfort in their faces, as if it were a new world.

The second point was, that I let them know how his majesty at his going gave me charge to call and receive from them the accounts of their circuits, according to his majesty's former prescript, to be set down in writing. And that I was to transmit the writings themselves to his majesty, and accordingly as soon as I have received them, I will send them to his majesty.

Some two days before I had a conference with some judges (not all, but such as I did choose), touching the high commission, and the extending of the same in some points, which I see I shall be able to dispatch by consent, without his majesty's further trouble.

I did call upon the committees also for the proceeding in the purging of Sir Edward Coke's Reports, which I see they go on with seriously.*

Thanks be to God, we have not much to do for matters of counsel; and I see now that his majesty is as well able by his letters to govern England from Scotland, as he was to govern Scotland from England.

---

* During the time that my Lord Chief Justice Coke lay under the displeasure of the court, for the reasons I have mentioned in the Discourse preceding these Letters, some information was given to the king, that he, having published eleven books of Reports, had written many things against his majesty's prerogative. And being commanded to explain some of them, my Lord Chancellor Ellesmere doth thereupon, in his letter of 22d of October, 1616, write thus to the king: According to your majesty's directions signified unto me by Mr. Solicitor, I called the lord chief justice before me on Thursday, the 17th instant, in presence of Mr. Attorney and others of your learned counsel. I did let him know your majesty's acceptance of the few animadversions, which upon review of his own labours, he had sent, though fewer than you expected, and his excuses other than you expected. And did at the same time inform him, that his majesty was dissatisfied with several other passages therein; and those not the principal points of the cases judged, but delivered by way of expatiation, and which might have been omitted without prejudice to the judgment: of which sort the attorney and solicitor general did for the present only select five, which being delivered to the chief justice on the 17th of October, he returns his answers at large upon the 21st of the same month, the which I have seen under his own hand. It is true the lord chancellor wished he might have been spared all service concerning the chief justice, as remembering the fifth petition of *dimitte nobis debita nostra*, &c. Insomuch that though a committee of judges was appointed to consider these books, yet the matter seems to have slept, till after Sir Francis Bacon was made lord keeper, it revived, and two judges more were added to the former. Whereupon Sir Edward Coke doth, by his letter, make his humble suit to the Earl of Buckingham. I. That if his majesty shall not be satisfied with his former offer, viz. by the advice of the judges, to explain and publish those points, so as no shadow may remain against his prerogative; that then all the judges of England may be called thereto. 2. That they might certify also what cases he had published for his majesty's prerogative and benefit, for the good of the church and quieting men's inheritances, and good of the commonwealth. But Sir Edward, being then or soon after coming into favour by the marriage of his daughter, I conceive there was no farther proceedings in this affair. It will be needless for me to declare what reputation these books have among the professors of the law; but I cannot omit upon this occasion to take notice of a character Sir Francis Bacon had some time before given them in his proposition to the king touching the compiling and amendment of the laws of England. "To give every man his due, had it not been for Sir Edward Coke's Reports, which though they may have errors, and some peremptory and extrajudicial resolutions more than are warranted, yet they contain infinite good decisions and rulings over of cases, the law by this time had been almost like a ship without ballast; for that the cases of modern experience are fled from those that are adjudged and ruled in former time."

LAW TRACTS.

THE ELEMENTS OF THE COMMON LAVVES OF ENGLAND,

Branched into a Double Tract:

THE ONE

Containing a Collection of some principall Rules and Maximes of the Common Law, with their Latitude and Extent.

Explicated for the more facile Introduction of such as are studiously addicted to that noble Profession.

THE OTHER

The Use of the Common Law, for the preservation of our Persons, Goods, and Good Names.

According to the Lawes and Customes of this Land.

By the late Sir *Francis Bacon* Knight, Lo: Verulam, and Viscount S. Alban.

Videre Vtilitas.

LONDON,
Printed by the Assignes of *Iohn More* Esquire.
1630.

A

COLLECTION

OF SOME PRINCIPAL

RULES and MAXIMES of the

Common Lawes of

ENGLAND,

WITH THEIR LATI-

TUDE and EXTENT:

Explicated for the more facile Introduction of such as are studiously addicted to that noble Profession.

By Sir FRANCIS BACON, then Sollicitor *generall to the late renowned Queene* Elizabeth, *and since Lord Chancellor of* ENGLAND.

Orbe parvo, sed non occiduo.

LONDON,

Printed by the Assignes of *J. More* Esq. 1630.

TO HER

SACRED MAJESTY.

I DO here most humbly present and dedicate to your sacred Majesty a sheaf and cluster of fruit of the good and favourable season, which, by the influence of your happy government, we enjoy; for if it be true that *silent leges inter arma*, it is also as true, that your Majesty is, in a double respect, the life of our laws; once, because without your authority they are but *litera mortua;* and again, because you are the life of our peace, without which laws are put to silence. And as the vital spirits do not only maintain and move the body, but also contend to perfect and renew it, so your sacred Majesty, who is *anima legis,* doth not only give unto your laws force and vigour, but also hath been careful of their amendment and reforming; wherein your Majesty's proceeding may be compared, as in that part of your government, for if your government be considered in all the parts, it is incomparable, with the former doings of the most excellent princes that ever have reigned, whose study altogether hath been always to adorn and honour times of peace with the amendment of the policy of their laws. Of this proceeding in Augustus Cæsar the testimony yet remains.

Pace data terris, animum ad civilia vertit
Jura suum; legesque tulit justissimus auctor.

Hence was collected the difference between *gesta in armis* and *acta in toga,* whereof he disputeth thus:

Ecquid est, quod tam propriè dici potest actum ejus qui togatus in republica cum potestate imperioque versatus sit quam lex? quære acta Gracchi? leges Sempronii proferantur. Quære Syllæ: Corneliæ? Quid? Cn. Pom. tertius consulatus in quibus actis consistet? nempe in legibus: à Cæsare ipso si quæreres quidnam egisset in urbe, et in toga: Phil i. c. 7. *leges multas se responderet, et præclaras tulisse.*

The same desire long after did spring in the emperor

Justinian, being rightly called *ultimus imperatorum Romanorum*, who, having peace in the heart of his empire, and making his wars prosperously in the remote places of his dominions by his lieutenants, chose it for a monument and honour of his government, to revise the Roman laws, from infinite volumes and much repugnancy, into one competent and uniform corps of law; of which matter himself doth speak gloriously, and yet aptly calling it, *proprium et sanctissimum templum justitiæ consecratum:* a work of great excellency indeed, as may well appear, in that France, Italy, and Spain, which have long since shaken off the yoke of the Roman empire, do yet nevertheless continue to use the policy of that law: but more excellent had the work been, save that the more ignorant and obscure time undertook to correct the more learned and flourishing time. To conclude with the domestical example of one of your Majesty's royal ancestors: King Edward I. your Majesty's famous progenitor, and the principal lawgiver of our nation, after he had in his younger years given himself satisfaction in the glory of arms, by the enterprise of the Holy Land, and having inward peace, otherwise than for the invasions which himself made upon Wales and Scotland, parts far distant from the centre of the realm, he bent himself to endow his state with sundry notable and fundamental laws, upon which the government hath ever since principally rested. Of this example, and others the like, two reasons may be given; the one, because that kings, which, either by the moderation of their natures, or the maturity of their years and judgment, do temper their magnanimity with justice, do wisely consider and conceive of the exploits of ambitious wars, as actions rather great than good; and so, distasted with that course of winning honour, they convert their minds rather to do somewhat for the better uniting of human society, than for the dissolving or disturbing of the same. Another reason is, because times of peace, for the most part drawing with them abundance of wealth and finesse of cunning, do draw also, in further consequence, multitude of suits and controversies, and abuses of laws by evasions and devices; which inconveniences in such time growing more general, do more instantly solicit for the amendment of laws to restrain and repress them.

Your Majesty's reign having been blest from the Highest with inward peace, and falling into an age wherein, if science be increased, conscience is rather decayed; and if men's wits be great their wills be greater; and wherein also laws are multiplied in number, and slackened in vigour and execution; it was not possible but that not only suits in law should multiply and increase, whereof a great part are always unjust, but also that all the indirect courses and practices to abuse law and justice should have been much attempted and put in ure, which no doubt had bred greater enormities, had they not, by the royal policy of your Majesty, by the censure and foresight of your council table and star-chamber, and by the gravity and integrity of your benches, been repressed and restrained: for it may be truly observed, that, as concerning frauds in contracts, bargains, and assurances, and abuses of laws by delays, covins, vexations, and corruptions in informers, jurors, ministers of justice, and the like, there have been sundry excellent statutes made in your Majesty's time, more in number, and more politic in provision, than in any your Majesty's predecessors' times.

But I am an unworthy witness to your Majesty of a higher intention and project, both by that which was published by your Chancellor in full parliament from your royal mouth, in the five and thirtieth of your happy reign; and much more by that which I have been since vouchsafed to understand from your Majesty, imparting a purpose for these many years infused into your Majesty's breast, to enter into a general amendment of the states of your laws, and to reduce them to more brevity and certainty, that the great hollowness and unsafety in assurances of lands and goods may be strengthened, the swarving penalties, that lie upon many subjects, removed, the execution of many profitable laws revived, the judge better directed in his sentence, the counsellor better warranted in his counsel, the student eased in his reading, the contentious suitor, that seeketh but vexation, disarmed, and the honest suitor, that seeketh but to obtain his right, relieved; which purpose and intention, as it did strike me with great admiration when I heard it, so it might be acknowledged to be one of the most chosen works, and of the highest merit and beneficence towards the subject, that ever entered into the mind of any king; greater than we can imagine, because the imperfections and dangers of the laws are covered under the clemency and excellent temper of your Majesty's government. And though there be rare precedents of it in government, as it cometh to pass in things so excellent, there being no precedent full in view but of Justinian; yet I must say as Cicero said to Cæsar, *Nihil vulgatum te dignum videri potest*;

and as it is no doubt a precious seed sown in your Majesty's heart by the hand of God's divine majesty, so, I hope, in the maturity of your Majesty's own time it will come up and bear fruit. But to return thence whither I have been carried; observing in your Majesty, upon so notable proofs and grounds, this disposition in general of a prudent and royal regard to the amendment of your laws, and having, by my private labour and travel, collected many of the grounds of the common laws, the better to establish and settle a certain sense of law, which doth now too much waver in incertainty, I conceived the nature of the subject, besides my particular obligation, was such, as I ought not to dedicate the same to any other than to your sacred majesty; both because though the collection be mine, yet the laws are yours; and because it is your Majesty's reign that hath been as a goodly seasonable spring weather to the advancing of all excellent arts of peace. And so concluding with a prayer answerable to the present argument, which is, that God will continue your Majesty's reign in a happy and renowned peace, and that he will guide both your policy and arms to purchase the continuance of it with surety and honour, I most humbly crave pardon, and commend your Majesty to the divine preservation.

Your Sacred Majesty's most humble
and obedient Subject and Servant,

FRANCIS BACON.

THE PREFACE.

I HOLD every man a debtor to his profession; from the which, as men of course do seek to receive countenance and profit, so ought they of duty to endeavour themselves, by way of amends, to be a help and ornament thereunto. This is performed in some degree by the honest and liberal practice of a profession, when men shall carry a respect not to descend into any course that is corrupt and unworthy thereof, and preserve themselves free from the abuses where-with the same profession is noted to be infected; but much more is this performed if a man be able to visit and strengthen the roots and foundation of the science itself; thereby not only gracing it in reputation and dignity, but also amplify-ing it in perfection and substance. Having, therefore, from the beginning, come to the study of the laws of this realm, with a desire no less, if I could attain unto it, that the same laws should be the better for my industry, than that myself should be the better for the knowledge of them; I do not find that, by mine own travel, without the help of authority, I can in any kind confer so profitable an addition unto that science, as by collecting the rules and grounds dispersed throughout the body of the same laws; for hereby no small light will be given in new cases, wherein the authorities do square and vary, to confirm the law, and to make it received one way; and in cases wherein the law is cleared by authority, yet nevertheless to see more profoundly into the reason of such judgments and ruled cases, and thereby to make more use of them for the decision of other cases more doubtful; so that the incertainty of law, which is the principal and most just challenge that is made to the laws of our nation at this time, will, by this new strength laid to the foundation, be somewhat the more settled and corrected. Neither will the use hereof be only in deciding of doubts, and helping soundness of judgment, but further in gracing of argument, in correcting unprofitable subtlety, and reducing the same to a more sound and substantial sense of law; in reclaiming vulgar errors, and generally the amendment in some measure of the very nature and complexion of the whole law: and, therefore, the conclusions of reason of this kind are worthily and aptly called by a great civilian *legum leges*, laws of laws, for that many *placita legum*, that is, particular and positive learnings of laws, do easily decline from a good temper of justice, if they be not rectified and governed by such rules.

Now for the manner of setting down of them, I have in all points, to the best of my understanding and foresight, applied myself not to that which might seem most for the ostentation of mine own wit or knowledge, but to that which may yield most use and profit to the students and professors of our laws.

And, therefore, whereas these rules are some of them ordinary and vulgar, that now serve but for grounds and plain songs to the more shallow and impertinent sort of arguments; other of them are gathered and extracted out of the harmony and congruity of cases, and are such as the wisest and deepest sort of lawyers have in judgment and use, though they be not able many times to express and set them down.

For the former sort, which a man that should rather write to raise a high opinion of himself, than to instruct others, would have omitted, as trite and within every man's compass; yet nevertheless I have not affected to neglect them, but have chosen out of them such as I thought good, I have reduced them to a true application, limiting and defining their bounds, that they may not be read upon at large, but restrained to point of difference; for as, both in the law and other sciences, the handling of questions by common-place, without aim or application, is the weakest; so yet, nevertheless, many common principles and generalities are not to be contemned, if they be well derived and reduced into particulars, and their limits and exclusions duly assigned; for there be two contrary faults and extremities in the debating and sifting out of the law, which may be best noted in two several manner of arguments. Some argue upon general grounds, and come not near the point in question: others, without laying any foundation of a ground or difference, do loosely put cases, which, though they go near the point, yet, being put so scattered, prove not, but rather serve to make the law appear more doubtful than to make it more plain.

Secondly, whereas some of these rules have a concurrence with the civil Roman law, and some others a diversity, and many times an opposition, such grounds which are common to our law and theirs, I have not affected to disguise into other words than the civilians use, to the end they might seem invented by me, and not borrowed or translated from them: no, but I took hold of it as a matter of great authority and majesty, to see and consider the concordance between the laws penned, and as it were dictated *verbatim*, by the same reason. On the other side, the diversities between the civil Roman rules of law and ours, happening either when there is such an indifferency of reason so equally balanced, as the one law embraceth one course, and the other the contrary, and both just, after either is once positive and certain, or where the laws vary in regard of accommodating the law to the different considerations of estate, I have not omitted to set down.

Thirdly, whereas I could have digested these rules into a certain method or order, which, I know, would have been more admired, as that which would have made every particular rule, through coherence and relation unto other rules, seem more cunning and deep; yet I have avoided so to do, because this delivering of knowledge in distinct and disjoined aphorisms doth leave the wit of man more free to turn and toss, and to make use of that which is so delivered to more several purposes and applications; for we see that all the ancient wisdom and science was wont to be delivered in that form, as may be seen by the parables of Solomon, and by the aphorisms of Hippocrates, and the moral verses of Theognes and Phocylides; but chiefly the precedent of the civil law, which hath taken the same course with their rules, did confirm me in my opinion.

Fourthly, whereas I know very well it would have been more plausible and more current, if the rules, with the expositions of them, had been set down either in Latin or in English; that the harshness of the language might not have disgraced the matter; and that civilians, statesmen, scholars, and other sensible men might not have been barred from them; yet I have forsaken that grace and ornament of them, and only taken this course: the rules themselves I have put in Latin, not purified further than the property of the terms of the law would permit; but Latin, which language I chose, as the briefest to contrive the rules compendiously, the aptest for memory, and of the greatest authority and majesty to be avouched and alleged in argument: and for the expositions and distinctions, I have retained the peculiar language of our law, because it should not be singular among the books of the same science, and because it is most familiar to the students and professors thereof, and because that it is most significant to express conceits of law; and to conclude, it is a language wherein a man shall not be enticed to hunt after words but matter; and for the excluding of any other than professed lawyers, it was better manners to exclude them by the strangeness of the language, than by the obscurity of the conceit; which is as though it had been written in no private and retired language, yet by those that are not lawyers would for the most part not have been understood, or, which is worse, mistaken.

Fifthly, whereas I might have made more flourish and ostentation of reading, to have vouched the authorities, and sometimes to have enforced or noted upon them, yet I have abstained from that also; and the reason is, because I judged it a matter undue and preposterous to prove rules and maxims; wherein I had the example of Mr. Littleton and Mr. Fitzherbert, whose writings are the institutions of the laws of England; whereof the one forbeareth to vouch any authority altogether; the other never reciteth a book, but when he thinketh the case so weak of credit in itself as it needs a surety; and these two I did far more esteem than Mr. Perkins or Mr. Standford, that have done the contrary. Well will it appear to those that are learned in the laws, that many of the cases are judged cases, either within the books, or of fresh report, and most of them fortified by judged cases and similitude of reason; though, in some few cases, I did intend expressly to weigh down the authority by evidence of reason, and therein rather to correct the law, than either to soothe a received error, or by unprofitable subtlety, which corrupteth the sense of law, to reconcile contrarieties. For these reasons I resolved not to derogate from the authority of the rules, by vouching of any of the authority of the cases, though in mine own copy I had them quoted: for although the meanness of mine own person may now at first extenuate the authority of this collection, and that every man is adventurous to control; yet, surely, according to Gamaliel's reason, if it be of weight, time will settle and authorise it; if it be light and weak, time will reprove it. So that, to conclude, you have here a work without any glory of affected novelty, or of method, or of language, or of quotations and authorities, dedicated only to use, and submitted only to the censure of the learned, and chiefly of time.

Lastly, there is one point above all the rest I account the most material for making these reasons indeed profitable and instructing; which is, that they be not set down alone, like short dark oracles, which every man will be content still to allow to be true, but in the mean time they give little light or direction; but I have attended them, a matter not practised, no not in the civil·law to any purpose, and for want whereof, indeed, the rules are but as proverbs, and many times plain fallacies, with a clear and perspicuous exposition, breaking them into cases, and opening them with distinctions, and sometimes showing the reasons above whereupon they depend, and the affinity they have with other rules. And though I have thus, with as good discretion and foresight as I could, ordered this work, and, as I might say, without all colours or shows, husbanded it best to profit; yet, nevertheless, not wholly trusting to mine own judgment; having collected three hundred of them, I thought good, before I brought them all into form, to publish some few, that, by the taste of other men's opinions in this first, I might receive either approbation in mine own course, or better advice for the altering of the other which remain; for it is great reason that that which is intended to the profit of others should be guided by the conceits of others.

REGULÆ.

1. In jure non remota causa, sed proxima spectatur.
2. Non potest adduci exceptio ejusdem rei, cujus petitur dissolutio.
3. Verba fortius accipiuntur contra proferentem.
4. Quod sub certa forma concessum vel reservatum est, non trahitur ad valorem vel compensationem.
5. Necessitas inducit privilegium quoad jura privata.
6. Corporalis injuria non recipit æstimationem de futuro.
7. Excusat aut extenuat delictum in capitalibus, quod non operatur idem in civilibus.
8. Æstimatio præteriti delicti ex post facto nunquam crescit.
9. Quod remedio destituitur ipsa re valet, si culpa absit.
10. Verba generalia restringantur ad habilitatem rei vel personæ.
11. Jura sanguinis nullo jure civili dirimi possunt.
12. Receditur a placitis juris potius quam injuria, ne delicta maneant impunita.
13. Non accipi debent verba in demonstrationem falsam, quæ competunt in limitationem veram.
14. Licet dispositio de interesse futuro sit inutilis, tamen potest fieri declaratio præcedens quæ fortiatur effectum interveniente novo actu.
15. In criminalibus sufficit generalis malitia intentionis cum facto paris gradus.
16. Mandata licita recipiunt strictam interpretationem, sed illicita latam et extensivam.
17. De fide et officio judicis non recipitur quæstio, sed de scientia, sive error sit judicis sive facti.
18. Persona conjuncta æquiparatur interesse proprio.
19. Non impedit clausula derogatoria qua minus ab eadem potestate res dissolvantur a quibus constituuntur.

20. Actus inceptus, cujus perfectio pendet ex voluntate partium revocari potest, si autem pendet ex voluntate tertiæ personæ vel ex contingenti, revocari non potest.

21. Clausula vel dispositio inutilis per præsumptionem remotam vel causam ex post facto non fulcitur.

22. Non videtur consensum retinuisse, si quis ex præscripto minantis aliquid immutavit.

23. Ambiguitas verborum latens verificatione suppletur, nam quod ex facto oritur ambiguum verificatione facti tollitur.

24. Licita bene miscentur, formula nisi juris obstet.

25. Præsentia corporis tollit errorem nominis, et veritas nominis tollit errorem demonstrationis.

THE

MAXIMS OF THE LAW.

REGULA I.

In jure non remota causa, sed proxima spectatur.

It were infinite for the law to judge the causes of causes, and their impulsions one of another; therefore it contenteth itself with the immediate cause, and judgeth of acts by that, without looking to any further degree.

As if an annuity be granted *pro consilio impenso et impendendo*, and the grantee commit treason, whereby he is imprisoned, so that the grantor cannot have access unto him for his counsel; yet, nevertheless, the annuity is not determined by this *non-feasance;* yet it was the grantee's act and default to commit the treason, whereby the imprisonment grew: but the law looketh not so far, but excuseth him, because the not giving counsel was compulsory, and not voluntary, in regard of the imprisonment. 6 H. 8 Dy. fo. 1. et 2.

So if a parson make a lease, and be deprived, or resign, the successors shall avoid the lease; and yet the cause of deprivation, and more strongly of a resignation, moved from the party himself: but the law regardeth not that, because the admission of the new incumbent is the act of the ordinary. Litt. cap. Discont. 2 H. 4. 3. 26 H. 8. 2.

So if I be seised of an advowson in gross, and a usurpation be had against me, and at the next avoidance I usurp arere, I shall be remitted: and yet the presentation, which is the act remote, is mine own act; but the admission of my clerk, whereby the inheritance is reduced to me, is the act of the ordinary.

5 H. 7. 25. So if I covenant with I. S. a stranger, in consideration of natural love to my son, to stand seised to the use of the said I. S. to the intent he shall enfeoff my son; by this no use ariseth to I. S. because the law doth respect that there is no immediate consideration between me and I. S.

12 H. 4. 4 H. 8. Dy. f. 1. So if I be bound to enter into a statute before the mayor of the staple at such a day, for the security of one hundred pounds, and the obligee, before the day, accept of me a lease of a house in satisfaction; this is no plea in debt upon my obligation: and yet the end of that statute was but security of money; but because the entering into this statute itself, which is the immediate act whereto I am bound, is a corporal act which lieth not in satisfaction, therefore the law taketh no consideration that the remote intent was for money.

M. 40 et 41. El. Julius Winnington's case, or report per le tres reverend Judgel, e Sur Coke, lib. 2. So if I make a feoffment in fee, upon condition that the feoffee shall enfeoff over, and the feoffee be disseised, and a descent cast, and then the feoffee bind himself in a statute, which statute is discharged before the recovery of the land: this is no breach of the condition, because the land was never liable to the statute, and the possibility that it should be liable upon the recovery the law doth not respect.

So if I enfeoff two, upon condition to enfeoff, and one of them take a wife, the condition is not broken; and yet there is a remote possibility that the joint-tenant may die, and then the feme is intitled to dower.

So if a man purchase land in fee-simple, and die without issue; in the first degree the law respecteth dignity of sex, and not proximity; and therefore the remote heir, on the part of the father, shall have it before the near heir on the part of the mother: but, in any degree paramount the first the law respecteth not, and therefore the near heir by the grandmother, on the part of the father, shall have it, before the remote heir of the grandfather on the part of the father.

This rule faileth in covinous acts, which though they be conveyed through many degrees and reaches, yet the law taketh heed to the corrupt beginning, and counteth all as one entire act.

37 R. Dacre's case, obiter. As if a feoffment be made of lands held by knight's service to I. S. upon condition that he, within a certain time, shall enfeoff I. D. which feoffment to I. D. shall be to the use of the wife of the first feoffer for her jointure, &c.; this

feoffment is within the statute of 32 H. VIII. *nam dolus circuitu non purgatur.*

In like manner this rule holdeth not in criminal acts, except they have a full interruption; because when the intention is matter of substance, and that which the law doth principally behold, there the first motive will be principally regarded, and not the last impulsion. As if I. S. of malice prepense discharge a pistol at I. D. and miss him, whereupon he throws down his pistol and flies, and I. D. pursueth him to kill him, whereupon he turneth and killeth I. D. with a dagger; if the law should consider the last impulsive cause, it should say that it was in his own defence: but the law is otherwise, for it is but a pursuance and execution of the first murderous intent. Op. Cattelyn et autres in case de Stoel.

But if I. S. had fallen down, his dagger drawn, and I. D. had fallen by haste upon his dagger, there I. D. had been *felo de se*, and I. S. shall go quit. 44 Ed. 3.

Also you may not confound the act with the execution of the act; nor the entire act with the last part, or the consummation of the act.

For if a disseisor enter into religion, the immediate cause is from the party, though the descent be cast in law; but the law doth but execute the act which the party procureth, and therefore the descent shall not bind, *et sic è converso.* Lit. cap. de discent.

If a lease for years be made rendering a rent, and the lessee make a feoffment of part, and the lessor enter, the immediate cause is from the law in respect of the forfeiture, though the entry be the act of the party; but that is but the pursuance and putting in execution of the title which the law giveth: and therefore the rent or condition shall be apportioned. 21 Eliz. 24 H. 8. fo. 4. Dy. 21 R.

So in the binding of a right by a descent, you are to consider the whole time from the disseisin to the descent cast; and if, at all times, the person be not privileged, the descent binds.

And, therefore, if a feme covert be disseised, and the baron dieth, and she taketh a new husband, and then the descent is cast: or if a man that is not *infra quatuor maria*, be disseised, and return into England, and go over sea again, and then a descent is cast, this descent bindeth, because of the *interim* when the persons might have entered; and the law respecteth not the state of the person at the 9 H. 7. 24. 3 et 4 P. et M. Dr 143.

last time of the descent cast, but a continuance from the very disseised to the descent.

4 et 5 P. et M. Dy. 159. So if baron and feme be, and they join in a feoffment of the wife's land rendering a rent, and the baron die, and the feme take a new husband before any rent-day, and he accepteth the rent, the feoffment is affirmed for ever.

REGULA II.

Non potest adduci exceptio ejusdem rei, cujus petitur dissolutio.

It were impertinent and contrary in itself, for the law to allow of a plea in bar of such matter as is to be defeated by the same suit; for it is included: otherwise a man should never come to the end and effect of his suit, but be cut off in the way.

And, therefore, if tenant in tail of a manor, whereunto a villain is regardant, discontinue and die, and the right of the entail descend unto the villain himself, who brings *formedon*, and the discontinuee pleadeth villanage; this is no plea, because the divesting of the manor, which is the intent of the suit, doth include this plea, because it determineth the villanage.

50 E. 3. So if tenant in ancient demesne be disseised by the lord, whereby the seigniory is suspended, and the disseisee bring his assize in the court of the lord, frank fee is no plea, because the suit is brought to undo the disseisin, and so to revive the seigniory in ancient demesne.

7 H. 4. 39. 7 H. 6. 44. So if a man be attainted and executed, and the heir bring error upon the attainder, and corruption of blood by the same attainder be pleaded, to interrupt his conveying in the same writ of error; this is no plea, for then he were without remedy ever to reverse the attainder.

38 Ed. 3. 32. So if tenant in tail discontinue for life rendering rent, and the issue brings *formedon*, and the warranty of his ancestor with assets is pleaded against him, and the assets is layed to be no other but his reversion with the rent; this is no plea, because the *formedon*, which is brought to undo this discontinuance, doth inclusively undo this new reversion in fee, with the rent thereunto annexed.

But whether this rule may take place where the matter of the plea is not to be avoided in the same suit, but another suit, is doubtful; and I rather take the law to be, that this rule doth extend to such cases; for otherwise the party were at a mischief, in respect the exceptions and bars might be pleaded cross, either of them, in the contrary suit; and so the party altogether prevented and intercepted to come by his right.

So if a man be attainted by two several attainders, and there is error in them both, there is no reason but there should be a remedy open for the heir to reverse those attainders being erroneous, as well if they be twenty as one.

And, therefore, if in a writ of error brought by the heir of one of them, the attainder should be a plea peremptorily; and so again, if in error brought of that other, the former should be a plea; these were to exclude him utterly of his right: and therefore it shall be a good replication to say, that he hath a writ of error depending of that also, and so the court shall proceed: but no judgment shall be given till both pleas be discussed; and if either plea be found without error, there shall be no reversal either of the one or of the other; and if he discontinue either writ, then shall it be no longer a plea; and so of several outlawries in a personal action.

And this seemeth to me more reasonable, than that generally an outlawry or an attainder should be no plea in a writ of error brought upon a diverse outlawry or attainder, as 7 H. IV. and 7. H. VI. seem to hold; for that is a remedy too large for the mischief; for there is no reason but if any of the outlawries or attainders be indeed without error, but it should be a peremptory plea to the person in a writ of error, as well as in any other action.

But if a man levy a fine *sur conusaunce de droit come ceo que il ad de son done*, and suffer a recovery of the same lands, and there be error in them both, he cannot bring error first of the fine, because, by the recovery, his title of error is discharged and released in law *inclusivè* but he must begin with the error upon the recovery, which he 37 R.
may do, because a fine executed barreth no titles that accrue *de puisne tems* after the fine levied, and so restore himself to his title of error upon the fine: but so it is not in the former case of the attainder; for a writ of error to a former attainder is not given away by a second, except it be by express words of an act of parliament, but only it remaineth a plea to his person while he liveth, and to the conveyance of his heir after his death.

But if a man levy a fine where he hath nothing in the land, which inureth by way of conclusion only, and is executory against all purchases and new titles which shall grow to the conusor afterwards, and he purchase the land,

and suffer a recovery to the conusee, and in both fine and recovery there is error; this fine is *Janus bifrons*, and will look forwards, and bar him of his writ of error brought of the recovery; and therefore it will come to the reason of the first case of the attainder, that he must reply, that he hath a writ also depending of the same fine, and so demand judgment.

16 E. 3. Fitz. age, 45. To return to our first purpose, like law is it if tenant in tail of two acres make two several discontinuances to several persons for life rendering a rent, and bringeth a *formedon* of both, and in *formedon* brought of white acre the reversion and rent reserved upon black acre is pleaded, and so contrary: I take it to be a good replication, that he hath *formedon* also upon that depending, whereunto the tenant hath pleaded the descent of the reversion of white acre; and so neither shall be a bar: and yet there is no doubt but if in a *formedon* the warranty of tenant in tail with assets be pleaded, it is no replication for the issue to say, that a *præcipe* dependeth brought by I. S. to evict the assets.

But the former case standeth upon the particular reason before mentioned.

REGULA III.

Verba fortius accipiuntur contra proferentem.

THIS rule, that a man's deeds and his words shall be taken strongliest against himself, though it be one of the most common grounds of the law, it is notwithstanding a rule drawn out of the depth of reason; for, first, it is a schoolmaster of wisdom and diligence in making men watchful in their own business; next, it is author of much quiet and certainty, and that in two sorts; first, because it favoureth acts and conveyances executed, taking them still beneficially for the grantees and possessors: and secondly, because it makes an end of many questions and doubts about construction of words; for if the labour were only to pick out the intention of the parties, every judge would have a several sense; whereas this rule doth give them a sway to take the law more certainly one way.

But this rule, as all other which are very general, is but a sound in the air, and cometh in sometimes to help and make up other reasons without any great instruction or direction; except it be duly conceived in point of difference, where it taketh place, and where not. And first we will examine it in grants, and then in pleadings.

The force of this rule is in three things, in ambiguity of

words, in implication of matter, and deducing or qualifying the exposition of such grants as were against the law, if they were taken according to their words.

And, therefore, if I. S. submit himself to arbitrement of all actions and suits between him and I. D. and I. N. it rests ambiguous whether this submission shall be intended *collectivè* of joint actions only, or *distributivè* of several actions also; but because the words shall be strongliest taken against I. S. that speaks them, it shall be understood of both: for if I. S. had submitted himself to arbitrement of all actions and suits which he hath now depending, except it be such as are between him and I. D. and I. N. now it shall be understood *collectivè* only of joint actions, because in the other case large construction was hardest against him that speaks, and in this case strict construction is hardest. 2 R. 3. 18. 21 H. 7. 29.

So if I grant ten pounds rent to baron and feme, and if the baron die that the feme shall have three pounds rent, because these words rest ambiguous whether I intend three pounds by way of increase, or three pounds by way of restraint and abatement of the former rent of ten pounds, it shall be taken strongliest against me that am the grantor, that is three pounds addition to the ten pounds: but if I had let lands to baron and feme for three lives, reserving ten pounds per annum, and, if the baron die, reserving three pounds; this shall be taken contrary to the former case, to abridge my rent only to three pounds. 8 Ass. p. 10.

So if I demise *omnes boscos meos in villa de Dale* for years, this passeth the soil; but if I demise all my lands in Dale *exceptis boscis*, this extendeth to the trees only, and not to the soil. 14 H. 8. 28 H. 8. Dr. 19.

So if I sow my land with corn, and let it for years, the corn passeth to the lessee, if I except it not; but if I make a lease for life to I. S. upon condition that upon request he shall make me a lease for years, and I. S. sow the ground, and then I make request, I. S. may well make me a lease excepting his corn, and not break the condition.

So if I have free warren in my own land, and let my land for life, not mentioning the warren, yet the lessee, by implication, shall have the warren discharged and extract during his lease: but if I let the land *una cum libera warrena*, excepting white acre, there the warren is not by implication reserved unto me either to be enjoyed or extinguished; but the lessee shall have warren against me in white acre. 8 H. 7. 8 H. 9. 5. 32 H. 6. 24. 28 H. 8. Dy. 30. 6.

So if I. S. hold of me by fealty and rent only, and I 29. Ass. pl. 10.

grant the rent, not speaking of the fealty; yet the fealty by implication shall pass, because my grant shall be taken strongly as of a rent service, and not of a rent secke.

44 Ed. 3. 19. Otherwise had it been if the seigniory had been by homage, fealty, and rent, because of the dignity of the service, which could not have passed by intendment by the grant of the rent: but if I be seised of the manor of Dale in fee, whereof I. S. holds by fealty and rent, and I grant the manor, excepting the rent, the fealty shall pass to the grantee, and I. S. shall have but a rent secke.

26 Ass. pl. 66.

So in grants against the law, if I give land to I. S. and his heirs males, this is a good fee-simple, which is a larger estate than the words seem to intend, and the word "males" is void. But if I make a gift in tail, reserving rent to me and the heirs of my body, the words "of my body" are not void, and to leave it rent in fee-simple; but the words "heirs and all" are void, and leave it but a rent for life; except, that you will say, it is but a limitation to any my heir in fee-simple which shall be heir of my body; for it cannot be rent in tail by reservation.

45 Ed. 3. 290. 24 R.* But if I give land with my daughter in frank marriage, the remainder to I. S. and his heirs, this grant cannot be good in all parts, according to the words: for it is incident to the nature of a gift in frank marriage, that the donee hold of the donor; and therefore my deed shall be taken so strongly against myself, that rather than the remainder shall be void, the frank marriage, though it be first placed in the deed, shall be void as a frank marriage.

But if I give land in frank marriage, reserving to me and my heirs ten pounds rent, now the frank marriage stands good, and the reservation is void, because it is a limitation of a benefit to myself, and not to a stranger.

So if I let white acre, black acre, and green acre to I. S. excepting white acre, this exception is void, because it is repugnant; but if I let the three acres aforesaid, rendering twenty shillings rent, viz. for white acre ten shillings, and for black acre ten shillings, I shall not distrain at all in green acre, but that shall be discharged of my rent.

4 H. 6. 22. So if I grant a rent to I. S. and his heirs out of my

---

* Quære car le ley sémble déi le contrary en tant que in un grant quant lun part del fait ne poit estoier oue lauter le darr: serra void, auterment in un devise et accordant fuit lopin: de Sur Anderson et Owen Just: contra Walmesley Just. P. 40. Eliz. in le case de Comtesse de Warwick et Sur Barkley in com. banco.

manor of Dale, *et obligo manerium prædictum et omnia bona et catalla mea super manerium prædictum existentia ad distringendum per ballivos domini regis:* this limitation of the distress to the king's bailiffs is void, and it is good to give a power of distress to I. S. the grantee, and his bailiffs. 26 Ass. pl. 66. 46 E. 3. 18.

But if I give land in tail *tenendo de capitalibus dominis per redditum viginti solidorum per fidelitatem:* this limitation of tenure to the lord is void; and it shall not be good, as in the other case, to make a reservation of twenty shillings good unto myself; but it shall be utterly void, as if no reservation at all had been made: and if the truth be that I, that am the donor, hold of the lord paramount by ten shillings only, then there shall be ten shillings only reserved upon the gift in tail as for ovelty. 2 Ed. 4. 5.

So if I give land to I. S. and the heirs of his body, and for default of such issue *quod tenementum prædictum revertatur ad I. N.* yet these words of reservation will carry a remainder to a stranger. But if I let white acre to I. S. excepting ten shillings rent, these words of exception to mine own benefit shall never inure to words of reservation. 21 Ed. 3. 49. 31 et 32 H. 8. Dyer 46. Plow. fo. 37. 35 H. 6. 34.

But now it is to be noted, that this rule is the last to be resorted to, and is never to be relied upon but where all other rules of exposition of words fail; and if any other rule come in place, this giveth place. And that is a point worthy to be observed generally in the rules of the law, that when they encounter and cross one another in any case, it be understood which the law holdeth worthier, and to be preferred; and it is in this particular very notable to consider, that this being a rule of some strictness and rigour, doth not, as it were, his office, but in absence of other rules which are of more equity and humanity; which rules you shall find afterwards set down with their expositions and limitations.

But now to give a taste of them to this present purpose: it is a rule, that general words shall never be stretched too far in intendment, which the civilians utter thus: *Verba generalia restringuntur ad habilitatem personæ, vel ad aptitudinem rei.*

Therefore, if a man grant to another, common *intra metas et bundas villæ de Dale*, and part of the ville is his several, and part is his waste and common; the grantee shall not have common in the several; and yet that is the strongest exposition against the grantor. 14 Ass. pl. 21.

So it is a rule, *Verba ita sunt intelligenda, ut res magis valeat, quam pereat:* and therefore if I give land to I. S. Lit. cap. cond.

and his heirs, *reddendo quinque libras annuatim* to I. D. and his heirs, this implies a condition to me that am the grantor; yet it were a stronger exposition against me, to say the limitation should be void, and the feoffment absolute.

10 Ed. 4. 1. So it is a rule, that the law will not intend a wrong, which the civilians utter thus: *Ea est accipienda interpretatio, quæ vitio caret.* And therefore if the executors of I. S. grant *omnia bona et catalla sua,* the goods which they have as executors will not pass, because *non constat* whether it may not be a devastation, and so a wrong; and yet against the trespassor that taketh them out of their hand, they shall declare *quod bona sua cepit.*

So it is a rule, words are to be understood that they work somewhat, and be not idle and frivolous: *Verba aliquid operari debent, verba cum effectu sunt accipienda.* And therefore if I buy and sell you four parts of my manor of Dale, and say not in how many parts to be divided, this shall be construed four parts of five, and not of six nor seven, &c. because that it is the strongest against me; but on the other side, it shall not be intended four parts of four parts, that is whole of four quarters; and yet that were strongest of all, but then the words were idle and of none effect.

3 H. 6. 20. So it is a rule, *Divinatio non interpretatio est, quæ omnino recedit a litera:* and therefore if I have a fee farm-rent issuing out of white acre of ten shillings, and I reciting the same reservation do grant to I. S. the rent of five shillings *percipiend' de reddit' prædict' et de omnibus terris et tenementis meis in Dale,* with a clause of distress, although there be atturnement, yet nothing passeth out of my former rent; and yet that were strongest against me to have it a double rent, or grant of part of that rent with an enlargement of a distress in the other land, but for that it is against the words, because *copulatio verborum inclinat exceptionem in eodem sensu,* and the word *de, anglicè* out of, may be taken in two senses, that is, either as a greater sum out of a less, or as a charge out of land, or other principal interest; and that the coupling of it with lands and tenements, *viz.* I reciting that I am seised of such a rent of ten shillings, do grant five shillings *percipiend' de eodem reddit',* it is good enough without atturnement; because *percipiend' de, etc.* may well be taken for *parcella de, etc.* without violence to the words; but if it had been *percipiend' de,* I. S. without saying *de redditibus prædict',* although I. S.

be the person that payeth me the foresaid rent of ten shillings, yet it is void; and so it is of all other rules of exposition of grants, when they meet in opposition with this rule, they are preferred.

Now to examine this rule in pleadings as we have done in grants, you shall find that in all imperfections of pleadings, whether it be in ambiguity of words and double intendments, or want of certainty and averments, the plea shall be strictly and strongly against him that pleads.

For ambiguity of words, if in a writ of entry upon disseisin, the tenant pleads jointenancy with I. S. of the gift and feoffment of I. D. judgment *de briefe*, the demandant saith that long time before I. D. any thing had, the demandant himself was seised in fee *quousque prædict' I. D. super possessionem ejus intravit*, and made a joint feoffment, whereupon he the demandant reentered, and so was seised until by the defendant alone he was disseised; this is no plea, because the word *intravit* may be understood either of a lawful entry, or of a tortious; and the hardest against him shall be taken, which is, that it was a lawful entry; therefore he should have alleged precisely that I. D. *disseisivit*. 22 H. 6. 43.

So upon ambiguity that grows by reference, if an action of debt be brought against I. N. and I. P. sheriffs of London, upon an escape, and the plaintiff doth declare upon an execution by force of a recovery in the prison of Ludgate *sub custodia* I. S. *et* I. D. then sheriffs in 1 K. H. VIII. and that he so continued *sub custodia* I. B. *et* I. G. in 2 K. H. VIII. and so continued *sub custodia* I. N. *et* I. L. in 3 K. H. VIII. and then was suffered to escape; I. N. and I. L. plead, that before the escape, supposed at such a day *anno superius in narratione specificato*, the said I. D. and I. S. *ad tunc vicecomites* suffered him to escape; this is no good plea, because there be three years specified in the declaration, and it shall be hardest taken that it was 1 or 3 H. VIII. when they were out of office; and yet it is nearly induced by the *ad tunc vicecomites*, which should leave the intendment to be of that year in which the declaration supposeth that they were sheriffs; but that sufficeth not, but the year must be alleged in fact, for it may be it was mislaid by the plaintiff, and therefore the defendants meaning to discharge themselves by a former escape, which was not in their time, must allege it precisely. 3 Ed. 6. Dy. 66.

For incertainty of intendment, if a warranty collateral be pleaded in bar, and the plaintiff by replication, to avoid 26 H. 8.

warranty, saith, that he entered upon the possession of the defendant, *non constat* whether this entry was in the life of the ancestor, or after the warranty attached; and therefore it shall be taken in hardest sense, that it was after the warranty descended, if it be not otherwise averred.

38 H. 6. 18. 39 H. 6. 5. For impropriety of words, if a man plead that his ancestors died by protestation seised, and that I. S. abated &c. this is no plea, for there can be no abatement except there be a dying seised alleged in fact; and an abatement shall not be improperly taken for disseissin in pleading, *car parols sont pleas.*

9 R. Dy. fo. 256 For repugnancy, if a man in avowry declare that he was seised in his demesne as of fee of white acre, and being so seised did demise the same white acre to I. S. *habendum* the moiety for twenty-one years from the date of the deed, the other moiety from the surrender, expiration, or determination of the estate of I. D. *qui tenet prædict' medietatem ad terminum vitæ suæ reddend'* 40*s*. rent: this declaration is insufficient, because the seisin that he hath alleged in himself in his demesne as of fee in the whole, and the state for life of a moiety, are repugnant; and it shall not be cured by taking the last, which is expressed to control the former, which is but general and formal; but the plea is naught, and yet the matter in law had been good to have entitled to have distrained for the whole rent.

But the same restraint follows this rule in pleading that was before noted in grants: for if the case be such as falleth within another rule of pleadings, then this rule may not be urged.

9. Ed. 4. 4 Ed. 6. Plow. And therefore it is a rule that a bar is good to a common intent, though not to every intent. As if a debt be brought against five executors, and three of them make default, and two appear and plead in bar a recovery had against them two of three hundred pounds, and nothing in their hands over and above that sum: if this bar should be taken strongliest against them, it should be intended that they might have abated the first suit, because the other three were not named, and so the recovery not duly had against them; but because of this other rule the bar is good: for that the more common intent will say, that they two did only administer, and so the action well considered; rather than to imagine, that they would have lost the benefit and advantage of abating the writ.

So there is another rule, that in pleading a man shall not disclose that which is against himself: and therefore if it be a matter that is to be set forth on the other side, then the plea shall not be taken in the hardest sense, but in the most beneficial, and to be left unto the contrary party to allege.

And, therefore, if a man be bound in an obligation, that 28 H. 8.
if the feme of the obligee do decease before the Feast of Dy. fo. 17.
St. John the Baptist, which shall be in the year of our Lord God 1598, without issue of her body by her husband lawfully begotten then living, that then the bond shall be void; and in debt brought upon this obligation the defendant pleads that the feme died before the said feast without issue of her body then living: if this plea should be taken strongliest against the defendant, then should it be taken that the feme had issue at the time of her death, but this issue died before the feast; but that shall not be so understood, because it makes against the defendant, and it is to be brought in on the plaintiff's side, and that without traverse.

So if in a detinue brought by a feme against the execu- 30 E. 3.
tors of her husband for her reasonable part of the goods of her husband, and her demand is of a moiety, and she declares upon the custom of the realm, by which the feme is to have a moiety, if there be no issue between her and her husband, and the third part if there be issue had, and declareth that her husband died without issue had between them; if this count should be hardliest construed against the party, it should be intended that her husband had issue by another wife, though not by her, in which case the feme is but to have the third part likewise; but that shall not be so intended, because it is matter of reply to be showed of the other side.

And so it is of all other rules of pleadings, these being sufficient not only for the exact expounding of these other rules, but *obiter* to show how this rule which we handle is put by when it meets with any other rule.

As for acts of parliament, verdicts, judgments, &c. which are not words of parties, in them this rule hath no place at all, neither in devises and wills, upon several reasons; but more especially it is to be noted, that in evidence it hath no place, which yet seems to have some affinity with pleadings, especially when demurrer is joined upon the evidence.

And, therefore, if land be given by will by H. C. to his 13. 14 R. P.
son I. C. and the heirs males of his body begotten; the re- 412.
mainder to F. C. and the heirs males of his body begotten: the remainder to the heirs males of the body of the devisor:

the remainder to his daughter S. C. and the heirs of her body, with a clause of perpetuity; and the question comes upon the point of forfeiture in an assize taken by default, and evidence is given, and demurrer upon evidence, and in the evidence given to maintain the entry of the daughter upon a forfeiture, it is not set forth nor averred that the devisor had no other issue male, yet the evidence is good enough, and it shall be so intended; and the reason thereof cannot be, because a jury may take knowledge of matters not within the evidence; and the court contrariwise cannot take knowledge of any matter not within the pleas; for it is clear that if the evidence had been altogether remote, and not proving the issue, there although the jury might find it, yet a demurrer might well be taken upon the evidence.

But if I take the reason of difference to be between pleadings, which are but openings of the case, and evidences which are the proofs of an issue; for pleadings being but to open the verity of the matter in fact indifferently on both parts have no scope and conclusion to direct the construction and intendment of them, and therefore must be certain; but in evidence and proofs the issue, which is the state of the question and conclusion, shall incline and apply all the proofs as tending to that conclusion.

Another reason is, that pleadings must be certain, because the adverse party may know whereto to answer, or else he were at a mischief, which mischief is remedied by a demurrer; but in evidence if it be short, impertinent, or uncertain, the adverse party is at no mischief, because it is to be thought that the jury will pass against him; yet, nevertheless, because the jury is not compellable to supply the defect of evidence out of their own knowledge, though it be in their liberty so to do; therefore the law alloweth a demurrer upon evidence also.

REGULA IV.

Quod sub certa forma concessum vel reservatùm est non trahitur ad valorem vel compensationem.

The law permitteth every man to part with his own interest, and to qualify his own grant, as it pleaseth himself; and, therefore, doth not admit any allowance or recompense, if the thing be not taken as it is granted.

17 H. 6. 10. So in all profits *a prendre*, if I grant common for ten beasts, or ten loads of wood out of my coppice, or ten loads

of hay out of my meads, to be taken for three years; he shall not have common for thirty beasts, or thirty loads of wood or hay, the third year, if he forbear for the space of two years; here the time is certain and precise.

So if the place be limited, or if I grant estovers to be spent in such a house, or stone towards the reparation of such a castle; although the grantee do burn of his fuel and repair of his own charge, yet he can demand no allowance for that he took it not.

So if the kind be specified, as if I let my park reserving to myself all the deer and sufficient pasture for them, if I do decay the game, whereby there is no deer, I shall not have quantity of pasture answerable to the feed of so many deer as were upon the ground when I let it; but am without any remedy, except I will replenish the ground again with deer.

But it may be thought that the reason of these cases is the default and laches of the grantor, which is not so.

For put the case that the house where the estovers should be spent be overthrown by the act of God, as by tempest, or burnt by the enemies of the king, yet there is no recompense to be made.

And in the strongest case, where it is in default of the grantor, yet he shall make void his own grant rather than the certain form of it should be wrested to an equity or valuation.

As if I grant common *ubicunque averia mea ierint*, the 9 H. 6. 36.
commoner cannot otherwise entitle himself, except that he aver that in such grounds my beasts have gone and fed; and if I never put in any, but occupy my grounds otherwise, he is without remedy; but if I put in, and after by poverty or otherwise desist, yet the commoner may continue; contrariwise, if the words of the grant had been *quandocunque averia mea ierint*, for there it depends continually upon the putting in of my beasts, or at least the general seasons when I put them in, not upon every hour or moment.

But if I grant *tertiam advocationem* to I. S. if he neglect to take his turn *ea vice*, he is without remedy: but if my wife be before entitled to dower, and I die, then my heir shall have two presentments, and my wife the third, and my grantee shall have the fourth; and it doth not impugn this rule at all, because the grant shall receive that construction at the first that it was intended such an avoidance as may be taken and enjoyed; as if I grant *proximam* 29 H. 8.
advocationem to I. D. and then grant *proximam advocationem* Dy. 38.

to I. S. this shall be intended the next to the next, which I may lawfully grant or dispose. *Quære.*

But if I grant *proximam advocationem* to I. S. and I. N. is incumbent, and I grant by precise words, *illam advocationem, quam post mortem, resignationem translationem vel deprivationem I. N. immediate fore contigerit;* now this grant is merely void, because I had granted that before, and it cannot be taken against the words.

REGULA V.

Necessitas inducit privilegium quoad jura privata.

THE law chargeth no man with default where the act is compulsory and not voluntary, and where there is not a consent and election; and, therefore, if either there be an impossibility for a man to do otherwise, or so great a perturbation of the judgment and reason as in presumption of law man's nature cannot overcome, such necessity carrieth a privilege in itself.

4 Ed. 6. cond. 9. 6.

Necessity is of three sorts, necessity of conservation of life, necessity of obedience, and necessity of the act of God, or a stranger.

Stamf.

First, for conservation of life: if a man steal viands to satisfy his present hunger, this is no felony nor larceny.

So if divers be in danger of drowning by the casting away of some boat or bark, and one of them get to some plank, or on the boat's side to keep himself above water, and another to save his life thrust him from it, whereby he is drowned; this is neither *se defendendo* nor by misadventure, but justifiable.

Con. 13. per Brooke. 15 H. 7. 2. per Keble.

So if divers felons be in a gaol, and the gaol by casualty is set on fire, whereby the prisoners get forth; this is no escape, nor breaking of prison.

14 H. 7. 29. per Read.

So upon the statute, that every merchant that setteth his merchandise on land without satisfying the customer or agreeing for it, which agreement is construed to be in certainty, shall forfeit his merchandise, and it is so that, by tempest, a great quantity of the merchandise is cast overboard, whereby the merchant agrees with the customer by estimation, which falleth out short of the truth, yet the over quantity is not forfeited; where note, that necessity dispenseth with the direct letter of a statute law.

4 Ed. 6. pl. condition. 4 Ed. 6. 20. condition.

So if a man have right to land, and do not make his entry for terror of force, the law allows him a continual claim, which shall be as beneficial to him as an entry; so shall a man save his default of appearance by *crestine de*

Lit. pl. 4. 19. 12 H. 4. 20. 14 H. 4. 30. B. 38 H. 6. 11.

eau, and avoid his debt by *duresse,* whereof you shall find proper cases elsewhere.

28 H. 6. 8. 39 H. 6. 50.

The second necessity is of obedience; and, therefore, where baron and feme commit a felony, the feme can neither be principal nor accessory; because the law intends her to have no will, in regard of the subjection and obedience she owes to her husband.

Stanmf. 26. 2. Ed. 3. 160. Cor. Fitzh.

So one reason amongst others why ambassadors are used to be excused of practices against the state where they reside, except it be in point of conspiracy, which is against the law of nations and society is, because *non constat* whether they have it in *mandatis,* and then they are excused by necessity of obedience.

So if a warrant or precept come from the king to fell wood upon the ground whereof I am tenant for life or for years, I am excused in waste.

B. 42 Ed. 3. 6.

The third necessity is of the act of God, or of a stranger; as if I be particular tenant for years of a house, and it be overthrown by grand tempest, or thunder and lightning, or by sudden floods or by invasion of enemies, or if I have belonging unto it some cottage which hath been infected, whereby I can procure none to inhabit them, no workmen to repair them, and so they fall down; in all these cases I am excused in waste: but of this last learning, when and how the act of God and strangers do excuse, there be other particular rules.

B. Wast. 31. 42. Ed. 3. 6. 19. Ed. 3. per Fitzh. Wast. 30. 32 Ed. 3. Fitzh. Wast 105. 44 Ed. 3. 21.

But then it is to be noted, that necessity privilegeth only *quoad jura privata,* for, in all cases, if the act that should deliver a man out of the necessity be against the commonwealth, necessity excuseth not; for *privilegium non valet contra rempublicam:* and as another saith, *necessitas publica major est quam privata:* for death is the last and farthest point of particular necessity, and the law imposeth it upon every subject, that he prefer the urgent service of his prince and country before the safety of his life: as if in danger of tempest those that are in a ship throw over other men's goods, they are not answerable; but if a man be commanded to bring ordnance or munition to relieve any of the king's towns that are distressed, then he cannot for any danger of tempest justify the throwing of them overboard; for there it holdeth which was spoken by the Roman, when he alleged the same necessity of weather to hold him from embarking, *necesse est ut eam, non ut vivam.* So in the case put before of husband and wife, if they join in committing treason, the necessity of obedience doth not excuse the offence as it doth in felony, because it is against the commonwealth.

13 H. 8. 16. per Shelly. So if a fire be taken in a street, I may justify the pulling down of the wall or house of another man to save the row from the spreading of the fire; but if I be assailed in my house, in a city or town, and distressed, and to save my life 12 H. 8. 10. per Brooke. 22 Ass. pl. 56. 6 E. 4. 7. per Sares. I set fire on mine own house, which spreadeth and taketh hold upon other houses adjoining, this is not justifiable, but I am subject to their action upon the case, because I cannot rescue mine own life by doing any thing which is against the commonwealth: but if it had been but a private trespass, as the going over another's ground, or the breaking of his inclosure when I am pursued, for the safeguard of my life, it is justifiable.

This rule admitteth an exception when the law intendeth some fault or wrong in the party that hath brought himself into the necessity; so that it is *necessitas culpabilis.* This I take to be the chief reason why *seipsum defendendo* is not matter of justification, because the law intends it hath a commencement upon an unlawful cause, because quarrels are not presumed to grow without some wrongs either in words or deeds on either part, and the law that thinketh 4 H. 7. 2. Stamford, 21. qu. 15. it a thing hardly triable in whose default the quarrel began, supposeth the party that kills another in his own defence not to be without malice; and therefore as it doth not touch him in the highest degree, so it putteth him to sue out his pardon of course, and punisheth him by forfeiture of goods: for where there cannot be any malice nor wrong presumed, as where a man assails me to rob me, and I kill him that assaileth me; or if a woman kill him that assaileth her to ravish her, it is justifiable without any pardon.

21 H. 7. 13. Stamf. 16. So the common case proveth this exception, that is, if a madman commit a felony, he shall not lose his life for it, because his infirmity came by the act of God: but if a drunken man commit a felony, he shall not be excused, because his imperfection came by his own default; for the reason and loss of deprivation of will and election by necessity and by infirmity is all one, for the lack of *arbitrium solutum* is the matter: and therefore as *infirmitas culpabilis* excuseth not, no more doth *necessitas culpabilis.*

REGULA VI.

Corporalis injuria non recipit æstimationem de futuro.

THE law, in many cases that concern lands or goods, doth deprive a man of his present remedy, and turneth him over to a further circuit of remedy, rather than to suffer an inconvenience: but if it be question of personal pain, the law will not compel him to sustain it and expect remedy, because it holdeth no damage a sufficient recompense for a wrong which is corporal.

As if the sheriff make a false return that I am summoned, whereby I lose my land; yet because of the inconvenience of drawing all things to incertainty and delay, if the 5 Ed. 4. 80. sheriff's return should not be credited, I am excluded of my averment against it, and am put to mine action of deceit against the sheriff and summoners; but if the sheriff 3 H. 6. 3. upon a *capias* return a *cepi corpus et quod est languidus in prisona*, there I may come in and falsify the return of the sheriff to save my imprisonment.

So if a man menace me in my goods, and that he will burn certain evidences of my land which he hath in his hand, if I will not make unto him a bond, yet if I enter into bond by this terror, I cannot avoid it by plea, because the law holdeth it an inconvenience to avoid a specialty by such matter of averment; and therefore I am put to mine action against such a menacer: but if he restrain my person, or threaten me with a battery, or with the burning of my 7 Ed. 4. 21. house, which is a safety and protection to my person, or with burning an instrument of manumission, which is an evidence of my enfranchisement; if upon such menace or duresse I make a deed, I shall avoid it by plea.

So if a trespasser drive away my beasts over another's 13 H. 8. 15. ground, I pursue them to rescue them, yet am I a trespasser 21 H. 7. 28. to the stranger upon whose ground I came: but if a man assail my person, and I fly over another's ground, now am I no trespasser.

This ground some of the canonists do aptly infer out of Christ's sacred mouth, *Amen, est corpus supra vestimentum*, where there say *vestimentum* comprehendeth all outward things appertaining to a man's condition, as lands and goods, which, they say, are not in the same degree with that which is corporal; and this was the reason of the ancient *lex talionis, oculus pro oculo, dens pro dente*, so that by that law *corporalis injuria de præterito non recipit æstimationem:* but our law, when the injury is already executed and inflicted, thinketh it best satisfaction to the party grieved to relieve him in damage, and to give him rather profit than revenge; but it will never force a man to tolerate a corporal hurt, and to depend upon that inferior kind of satisfaction, *ut in damagiis*.

REGULA VII.

Excusat aut extenuat delictum in capitalibus, quod non operatur idem in civilibus.

In capital causes *in favorem vitæ*, the law will not punish in so high a degree, except the malice of the will and intention appear; but in civil trespasses and injuries that are of an inferior nature, the law doth rather consider the damage of the party wronged, than the malice of him that was the wrong-doer: and therefore,

The law makes a difference between killing a man upon malice, forethought, and upon present heat: but if I give a man slanderous words, whereby I damnify him in his name and credit, it is not material whether I use them upon sudden choler and provocation, or of set malice, but in an action upon the case I shall render damages alike.

So if a man be killed by misadventure, as by an arrow at butts, this hath a pardon of course; but if a man be hurt or maimed only, an action of trespass lieth, though it be done against the party's mind and will, and he shall be punished in the law as deeply as if he had done it of malice.

Stamf. 16. 6 E. 4. 7.

So if a surgeon authorised to practise, do, through negligence in his cure, cause the party to die, the surgeon shall not be brought in question of his life; and yet if he do only hurt the wound, whereby the cure is cast back, and death ensues not, he is subject to an action upon the case for his misfaisance.

Stamf. 16. B.

So if baron and feme be, and they commit felony together, the feme is neither principal nor accessory, in regard of her obedience to the will of her husband: but if baron and feme join in committing a trespass upon land or otherwise, the action may be brought against them both.

So if an infant within years of discretion, or a madman, kill another, he shall not be impeached thereof: but if they put out a man's eye, or do him like corporal hurt, he shall be punished in trespass.

B. 3. H. 7. 1. Stamf. 16. B. 35 H. 6. 11.

So in felonies the law admitteth the difference of principal and accessory, and if the principal die, or be pardoned, the proceeding against the accessory faileth; but in a trespass, if one command his man to beat you, and the servant after the battery die, yet your action of trespass stands good against the master.

17 H. 4. 19. Com. 98.

REGULA VIII.

Æstimatio præteriti delicti ex post facto nunquam crescit.

THE law construeth neither penal laws nor penal facts by intendments, but considereth the offence in degree, as it standeth at the time when it is committed; so as if any circumstance or matter be subsequent, which laid together with the beginning should seem to draw to it a higher nature, yet the law doth not extend or amplify the offence.

Therefore, if a man be wounded, and the percussor is 11 H. 4. 12. voluntarily let go at large by the gaoler, and after death ensueth of the hurt, yet this is no felonious escape in the gaoler.

So if the villain strike the heir apparent of the lord, and the lord dieth before, and the person hurt, who succeedeth to be lord to the villain dieth after, yet this is no petty treason.

So if a man compass and imagineth the death of one that after cometh to be king of the land, not being any person mentioned within the statute of 25 Ed. III. this imagination precedent is not high treason.

So if a man use slanderous words of a person upon whom some dignity after descends that maketh him a peer of the realm, yet he shall have but a simple action of the case, and not in the nature of a *scandalum magnatum* upon the statute.

So if John Stile steal sixpence from me in money, and the king by his proclamation doth raise monies, that the weight of silver in the piece now of sixpence should go for twelve pence, yet this shall remain petty larceny, and not felony: and yet in all civil reckonings the alteration shall take place; as if I contract with a labourer to do some work for twelve pence, and the enhancing of money cometh before I pay him, I shall satisfy my contract with a sixpenny piece so raised.

So if a man deliver goods to one to keep, and after retain the same person into his service, who afterwards goeth away with his goods, this is no felony by the statute of 28 H. 8. pl. 2. 21 H. VIII. because he was not servant at that time.

In like manner if I deliver goods to the servant of I. S. to keep and after die, and make I. S. my executor; and before any new commandment of I. S. to his servant for the custody of the same goods, his servant goeth away with them, this is also out of the same statute. *Quod nota.*

But note that it is said *præteriti delicti;* for any acces-

sory before the act is subject to all the contingencies pregnant of the fact, if they be pursuances of the same fact;
18 Eliz. com. 175. as if a man command or counsel one to rob a man, or beat him grievously, and murder ensue, in either case he is accessory to the murder, *quia in criminalibus præstantur accidentia.*

REGULA IX.

Quod remedio destituitur ipsa re valet si culpa absit.

The benignity of the law is such, as, when to preserve the principles and grounds of law it depriveth a man of his remedy without his own fault, it will rather put him in a better degree and condition than in a worse; for if it disable him to pursue his action, or to make his claim, sometimes it will give him the thing itself by operation of law without any act of his own, sometimes it will give him a more beneficial remedy.

Lit. pl. 683. And therefore if the heir of the disseisor which is in by descent make a lease for life, the remainder for life unto the disseisee, and the lessee for life die, now the frank tenement is cast upon the disseisee by act in law, and thereby he is disabled to bring his *præcipe* to recover his right; whereupon the law judgeth him in of his ancient right as strongly as if it had been recovered and executed by action, which operation of law is by an ancient term and word of law called a *remitter;* but if there may be assigned any default or laches in him, either in accepting the freehold or in accepting the interest that draws the freehold, then the law denieth him any such benefit.

Lit. pl. 682. And therefore if the heir of the disseisor make a lease for years, the remainder in fee to the disseisee, the disseisee is not remitted, and yet the remainder is in him without his own knowledge or assent: but because the freehold is not cast upon him by act in law, it is no remitter. *Quod nota.*

Lit. pl. 685. So if the heir of the disseisor infeoff the disseisee and a stranger, and make livery to the stranger, although the stranger die before any agreement or taking of the profits by the disseisee, yet he is not remitted; because though a moiety be cast upon him by survivor, yet that is but *jus accrescendi,* and it is no casting of the freehold upon him by act in law, but he is still as an immediate purchaser, and therefore no remitter.

So if the husband be seised in the right of his wife, and discontinue and dieth, and the feme takes another husband, who takes a feoffment from the discontinuee to him and his wife, the feme is not remitted; and the reason is, because she was once sole, and so a laches in her for not pursuing her right; but if the feoffment taken back had been to the first husband and herself, she had been remitted. Semble in cest case cleiement le ley deeme contraie. Lit. pl. 665.

Yet if the husband discontinue the lands of the wife, and the discontinuee make a feoffment to the use of the husband and wife she is not remitted; but that is upon a special reason, upon the letter of the statute of 27 H. VIII. of uses, that willeth that the *cestuy que use* shall have the possession in quality and degree, as he had the use; but that holdeth place only upon the first vesting of the use; for when the use is absolutely executed and vested, then it doth insue merely the nature of possessions; and if the discontinuee had made a feoffment in fee to the use of I. S. for life, the remainder to the use of baron and feme, and lessee for life die, now the feme is remitted, *causa qua supra*. 2 M. Condic. 3. 34 H. 8. Dy. 3. 19.

Also, if the heir of the disseisor make a lease for life, the remainder to the disseisee, who chargeth the remainder, and lessee for life dies, the disseisee is not remitted; and the reason is, his intermeddling with the wrongful remainder, whereby he hath affirmed the same to be in him, and so accepted it: but if the heir of the disseisor had granted a rent charge to the disseisee, and afterwards made a lease for life, the remainder to the disseisee, and the lessee for life had died, the disseisee had been remitted; because there appeareth no assent or acceptance of any estate in the freehold, but only of a collateral charge.

So if the feme be disseised, and intermarry with the disseisor, who makes a lease for life, rendering rent, and dieth, leaving a son by the same feme, and the son accepts the rent of the lessee for life, and then the feme dies, and the lessee for life dies, the son is not remitted; yet the frank tenement was cast upon him by act in law, but because he had agreed to be in the tortious reversion by acceptance of the rent, therefore no remitter. 6 Ed. 3. 4. Cond. 3. 67. 28 H. 8. pl. 207.

So if tenant in tail discontinue, and the discontinuee make a lease for life, the remainder to the issue in tail being within age, and at full age the lessee for life surrendereth to the issue in tail, and tenant in tail die, and lessee for life dies, yet the issue is not remitted: and yet if the issue had accepted a feoffment within age, and had continued the taking of the profits when he came of full age, and then the tenant in tail had died, notwithstanding his taking of the profits, he had been remitted; for that which guides the remitter, is, if he be once in of the freehold without any laches: as if the heir of the disseisor enfeoffs the heir of the disseisee, who dies, and it descends to a second heir, upon whom the frank tenement is cast by descent, who enters and takes the profits, and then the disseisee dies, this is a remitter, *causa qua supra.*

Lit. pl. 3. 6. Also if tenant in tail discontinue for life, and take a surrender of the lessee, now he is remitted and seised again by force of the tail, and yet he cometh in by his own act: but this case differeth from all other cases; because the discontinuance was but particular at first, and the new gained reversion is but by intendment and necessity of law; and, therefore, is but, as it were, *ab initio,* with a limitation to determine whensoever the particular discontinuance endeth, and the estate cometh back to the ancient right.

To proceed from cases of remitter, which is a great branch of this rule, to other cases: if executors do redeem goods pledged by their testator with their own money, the law doth convert so much goods as doth amount to the value of that they laid forth, to themselves in property, and upon a plea of fully administered it shall be allowed: and the reason is, because it may be matter of necessity for the well administering of the goods of the testator, and executing their trust, that they disburse money of their own: for else perhaps the goods would be forfeited, and he that had them in pledge would not accept other goods but money, and so it is a liberty which the law gives them, and they cannot have any suit against themselves; and, therefore, the law gives them leave to retain so much goods by way of allowance: and if there be two executors, and one of them pay the money, he may likewise retain against his companion, if he have notice thereof.

6 H. 8. pl. 3. Dy.

3 Eliz. 187, pl. 6. But if there be an overplus of goods, above the value of that he shall disburse, then ought he by his claim to determine what goods he doth elect to have in value; or else before such election, if his companion do sell all the goods he hath no remedy but in spiritual court: for to say he should be tenant in common with himself and his companion *pro rata* of that he doth lay out the law doth reject that course for intricateness.

29 H. 8. pl. 7. in fine. 22 Ass. 52 F. Rec. in value 23. So if I. S. have a lease for years worth twenty pounds by the year, and grant unto I. D. a rent of ten pounds a year, and after make him my executor; now I. D. shall be charged with assets ten pounds only, and the other ten pounds shall be allowed and considered to him: and the reason is, because the not refusing shall be accounted no

laches to him, because an executorship is *pium officium*, and matter of conscience and trust, and not like a purchase to a man's own use.

Like law is, where the debtor makes the debtee his executor, the debt shall be considered in the assets, notwithstanding it be a thing in action. 12 H. 4. 22. Cond. 185. 2 H. 7. 5. 37. H. 6. 32.

So if I have a rent charge, and grant that upon condition, now though the condition be broken, the grantee's estate is not defeated till I have made my claim; but if after any such grant my father purchase the land, and it descend to me; now, if the condition be broken, the rent ceaseth without claim: but if I had purchased the land myself then I had extincted mine own condition, because I had disabled myself to make my claim: and yet a condition collateral is not suspended by taking back an estate; as if I make a feoffment in fee, upon condition that I. S. shall marry my daughter, and take a lease for life from my feoffee, if the feoffee break the condition I may claim to hold in by my fee-simple; but the case of the charge is otherwise, for if I have a rent charge issuing out of twenty acres, and grant the rent over upon condition, and purchase but one acre, the whole condition is extinct, and the possibility of the rent, by reason of the condition, is as fully destroyed as if there had been no rent in *esse*. 6 E. 6. Cond. 133. 6. Lit. pl. 352. 20 H. 7. per Pol. 35 H. 6. Fitz. Barr. 162.

So if the King grant to me the wardship of I. S. the son and heir of I. S. when it falleth; because an action of covenant lieth not against the King, I shall have the thing myself in interest. 30 H. 6. Fitz. Grants 91.

But if I let land to I. S. rendering a rent with condition of re-entry, and I. S. be attainted whereby the lease comes to the King, now the demand upon this land is gone, which should give me benefit of re-entry, and yet I shall not have it reduced without demand; and the reason of difference is, because my condition in this case is not taken away in right, but only suspended by the privilege of the possession: for if the King grant the lease over, the condition is revived as it was. 7 H. 6. 40.

Also if my tenant for life grant his estate to the King, now if I will grant my reversion over, the King is not compellable to attürn, therefore it shall pass by grant by deed without atturnment.

So if my tenant for life be, and I grant my reversion *pur autre vie*, and the grantee die, living *cestui que vie*, now the privity between tenant for life and me is not restored, and I have no tenant in *esse* to atturn; therefore I may pass my reversion without atturnment. *Quod nota*. 9 Ed. 2. Fitz. Atturnments 18.

So if I have a nomination to a church, and another hath the presentation, and the presentation comes to the King, now because the King cannot be attendant, my nomination is turned to an absolute patronage.

6 Ed. 6. Dy. 72.* So if a man be seised of an advowson, and take a wife, and after title of dower given he join in impropriating the church and dieth; now because the feme cannot have the turn, because of the perpetual incumbency, she shall have all the turns during her life; for it shall not be disimpropriated to the benefit of the heir contrary to the grant of tenant in fee-simple.

But if a man grant the third presentment to I. S. and his heirs, and impropriate the advowson, now the grantee is without remedy, for he took his grant subject to that mischief at the first: and, therefore, it was his laches, and therefore not like the case of the dower; and this grant of the third avoidance is not like *tertia pars advocationis*, or *medietas advocationis* upon a tenancy in common of the advowson; for if two tenants in common be, and a usurpation be had against them, and the usurper do impropriate, and one of the tenants in common do release, and the other bring his writ of right *de medietate advocationis*, and recover; now I take the law to be, that because tenants in common ought to join in presentments, which cannot now be, he shall have the whole patronage: for neither can there be an apportionment that he should present all the turns, and his incumbent but to have a moiety of the profits, nor yet the act of impropriation shall not be defeated.

45 Ed. 3. 10. But as if two tenants in common be of a ward, and they join in a writ of right of ward, and one release, the other shall recover the entire ward, because it cannot be divided: so shall it be in the other case, though it be of inheritance, and though he bring his action alone.

As if a disseisor be disseised, and the first disseisee released to the second disseisor upon condition, and a descent be cast, and the condition broken; now the mean disseisor, whose right is revived, shall enter notwithstanding this descent, because his right was taken away by the act of a stranger.

41 Ed. 3. 10. Le contrary fuit resoli in Martin Trott's case, pa. 32 Eliz. But if I devise land by the statute of 32 H. VIII. and the heir of the devisor enters and makes a feoffment in fee, and feoffee dieth seised, this descent bindeth, and there shall not be a perpetual liberty of entry, upon the reason that he

---

* Vide contra, 2 E. 3. fol. 8. Que presentmét del feme l'advowson est deveign disimpropriate a touts jours quel est agree in sur Cok. Rep. 7. fo. 8. a.

never had seisin whereupon he might ground his action, but he is at a mischief by his own laches: and the like law of the King's patentee; for I see no reasonable difference between them and him in the remainder, which is Littleton's case. in Com. Banco, and Pa. 1. Jac. ib. vide 7. R. 2. Scire fac. 3.

But note, that the law by operation and matter in fact will never countervail and supply a title grounded upon a matter of record; and therefore if I be entitled unto a writ of error, and the land descend unto me, I shall never be remitted, no more shall I be unto an attaint, except I may also have a writ of right. 41 E. 3. 14. per Finchden.

So if upon my avowry for services, my tenant disclaim where I may have a writ of right as upon disclaimer, if the land after descend to me, I shall never be remitted. 25 H. 8. Dy. 1. 7.

REGULA X.

Verba generalia restringunter ad habilitatem rei vel personæ.

It is a rule that the King's grants shall not be taken or construed to a special intent; it is not so with the grants of a common person, for they shall be extended as well to a foreign intent as to a common intent; yet, with this exception, that they shall never be taken to an impertinent or a repugnant intent: for all words whether they be in deeds or statutes, or otherwise, if they be general and not express and precise, shall be restrained unto the fitness of the matter or person.

As if I grant common *in omnibus terris meis* in D. and I have in D. both open grounds and several, it shall not be stretched to my common in several, much less in my gardens and orchards. Perk. pl. 108.

So if I grant to a man *omnes arbores meas crescentes supra terras meas in* D. he shall not have apple-trees, nor other fruit-trees growing in my gardens, or orchards, if there be any other trees upon my grounds. 14 H. 8. 2.

So if I grant to I. S. an annuity of ten pounds a year *pro consilio impenso et impendendo*, if I. S. be a physician, it shall be understood of his counsel in physic; and if he be a lawyer, of his counsel in law. 41 Ed. 3. 6. et 19.

So if I do let a tenement to I. S. near by my dwelling-house in a borough, provided that he shall not erect or use any shop in the same without my license, and afterwards I license him to erect a shop, and I. S. is then a miller, he shall not by virtue of these general words, erect a joiner's shop.

So the statute of chantries, that willeth all lands to be forfeited, given or employed to a superstitious use, shall 26 E. 337. Dy.

16 Eliz. 337. Dyer. not be construed of the glebe lands of parsonages: nay farther, if the lands be given to the parson of D. to say a mass in his church of D. this is out of the statute, because it shall be intended but as augmentation of his glebe; but otherwise it had been, if it had been to say a mass in any other church than his own.

So in the statute of wrecks, that willeth that goods wrecked where any live domestical creature remains in the vessel, shall be preserved and kept to the use of the owner that shall make his claim by the space of one year, doth not extend to fresh victuals or the like, which is impossible to keep without perishing or destroying it; for in these and the like cases general words may be taken, as was said to a rare foreign intent, but never to an unreasonable intent.

REGULA XI.

Jura sanguinis nullo jure civili dirimi possunt.

THEY be the very words of the civil law, which cannot be amended, to explain this rule, *hæres est nomen juris, Filius est nomen naturæ:* therefore corruption of blood taketh away the privity of the one, that is of the heir, but not of other, that is of the son; therefore if a man be attainted and be murdered by a stranger, the eldest son shall not have appeal, because the appeal is given to the heir, for the youngest sons who are equal in blood shall not have it; but if an attainted person be killed by his son, this is petty treason, for that the privity of a son remaineth: for I admit the law to be that if the son kill his father or mother it is petty treason, and that there remaineth so much in our laws of the ancient footsteps of *potestas patriæ* and natural obedience, which by the law of God is the very instance itself; and all other government and obedience is taken but by equity, which I add because some have sought to weaken the law in that point.

36 H. 6. 57, 58. 21 Ed. 3. 17.

Lamb. Jus. p. 293. Fitz. crown. 447.

So if land descend to the eldest son of a person attainted from his ancestor of the mother held in knight's service, the guardian shall enter, and oust the father, because the law giveth the father that prerogative in respect he is his son and heir; for of a daughter or a special heir in tail he shall not have it: but if the son be attainted, and the father covenant in consideration of natural love to stand seised of land to his use, this is good enough to raise a use, because the privity of a natural affection remaineth.

F. N. Br. fo. 143. De Droit.

26 E. 337. Dy. So if a man be attainted and have charter of pardon, and be returned of a jury between his son and I. S. the challenge remaineth; so may he maintain any suit of his son, notwithstanding the blood be corrupted.

So by the statute of 21 H. VIII. the ordinary ought to commit the administration of his goods that was attainted and purchase his charter of pardon, to his children, though born before the pardon, for it is no question of inheritance: for if one brother of the half blood die, the administration 5 Ed. 6. ought to be committed to his other brother of the half blood, Adm. 47. if there be no nearer by the father.

So if the uncle by the mother be attainted, and pardoned, 33 H 6. 55 and land descend from the father to the son within age held in socage, the uncle shall be guardian in socage; for that savoureth so little of the privity of heir, as the possibility to inherit shutteth not.

But if a feme tenant in tail assent to the ravisher, and have no issue, and her cousin is attainted, and pardoned, and purchaseth the reversion, he shall not enter for a for- 5 Ed. 4. 50. feiture. For though the law giveth it not in point of inheritance, but only as a perquisite to any of the blood, so he be next in estate; yet the recompense is understood for the stain of his blood, which cannot be considered when itis once wholly corrupted before.

So if a villain be attainted, yet the lord shall have the issues of his villain born before or after the attainder; for the lord hath them *jure naturæ* but as the increase of a flock.

Query, Whether if the eldest son be attainted and par- F. N. Br. doned, the lord shall have aid of his tenants to make him 82. G. a knight, and it seemeth he shall; for the words of the writ Register, fol. 87. hath *filium primogenitum*, and not *filium et hæredem*, and the like writ hath *pur file marrier* who is no heir.

REGULA XII.

Receditur à placitis juris, potius quàm injuriæ et delicta maneant impunita.

THE law hath many grounds and positive learnings, which are not of the maxims and conclusions of reason; but yet are learnings received with the law, set down, and will not have called in question; these may be rather called *placita juris* than *regulæ juris;* with such maxims the law will dispense, rather than crimes and wrongs should be unpunished, *quia salus populi suprema lex;* and *salus populi* is contained in the repressing offences by punishment.

Therefore if an advowson be granted to two, and the Fitz. N. B. 30. heirs of one of them, and a usurpation be had, they both shall join in a writ of right of advowson; and yet it is a ground in law, that a writ of right lieth of no less estate than of a fee-simple; but because the tenant for life hath no other several action in the law given him, and also that the jointure is not broken, and so the tenant in fee-simple cannot bring his writ of right alone; therefore rather than he shall be deprived wholly of remedy, and this wrong unpunished, he shall join his companion with him, notwithstanding the feebleness of his estate.

46 Ed. 3. 21. But if lands be given to two, and to the heirs of one of them, and they lease in a *præcipe* by default, now they shall not join in a writ of right, because the tenant for life hath a several action, namely, a *Quod ei deforciat*, in which respect the jointure is broken.

27 H. 8. 13. So if tenant for life and his lessor join in a lease for years, and the lessee commit waste, they shall join in punishing this waste, and *locus vastatus* shall go to the tenant for life, and the damages to him in reversion; and yet an action of waste lieth not for tenant for life; but because he in the reversion cannot have it alone, because of the mean estate for life, therefore rather than the waste shall be unpunished, they shall join.

45 Ed. 3. 3. 22 H. 6. 24. So if two coparceners be, and they lease the land, and one of them die, and hath issue, and the lessee commit waste, the aunt and the issue shall join in punishing this waste, and the issue shall recover the moiety of the place wasted, and the aunt the other moiety and the entire damages; and yet *actio injuriarum moritur cum persona* but *in favorabilibus magis attenditur quod prodest, quàm quod nocet.*

20 Ed. 2. Fitz. F. descent. 16. So if a man recovers by erroneous judgment, and hath issue two daughters, and one of them is attainted, the writ of error shall be brought against the parceners notwithstanding the privity fail in the one.

33 Eliz. Also it is a positive ground, that the accessory in felony cannot be proceeded against, until the principal be tried; yet if a man upon subtlety and malice set a madman by some device to kill him, and he doth so; now forasmuch as the madman is excused because he can have no will nor malice, the law accounteth the inciter as principal, though he be absent, rather than the crime shall go unpunished.

Fitz. Corone, 459. Ed. 4. M. 28. 6. Stamf. lib. 2. fol. 60. So it is a ground of the law, that the appeal of murder goeth not to the heir where the party murdered hath a wife, nor to the younger brother where there is an elder; yet if the wife murder her husband, because she is the party offendor, the appeal leaps over to the heir; and so if the son and heir murder his father, it goeth to the second brother.

But if the rule be one of the higher sort of maxims that are *regulæ rationales*, and not *positivæ*, then the law will rather endure a particular offence to escape without punishment, than violate such a rule.

As it is a rule that penal statutes shall not be taken by equity, and the statute of 1 Ed. VI. enacts that those that are attainted for stealing of horses shall not have their clergy, the judges conceived that this did not extend to him that stole but one horse, and therefore procured a new act for it, 2 Ed. VI. cap. 33. And they had reason for it, as I take the law; for it is not like the case upon the statute of Glocest. that gives an action of waste against him that holds *pro termino vitæ vel annorum*. It is true, if a man hold but for a year he is within the statute; for it is to be noted, that penal statutes are taken strictly and literally only in the point of defining and setting down the fact and the punishment, and in those clauses that do concern them; and not generally in words that are but circumstances and conveyance in the putting of the case: and so see the diversity; for if the law be, that for such an offence a man shall lose his right hand, and the offender hath had his right hand before cut off in the wars, he shall not lose his left hand, but the crime shall rather pass without the punishment which the law assigned, than the letter of the law shall be extended; but if the statute of 1 Ed. VI. had been, that he that should steal a horse should be ousted of his clergy, then there had been no question at all, but if a man had stolen more horses than one, but that he had been within the statute, *quia omne majus continet in se minus.*

Cap. 12. Stamf. 2. fol. 125.

Plow. 167. Litt. cap. 46. Ed. 3. 31.

REGULA XIII.

Non accipi debent verba in demonstrationem falsam quæ competunt in limitationem veram.

THOUGH falsity of addition or demonstration doth not hurt where you give the thing the proper name, yet nevertheless if it stand doubtful upon the words, whether they import a false reference and demonstration, or whether they be words of restraint that limit the generality of the former name, the law will never intend error or falsehood.

And, therefore, if the parish of Hurst do extend into the counties of Wiltshire and Berkshire, and I grant my close called Callis, situate and lying in the parish of Hurst in the county of Wiltshire, and the truth is, that the whole close

12 Eliz. 21. Dyer, 291. 23 Eliz. Dy. 376. 7 Ed. 6. Dy. 56.

lieth in the county of Berkshire; yet the law is, that it passeth well enough, because there is a certainty sufficient in that I have given it a proper name which the false reference doth not destroy, and not upon the reason that these words, "in the county of Wiltshire," shall be taken to go to the parish only, and so to be true in some sort, and not to the close, and so to be false: for if I had granted *omnes terras meas in parochia de Hurst in com. Wiltshire*, and I had no lands in Wiltshire but in Berkshire, nothing had past.

9 Ed. 4. 7. 21 Ed. 3. 18. 18 Eliz. But in the principal case, if the close called Callis had extended part into Wiltshire and part into Berkshire, then only that part had passed which lay in Wiltshire.

29 Reg. So if I grant *omnes et singulas terras meas in tenura I. D. quas perquisivi de I. N. in indentura dimissionis fact' I. B. specificat.* If I have land wherein some of these references are true and the rest false, and no land wherein they are all true, nothing passeth: as if I have land in the tenure of I. D. and purchased of I. N. but not specified in the indenture to I. B. or if I have land which I purchased of I. N. and specified in the indenture of demise to I. B. and not in the tenure of I. D.

But if I have some land wherein all these demonstrations are true, and some wherein part of them are true and part false, then shall they be intended words of true limitation to pass only those lands wherein all those circumstances are true.

REGULA XIV.

Licet dispositio de interesse futuro sit inutilis, tamen potest fieri declaratio præcedens quæ sortiatur effectum interveniente novo actu.

THE law doth not allow of grants except there be a foundation of an interest in the grantor; for the law that will not accept of grants of titles, or of things in action which are imperfect interests, much less will it allow a man to grant or incumber that which is no interest at all, but merely future.

But of declarations precedent before any interest vested the law doth allow, but with this difference, so that there be some new act or conveyance to give life and vigour to the declaration precedent.

Now the best rule of distinction between grants and declarations is, that grants are never countermandable, not in respect of the nature of the conveyance or instrument, though sometime in respect of the interest granted they are, whereas declarations evermore are countermandable in their natures.

And therefore if I grant unto you, that if you enter into an obligation to me of one hundred pounds, and after do procure me such a lease, that then the same obligation shall be void, and you enter into such an obligation unto me, and afterwards do procure such a lease, yet the obligation is simple, because the defeisance was made of that which was not. 20 Eliz. 19 H. 6. 62.

So if I grant unto you a rent charge out of white acre, and that it shall be lawful for you to distrain in all my other lands whereof I am now seised, and which I shall hereafter purchase; although this be but a liberty of distress, and no rent, save only out of white acre, yet as to the lands afterwards to be purchased the clause is void. 27 Ed. 3.

So if a reversion be granted to I. S. and I. D. a stranger by his deed do grant to I. S. that if he purchase the particular estate, he will atturne to the grant, this is a void atturnment, notwithstanding he doth afterwards purchase the particular estate. 29 Ed. 3. 6. 24 Eliz.

But of declarations the law is contrary; as if the disseisee make a charter of feoffment to I. S. and a letter of attorney to enter and make livery and seisin, and deliver the deed of feoffment, and afterwards livery and seisin is made accordingly, this is a good feoffment; and yet he had no other thing than a right at the time of the delivery of the charter; but because a deed of feoffment is but matter of declaration and evidence, and there is a new act which is the livery subsequent, therefore it is good in law. 13, 14 Eliz. 20, 21 Eliz. 25 Eliz. M. 38. et 39 Eliz.

So if a man make a feoffment to I. S. upon condition to enfeoff I. N. within certain days, and there are deeds made both of the first feoffment and the second, and letters of attorney accordingly, and both those deeds of feoffment and letters of attorney are delivered at a time, so that the second deed of feoffment and letters of attorney are delivered when the first feoffee had nothing in the land; and yet if both liveries be made accordingly, all is good. 36 Eliz.

So if I covenant with I. S. by indenture, that before such a day I will purchase the manor of D. and before the same day I will levy a fine of the same land, and that the same fine shall be to certain uses which I express in the same indenture; this indenture to lead uses being but matter of declaration, and countermandable at my pleasure, will suffice, though the land be purchased after; because there is a new act to be done, *viz.* the fine.

25 Eliz. 27 Eliz. But if there were no new act, then otherwise it is; as if I covenant with my son in consideration of natural love, to stand seised unto his use of the lands which I shall afterwards purchase, yet the use is void: and the reason is, because there is no new act, nor transmutation of possession following to perfect this inception; for the use must be limited by the feoffor, and not the feoffee, and he had nothing at the time of the covenant.

Com. Plowd. Rigden's case. So if I devise the manor of D. by special name, of which at that time I am not seised, and after I purchase it, except I make some new publication of my will, this devise is void; and the reason is, because that my death, which is the consummation of my will, is the act of God, and not my act, and therefore no such act as the law requireth.

But if I grant unto I. S. authority by my deed to demise for years the land whereof I am now seised, or hereafter shall be seised; and after I purchase the lands, and I. S. my attorney doth demise them: this is a good demise, because the demise of my attorney is a new act, and all one with a demise by myself.

21 Eliz. But if I mortgage land, and after covenant with I. S. in consideration of money which I receive of him, that after I have entered for the condition broken, I will stand seised to the use of the same I. S. and I enter, and this deed is enrolled, and all within the six months, yet nothing passeth away, because this enrolment is no new act, but a perfective ceremony of the first deed of bargain and sale; and the law is more strong in that case, because of the vehement relation which the enrolment hath to the time of the bargain and sale, at what time he had nothing but a naked condition.

6 Ed. 6. Br. So if two joint tenants be, and one of them bargain and sell the whole land, and before the enrolment his companion dieth, nothing passeth of the moiety accrued unto him by survivor.

REGULA XV.

In criminalibus sufficit generalis malitia intentionis cum facto paris gradus.

All crimes have their conception in a corrupt intent, and have their consummation and issuing in some particular fact; which though it be not the fact at which the intention of the malefactor levelled, yet the law giveth him no advantage of that error, if another particular ensue of as high a nature.

Therefore if an impoisoned apple be laid in a place to poison I. S. and I. D. cometh by chance and eateth it, this is murder in the principal that is actor, and yet the malice *in individuo* was not against I. D. 18 Eliz. Sander's case, com. 474.

So if a thief find the door open, and come in by night and rob a house, and be taken with the manner, and break a door to escape, this is burglary; yet the breaking of the door was without any felonious intent, but it is one entire act. Cr. J. peace, 30.

So if a caliver be discharged with a murderous intent at I. S. and the piece break and strike into the eye of him that dischargeth it, and killeth him, he is *felo de se*, and yet his intention was not to hurt himself; for *felonia de se*, and murder are *crimina paris gradus*. For if a man persuade another to kill himself, and be present when he doth so, he is a murderer. Cave.

But *quære*, if I. S. lay impoisoned fruit for some other stranger his enemy, and his father or mother come and eat it, whether this be petty treason, because it is not altogether *crimen paris gradus*. Cr. Just. peace, fol. 18, 19.

REGULA XVI.

Mandata licita recipiunt strictam interpretationem, sed illicita latam et extensam.

In committing of lawful authority to another, a man may limit it as strictly as it pleaseth him, and if the party authorised do transgress his authority, though it be but in circumstance expressed, it shall be void in the whole act.

But when a man is author and monitor to another to commit an unlawful act, then he shall not excuse himself by circumstances not pursued.

Therefore if I make a letter of attorney to I. S. to deliver livery and seisin in the capital messuage, and he doth it in another place of the land; or between the hours of two and three, and he doth it after or before; or if I make a charter of feoffment to I. D. and I. B. and express the seisin to be delivered to I. D. and my attorney deliver it to I. B. in all these cases the act of the attorney, as to execute the estate, is void; but if I say generally to I. D. whom I mean only to enfeoff, and my attorney make it to his attorney, it shall be intended, for it is a livery to him in law. 10 H. 7. 19. 15, 16. 16 El. Dy. 337. 16 El. Dy. 337. 11 El. Dy. 283. 38 H. 8. 68. Dy.

18 El. Sander's case, com. 175. But on the other side, if a man command I. S. to rob I. D. on Shooters-hill, and he doth it on Gads-hill; or to rob him such a day, and he doth it not himself but procureth I. B. to do it; or to kill him by poison, and he doth it by violence; in all these cases, notwithstanding the fact be not executed, yet he is accessory nevertheless.

Ibidem. But if it be to kill I. S. and he killeth I. D. mistaking him for I. S. then the acts are distant in substance, and he is not accessory.

And be it that the facts be of differing degrees, and yet of a kind.

As if a man bid I. S. to pilfer away such things out of a house, and precisely restrain him to do it sometimes when he is gotten in without breaking of the house, and yet he breaketh the house; yet he is accessory to the burglary; for a man cannot condition with an unlawful act, but he must at his peril take heed how he putteth himself into another man's hands.

18 Eliz. in Sander's case. pl. com. 475. But if a man bid one rob I. S. as he goeth to Sturbridge-fair, and he rob him in his house, the variance seems to be of substance, and he is not accessory.

REGULA XVII.

De fide et officio judicis non recipitur quæstio; sed de scientia, sive error sit juris sive facti.

The law doth so much respect the certainty of judgment, and the credit and authority of judges, as it will not permit any error to be assigned that impeacheth them in their trust and office, and in wilful abuse of the same; but only in ignorance, and mistaking either of the law or of the case and matter in fact.

F. N. br. fo. 21. 7 H. 7. 4. And therefore if I will assign for error, that whereas the verdict passed for me, the court received it contrary, and so gave judgment against me, this shall not be accepted.

3 H. 6. Ass. 3. So if I will allege for error, that whereas I. S. offered to plead a sufficient bar, the court refused it, and drave me from it, this error shall not be allowed.

2 M. Dy. 114. But the greatest doubt is where the court doth determine of the verity of the matter in fact; so that is rather a point of trial than a point of judgment, whether it shall be re-examined in error.

1 Mar. 5. 28 Ass. pl. 15. 21 H. 7. 40. 35. As if an appeal of maim be brought, and the court, by the assistance of the chirurgeons, adjudge it to be a maim, whether the party grieved may bring a writ of error; and I hold the law to be he cannot.

So if one of the prothonotaries of the Common Pleas 8 H. 4. 3.
bring an assize of his office, and allege fees belonging to
the same office in certainty, and issue is taken upon these 1 Mar. Dy.
fees, this issue shall be tried by the judges by way of ex- 89. 5 Mar. Dy.
amination, and if they determine it for the plaintiff, and he 163.
have judgment to recover arrerages accordingly, the defendant can bring no writ of error of this judgment, though the fees in truth be other.

So if a woman bring a writ of dower, and the tenant 8 H. 6. 23.
plead her husband was alive, this shall be tried by proofs 2 El. 285. Dy. 43 Ass. 26.
and not by jury, and upon judgment given on either side 41 Ass. 5.
no error lies. 39 Ass. 9.

So if *nul tiel record* be pleaded, which is to be tried by 5 Ed. 4. 3. 9 H. 7. 2.
the inspection of the record, and judgment be thereupon 19 H. 6. 52.
given, no error lieth.

So if in the assize the tenant saith, he is *Counte de dale*, 22 Ass. pl. 24.
et nient nosme counte, in the writ, this shall be tried by the 19 Ed. 4. 6.
records of the chancery, and upon judgment given no error lieth.

So if a felon demand his clergy, and read well and distinctly, and the court who is judge thereof do put him from his clergy wrongfully, error shall never be brought upon this attainder.

So if upon judgment given upon confession for default, 9 Ass. 8.
and the court do assess damages, the defendant shall never F. N. Br. 21.
bring a writ, though the damage be outrageous.

And it seemeth in the case of maim, and some other cases, that the court may dismiss themselves of discussing the matter by examination, and put it to a jury, and then the party grieved shall have his attaint; and therefore it seemeth that the court that doth deprive a man of his action, should be subject to an action; but that notwithstanding the law will not have, as was said in the beginning, the judges called in question in the point of their office when they undertake to discuss the issue, and that is the true reason: for to say that the reason of these cases should be, because
trial by the court should be peremptory as trial by certifi- 21 Ass. 24.
cate, (as by the bishop in case of bastardy, or by the mar- 11 H. 4. 41. 7 H. 6. 37.
shal of the king, &c.) the cases are nothing alike; for the reason of those cases of certificate is, because if the court should not give credit to the certificate, but should reexamine it, they have no other mean but to write again to the same lord bishop, or the same lord marshal, which were frivolous, because it is not to be presumed they

would differ from their former certificate; whereas in these other cases of error the matter is drawn before a superior court, to reexamine the errors of an inferior court: and therefore the true reason, as was said, that to examine again that which the court had tried were in substance to attaint the court.

And therefore this is a certain rule in error, that error in law is ever of such matters as were not crossed by the record; as to allege the death of the tenant at the time of the judgment given, nothing appeareth upon record to the contrary.

F.N.Br.21. So when the infant levies a fine, it appeareth not upon the record that he is an infant, therefore it is an error in fact, and shall be tried by inspection during nonage.

But if a writ of error be brought in the King's Bench of a fine levied by an infant, and the court by inspection and examination doth affirm the fine, the infant, though it be during his infancy, shall never bring a writ of error in the
2 R. 3. 20. parliament upon this judgment; not but that error lies after error, but because it doth now appear upon the record
F.N.Br.21. that he is now of full age, therefore it can be no error in fact. And therefore if a man will assign for error that fact,
9 Ed. 4. 3. that whereas the judges gave judgment for him, the clerks entered it in the roll against him, this error shall not be allowed; and yet it doth not touch the judges but the clerks: but the reason is, if it be an error, it is an error in fact; and you shall never allege an error in fact contrary to the record.

REGULA XVIII.

Persona conjuncta æquiparatur interesse proprio.

THE law hath that respect of nature and conjunction of blood, as in divers cases it compareth and matcheth nearness of blood with consideration of profit and interest; yea, and in some cases alloweth of it more strongly.

7 et 8 Eliz. Therefore if a man covenant, in consideration of blood, to stand seised to the use of his brother, or son, or near kinsman, a use is well raised of this covenant without transmutation of possession; nevertheless it is true, that consideration of blood is not to ground a personal contract upon; as if I contract with my son, that in consideration of blood I will give unto him such a sum of money, this is a *nudum pactum*, and no *assumpsit* lieth upon it; for to subject me to an action, there needeth a consideration

of benefit; but the use the law raiseth without suit or action; and besides, the law doth match real considerations with real agreements and covenants.

So if a suit be commenced against me, my son, or brother, I may maintain as well as he in remainder for his interest, or his lawyer for his fee; and if my brother have a suit against my nephew or cousin, yet it is at my election to maintain the cause of my nephew or cousin, though the adverse party be nearer unto me in blood.

19 Ed. 4. 5. 19 Ed. 4. 22. 22 H. 6. 35. 21 H. 6. 15. 16. 22 H. 6. 5. 20 H. 6. 14 H. 6. 6.

So in challenges of juries, challenge of blood is as good as challenge within distress, and it is not material how far off the kindred be, so the pedigree can be conveyed in a certainty, whether it be of the half blood or whole.

14 H. 7. 2. 14 et 15 El. 21 Ed. 4. 75. Com. 425.

So if a man menace me, that he will imprison or hurt in body my father, or my child, except I make such an obligation, I shall avoid this duresse, as well as if the duresse had been to mine own person: and yet if a man menace me, by taking away or destruction of my goods, this is no good duresse to plead: and the reason is, because the law can make me reparation of that loss, and so it cannot of the other.

15 H. 6. 17. 39 H. 6. 50. 21 Ed. 4. 13. 18 H. 6. 21. 15 Ed. 4. 1. 39 H. 6. 91. 7 Ed. 4. 21. 20 Ass. 14.

So if a man under the years of twenty-one contract for the nursing of his lawful child, this contract is good, and shall not be avoided by infancy, no more than if he had contracted for his own aliments or erudition.

Perk. 4. D. cap. 28.

REGULA XIX.

Non impedit clausula derogatoria, quo minùs ab eadem potestate res dissolvantur, à quibus constituuntur.

Acts which are in their natures revocable, cannot by strength of words be fixed or perpetuated; yet men have put in use two means to bind themselves from changing or dissolving that which they have set down, whereof one is *clausula derogatoria*, the other *interpositio juramenti*, whereof the former is only pertinent to this present purpose.

This *clausula derogatoria* is by the common practical term called *clausula non obstante, de futuro esse*, the one weakening and disannulling any matter past to the contrary, the other any matter to come; and this latter is that only whereof we speak.

The *clausula de non obstante de futuro*, the law judgeth to be idle and of no force, because it doth deprive men of that which of all other things is most incident to human condition, and that is alteration or repentance.

Therefore if I make my will, and in the end thereof do add such like clause [Also my will is, if I shall revoke this present will, or declare any new will, except the same shall be in writing, subscribed with the hands of two witnesses, that such revocation or new declaration shall be utterly void; and by these presents I do declare the same not to be my will, but this my former will to stand] any such pretended will to the contrary notwithstanding; yet nevertheless this clause or any the like never so exactly penned, and although it do restrain the revocation but in circumstance and not altogether, is of no force or efficacy to fortify the former will against the second; but I may by parole without writing repeal the same will and make a new.

28 Ed. 3. cap. 7. 24 Ed. 3. cap. 9. 2 H. 7. 6.

So if there be a statute made that no sheriff shall continue in his office above a year, and if any patent be made to the contrary, it shall be void; and if there be any *clausula de non obstante* contained in such patent to dispense with this present act, that such clause also shall be void; yet nevertheless a patent of the sheriff's office made by the king, with a *non obstante*, will be good in law contrary to such statute, which pretendeth to exclude *non obstantes;* and the reason is, because it is an inseparable prerogative of the crown to dispense with politic statutes, and of that kind; and then the derogatory clause hurteth not.

So if an act of parliament be made, wherein there is a clause contained that it shall not be lawful for the king, by authority of parliament, during the space of seven years, to repeal and determine the same act, this is a void clause, and such act may be repealed within the seven years; and yet if the parliament should enact in the nature of the ancient *lex regia*, that there should be no more parliaments held, but that the king should have the authority of the parliament; this act were good in law, *quia potestas suprema seipsum dissolvere potest, ligare non potest;* for as it is in the power of a man to kill a man, but it is not in his power to save him alive, and to restrain him from breathing or feeling; so it is in the power of a parliament to extinguish or transfer their own authority, but not, whilst the authority remains entire, to restrain the functions and exercises of the same authority.

So in the 28 of K. H. VIII. chap. 17, there was a statute made, that all acts that passed in the minority of kings, reckoning the same under the years of twenty-four, might be annulled and revoked by their letters patents when they came to the same years; but this act in the first of K. Ed. VI. who was then between the years of ten and eleven, cap. 11, was repealed, and a new law surrogate in place thereof, wherein a more reasonable liberty was given; and wherein, though other laws are made revocable according to the provision of the former law with some new form prescribed, yet that very law of revocation, together with pardons, is made irrevocable and perpetual, so that there is a direct contrariety between these two laws; for if the former stands, which maketh all latter laws during the minority of kings revocable without exception of any law whatsoever, then that very law of repeal is concluded in the generality, and so itself made revocable: on the other side, that law making no doubt of the absolute repeal of the first law, though itself were made during the minority, which was the very case of the former law in the new provision which it maketh, hath a precise exception, that the law of repeal shall not be repealed.

14 El. Dy. 313.
P. Comm. 563.

But the law is, that the first law by the impertinency of it was void *ab initio et ipso facto* without repeal, as if a law were made, that no new statute should be made during seven years, and the same statute be repealed within the seven years, if the first statute should be good, then the repeal could not be made thereof within that time; for the law of repeal were a new law, and that were disabled by the former law; therefore it is void in itself, and the rule holds, *perpetua lex est, nullam legem humanam ac positivam perpetuam esse; et clausula quæ abrogationem excludit initio non valet.*

Neither is the difference of the civil law so reasonable as colourable, for they distinguish and say that a derogatory clause is good to disable any latter act, except you revoke the same clause before you proceed to establish any later disposition or declaration; for they say, that *clausula derogatoria ad alias sequentes voluntates posita in testamento, (viz. si testator dicat quod si contigerit eum facere aliud testamentum non vult illud valere) operatur quod sequens dispositio ab ipsa clausula reguletur, et per consequens quod sequens dispositio duretur sine voluntate, et sic quod non sit attendendum.* The sense is, that where a former will is made, and after a later will, the reason why, without an express revocation of the former will, it is by implication revoked, is because of the repugnancy between the disposition of the former and the later.

But where there is such a derogatory clause, there can be gathered no such repugnancy: because it seemeth that the testator had a purpose at the making of the first will to make some shew of a new will, which nevertheless his intention was should not take place: but this was answered before; for if that clause were allowed to be good until a revocation, then would no revocation at all be made, therefore it must needs be void by operation of law at first. Thus much of *clausula derogatoria.*

REGULA XX.

Actus inceptus, cujus perfectio pendet ex voluntate partium, revocari potest; si autem pendet ex voluntate tertiæ personæ, vel ex contigenti, non potest.

In acts that are fully executed and consummate, the law makes this difference, that if the first parties have put it in the power of a third person, or of a contingency, to give a perfection to their acts, then they have put it out of their own reach and liberty; therefore there is no reason they should revoke them; but if the consummation depend upon the same consent, which was the inception, then the law accounteth it in vain to restrain them from revoking of it; for as they may frustrate it by omission and *non feisance,* at a certain time, or in a certain sort or circumstance, so the law permitteth them to dissolve it by an express consent before that time, or without that circumstance.

Therefore if two exchange land by deed, or without deed, and neither enter, they may make a revocation or dissolution of the same exchange by mutual consent, so it be by deed, but not by parole; for as much as the making of an exchange needeth no deed, because it is to be perfected by entry, which is a ceremony notorious in the nature of a livery; but it cannot be dissolved but by deed, because it dischargeth that which is but title.

F. N. Br. 36. 13 H. 7. 13, 14.

So if I contract with I. D. that if he lay me into my cellar three tuns of wine before Mich. that I will bring into his garner twenty quarters of wheat before Christmas, before either of these days the parties may by assent dissolve the contract; but after the first day there is a perfection given to the contract by action on the one side, and they may make cross releases by deed or parole, but never dissolve the contract; for there is a difference between dissolving the contract, and release or surrender of the thing contracted for: as if lessee for twenty years make a lease for ten years, and after he take a lease for five years,

F. 36. Eliz.

yet this cannot inure by way of surrender: for a petty lease derived out of a greater cannot be surrendered back again, but inureth only by dissolution of contract; for a lease of land is but a contract executory from time to time of the profits of the land, to arise as a man may sell his corn or his tithe to spring or to be perceived for divers future years.

But to return from our digression: on the other side, if I contract with you for cloth at such a price as I. S. shall name; there if I. S. refuse to name, the contract is void; but the parties cannot discharge it, because they have put it in the power of the third person to perfect.

So if I grant my reversion, though this be an imperfect act before atturnment; yet because the atturnment is the act of a stranger, this is not simply revocable, but by a policy or circumstance in law, as by levying a fine, or making a bargain and sale, or the like.

11 H. 7. 19. 1 R. 2. F. atturnment, 8.

So if I present a clerk to the bishop, now can I not revoke this presentation, because I have put it out of myself, that is, the bishop, by admission, to perfect my act begun.

31 Ed. 1. F. Q. Imp. 185. 14 Ed. 4. 2. 38 Ed. 3. 35.

The same difference appeareth in nominations and elections; as if I enfeoff such a one as I. D. shall name within a year, and I. D. name I. B. yet before the feoffment, and within the year, I. D. may countermand his nomination, and name again, because no interest passeth out of him. But if I enfeoff I. S. to the use of such a one as I. D. shall name within a year, then if I. D. name I. B. it is not revocable, because the use passeth presently by operation of law.

14 Ed. 4. 2.

So in judicial acts the rule of the civil law holdeth *sententia interlocutoria revocari potest*, that is, that an order may be revoked, but a judgment cannot; and the reason is, because there is title of execution or bar given presently unto the party upon judgment, and so it is out of the judge to revoke, in courts ordered by the common law.

REGULA XXI.

Clausula vel dispositio inutilis per presumptionem remotam vel causam ex post facto non fulcitur.

Clausula vel dispositio inutilis are said, when the act or the words do work or express no more than the law by intendment would have supplied; and therefore the doubling or iterating of that and no more, which the conceit of law doth in a sort prevent and preoccupate, is reputed nugation, and is not supported and made of substance either by a foreign intendment of some purpose, in regard whereof it might be material, nor upon any cause emerging afterwards, which may induce an operation of those idle words.

32 H. 8. Goord. 39. Ber. 2. M. Br. devises, 41. And therefore if a man demise land at this day to his son and heir, this is a void devise, because the disposition of law did cast the same upon the heir by descent; and yet if it be knight's service land, and the heir within age, if he take by the devise, he shall have two parts of the profits to his own use, and the guardian shall have benefit but of the third; but if a man devise land to his two daughters, having no sons, then the devise is good, because he doth
29 H. 8. alter the disposition of law; for by the law they shall take
Dy. 12. in copercenary, but by the devise they shall take jointly; and this is not any foreign collateral purpose, but in point of taking of estate.

So if a man make a feoffment in fee to the use of his last will and testament, these words of special limitation are void, and the law reserveth the ancient use to the feoffor and his heirs; and yet if the words might stand, then might it be authority by his will to declare and appoint uses, and then though it were knight's service land, he might dispose the whole. As if a man make a feoffment in fee, to the use of the will and testament of a stranger, there the stranger may declare a use of the whole by his will, notwithstanding it be knight's service land; but the reason of the principal case is, because uses before the statute of 27 H. 8. were to have been disposed by will, and therefore before that statute a use limited in the form aforesaid, was but a frivolous limitation, in regard of the old use that the law reserved was deviseable; and the
19 H. 8. 11. statute of 27 altereth not the law, as to the creating and
5 Ed. 4. 8. limiting of any use, and therefore after that statute, and before the statute of wills, when no land could have been devised, yet was it a void limitation as before, and so continueth to this day.

But if I make a feoffment in fee to the use of my last will and testament, thereby to declare an estate tail and no greater estate, and after my death, and after such estate declared shall expire, or in default of such declaration then to the use of I. S. and his heirs, this is a good limitation;
19 H. 8. 11. and I may by my will declare a use of the whole land to
6 Ed. 4. 8. a stranger, though it be held in knight's service, and yet I have an estate in fee simple by virtue of the old use during life.

So if I make a feoffment in fee to the use of my right 32 H. 8. 43. Dy.
heirs, this is a void limitation, and the use reserved by the 20 H. 8. 8. Dy.
law doth take place: and yet if the limitation should be 7 Eliz. 237.
good the heir should come in by way of purchase, who Dy.
otherwise cometh in by descent; but this is but a circumstance which the law respecteth not, as was proved before.

But if I make a feoffment in fee to the use of my right heirs, and the right heirs of I. S. this is a good use, because 10 El. 274.
I have altered the disposition of law; neither is it void for Dy.
a moiety, but both our right heirs when they come in being shall take by joint purchase; and he to whom the first 2 Ed. 3. 29.
falleth shall take the whole, subject nevertheless to his 30 E. 1. Fitz
companion's title, so it have not descended from the first Devise. 9.
heir to the heir of the heir: for a man cannot be joint-tenant claiming by purchase, and the other by descent, because they be several titles.

So if a man having land on the part of his mother make a feoffment in fee to the use of himself and his heirs, this use, though expressed, shall not go to him and the heirs of the part of his father as a new purchase, no more than 4 M. 133. pl.
it should have done if it had been a feoffment in fee nakedly 6. Dyer.
without consideration, for the intendment is remote. But if baron and feme be, and they join in a fine of the feme's land, and express a use to the husband and wife and their heirs: this limitation shall give a joint estate by intierties to them both, because the intendment of law would have conveyed the use to the feme alone. And thus much 5 Ed. 4. 8.
touching foreign intendments. 19 H. 8. 11.

For matter *ex post facto*, if a lease for life be made to two, and the survivor of them, and they after make partition: now these words (and the survivor of them) should seem to carry purpose as a limitation, that either of them should be stated of his part for both their lives severally; but yet the law at the first construeth the words but words 30 Ass. 8. Fitz.
of dilating to describe a joint estate; and if one of them Part 16.
die after partition, there shall be no occupant, but his part 31 H. 8. 46.
shall revert. Pl. 7. Dy.

So if a man grant a rent charge out of ten acres, and grant further that the whole rent shall issue out of every acre, and distress accordingly, and afterwards the grantee purchase an acre: now this clause should seem to be material to uphold the rent; but yet nevertheless the law at first accepteth of these words but as words of explanation, and then notwithstanding the whole rent is extinct.

4 Ed. 6. Com. 33. per Hinde. 27 H. 8. 6. So if a gift in tail be made upon condition, that if tenant in tail die without issue, it shall be lawful for the donor to enter; and the donee discontinue and die without issue: now this condition should seem material to give him benefit of entry, but because it did at the first limit the estate according to the limitation of law, it worketh nothing upon this matter emergent afterward.

22 Ass. Pl. 52. So if a gift in tail be made of lands held in knight's service with an express reservation of the same service, whereby the land is held over, and the gift is with warranty, and the land is evicted, and other land recovered in value against the donor, held in socage, now the tenure which the law makes between the donor and donee shall be in socage, and not in knight's service, because the first reservation was according to the owelty of service, which was no more than the law would have reserved.

But if a gift in tail had been made of lands held in socage with a reservation of knight's service tenure, and with warranty, then, because the intendment of law is altered, the new land shall be held by the same service the last land was, without any regard at all to the tenure paramount: and thus much of matter *ex post facto*.

This rule faileth where that the law saith as much as the party, but upon foreign matter not pregnant and appearing upon the same act and conveyance, as if lessee for life be, and he lets for twenty years, if he live so long; this limitation (if he live so long) is no more than the law saith, but it doth not appear upon the same conveyance or act, that this limitation is nugatory, but it is foreign matter in respect of the truth of the state whence the lease is derived: and, therefore, if lessee for life make a feoffment in fee, yet 16 H. 7. 4. per Keble. 24 Ed. 3. 28. Fitz. pl. 98. the state of the lease for years is not enlarged against the feoffee; otherwise had it been if such limitation had not been, but that it had been left only to the law.

So if tenant after possibility make a lease for years, and the donor confirms to the lessee to hold without impeachment of waste during the life of tenant in tail, this is no more than the law saith; but the privilege of tenant after possibility is foreign matter, as to the lease and confirmation: and therefore if tenant after possibility do surrender, yet the lessee shall hold dispunishable of waste; otherwise had it been if no such confirmation at all had been made.

Also heed must be given that it be indeed the same thing which the law intendeth, and which the party expresseth, and not like or resembling, and such as may stand both together: for if I let land for life rendering a rent, and by my deed warrant the same land, this warranty in law and warranty in deed are not the same thing, but may both stand together. 20 Ed. 2. Fitz. 7. 21 Ed. 1. Zouch. 289.

There remaineth yet a great question on this rule.

A principal reason whereupon this rule is built, should seem to be, because such acts or clauses are thought to be but declaratory, and added upon ignorance and *ex consuetudine clericorum*, upon observing of a common form, and not upon purpose or meaning, and therefore whether by particular and precise words a man may not control the intendment of the law.

To this I answer, that no precise or express words will control this intendment of law; but as the general words are void, because they say contrary to that the law saith; so are they which are thought to be against the law: and therefore if I demise my land being knight's service tenure to my heir, and express my intention to be, that the one part should descend to him as the third appointed by statute, and the other he shall take by devise to his own use; yet this is void: for the law saith, he is in by descent of the whole, and I say he shall be in by devise, which is against the law.

But if I make a gift in tail, and say upon condition, that if tenant in tail discontinue and after die without issue, it shall be lawful for me to enter; this is a good clause to make a condition, because it is but in one case, and doth not cross the law generally: for if the tenant in tail in that case be disseised, and a descent cast, and die without issue, I that am the donor shall not enter. Lit. pl. 362.

But if the clause had been provided, that if tenant in tail discontinue, or suffer a descent, or do any other fact whatsoever, that after his death without issue it shall be lawful for me to enter: now this is a void condition, for it importeth a repugnancy to law; as if I would over-rule that where the law saith I am put to my action, I nevertheless will reserve to myself an entry.

REGULA XXII.

Non videtur consensum retinuisse si quis ex præscripto minantis aliquid immutavit.

ALTHOUGH choice and election be a badge of consent, yet if the first ground of the act be duresse, the law will not construe that the duresse doth determine, if the party duressed do make any motion or offer.

Therefore if a party menace me, except I make unto him a bond of forty pounds, and I tell him that I will not do it, but I will make unto him a bond of twenty pounds, the law shall not expound this bond to be voluntary, but shall rather make construction that my mind and courage is not to enter into the greater bond for any menace, and yet that I enter by compulsion notwithstanding into the lesser.

But if I will draw any consideration to myself, as if I had said, I will enter into your bond of forty pounds, if you will deliver me that piece of plate, now the duresse is discharged; and yet if it had been moved from the duressor, who had said at the first, You shall take this piece of plate, and make me a bond of forty pounds, now the gift of the plate had been good, and yet the bond shall be avoided by duresse.

REGULA XXIII.

Ambiguitas verborum latens verificatione suppletur; nam quod ex facto oritur ambiguum verificatione facti tollitur.

There be two sorts of ambiguities of words, the one is *ambiguitas patens,* and the other *latens. Patens* is that which appears to be ambiguous upon the deed or instrument; *latens* is that which seemeth certain and without ambiguity, for any thing that appeareth upon the deed or instrument; but there is some collateral matter out of the deed that breedeth the ambiguity.

Ambiguitas patens is never holpen by averment, and the reason is, because the law will not couple and mingle matter of specialty, which is of the higher account, with matter of averment, which is of inferior account in law; for that were to make all deeds hollow, and subject to averments, and so in effect, that to pass without deed, which the law appointeth shall not pass but by deed.

Therefore if a man give land to *I. D. et I. S. et hæredibus,* and do not limit to whether of their heirs, it shall not be supplied by averment to whether of them the intention was the inheritance should be limited.

So if a man give land in tail, though it be by will, the remainder in tail, and add a *proviso* in this manner: Provided that if he, or they, or any of them do any, &c. according to the usual clauses of perpetuities, it cannot be averred upon the ambiguities of the reference of this clause, that the intent of the devisor was, that the restraint should go only to him in the remainder, and the heirs of his body;

and that the tenant in tail in possession was meant to be at large.

Of these infinite cases might be put, for it holdeth generally that all ambiguity of words by matter within the deed, and not out of the deed, shall be holpen by construction, or in some case by election, but never by averment, but rather shall make the deed void for uncertainty.

But if it be *ambiguitas latens*, then otherwise it is: as if I grant my manor of S. to I. F. and his heirs, here appeareth no ambiguity at all; but if the truth be, that I have the manors both of South S. and North S. this ambiguity is matter in fact, and therefore it shall be holpen by averment, whether of them was that the party intended should pass.

So if I set forth my land by quantity, then it shall be supplied by election, and not averment.

As if I grant ten acres of wood in sale, where I have a hundred acres, whether I say it in my deed or no, that I grant out of my hundred acres, yet here shall be an election in the grantee, which ten he will take.

And the reason is plain, for the presumption of the law is, where the thing is only nominated by quantity, that the parties had indifferent intentions which should be taken, and there being no cause to help the uncertainty by intention, it shall be holpen by election.

But in the former case the difference holdeth, where it is expressed and where not; for if I recite, Whereas I am seised of the manor of North S. and South S. I lease unto you *unum manerium de S.* there it is clearly an election. So if I recite, Where I have two tenements in St. Dunstan's, I lease unto you *unum tenementum*, there it is an election, not averment of intention, except the intent were of an election, which may be specially averred.

Another sort of *ambiguitas latens* is correlative unto these: for this ambiguity spoken of before, is when one name and appellation doth denominate divers things, and the second, when the same thing is called by divers names.

As if I give lands to Christ-Church in Oxford, and the name of the corporation is *Ecclesia Christi in Universitate Oxford*, this shall be holpen by averment, because there appears no ambiguity in the words: for this variance is matter in fact, but the averment shall not be of intention, because it doth stand with the words.

For in the case of equivocation the general intent includes both the special, and therefore stands with the words:

but so it is not in variance, and therefore the averment must be of matter, that do endure quantity, and not intention.

As to say, of the precinct of Oxford, and of the University of Oxford, is one and the same, and not to say that the intention of the parties was, that the grant should be to Christ-Church in that University of Oxford.

REGULA XXIV.

Licita bene miscentur, formula nisi juris obstet.

THE law giveth that favour to lawful acts, that although they be executed by several authorities, yet the whole act is good.

As when tenant for life is the remainder in fee, and they join in a livery by deed or without, this is one good entire livery drawn from them both, and doth not inure to a surrender of the particular estate, if it be without deed* or confirmation of those in the remainder, if it be by deed; but they are all parties to the livery.

So if tenant for life the remainder in fee be, and they join in granting a rent, this is one solid rent out of both their estates, and no double rent, or rent by confirmation.

So if tenant in tail be at this day, and he make a lease for three lives, and his own, this is a good lease, and warranted by the statute of 32 H. VIII. and yet it is good in part by the authority which tenant in tail hath by the common law, that is for his own life, and in part by the authority which he hath by the statute, that is, for the other three lives.

Quære.

So if a man, seised of lands deviseable by custom, and of other land held in knight's service, and devise all his lands, this is a good devise of all the land customary by the common law, and of two parts of the other land by the statutes.

So in the Star-chamber a sentence may be good, grounded in part upon the authority given the court by the statute of 3 H. VII. and in part upon that ancient authority which the court hath by the common law, and so upon several commissions.

But if there be any form which the law appointeth to be

* Semble cleerement le ley d'estre contrary in ambideux cases, car lou est sans fait est livery solement de cestui in le rem' et surr' de partic' ten' auterment serra forfeiture de son estate, et lou est per fait, le livery passa solement de tenant, car il ad le frank tenement, vide accordant. Snr. Co. lib. 1. 76. b. 77. a. Com. Plow. 59. A. 140. 2 H. 5. 7. 13 H. 7. 14. 13 Ed. 4. 4. a. 27 H. 8. 13. M. 16 et 17. El. Dy. 339.

observed, which cannot agree with the diversities of authorities, then this rule faileth.

As if three coparceners be, and one of them alien her purparty, the feoffee and one of the sisters cannot join in a writ *de part' facienda*, because it behoveth the feoffee to mention the statute in his writ. Vide 1 Instit. 166. b.

REGULA XXV.

Præsentia corporis tollit errorem nominis, et veritas nominis tollit errorem demonstrationis.

THERE be three degrees of certainty.

1. Presence.
2. Name.
3. Demonstration or reference.

Whereof the presence the law holdeth of greatest dignity, the name in the second degree, and the demonstration or reference in the lowest, and always the error or falsity in the less worthy.

And therefore if I give a horse to I. D. being present, and say unto him, I. S. take this, this is a good gift, notwithstanding I call him by a wrong name: but so had it not been if I had delivered him to a stranger to the use of I. S. where I meant I. D.

So if I say unto I. S. Here I give you my ring with the ruby, and deliver it with my hand, and the ring bear a diamond and no ruby, this is a good gift notwithstanding I name it amiss.

So had it been if by word or writing, without the delivery of the thing itself, I had given the ring with the ruby, although I had no such, but only one with a diamond, which I meant, yet it would have passed.

So if I by deed grant unto you, by general words, all the lands that the king hath passed unto me by letters patents, dated 10 May, unto this present indenture annexed, and the patent annexed have date 10 July, yet if it be proved that that was the true patent annexed, the presence of the patent maketh the error of the date recited not material; yet if no patent had been annexed, and there had been also no other certainty given, but the reference of the patent, the date whereof was misrecited, although I had no other patent ever of the king, yet nothing would have passed.

Like law is it, but more doubtful, where there is not a presence, but a kind of representation, which is less worthy than a presence, and yet more worthy than a name or reference.

As if I covenant with my ward, that I will tender unto him no other marriage than the gentlewoman whose picture I delivered him, and that picture hath about it *ætatis suæ anno* 16, and the gentlewoman is seventeen years old; yet nevertheless, if it can be proved that the picture was made for that gentlewoman, I may, notwithstanding this mistaking, tender her well enough.

So if I grant you for life a way over my land, according to a plot intended between us, and after I grant unto you and your heirs a way according to the first plot intended, whereof a table is annexed to these presents, and there be some special variance between the table and the original plot, yet this representation shall be certainty sufficient to lead unto the first plot; and you shall have the way in fee nevertheless, according to the first plot, and not according to the table.

So if I grant unto you by general words the land which the king hath granted me by his letters patents, *quarum tenor sequitur in hæc verba*, &c. and there be some mistaking in the recital and variance from the original patent, although it be in a point material, yet the representation of this whole patent shall be as the annexing of the true patent, and the grant shall not be void by this variance.

Now for the second part of this rule, touching the name and the reference, for the explaining thereof, it must be noted what things sound in demonstration or addition: as first in lands, the greatest certainty is, where the land hath a name proper, as, the manor of Dale, Grandfield, &c. the next is equal to that, when the land is set forth by bounds and abuttals, as a close of pasture bounding on the east part upon Emsden Wood, on the south upon, &c. It is also a sufficient name to lay the general boundary, that is, some place of larger precinct, if there be no other land to pass in the same precinct, as all my lands in Dale, my tenement in St. Dunstan's parish, &c.

A farther sort of denomination is to name land by the attendancy they have to other lands more notorious, as parcel of my manor of D. belonging to such a college lying upon Thames' Bank.

All these things are notes found in denomination of lands, because they be signs to call, and therefore of property to signify and name a place: but these notes that sound only in demonstration and addition, are such as are but transitory and accidental to the nature of the place.

As *modo in tenura et occupatione* of the proprietary, tenure or possessor is but a thing transitory in respect of land; *Generatio venit, generatio migrat, terra autem manet in æternum.*

So likewise matter of conveyance, title, or instrument.

As, *quæ perquisivi de I. D. quæ descendebant à I. N. patre meo*, or, *in prædicta indentura dimissionis*, or, *in prædictis literis patentibus specificat'.*

So likewise, *continent' per æstimationem 20 acras*, or if *(per æstimationem)* be left out, all is one, for it is understood, and this matter of measure, although it seem local, yet it is indeed but opinion and observation of men.

The distinction being made, the rule is to be examined by it.

Therefore if I grant my close called Dale, in the parish of Hurst, in the county of Southampton, and the parish likewise extendeth into the county of Berkshire, and the whole close of Dale lieth in the county of Berkshire; yet because the parcel is especially named, the falsity of the addition hurteth not, and yet this addition is found in name, but (as it was said) it was less worthy than a proper name.

So if I grant *tenementum meum*, or *omnia tenementa mea*, (for the universal and indefinite to this purpose are all one) *in parochia Sancti Butolphi extra Aldgate* (where the verity is *extra Bishopsgate) in tenura Guilielmi*, which is true, yet this grant is void, because that which sounds in denomination is false, which is the more worthy; and that which sounds in addition is true, which is the less;* and though *in tenura Guilielmi*, which is true, had been first placed, yet it had been all one.

But if I grant *tenementum meum quod perquisivi de R. C. in Dale*, where the truth was T. C. and I have no other tenements in D. but one, this grant is good, because that which soundeth in name (namely, *in Dale)* is true, and that which sounded in addition *(viz. quod perquisivi*, &c.) is only false.

Vide ib. quæ contraria est lex, car icy auxl le primer certainty est faux.

So if I grant *prata mea in Sale continentia* 10 *acras*, and they contain indeed 20 acres, the whole twenty pass.

So if I grant all my lands, being parcels *manerii de D. in*

* Semble icy le grant ust este assets bon, come fuit resolu per Cur', Co. lib. 3. fol. 10. a. vide. 33 H. 8. Dy. 50. b. 12 El. ib. 292. b. et Co. lib. 2. fo. 33. a.

prædictis literis patentibus specificat', and there be no letters patents, yet the grant is good enough.

The like reason holds in demonstrations of persons, that have been declared in demonstration of lands and places, the proper name of every one is in certainty worthiest: next are such appellations as are fixed to his person, or at least of continuance, as, son of such a man, wife of such a husband; or addition of office, as, clerk of such a court, &c. and the third are actions or accidents, which sound no way in appellation or name, but only in circumstance, which are less worthy, although they may have a poor particular reference to the intention of the grant.

And therefore if an obligation be made to I. S. *filio et hæredi G. S.* where indeed he is a bastard, yet this obligation is good.

So if I grant land *Episcopo nunc Londinensi qui me erudivit in pueritia*, this is a good grant, although he never instructed me.

But *è converso*, if I grant land to I. S. *filio et hæredi G. S.* and it be true that he is son and heir unto G. S. but his name is Thomas, this is a void grant.

Or if in the former grant it was the Bishop of Canterbury who taught me in my childhood, yet shall it be good (as was said) to the Bishop of London, and not to the Bishop of Canterbury.

The same rule holdeth of denomination of times, which are such a day of the month, such a day of the week, such a Saint's day or eve, to-day, to-morrow; these are names of times.

But the day that I was born, the day that I was married; these are but circumstances and addition of times.

And therefore if I bind myself to do some personal attendance upon you upon Innocents' day, being the day of your birth, and you were not born that day, yet shall I attend.

There resteth two questions of difficulty yet upon this rule: first, Of such things whereof men take not so much note as that they shall fail of this distinction of name and addition.

As, my box of ivory lying in my study sealed up with my seal of arms; my suit of arras with the story of the nativity and passion: of such things there can be no name but all is of description, and of circumstance, and of these I hold the law to be, that precise truth of all recited circumstances is not required.

But in such things *ex multitudine signorum colligitur identitas vera*, therefore though my box were sealed, and although the arras had the story of the nativity, and not of the passion, if I had no other box, nor no other suit, the gifts are good; and there is certainty sufficient, for the law doth not expect a precise description of such things as have no certain denomination.

Secondly, Of such things as do admit the distinction of name and addition, but the notes fall out to be of equal dignity all of name or addition.

As *prata mea juxta communem fossam in D.* whereof the one is true, the other false; or *tenementum meum in tenura Guilielmi quod perquisivi de R. C. in prædict' indent' specificat'*, whereof one is true, and two are false; or two are true, and one false.

So *ad curiam quam tenebat die Mercurii tertio die Martii*, whereof the one is true, the other false.

In these cases the former rule, *ex multitudine signorum*, &c. holdeth not; neither is the placing of the falsity or verity first or last material, but all must be true, or else the grant is void; always understood, that if you can reconcile all the words, and make no falsity, that is quite out of this rule, which hath place only where there is a direct contrariety or falsity not to be reconciled to this rule.

Vide livers avant dit pur cest auxi.

As if I grant all my land in D. *in tenura I. S.* which I purchased of I. N. specified in a devise to I. D. and I have land in D. whereof in part of them all these circumstances are true, but I have other lands in D. wherein some of them fail, this grant will not pass all my land in D. for there these are references, and no words of falsity or error, but of limitation and restraint.

THE VSE OF THE LAW.

Provided for Preservation

OF

Our { *Persons*, *Goods*, and *Good Names*.

According to the Practice

OF

The { *Lawes and Customes* } *of this Land.*

By the Lord Verulam Viscount of S. *Albons*, &c.

LONDON,
Printed by the Assignes of IOHN MOORE Esquire. 1635.

Cum Privilegio.

A TABLE

OF THE

CONTENTS OF THIS ENSUING TREATISE.

THE

USE OF THE LAW,

AND WHEREIN IT PRINCIPALLY CONSISTETH.

THE use of the law consisteth principally in these three things:

I. To secure men's persons from death and violence.

II. To dispose the property of their goods and lands.

III. For preservation of their good names from shame and infamy.

Surety to keep the peace.

For safety of persons, the law provideth that any man standing in fear of another may take his oath before a justice of peace, that he standeth in fear of his life, and the justice shall compel the other to be bound with sureties to keep the peace.

Action of the case, for slander, battery, &c.

If any man beat, wound, or maim another, or give false scandalous words that may touch his credit, the law giveth thereupon an action of the case, for the slander of his good name; and an action of battery, or an appeal of maim, by which recompense shall be recovered, to the value of the hurt, damage, or danger.

Appeal of murder given to the next of kin.

If any man kill another with malice, the law giveth an appeal to the wife of the dead, if he had any, or to the next of kin that is heir in default of a wife, by which appeal the defendant convicted is to suffer death, and to lose all his lands and goods. But if the wife or heir will not sue or be compounded withal, yet the king is to punish the offence by indictment or presentment of a lawful inquest and trial of the offenders before competent judges; whereupon being found guilty, he is to suffer death, and to lose his lands and goods.

Manslaughter, and when a forfeiture of goods, and when not.

If one kill another upon a sudden quarrel, this is manslaughter, for which the offender must die, except he can read; and if he can read, yet must he lose his goods, but no lands.

And if a man kill another in his own defence, he shall not lose his life, nor his lands, but he must lose his goods, except the party slain did first assault him, to kill, rob, or trouble him by the highway side, or in his own house, and then he shall lose nothing.

Felon. de se.

And if a man kill himself, all his goods and chattels are forfeited, but no lands.

Felony by mischance.

If a man kill another by misfortune, as shooting an arrow at a butt or mark, or casting a stone over a house, or the like, this is loss of his goods and chattels, but not of his lands, nor life.

Deodand.

If a horse, or cart, or a beast, or any other thing do kill a man, the horse, beast, or other thing, is forfeited to the crown, and is called a deodand, and usually granted and allowed by the king to the Bishop Almner, as goods are of those that kill themselves.

Cutting out of tongues, and putting out of eyes, made felony.

The cutting out of a man's tongue, or putting out his eyes maliciously, is felony; for which the offender is to suffer death, and lose his lands and goods.

But for that all punishment is for example's sake; it is good to see the means whereby offenders are drawn to their punishment; and first for the matter of the peace.

THE ancient laws of England planted here by the Conqueror were, that there should be officers of two sorts in all the parts of this realm to preserve the peace:—

1. *Constabularii* } *Pacis.*
2. *Conservatores* }

The office of the constable.

The office of the constable was, to arrest the parties that he had seen breaking the peace, or in fury ready to break the peace, or was truly informed by others, or by their own confession, that they had freshly broken the peace; which persons he might imprison in the stocks, or in his own house, as his or their quality required, until they had become bounden with sureties to keep the peace; which obligation from thenceforth was to be sealed and delivered to the constable to the use of the king. And that the constable was to send to the king's Exchequer or Chancery, from whence process should be awarded to levy the debt, if the peace were broken.

But the constable could not arrest any, nor make any put in bond upon complaint of threatening only, except they had seen them breaking the peace, or had come freshly after the peace was broken. Also, these constables should keep watch about the town for the apprehension of rogues and vagabonds, and night-walkers, and eves-droppers, scouts, and such like, and such as go armed. And they ought likewise to raise hue and cry against murderers, manslayers, thieves, and rogues.

Of this office of constable there were high constables, two of every hundred; petty constables, one in every village; they were, in ancient time, all appointed by the sheriff of the shire yearly, in his court called the Sheriff's Tourn, and there they received their oath. But at this day they are appointed either in the law-day of that precinct wherein they serve, or else by the high constable in the sessions of the peace.

2. High constables for every hundred.
1. Petty constable for every village.

The Sheriff's Tourn is a court very ancient, incident to his office. At the first, it was erected by the Conqueror, and called the King's Bench, appointing men studied in the knowledge of the laws to execute justice, as substitutes to him in his name, which men are to be named, *Justiciarii ad placita coram Rege assignati*. One of them being *Capitalis Justiciarius* called to his fellows; the rest in number as pleaseth the king, of late but three *Justiciarii*, holden by patent. In this court every man above twelve years of age was to take his oath of allegiance to the king, if he were bound, then his lord to answer for him. In this court the constables were appointed and sworn; breakers of the peace punished by fine and imprisonment, the parties beaten or hurt recompensed upon complaints of damages; all appeals of murder, maim, robbery, decided; contempts against the crown, public annoyances against the people, treasons and felonies, and all other matters of wrong, betwixt party and party, for lands and goods.

The King's Bench first instituted, and in what matters they anciently had jurisdiction.

But the king seeing the realm grow daily more and more populous, and that this one court could not dispatch all, did first ordain that his marshal should keep a court for controversies arising within the virge; which is within twelve miles of the chiefest tunnel of the court, which did but ease the King's Bench in matters only concerning debts, covenants, and such like, of those of the king's household only, never dealing in breaches of the peace, or

Court of Marshalsea erected, and its jurisdiction within twelve miles of the chief tunnel of the king, which is the full extent of the virge.

concerning the crown by any other persons, or any pleas of lands. Insomuch as the king, for further ease, having divided this kingdom into counties, and committing the charge of every county to a lord or earl, did direct that those earls, within their limits, should look to the matter of the peace, and take charge of the constables, and reform public annoyances, and swear the people to the crown, and take pledges of the freemen for their allegiance, for which purpose the county did once every year keep a court, called the Sheriff's Tourn; at which all the county (except women, clergy, children under twelve, and not aged above sixty) did appear to give or renew their pledges of allegiance. And the court was called *Curia Franci Plegii*, a View of the Pledges of Freemen; or, *Turnus Comitatus*.

Sheriff's Tourn instituted upon the division of England into counties, the charge of this court was committed to the earl of the same county: this was likewise called *Curia Visus fra. pleg.*

Subdivision of the county court into hundreds.

At which meeting or court there fell, by occasion of great assemblies, much bloodshed, scarcity of victuals, mutinies, and the like mischiefs which are incident to the congregations of people, by which the king was moved to allow a subdivision of every county into hundreds, and every hundred to have a court, whereunto the people of every hundred should be assembled twice a year for survey of pledges, and use of that justice which was formerly executed in that grand court for the county; and the count or earl appointed a bailiff under him to keep the hundred court. But in the end, the kings of this realm found it necessary to have all execution of justice immediately from themselves, by such as were more bound than earls to that service, and readily subject to correction for their negligence or abuse; and therefore took to themselves the appointing of a sheriff yearly in every county, calling them *vicecomites*, and to them directed such writs and precepts for executing justice in the county as fell out needful to have been dispatched, committing to the sheriff *custodium comitatus;* by which the earls were spared of their toils and labours, and that was laid upon the sheriffs. So as now the sheriff doth all the king's business in the county, and that is now called the Sheriff's Tourn; that is to say, he is judge of this grand court for the county, and also of all hundred courts not given away from the crown.

The charge of the county taken from the earls, and committed yearly to such persons as it pleased the king.

The sheriff is judge of all hundred courts not given away from the crown.

County Court kept monthly by the sheriff.

He hath another court, called the County Court, belonging to his office, wherein men may sue monthly for any debt or damages under forty pounds, and may have writs for to replevy their cattle distrained and impounded by others, and there try the cause of their distress; and by a writ called *Justicies*, a man may sue for any sum; and in this court the sheriff, by a writ called an exigent, doth proclaim men sued in courts above to render their bodies, or else they be outlawed.

This sheriff doth serve the king's writs of process, be they summons, attachments to compel men to answer to the law, and all writs of execution of the law, according to judgments of superior court, for taking of men's goods, lands, or bodies, as the cause requireth. The office of the sheriff.

The hundred courts were most of them granted to religious men, noblemen, and others of great place. And also many men of good quality have attained by charter, and some by usage, within manors of their own liberty, of keeping law days, and to use there justice appertaining to a law day. Hundred courts to whom they were at first granted.

Whosoever is lord of the hundred court is to appoint two high constables of the hundred, and also is to appoint in every village a petty constable, with a tithing man to attend in his absence, and to be at his commandment when he is present in all services of his office for his assistance. Lord of the hundred to appoint two high constables.

There have been by use and statute law (besides surveying of the pledges of freemen, and giving the oath of allegiance, and making constables) many additions of powers and authority given to the stewards of leets and law-days to be put in ure in their courts; as for example, they may punish innkeepers, victuallers, bakers, butchers, poulterers, fishmongers, and tradesmen of all sorts selling with under weights or measures, or at excessive prices, or things unwholesome, or ill made in deceit of the people. They may punish those that do stop, straiten, or annoy the highways, or do not, according to the provision enacted, repair or amend them, or divert water courses, or destroy fry of fish, or use engines or nets to take deer, conies, pheasants, or partridges, or build pigeon houses, except he be lord of the manor, or parson of the church. They may also take presentment upon oath of the twelve sworn jury before them of all felonies; but they cannot try the malefactors, only they must by indenture deliver over those presentments of felony to the judges, when they come their circuits into that county. All those courts before mentioned are in use, and exercised as law at this day, concerning the sheriffs' law days and leets, and the offices of high constables, petty constables, and tithing men; howbeit, with some further additions by statute laws, laying charge upon them for taxation for poor, for soldiers, and the like, and dealing without corruption, and the like. Of what matters they inquire of in leets and law-days.

Conservators of the peace called by the king's writ for term of their lives, or at the king's pleasure.

Conservators of the peace were in ancient times certain, which were assigned by the king to see the peace maintained, and they were called to the office by the king's writ, to continue for term of their lives, or at the king's pleasure.

Conservators of the peace, and what their office was.

For this service, choice was made of the best men of calling in the country, and but few in the shire. They might bind any man to keep the peace, and to good behaviour, by recognizance to the king, with sureties; and they might by warrant send for the party, directing their warrant to the sheriff or constable, as they please, to arrest the party, and bring him before them. This they used to do when complaint was made by any that he stood in fear of another, and so took his oath; or else, where the conservator himself did, without oath or complaint, see the disposition of any man inclined to quarrel and breach of the peace, or to misbehave himself in some outrageous manner of force or fraud, there, by his own discretion, he might send for such a fellow, and make him find sureties of the peace, or of his good behaviour, as he should see cause; or else commit him to the gaol if he refused.

Conservators of the peace by virtue of their office.

The judges of either bench in Westminster, barons of the Exchequer, master of the rolls, and justices in eyre and assizes in their circuits, were all, without writ, conservators of the peace in all shires of England, and continue to this day.

Justices of peace ordained in lieu of conservators. Power of placing and displacing just. of peace by use delegated from the king to the chancellor.

But now at this day conservators of the peace are out of use, and in lieu of them there are ordained justices of peace, assigned by the king's commissions in every county, which are moveable at the king's pleasure; but the power of placing and displacing justices of the peace is by use delegated from the king to the chancellor.

That there should be justices of peace by commissions, it was first enacted by a statute made 1 Edward III. and their authority augmented by many statutes made since in every king's reign.

The power of the justices of peace, to fine the offenders to the crown, and not to recompense the party grieved.

They are appointed to keep four sessions every year; that is, every quarter one. These sessions are a sitting of the justices to dispatch the affairs of their commissions. They have power to hear and determine in their sessions all felonies, breaches of the peace, contempts, and trespasses, so far as to fine the offender to the crown, but not to award recompense to the party grieved.

Parl. Stat. 17. R. 2. cap. 10. & v. *Dier*, 69. b. Ils. ount poiar d'inquier de murder car. ce felon.

They are to suppress riots and tumults, to restore possessions forcibly taken away, to examine all felons apprehended and brought before them; to see impotent poor people, or maimed soldiers provided for according to the laws, and rogues, vagabonds, and beggars punished. They are both to license and suppress alehouses, badgers of corn and victuals, and to punish forestallers, regrators, and engrossers.

Authority of the justices of peace, through whom run all the county services unto the crown.

Through these in effect run all the county services to the crown, as taxations of subsidies, mustering men, arming them, and levying forces, that is done by a special commission or precept from the king. Any of these justices, by oath taken by a man that he standeth in fear that another man will beat him, or kill him, or burn his house, are to send for the party by warrant of attachment, directed to the sheriff or constable, and then to bind the party with sureties by recognizance to the king to keep the peace, and also to appear at the next sessions of the peace; at which next sessions, when every justice of peace hath therein delivered all their recognizances so taken, then the parties are called, and the cause of binding to the peace examined, and both parties being heard, the whole bench is to determine as they see cause, either to continue the party so bound, or else to discharge him.

Beating, killing, burning of houses, attachments for surety of the peace.

Recognizance of the peace delivered by the justices at their sessions.

The justices of peace in their sessions are attended by the constables and bailiffs of all hundreds and liberties within the county, and by the sheriff or his deputy, to be employed as occasion shall serve in executing the precepts and directions of the court. They proceed in this sort: the sheriff doth summon twenty-four freeholders, discreet men of the said county, whereof some sixteen are selected and sworn, and have their charge to serve as the grand jury, the party indicted is to traverse the indictment, or else to confess it, and so submit himself to be fined as the court shall think meet (regard had to the offence), except the punishment be certainly appointed, as often it is, by special statutes.

Quarter sessions held by the justices of the peace.

The justices of peace are many in every county, and to them are brought all traitors, felons, and other malefactors of any sort upon their first apprehension, and that justice to whom they are brought examineth them, and heareth their accusations, but judgeth not upon it; only if he find the suspicion but light, then he taketh bond, with sureties of the accused, to appear either at the next assizes, if it be a matter of treason or felony, or else at the quarter sessions, if it be concerning riot or misbehaviour, or some other small offence. And he also then bindeth to appear those that give testimony and prosecute the accusation, all the accusers and witnesses, and so setteth the party at large. And at the assizes or sessions (as the case falleth out) he certifieth the recognizances taken of the accused, accusers, and witnesses, who being there are called, and appearing, the cause of the accused is debated according to law for his clearing or condemning.

The authority of justices of the peace out of their sessions.

But if the party accused seem upon pregnant matter in the accusation, and to the justice to be guilty, and the offence heinous, or the offender taken with the manner, then the justice is to commit the party by his warrant called a *mittimus* to the gaoler of the common gaol of the county, there to remain until the assizes. And then the justice is to certify his accusation, examination, and recognizance taken for the appearances and prosecution of the witnesses, so as the judges may, when they come, readily proceed with him as the law requireth.

Judges of assize come in place of the ancient judges in eyre about the time of R. 2.

The judges of the assizes, as they be now become into the place of the ancient justices in eyre, called *justiciarii itinerantes*, which, in the prime kings after the conquest, until Henry the Third's time especially, and after, in lesser measure, even to Richard the Second's time, did execute the justice of the realm; they began in this sort.

The authority of tourns, leets, hundreds, and law-days, as it was confirmed to some special causes touching the public good.

The king, not able to dispatch business in his own person, erected the Court of King's Bench;* that not able to receive all, nor meet to draw the people all to one place, there were ordained counties and the sheriff's tourns, hundred courts, and particular leets, and law-days, as before mentioned, which dealt only with crown matters for the public; but not the private titles of lands or goods, nor the trial of grand offences, of treasons, and felonies, but all the counties of the realm were divided into six circuits. And two learned men well read in the laws of the realm were assigned by the king's commission to every circuit, and to ride twice a year through those shires allotted to that circuit, making proclamation beforehand, a convenient time in

* 1. King's Bench. 2. Marshal's Court. 3. County Court. 4. Sheriff's Tourns. 5. Hundred Leets and Law-days. All which dealt only in crown matters; but the Justice in eyre dealt in private titles of lands or goods, and in all treasons and felonies, of whom there were twelve in number, the whole realm being divided into six circuits. England divided into six circuits, and two learned men in the laws, assigned by the king's commission to ride twice a year through those shires allotted to that circuit, for their trial of private titles to lands and goods, and all treasons and felonies, which the county courts meddle not in.

every county, of the time of their coming, and place of their sitting, to the end the people might attend them in every county of that circuit.

They were to stay three or four days in every county, and in that time all the causes of that county were brought before them by the parties grieved, and all the prisoners of the said gaol in every shire, and whatsoever controversies arising concerning life, lands, or goods.

The authority of these judges in eyre is in part translated by act of parliament to justices of assize, which be now the judges of circuits, and they do use the same course that justices in eyre did, to proclaim their coming every half year, and the place of their sitting.

The authority translated by parliament to justices of assize.

The business of the justices in eyre, and of the justices of assize at this day is much lessened, for that, in Henry the Third's time, there was erected the Court of Common Pleas at Westminster, in which court have been ever since, and yet are begun and handled the great suits of lands, debts, benefices, and contracts, fines for assurance of lands and recoveries, which were wont to be either in the King's Bench, or else before the justices in eyre. But the statute of *Mag. Char. cap.* 11. 5. is negative against it, *viz. Communia placita non sequantur curiam nostram, sed teneantur in aliquo loco Certo;* which *locus Certus* must be the Common pleas; yet the judges of circuits have now five commissions by which they sit.

The authority of the justices of assizes much lessened by the court of Common Pleas, erected in H. 3. time.

The justices of assize have at this day five commissions by which they sit.

The first is a commission of oyer and terminer, directed unto them, and many others of the best account, in their circuits; but in this commission the judges of assize are of the *quorum*, so as without them there can be no proceeding.

1. Oyer & term. 2. Gaol delivery. 3. To take assizes. 4. To take Nisi Prius. 5. Of the peace.

This commission giveth them power to deal with treasons, murders, and all manner of felonies and misdemeanors whatsoever; and this is the largest commission that they have.

Oyer and terminer, in which the judges are of the quorum, and this is the largest commission they have.

The second is a commission of gaol delivery; that is, only to the judges themselves, and the clerk of the assize associate: and by this commission they are to deal with every prisoner in the gaol, for what offence soever he be there; and to proceed with him according to the laws of the realm, and the quality of his offence: and they cannot, by this commission, do any thing concerning any man but those that are prisoners in the gaol. The course now in use of execution of this commission of gaol delivery is this. There is no prisoner but is committed by some justice of

Gaol delivery directed only to judges themselves, and the clerk of the assize.

peace, who, before he committed him, took his examination, and bound his accusers and witnesses to appear and prosecute at the gaol delivery. This justice doth certify these examinations and bonds, and thereupon the accuser is called solemnly into the court, and when he appeareth he is willed to prepare a bill of indictment against the prisoner, and go with it to the grand jury, and give evidence upon their oaths, he and the witnesses, which he doth; and then the grand jury write thereupon either *billa vera,* and then the prisoner standeth indicted, or else *ignoramus,* and then he is not touched. The grand jury deliver these bills to the judges in their court, and so many as they find indorsed *billa vera,* they send for those prisoners, then is every man's indictment put and read to him, and they ask him whether he be guilty or not. If he saith guilty, his confession is recorded; if he say not guilty, then he is asked how he will be tried; he answereth, by the country. Then the sheriff is commanded to return the nâmes of twelve freeholders to the court, which freeholders be sworn to make true delivery between the king and the prisoner, and then the indictment is again read, and the witnesses sworn to speak their knowledge concerning the fact, and the prisoner is heard at large what defence he can make, and then the jury go together and consult. And after a while they come in with a verdict of guilty or not guilty, which verdict the judges do record accordingly. If any prisoner plead not guilty upon the indictment, and yet will not put himself to trial upon the jury (or stand mute), he shall be pressed.

The manner of the proceedings of the justices of circuits in their circuits.

The course now in use with the judges for the execution of the commission of gaol delivery.

The judges, when many prisoners are in the gaol, do in the end before they go peruse every one. Those that were indicted by the grand jury, and found not guilty by the select jury, they judge to be quitted, and so deliver them out of the gaol. Those that are found guilty by both juries they judge to death, and command the sheriff to see execution done. Those that refuse trial by the country, or stand mute upon the indictment, they judge to be pressed to death: some whose offences are pilfering under twelvepence value they judge to be whipped. Those that confess their indictments, they judge to death, whipping, or otherwise, as their offence requireth. And those that are not indicted at all, but their bill of indictment returned with *ignoramus* by the grand jury, and all other in the gaol against whom no bills at all are preferred, they do acquit by proclamation out of the gaol. That one way or other they rid the gaol of all the prisoners in it. But because some prisoners have their books, and be burned in the hand and so delivered, it is necessary to show the reason thereof. This having their books is called their clergy, which in ancient time began thus.

For the scarcity of the clergy, in the realm of England, to be disposed in religious houses, or for priests, deacons, and clerks of parishes, there was a prerogative allowed to the clergy, that if any man that could read as a clerk were to be condemned to death, the bishop of the diocess might, if he would, claim him as a clerk, and he was to see him tried in the face of the court.

Book allowed to clergy for the scarcity of them, to be disposed in religious houses.

Whether he could read or not, the book was prepared and brought by the bishop, and the judge was to turn to some place as he should think meet, and if the prisoner could read, then the bishop was to have him delivered over unto him to dispose of in some places of the clergy, as he should think meet. But if either the bishop would not demand him, or that the prisoner could not read, then was to be put to death.

And this clergy was allowable in the ancient times and law, for all offences whatsoever they were, except treason and robbing of churches, their goods and ornaments. But by many statutes made since, the clergy is taken away for murder, burglary, robbery, purse-cutting, horse-stealing, and divers other felonies particularized by the statutes to the judges; and lastly, by a statute made 18 Elizabeth, the judges themselves are appointed to allow clergy to such as can read, being not such offenders from whom clergy is taken away by any statute, and to see them burned in the hand, and so discharge them without delivering them to the bishop, howbeit the bishop appointeth the deputy to attend the judges with a book to try whether they could read or not.

Concerning the allowing of the clergy to the prisoner.

Clergy allowed in all offences except treason and robbing of churches, and now taken away by many statutes.
1. In treason.
2. In burglary.
3. Robbery.
4. Purse-cutting.
5. Horse-stealing, and in divers other offences particularized in several statutes. By the stat. of 18 Eliz. the judges are appointed to allow clergy, and to see them burned in the hand, and to discharge the prisoners without delivering them to the bishop.

The third commission that the judges of circuits have, is a commission directed to themselves only, and the clerk of assize to take assizes, by which they are called justices of assize, and the office of those justices is to do right upon writs called assizes, brought before them by such as are wrongfully thrust out of their lands. Of which number of writs there was far greater store brought before them in ancient times than now, for that men's seisins and possessions are sooner recovered by sealing leases upon the ground, and by bringing an *ejectione firme*, and trying their title so, than by the long suits of assizes.

4. Commission is to take Nisi Prius, and this is directed to two judges and the clerk of the assize.

Nisi Prius.

The fourth commission is a commission to take *Nisi Prius* directed to none but to the judges themselves and their clerks of assizes, by which they are called justices of *Nisi Prius*. These *Nisi Prius* happen in this sort, when a suit is begun for any matter in one of the three courts, the King's Bench, Common Pleas, or the Exchequer here above, and the parties in their pleadings do vary in a point of fact; as for example, if in an action of debt upon obligation, the defendant denies the obligation to be his debt, or in any action of trespass grown for taking away goods, the defendant denieth that he took them, or in an action of the case for slanderous words, the defendant denieth that he spake them, &c.

Then the plaintiff is to maintain and prove that the obligation is the defendant's deed, that he either took the goods, or spake the words; upon which denial and affirmation the law saith, that issue is joined betwixt them, which issue of the fact is to be tried by a jury of twelve men of the county where it is supposed by the plaintiff to be done, and for that purpose the judges of the court do award a writ of *venire facias* in the king's name to the sheriff of that county, commanding him to cause four and twenty discreet freeholders of his county, at a certain day, to try this issue so joined, out of which four and twenty only twelve are chosen to serve. And that double number is returned, because some may make default, and some be challenged upon kindred, alliance, or partial dealing.

The manner of proceeding of justices of circuits in their circuits.

The course the judges hold in their circuit in the execution of their commission concerning the taking of nisi prius.

These four and twenty the sheriff doth name and certify to the court, and withal that he hath warned them to come at the day according to their writ. But, because at his first summons their falleth no punishment upon the four and twenty if they come not, they very seldom or never appear upon the first writ, and upon their default there is another writ* returned to the sheriff, commanding him to distrain them by their lands to appear at a certain day appointed by the writ, which is the next term after, *Nisi Prius justiciarii nostri ad assizas capiendas venerint*, &c. of which words the writ is called a *nisi prius*, and the judges of the circuit of that county in that vacation and mean time before the day of appearance appointed for the jury above, here by their commission of *Nisi Prius* have authority to

* Distringas.

take the appearance of the jury in the county before them, and there to hear the witnesses and proofs on both sides concerning the issue of fact, and to take the verdict of the jury, and against the day they should have appeared above, to return the verdict read in the court above, which return is called a *postea*. Postea.

And upon this verdict clearing the matter in fact, one way or other, the judges above give judgment for the party for whom the verdict is found, and for such damages and costs as the jury do assess.

By those trials called *Nisi Prius*, the juries and the parties are eased much of the charge they should be put to, by coming to London with their evidences and witnesses, and the courts of Westminster are eased of much trouble they should have, if all the juries for trials should appear and try their causes in those courts; for those courts above have little leisure now; though the juries come not up, yet in matters of great weight, or where the title is intricate or difficult, the judges above, upon information to them, do retain those causes to be tried there, and the juries do at this day in such causes come to the bar at Westminster.

The fifth commission that the judges in their circuits do sit by, is the commission of the peace in every county of their circuit. And all the justices of the peace, having no lawful impediment, are bound to be present at the assizes to attend the judges, as occasion shall fall out; if any make default, the judges may set a fine upon him at their pleasure and discretions. Also the sheriff in every shire through the circuit is to attend in person, or by a sufficient deputy allowed by the judges, all that time they be within the county, and the judges may fine him if he fail, or for negligence or misbehaviour in his office before them; and the judges above may also fine the sheriff for not returning or not sufficient returning of writs before them.

5. Commission is a commission of the peace.

The justices of the peace and the sheriff are to attend the judges in their county.

Property in Lands is gotten and transferred by one to another, by these four manner of ways:

1. By Entry.
2. By Descent.
3. By Escheat.
4. Most usually by Conveyance.

1. Property by entry is, where a man findeth a piece of land that no other possesseth or hath title unto, and he that so findeth it doth enter, this entry gaineth a property; this law seemeth to be derived from this text, *terra dedit*

Of property of lands to be gained by entry.

filiis hominum, which is to be understood, to those that will till and manure it, and so make it yield fruit; and that is he that entereth into it, where no man had it before. But this manner of gaining lands was in the first days, and is not now of use in England, for that by the conquest all the land of this nation was in the Conqueror's hands, and appropriated unto him, except religious and church-lands, and the lands in Kent, which by composition were left to the former owners, as the Conqueror found them, so that no man but the bishopricks, churches, and the men of Kent, can at this day make any greater title than from the conquest to any lands in England; and lands possessed without any such title are in the crown, and not in him that first entereth; as it is by land left by the sea, this land belongeth to the king, and not to him that hath the lands next adjoining, which was the ancient sea banks. This is to be understood of the inheritance of lands; *viz.* that the inheritance cannot be gained by the first entry. But an estate for another man's life by out-laws may, at this day, be gotten by entry. As a man called A. having land conveyed unto him for the life of B. dieth without making any estate of it there, whosoever first entereth into the land after the decease of A. getteth the property in the land for time of the continuance of the estate which was granted to A. for the life of B. which B. yet liveth, and therefore the said land cannot revert till B. die. And to the heir of A. it cannot go, for that it is not any state of inheritance, but only an estate for another man's life; which is not descendable to the heir, except he be specially named in the grant: *viz.* to him and his heirs. As for the executors of A. they cannot have it, for it is not an estate testamentary, that it should go to the executors as goods and chattels should, so as in truth no man can entitle himself unto those lands; and therefore the law preferreth him that first entereth, and he is called *occupans*, and shall hold it during the life of B. but must pay the rent, perform the conditions, and do no waste. And he may by deed assign it to whom he please in his life time. But if he die before he assign it over, then it shall go again to whomsoever first entereth and holdeth. And so all the life of B. so often as it shall happen.

All lands in England were the Conqueror's, and appropriated to him upon the conquest of England, and held of him, except 1. Religious and church lands. 2. The lands of the men of Kent. Land left by the sea belongeth to the king.

Occupancy.

Likewise if any man doth wrongfully enter into another man's possession, and put the right owner of the freehold and inheritance from it, he thereby getteth the freehold and inheritance by disseisin, and may hold it against all men, but him that hath right, and his heirs, and is called a disseisor. Or if any one die seised of lands, and before his heir doth enter, one that hath no right doth enter into the lands, and holdeth them from the right heir, he is called an abator, and is lawful owner against all men but the right heir.

And if such person abator, or disseisor (so as the disseisor hath quiet possession five years next after the disseisin) do continue their possession, and die seised, and the land descend to his heir, they have gained the right to the possession of the land against him that hath right till he recover it by fit action real at the common law. And if it be not sued for at the common law within threescore years after the disseisin, or abatement committed, the right owner hath lost his right by that negligence. And if a man hath divers children, and the elder, being a bastard, doth enter into the land and enjoyeth it quietly during his life, and dieth thereof so seised, his heirs shall hold the land against all the lawful children and their issues.

Property of lands by descent.

Property of lands by descent is, where a man hath lands of inheritance, and dieth, not disposing of them, but leaving it to go (as the law casteth it) upon the heir. This is called a descent of law, and upon whom the descent is to light, is the question. For which purpose the law of inheritance preferreth the first child before all others, and amongst children the male before the female, and amongst males the first born. If there be no children, then the brother; if no brothers, then sisters; if neither brothers nor sisters, then uncles; and for lack of uncles, aunts; if none of them, then cousins in the nearest degree of consanguinity, with these three rules of diversities. 1. That the eldest male shall solely inherit; but if it come to females, then they, being all in an equal degree of nearness, shall inherit altogether, and are called parceners, and all they make but one heir to the ancestor. 2. That no brother nor sister of the half-blood shall inherit to his brother or sister, but as a child to his parents, as for example: If a man have two wives, and by either wife a son, the eldest son overliving his father is to be preferred to the inheritance of the father, being fee-simple; but if he entereth and dieth without a child, the brother shall not be his heir, because he is of the half-blood to him, but the uncle of the eldest brother or sister of the whole blood; yet if the eldest brother had died, or had not entered in the life of the father, either by such entry or conveyance, then the youngest brother should

Of descent, three rules.

Brother or sister of the half blood shall not inherit to his brother or sister, but only as a child to his parents.

inherit the land that the father had, although it were a child by the second wife, before any daughter by the first. The third rule about descents. That land purchased so by the party himself that dieth is to be inherited; first, by the heirs of the father's side; then, if he have none of that part, by the heirs of the mother's side. But lands descended to him from his father or mother are to go to that side only from which they came, and not to the other side.

Descent.

Those rules of descent mentioned before are to be understood of fee-simples, and not of entailed lands, and those rules are restrained by some particular customs of some particular places; as, namely, the custom of Kent, that every male of equal degree of childhood, brotherhood, or kindred, shall inherit equally, as daughters shall, being parceners; and in many borough towns of England, and the custom alloweth the youngest son to inherit, and so the youngest daughter. The custom of Kent is called gavelkind. The custom of boroughs, burgh English.

Customs of certain places.

And there is another note to be observed in fee-simple inheritance, and that is, that every heir having fee-simple land or inheritance, be it by common law or by custom of either gavelkind or burgh English, is chargeable so far forth as the value thereof extendeth with the binding acts of the ancestors from whom the inheritance descendeth; and these acts are collateral encumbrances, and the reason of this charge is, *qui sentit commodum, sentire debet et incommodum sive onus.* As for example, if a man bind himself and his heirs in an obligation, or do covenant by writing for him and his heirs, or do grant an annuity for him and his heirs, or do make a warranty of land, binding him and his heirs to warranty, in all these cases the law chargeth the heir, after the death of the ancestor, with this obligation, covenant, annuity, and warranty, yet with these three cautions: first, that the party must by special name bind himself and his heirs, or covenant, grant, and warrant for himself and his heirs, otherwise the heir is not to be touched. Secondly, that some action must be brought against the heir whilst the land or other inheritance resteth in him unaliened away: for if the ancestor die, and the heir, before an action be brought against him upon those bonds, covenants, or warranties, do alien away the land, then the heir is clean discharged of the burden, except the land was by fraud conveyed away of purpose to prevent the suit intended against him. Thirdly, that no heir is further to be charged than the value of the land descended unto him from the

Every heir having land is bound by the binding acts of his ancestors if he be named.

Dyer, 114. Plowd.

Dyer, 149. Plowd.

same ancestor that made the instrument of charge, and that land also not to be sold outright for the debt, but to be kept in extent, and at a yearly value, until the debt or damage be run out. Nevertheless if an heir that is sued upon such a debt of his ancestor do not deal clearly with the court when he is sued, that is, if he come not in immediately, and by way of confession set down the true quantity of his inheritance descended, and so submit himself therefore, as the law requireth, then that heir that otherwise demeaneth himself shall be charged of his own lands or goods, and of his money, for this deed of his ancestor. As for example; if a man bind himself and his heirs in an obligation of one hundred pounds, and dieth, leaving but ten acres of land to his heir, if his heir be sued upon the bond, and cometh in, and denieth that he hath any lands by descent, and it is found against him by the verdict that he hath ten acres, this heir shall now be charged by his false plea of his own lands, goods, and body, to pay the hundred pounds, although the ten acres be not worth ten pounds.

Day & Pepp's case.

Heir charged for his false plea.

Property of lands by escheat is where the owner died seised of the lands in possession without child or other heir, thereby the land, for lack of other heir, is said to escheat to the lord of whom it is holden. This lack of heir happeneth principally in two cases: first, where the lands' owner is a bastard. Secondly, where he is attainted of felony or treason. For neither can a bastard have any heir, except it be his own child, nor a man attainted of treason, although it be his own child.

Property of lands by escheat.

Two causes of escheat. 1. Bastardy. 2. Attainder of treason, felony.

Upon attainder of treason the king is to have the land, although he be not the lord of whom it is held, because it is a royal escheat. But for felony it is not so, for there the king is not to have the escheat, except the land be holden of him: and yet, where the land is not holden of him, the king is to have the land for a year and a day next ensuing the judgment of the attainder, with a liberty to commit all manner of waste all that year in houses, gardens, ponds, lands, and woods.

Attainder of treason entitleth the king, though lands be not holden of him, otherwise in attainder of felony, &c. for there the king shall have but *annum diem et vestum.*

In these escheats two things are especially to be observed; the one is the tenure of the lands, because it directeth the person to whom the escheat belongeth, viz. the lord of the manor of whom the land is holden. 2. The manner of such attainder which draweth with it the escheat. Concerning the tenures of lands, it is to be understood, that all lands are holden of the crown, either mediately or im-

In escheat two things are to be observed. 1. The tenure. 2. The manner of the attainder.

All lands are holden of the crown immediately or mediately by mesne lords, the reason. Concerning the tenure of lands. The Conqueror, by right of conquest, got all the lands of the realm into his hands, and as he gave it, he still reserved rents and services. Knight's service in *capite* first instituted. The reservations in knight's service tenure was four. 1. Marriage of the wards, male and female. 2. Horse for service. 3. Homage and fealty. 4. Primer seisin. The policy of the Conqueror in the reservation of services constituted in four particulars, was to have the marriage of his wards both male and female. Reservation that his tenant should keep a horse of service, and serve upon him himself, when the king went to wars, which is a part of that service called knight's service.

mediately, and that the escheat appertaineth to the immediate lord, and not to the mediate. The reason why all land is holden of the crown immediately, or by mesne lords, is this.

The Conqueror got, by right of conquest, all the land of the realm into his own hands, in demesne, taking from every man all estate, tenure, property, and liberty of the same (except religious and church lands, and the land in Kent) and still as he gave any of it out of his own hand, he reserved some retribution of rents, or services, or both, to him and to his heirs, which reservation is that which is called the tenure of land.

In which reservation he had four institutions, exceeding politic and suitable to the state of a conqueror.

1. Seeing his people to be part Normans, and part Saxons, the Normans he brought with him, the Saxons he found here, he bent himself to conjoin them by marriages in amity, and for that purpose ordains, that if those of his nobles, knights, and gentlemen to whom he gave great rewards of lands should die, leaving their heir within age, a male within twenty-one, and a female within fourteen years, and unmarried, then the king should have the bestowing of such heirs in marriage, in such a family,* and to such persons as he should think meet; which interest of marriage went still employed, and doth at this day in every tenure called knight's service.

The second was to the end that his people should still be conserved in warlike exercises, and able for his defence. When therefore he gave any good portion of lands, that might make the party of abilities or strength, he withal reserved this service: that that party and his heirs having such lands, should keep a horse of service continually, and serve upon him himself when the king went to wars, or else, having impediment to excuse his own person, should find another to serve in his place; which service of horse and man is a part of that tenure called knight's service at this day.

But if the tenant himself be an infant, the king is to hold this land himself until he come to full age, finding him meat, drink, apparel, and other necessaries, and finding a horse and a man with the overplus, to serve in the wars as the tenant himself should do if he were at full age.

But if this inheritance descend upon a woman, that

* Interest of marriage goeth employed in every tenure by knight's service.

cannot serve by her sex, then the king is not to have the lands, she being of fourteen years of age, because she is then able to have a husband that may do the service in person.

The third institution, that upon every gift of land the king reserved a vow and an oath to bind the party to his faith and loyalty:* that vow was called homage, the oath fealty. Homage is to be done kneeling, holding his hands between the knees of the lord, saying, in the French tongue, I become your man of life and limb, and of earthly honour. Fealty is to take an oath, upon a book, that he will be a faithful tenant to the king, and do his service, and pay his rents according to his tenure.

3. Institution of the Conqueror was, that his tenants by knight's service vow unto loyalty, which he called homage, and make unto him oath of his faith, which was called fealty.
1. Homage.
2. Fealty.

The fourth institution was, that for recognizon† of the king's bounty by every heir succeeding his ancestor in those knight's service lands, the king should have *primer seisin* of the lands, which is one year's profit of the lands, and until this be paid the king is to have possession of the land, and then to restore it to the heir; which continueth at this day in use, and is the very cause of suing livery, and that as well where the heir hath been in ward as otherwise.

4. Institution was for recognizon of the king's bounty, to be paid by every heir upon the death of his ancestor, which is one year's profit of the lands called *primer seisin*.

These beforementioned be the rights of the tenure called knight's service in capite, which is as much to say, as tenure *de persona regis*, and capite being the chiefest part of the person, it is called a tenure in capite, or in chief. And it is also to be noted, that as this tenure in *capite* by knight's service generally was a great safety to the crown, so also the Conqueror instituted other tenures in capite necessary to his estate; as, namely, he gave divers lands to be holden of him by some special service about his person, or by bearing some special office in his house, or in the field, which have knight's service and more in them, and these he called tenures by grand serjeanty. Also he provided, upon the first gift of lands, to have revenues by continual service of ploughing his land, repairing his houses, parks,

Knight's service in capite is a tenure *de persona Regis*.
Tenants by grand serjeanty were to pay relief at the full age of every heir, which was one year's value of the lands so held, *ultra Repriss.*
Grand serjeanty.
Petty serjeanty.

* Aid money to make the king's eldest son a knight, or to marry his eldest daughter, is likewise due to his majesty from every one of his tenants in knight's service, that hold by a whole fee, twenty shillings, and from every tenant in soccage if his land be worth twenty pounds per annum, twenty shillings, *vide* N. 3. fol. 82.

† Escuage was likewise due unto the king from his tenant by knight's service; when his majesty made a voyage royal to war against another nation, those of his tenants that did not attend him there for forty days, with horse and furniture fit for service, were to be assessed in a certain sum by act of parliament, to be paid unto his majesty; which assessment is called escuage.

pales, castles, and the like. And sometimes to a yearly provision of gloves, spurs, hawks, horses, hounds, and the like; which kind of reservations are called also tenures in chief, or in capite of the king, but they are not by knight's service, because they required no personal service, but such things as the tenants may hire another to do, or provide for his money. And this tenure is called a tenure by soccage in capite, the word *socagium* signifying the plough; howbeit, in this latter time, the service of ploughing the land is turned into money rent, and so of harvest works, for that the kings do not keep their demesne in their own hands as they were wont to do; yet what lands were *de antiquo dominico coronæ*, it well appeareth in the records of the Exchequer, called the Book of Doomsday. And the tenants by ancient demesne have many immunities and privileges at this day, that in ancient times were granted unto those tenants by the crown, the particulars whereof are too long to set down.

The institution of soccage in capite, and what it is now turned into money rents.

These tenures in capite, as well that by soccage as the others by knight's service, have this property, that the tenants cannot alien their lands without license of the king; if he do, the king is to have a fine for the contempt, and may seize the land, and retain it until the fine be paid. And the reason is, because the king would have a liberty in the choice of his tenant, so that no man should presume to enter into those lands, and hold them (for which the king was to have those special services done him) without the king's leave. This license and fine, as it is now digested, is easy and of course.

Office of alienation.

A license of alienation is the third part of one year's value of the land moderately rated.

There is an office called the office of alienation, where any man may have a license at a reasonable rate, that is, at the third part of one year's value of the land moderately rated. A tenant in cap. by knight's service or grand serjeanty, was restrained by ancient statute, that he should not give nor alien away more of his lands, than that with the rest he might be able to do the service due to the king; and this is now out of use.

Aid a sum of money ratably levied according to the proportion of the lands.

Every tenant by knight's service in capite, had to make the king's eldest son a knight, or to marry his eldest daughter.

And to this tenure by knight's service in chief was incident, that the king should have a certain sum of money, called aid, due to be ratably levied amongst all those tenants proportionably to his lands, to make his eldest son a knight, or to marry his eldest daughter.

Tenants by soccage in capite must sue livery and pay *primer seisin*, and not to be in ward for body or land.

And it is to be noted, that all those that hold lands by the tenure of soccage in capite (although not by knight's service) cannot alien without license; and they are to sue livery, and pay primer seisin, but not to be in ward for body or land.

By example and resemblance of the king's policy in these institutions of tenures, the great men and gentlemen of this realm did the like so near as they could: as for example, when the king had given to any of them two thousand acres of land, this party purposing in this place to make his dwelling, or, as the old word is, his mansion house, or his manor house, did devise how he might make his land a complete habitation to supply him with all manner of necessaries, and for that purpose, he would give of the outtermost parts of those two thousand acres one hundred or two hundred acres, or more or less, as he should think meet, to one of his most trusty servants, with some reservation of rent, to find a horse for the wars, and go with him when he went with the king to the wars, adding vow of homage, and the oath of fealty, wardship, marriage, and relief. This relief is to pay five pounds for every knight's fee, or after the rate for more or less at the entrance of every heir; which tenant,* so created and placed, was and is to this day called a tenant by knight's service, and not by his own person, but of his manors; of these he might make as many as he would. Then this lord would provide that the land which he was to keep for his own use should be ploughed, and his harvest brought home, his house repaired, his park paled, and the like: and for that end he would give some lesser parcels to sundry others, of twenty, thirty, forty, or fifty acres, reserving the service of ploughing a certain quantity (or so many days) of his land, and certain harvest works or days in the harvest to labour, or to repair the house, park, pale, or otherwise, or to give him, for his provision, capons, hens, pepper, commin, roses, gilliflowers, spurs, gloves, or the like; or to pay him a certain rent, and to be sworn to be his faithful tenant, which tenure was called a soccage tenure, and is so to this day, howbeit most of the ploughing and harvest services are turned into money rents.

How manors were at first created.

Manors created by great men in imitation of the policy of the king in the institutions of tenures. *A manere*, the word manor.

Knight's service tenure reserved to common persons.

Relief is five pound to be paid by every tenant by knight's service to his lord upon his entrance respectively for every knight's fee descended.

Soccage tenure reserved by the lord.

The tenants in soccage at the death of every tenant were to pay relief, which was not as knight's service is, five pounds a knight's fee.† But it was, and so is still, one year's rent of the land, and no wardship or other profit to the

Relief of tenant in soccage, one year's rent, and no wardship or other profit

* Knight's service tenure created by the lord is not a tenure by knight's service of the person of the lord, but of his manor.

† Aid money and escuage money is likewise due unto the lords of their tenants, *vide* N. 3. fol. 82 and 83.

upon the dying of the tenant.

lord. The remainder of the two thousand acres he kept to himself, which he used to manure by his bondmen, and appointed them at the courts of his manor how they should hold it, making an entry of it into the roll of the remembrances of the acts of his court, yet still in the lord's power to take it away; and, therefore, they were called tenants at will, by copy of court roll; being in truth bondmen at the beginning, but having obtained freedom of their persons, and gained a custom by use of occupying their lands, they now are called copyholders, and are so privileged that the lord cannot put them out, and all through custom. Some copyholders are for lives, one, two, or three successively; and some inheritances from heir to heir by custom, and custom ruleth these estates wholly, both for widow's estates, fines, harriots, forfeitures, and all other things.

Villenage or tenure by copy of court roll.

Court Baron, with the use of it.

Manors being in this sort made at the first, reason was that the lord of the manor should hold a court, which is no more than to assemble his tenants together at a time by him to be appointed; in which court he was to be informed, by oath of his tenants, of all such duties, rents, reliefs, wardships, copyholds, or the like, that had happened unto him, which information is called a presentment, and then his bailiff to seize and distrain for those duties, if they were denied or withholden, which is called a court baron: and herein a man may sue for any debt or trespass under forty pounds value, and the freeholders are to judge of the cause upon proof produced upon both sides. And therefore the freeholders of these manors, as incident to their tenures, do hold by suit of court, which is to come to the court, and there to judge between party and party in those petty actions; and also to inform the lord of duties, of rents, and services unpaid to him from his tenants. By this course it is discerned who be the lords of lands, such as if the tenants die without heir, or be attainted of felony or treason, shall have the land by escheat.

Suit to the court of the lord incident to the tenure of the freeholders.

What attainders shall give the escheat to the lord. Attainders, 1. By judgment. 2. By verdict or confession. 3. By outlawry, give the lands to the lord.

Now concerning what attainders shall give the escheat to the land, it is to be noted, that it must either be by judgment of death, given in some court of record, against the felon found guilty by verdict, or confession of the felony, or it must be by outlawry of him.

Of an attainder by outlawry.

The outlawry groweth in this sort: a man is indicted for felony, being not in hold, so as he cannot be brought in person to appear, and to be tried, insomuch that process of *capias* is therefore awarded to the sheriff, who, not finding him, returneth *non est inventus in Balliva mea;* and thereupon another *capias* is awarded to the sheriff, who likewise, not finding him, maketh the same return; then a writ called an *exigent* is directed to the sheriff, commanding him to proclaim him in his county court, five several court days, to yield his body, which if the sheriff do, and the party yield not his body, he is said by the default to be outlawed, the coroners there adjudging him outlawed, and the sheriff making the return of the proclamations and of the judgment of the coroners upon the back side of the writ. This is an attainder of felony, whereupon the offender doth forfeit his lands, by an escheat, to the lord of whom they are holden.

But note, that a man found guilty of felony by verdict or confession, and praying his clergy, and thereupon reading as a clerk, and so burnt in the hand and discharged, is not attainted, because he, by his clergy, preventeth the judgment of death, and is called a clerk convict, who loseth not his lands, but all his goods, chattels, leases, and debts. Prayer of clergy.

So a man indicted, that will not answer, nor put himself upon trial, although he be by this to have judgment of pressing to death, yet he doth forfeit no lands, but goods, chattels, leases, and debts, except his offence be treason, and then he forfeiteth his lands to the crown. He that standeth mute forfeiteth no lands, except for treason.

So a man that killeth himself shall not lose his lands, but his goods, chattels, leases, and debts. So of those that kill others in their own defence, or by misfortune. He that killeth himself forfeiteth but his chattels.

A man that being pursued for felony, and flyeth for it, loseth his goods for his flying, although he return and is tried, and found not guilty of the fact. Flying for felony a forfeiture of goods.

So a man indicted of felony, if he yield not his body to the sheriff until after the exigent of proclamation is awarded against him, this man doth forfeit all his goods for his long stay, although he be found not guilty of the felony; but none is attainted to lose his lands, but only such as have judgments of death, by trial upon verdict, or their own confession, or that they be by judgment of the coroners outlawed as before. He that yieldeth his body upon the exigent for felony forfeiteth his goods.

Besides the escheats of lands to the lords of whom they be holden for lack of heirs, and by attainder for felony (which only do hold place in fee-simple lands), there are also forfeiture of lands to the crown by attainder of treason; as namely, if one that hath entailed lands commit treason, he forfeiteth the profits of the lands for his life to the crown, but not to the lord. Lands entailed escheat to the king for treason. Stat. 26 H. 8.

And if a man, having an estate for life of himself or of Tenant for life committeth treason or felony, there shall be no escheat to the lord.

another, commit treason or felony, the whole estate is forfeited to the crown, but no escheat to the lord.

But a copyhold for fee-simple, or for life, is forfeited to the lord and not to the crown; and if it be entailed, the lord is to have it during the life of the offender only, and then his heir is to have it.

The custom of Kent is, that gavelkind land is not forfeitable nor escheatable for felony, for they have an old saying; the father to the bough, and the son to the plough.

The wife loseth no power notwithstanding the husband be attainted of felony.

If the husband was attainted, the wife was to lose her thirds in cases of felony and treason, but yet she is no offender; but, at this day, it is holden by statute law that she loseth them not for the husband's felony. The relation of these forfeits are these.

Attainder in felony or treason by verdict, confession, or outlawry, forfeiteth all they had from the time of the offence committed.

1. That men attainted* of felony or treason, by verdict or confession, do forfeit all the lands they had at the time of their offence committed, and the king or the lord, whosoever of them hath the escheat or forfeiture, shall come in and avoid all leases, statutes, or conveyances done by the offender, at any time since the offence done. And so is the law clear also if a man be attainted for treason by outlawry; but upon attainder of felony by outlawry it hath been much doubted by the law books whether the lord's title by escheat shall relate back to the time of the offence done, or only to the date or test of the writ of exigent for proclamation, whereupon he is outlawed; howbeit at this day it is ruled, that it shall reach back to the time of his fact, but for goods, chattels, and debts, the king's title shall look no further back than to those goods, the party attainted by verdict or confession had at the time of the verdict and confession given or made, and in outlawries at the time of the exigent, as well in treasons as felonies: wherein it is to be observed, that upon the parties first apprehension, the king's officers are to seize all the goods and chattels, and preserve them together, dispending only so much out of them as is fit for the sustentation of the person in prison, without any wasting, or disposing them until conviction, and then the property of them is in the crown, and not before.

And so it is upon an attainder of outlawry, otherwise it is in the attainder by verdict, confession, and outlawry, as to their relation for the forfeiture of goods and chattels.

The king's officers upon the apprehension of a felon are to seize his goods and chattels.

A person attainted may purchase, but it shall be to the king's use.

It is also to be noted, that persons attainted of felony or treason have no capacity in them to take, obtain, or purchase, save only to the use of the king, until the party be

* Of the relation of attainders, as to the forfeiture of lands and goods with the diversity.

pardoned. Yet the party giveth not back his lands or goods without a special patent of restitution, which cannot restore the blood without an act of parliament. So if a man have a son, and then is attainted of felony or treason, and pardoned, and purchaseth lands, and then hath issue another son, and dieth, the son he had before he had his pardon, although he be his eldest son, and the patent have the words of restitution to his lands, shall not inherit, but his second son shall inherit them, and not the first; because the blood is corrupted by the attainder, and cannot be restored by patent alone, but by act of parliament. And if a man have two sons, and the eldest is attainted in the life of his father, and dieth without issue, the father living, the second son shall inherit the father's lands; but if the eldest son have any issue, though he die in the life of his father, then neither the second son, nor the issue of the eldest, shall inherit the father's lands, but the father shall there be accounted to die without heir, and the land shall escheat, whether the eldest son have issue or not afterward or before, though he be pardoned after the death of his father.

There can be no restitution in blood without act of parliament, but a pardon enableth a man to purchase, and the heir begotten after shall inherit those lands.

Property of lands by conveyance is first distributed into estates for years, for life, in tail, and fee-simple.

THESE estates are created by word, by writing, or by record. For estates of years, which are commonly called leases for years, they are thus made; where the owner of the land agreeth with the other by word of mouth, that the other shall have, hold, and enjoy the land, to take the profits thereof for a time certain of years, months, weeks, or days, agreed between them, and this is called a lease parol; such a lease may be made by writing pole, or indented of devise, grant, and to farm let, and so also by fine of record; but whether any rent be reserved or no, it is not material. Unto these leases there may be annexed such exceptions, conditions, and covenants, as the parties can agree on. They are called chattels real, and are not inheritable by the heirs, but go to the executors and administrators, and be saleable for debts in the life of the owner, or in the executors' or administrators' hands by writs of execution upon statutes, recognizances, judgments of debts or damages. They be also forfeitable to the crown by outlawry, by attainder for treason, felony, or premunire, killing himself, flying for felony, although not guilty of the fact, standing out or refusing to be tried by the country, by conviction of

Property of land by conveyance divided into, 1. Estates in fees. 2. In tail. 3. For life. 4. For years.

Leases for years they go to the executors and not to the heirs.

Leases are to be forfeited by attainder. 1. In treason. 2. Felony. 3. Premunire. 4. By killing himself. 5. For flying. 6. Standing out, or mute, or refusing to be tried by the country. 7. By conviction. 8. Petty larceny.

9. Going beyond the sea without license. Extents upon stat.staple, merchant, elegit, wardship of body and lands are chattels, and forfeitable in the same manner as leases for years are.

felony, by verdict without judgment, petty larceny, or going beyond the sea without license.

They are forfeitable to the crown, in like manner as leases for years, or interest gotten in other men's lands, by extending for debt upon judgment in any court of record, stat. merchant, stat. staple, recognizances; which being upon statutes are called tenants by stat. merchant, or staple, the other tenants by elegit, and by wardship of body and lands, for all these are called chattels real, and go to the executors and administrators, and not to the heirs, and are saleable and forfeitable as leases for years are.

Lease for life is not forfeitable by outlawry except in cases of felony or premunire, and then to the king, and not to the lord by escheat; and it is not forfeited by any of the means before mentioned of leases for years. Lease for life not to be sold by the sheriff for debt, but extended yearly.

Leases for lives are also called freeholds, they may also be made by word or writing, there must be livery and seisin* given at the making of the lease, whom we call the lessor, who cometh to the door, backside, or garden, if it be a house, if not, then to some part of the land, and there he expresseth, that he doth grant unto the taker, called the lessee, for term of his life: and in seisin thereof, he delivereth to him a turf, twig, or ring of the door; and if the lease be by writing, then commonly there is a note written on the backside of the lease,† with the names of those witnesses who were present at the time of the livery of seisin made. This estate is not saleable by the sheriff for debt, but the land is to be extended for a yearly value, to satisfy the debt. It is not forfeitable by outlawry, except in cases of felony, nor by any of the means before mentioned, of leases for years; saving in an attainder for and felony, treason, premunire, and then only to the crown; not to the lords by escheat.

A man that hath bona felon. by charter, shall not have the means if leaser for life be attainted.

And though a nobleman or other have liberty, by charter, to have all felon's goods, yet a tenant holding for term of life, being attainted of felony, doth forfeit unto the king, and not to this nobleman.

Occupant.

If a man have an estate in lands for another man's life, and dieth, this land cannot go to his heir, nor to his executors, but to the party that first entereth, and he is called an occupant as before hath been declared.

Of estate tails, and how such an estate may be limited.

A lease for years, or for life, may be made also by fine of record, or bargain and sale, or covenant to stand seised upon good considerations of marriage, or blood, the reasons whereof are hereafter expressed.

Entails of lands are created by a gift, with livery and

* What livery of seisin is, and how it is requisite to every estate for life.
† Indorsement of livery upon the back of the deed, and witness of it.

seisin to a man, and to the heirs of his body; this word (body) making the entail may be demonstrated and restrained to the males or females, heirs of their two bodies; or of the body of either of them, or of the body of the grandfather or father.

By the stat. of West. 1. made in Ed. 1. time, estates in tail were so strengthened that they were not forfeitable by any attainder.

Entails of lands began by a statute made in Edward the First's time, by which also they are so much strengthened, as that the tenant in tail could not put away the land from the heir by any act of conveyance or attainder, nor let it, nor incumber it, longer than his own life.

The great inconvenience that ensued thereof.

But the inconvenience thereof was great, for, by that means, the land being so sure tied upon the heir, as that his father could not put it from him, it made the son to be disobedient, negligent, and wasteful, often marrying without the father's consent, and to grow insolent in vice, knowing that there could be no check of disinheriting him. It also made the owners of the land less fearful to commit murders, felonies, treasons, and manslaughters; for that they knew none of these acts could hurt the heir of his inheritance. It hindered men that had entailed lands, that they could not make the best of their lands by fine and improvement, for that none upon so uncertain an estate, as for term of his own life, would give him a fine of any value, nor lay any great stock upon the land that might yield rent improved.

The prejudice the crown received thereby.

Lastly, those entails did defraud the crown and many subjects of their debts; for that the land was not liable longer than his own life time, which caused that the king could not safely commit any office of account to such, whose lands were entailed, nor other men trust them with loan of money.

The stat. 4 H. 7. and 32 H. 8. to bar estates tail by fine.

These inconveniences were all remedied by acts of parliament; as namely, by acts of parliament later than the acts of entails, made 4 H. VII. 32 H. VIII. A tenant in tail may disinherit his son by a fine with proclamation, and may, by that means also, make it subject to his debts and sales.

26 H. 8.
32 H. 8.
33 H. 8.
13 & 39 Eliz.
Entails two privileges.
1. Not forfeitable for felony.
2. Not extendable for the debts of the

By a statute made, 26 H. VIII. a tenant in tail doth forfeit his lands for treason; and by another act of parliament, 32 H. VIII. he may make leases good against his heir for twenty-one years, or three lives; so that it be not of his chief houses, lands, or demesne, or any lease in reversion, nor less rent reserved than the tenants have paid most part of twenty-one years before, nor having any manner of discharge for doing wastes and spoils: by a statute made 33 H. VIII. tenants of entailed lands are liable to the

party after his death. *Proviso*, not to put away the land from his next heir. If he do, to forfeit his own estate, and that his next heir must enter.

king's debts by extent, and by a statute made 13 and 39 Eliz. they are saleable for the arrearages upon his account for his office. So that now it resteth, that entailed lands have two privileges only, which be these. First, not to be forfeited for felonies. Secondly, not to be extended for debts after the parties' death, except the entails be cut off by fine and recovery.

Of the new device called a perpetuity, which is an entail with an addition.

But it is to be noted, that since these notable statutes, and remedies prov e by statutes, do dock entails, there is start up a device called perpetuity, which is an entail with an addition of a proviso conditional, tied to his estate, not to put away the land from his next heir; and if he do, to forfeit his own estate. Which perpetuities, if they should stand, would bring in all the former inconveniences subject to entails, that were cut off by the former mentioned statutes, and far greater; for, by the perpetuity, if he that is in possession start away never so little, as in making a lease, or selling a little quillet, forgetting after two or three descents, as often they do, how they are tied, the next heir must enter, who, peradventure, is his son, his brother, uncle, or kinsman, and this raiseth unkind suits, setting all that kindred at jars, some taking one part, some another, and the principal parties wasting their time and money in suits of law. So that in the end they are both constrained by necessity to join both in a sale of the land, or a great part of it, to pay their debts, occasioned through their suits. And if the chiefest of the family, for any good purpose of well seating himself, by selling that which lieth far off is to buy that which is near, or for the advancement of his daughters or younger sons should have reasonable cause to sell, this perpetuity, if it should hold good, restraineth him. And more than that, where many are owners of inheritance of land not entailed may, during the minority of his eldest son, appoint the profits to go to the advancement of the younger sons and daughters, and pay debts; by entails and perpetuities the owners of these lands cannot do it, but they must suffer the whole to descend to his eldest son, and so to come to the crown by wardship all the time of his infancy.

These perpetuities would bring in all the former inconveniences of estates tails.

The inconveniences of those perpetuities.

Quære whether it be better to restrain men by these perpetuities from alienations, or to hazard the undoing of houses by

Wherefore, seeing the dangerous times and untowardly heirs, they might prevent those mischiefs of undoing their houses by conveying the land from such heirs, if they were not tied to the stake by those perpetuities, and restrained from forfeiting to the crown, and disposing it to their own or to their children's good; therefore it is worthy of consideration, whether it be better for the subject and sovereign to have the lands secured to men's names and bloods by perpetuities, with all the inconveniences abovementioned, or to be in hazard of undoing his house by unthrifty posterity.

unthrifty posterity.

The last and greatest estate of lands is fee-simple, and beyond this there is none of the former for lives, years, or entails; but beyond them is fee-simple. For it is the greatest, last, and uttermost degree of estates in land; therefore he that maketh a lease for life, or a gift in tail, may appoint a remainder when he maketh another for life or in tail, or to a third in fee-simple; but after a fee-simple he can limit no other estate. And if a man do not dispose of the fee-simple by way of remainder, when he maketh the gift in tail, or for lives, then the fee-simple resteth in himself as a reversion. The difference between a reversion and a remainder is this: The remainder is always a succeeding estate, appointed upon the gifts of a precedent estate, at the time when the precedent is appointed. But the reversion is an estate left in the giver, after a particular estate made by him for years, life, or entail; where the remainder is made with the particular estates, then it must be done by deeds in writing, with livery and seisin, and cannot be by words. And if the giver will dispose of the reversion after it remaineth in himself, he is to do it by writing, and not by word, and the tenant is to have notice of it, and to attu rn it, which is to give his assent by word, or paying rent, or the like; and except the tenant will thus atturn, the party to whom the reversion is granted cannot have the reversion, neither can he compel him by any law to atturn, except the grant of the reversion be by fine; and then he may by writ provided for that purpose: and if he do not purchase that writ, yet by the fine the reversion shall pass; and the tenant shall pay no rent, except he will himself, nor be punished for any wastes in houses, woods, &c. unless it be granted by bargain and sale by indenture enrolled. These fee-simple estates lie open to all perils of forfeitures, extents, incumbrances, and sales.

The last and greatest estate in land is fee-simple.

A remainder cannot be limited upon an estate in fee-simple.

The difference between a remainder and a reversion.

A reversion cannot be granted by word.

Atturnment must be had to the grant of the reversion.

The tenant not compellable to atturn but where the reversion is granted by fine.

Lands are conveyed by these six means: first, by feoffment,* which is, where by deed lands are given to one and his heirs, and livery and seisin made according to the form and effect of the deed; if a lesser estate than fee-simple be given, and livery of seisin made, it is not called a feoffment, except the fee-simple be conveyed, but is otherwise called a lease for life or gift entail as abovementioned.

* Lands may be conveyed six manner of ways. 1. By feoffment. 2. By fine. 3. By recovery. 4. By use. 5. By covenant. 6. By will.

A fine is a real agreement, beginning thus, *Hæc est finalis*

What a fine is,

and how lands may be conveyed hereby.

concordia, &c. This is done before the king's judges in the Court of Common Pleas, concerning lands that a man should have from another to him and his heirs, or to him for his life, or to him and the heirs males of his body, or for years certain, whereupon rent may be reserved, but no condition or covenants. This fine is a record of great credit, and upon this fine are four proclamations made openly in the Common Pleas; that is, in every term one for four terms together: and if any man, having right to the same, make not his claim within five years after the proclamations ended, he loseth his right for ever, except he be an infant, a woman covert, a madman, or beyond the seas, and then his right is saved; so that he claim within five years after the death of her husband's full age, recovery of his wits, or return from beyond the seas. This fine is called a feoffment of record, because that it includeth all that the feoffment doth, and worketh further of his own nature, and barreth entails peremptorily, whether the heir doth claim within five years or not, if he claim by him that levied the fine.

Five years non claim barreth not,
1. An infant.
2. Feme covert.
3. Madman.
4. Beyond sea.

Fine is a feoffment of record.

What recoveries are.

Recoveries are where, for assurances of lands, the parties do agree, that one shall begin an action real against the other, as though he had good right to the land, and the other shall not enter into defence against it, but allege that he bought the land of I. H. who had warranted unto him, and pray that I. H. may be called in to defend the title, which I. H. is one of the cryers of the Common Pleas, and is called the common voucher. This I. H. shall appear and make as if he would defend it, but shall pray a day to be assigned him in his matter of defence, which being granted him, at the day he maketh default, and thereupon the court is to give judgment against him, which cannot be for him to lose his lands, because he hath it not, but the party that he hath sold it to, hath that who vouched him to warrant it.

Common voucher one of the cryers of the court.

Judgment for the demandant against the tenant in tail.

Judgment for tenant to recover so much land in value of the common voucher.

Therefore the demandant who hath no defence made against it, must have judgment to have the land against him that he sued (who is called the tenant), and the tenant is to have judgment against I. H. to recover in value so much land of his, where, in truth, he hath none, nor never will. And by this device, grounded upon the strict principles of law, the first tenant loseth the land, and hath nothing for it; but it is by his own agreement, for assurance to him that bought it.

This recovery barreth entails, and all remainders and reversions that should take place after the entails, saving where the king is giver of the entail, and keepeth the reversion to himself, then neither the heir, nor the remainder, nor reversion is barred by the recovery.

A recovery barreth an escheat tail, and all reversions and remaindments thereupon.

The reason why the heirs, remainders, and reversions are thus barred is because in strict law the recompense adjudged against the cryer that was vouchee, is to go in succession of estate as the land should have done, and then it was not reason to allow the heir the liberty to keep the land itself, and also to have recompense; and, therefore, he loseth the land, and is to trust to the recompense.

The reason why a common recovery barreth those in remainder and reversions.

This sleight was first invented when entails fell out to be so inconvenient as is before declared, so that men made no conscience to cut them off if they could find law for it. And now by use, those recoveries are become common assurances against entails, remainders, and reversions, and are the greatest security purchasers have for their moneys; for a fine will bar the heir in tail, and not the remainder, nor reversion, but a common recovery will bar them all.

The many inconveniences of estates in tail brought in these recoveries, which are made now common conveyances and assurances for land.

Upon feoffments and recoveries, the estate doth settle as the use and intent of the parties is declared by word or writing, before the act was done; As for example; if they make a writing that one of them shall levy a fine, make a feoffment, or suffer a common recovery to the other, but the use and intent is, that one should have it for his life, and after his decease, a stranger to have it in tail, and then a third in fee-simple. In this case the land settleth in an estate according to the use and intent declared. And that by reason of the statute made 27 H. VIII. conveying the land in possession to him that hath interest in the use, or intent of the fine, feoffment, or recovery, according to the use and intent of the parties.

Upon fines, feoffments, and recoveries, the estate doth settle according to the intent of the parties.

Upon this statute is likewise grounded the fourth and fifth of the six conveyances, viz. bargains, sales, covenants, to stand seised to uses; for this statute, wheresoever it findeth a use, conjoineth the possession to it, and turneth it into like quality of estate, condition, rent, and the like as the use hath.

Bargains, sales, and covenants to stand sesied to a use, are all grounded upon one statute.

The use is but the equity and honesty to hold the land *in conscientia boni viri.* As for example; I and you agree that I shall give you money for your land, and you shall make me assurance of it. I pay you the money, but you made me no assurance of it. Here, although the estate of the land be still in you, yet the equity and honesty to have it

What a use is.

is with me; and this equity is called the use, upon which I had no remedy but in Chancery, until this statute was made of 27 H. VIII. and now this statute conjoineth and containeth the land to him that hath the use. I for my money paid to you have the land itself, without any other conveyance from you, and it is called a bargain and sale.

Before 27 H. 8. there was no remedy for a use, but in Chancery.

But the parliament that made that statute did foresee that it would be mischievous that men's lands should so suddenly, upon the payment of a little money, be conveyed from them, peradventure in an alehouse or a tavern, upon strainable advantages, did therefore gravely provide another act in the same parliament, that the land, upon payment of this money, should not pass away, except there were a writing indented made between the said two parties, and the said writing also within six months enrolled in some of the courts at Westminster, or in the sessions rolls in the shire where the land lieth, unless it be in cities or corporate towns where they did use to enrol deeds, and there the statute extendeth not.

The stat. of 27 H. 8. doth not pass land upon the payment of money without a deed indented and enrolled.

The stat. of 27 H. 8. extendeth not into cities and corporate towns where they did use to enrol deeds.

The fifth conveyance of a fine is a conveyance to stand seised to uses. It is in this sort; a man that hath a wife and children, brethren, and kinsfolk, may, by writing under his hand and seal, agree that for their or any of their preferment he will stand seised of his lands to their uses, either for life in tail or fee, so as he shall see cause; upon which agreement in writing there ariseth an equity or honesty, that the land should go according to those agreements; nature and reason allowing these provisions, which equity and honesty is the use. And the use being created in this sort, the statute of 27 H. VIII. beforementioned, conveyeth the estate of the land, as the use is appointed.

A conveyance to stand seised to a use.

Upon an agreement in writing to stand seised to the use of any of his kindred, a use may be created, and the estate of the land thereupon executed, by 27 H. 8.

And so this covenant to stand seised to uses is at this day, since the said statute, a conveyance of land, and with this difference from a bargain and sale; in that this needeth no enrolment as a bargain and sale doth, nor needeth it to be in writing indented, as bargain and sale must: and if the party to whose use he agreeth to stand seised of the land, be not wife, or child, cousin, or one that he meaneth to marry, then will no use rise, and so no conveyance; for although the law alloweth such weighty considerations of marriage and blood to raise uses, yet doth it not admit so trifling considerations as of acquaintance, schooling, services, or the like.

A covenant to stand seised to a use needeth no enrolment, as a bargain and sale to a use doth, so it be to the use of wife, child, or cousin, or one he meaneth to marry.

But where a man maketh an estate of his land to others by fine, feoffment, or recovery, he may then appoint the use

Upon a fine, feoffment, or recovery, a man

to whom he listeth, without respect of marriage, kindred, or other things; for in that case his own will and declaration guideth the equity of the estate. It is not so when he maketh no estate, but agreeth to stand seised, nor when he hath taken any thing, as in the cases of bargain, and sale, and covenant, to stand to uses.

may limit the use to whom he listeth, without consideration of blood, or money. Otherwise, in a bargain and sale, or covenant.

The last of the six conveyances is a will in writing, which course of conveyance was first ordained by statute made 32 H. VIII. before which statute no man might give land by will, except it were in a borough town, where there was an especial custom that men might give their lands by will; as in London, and many other places.

Of the continuance of land by will.

The not giving of land by will was thought to be a defect at common law; that men in wars, or suddenly falling sick, had not power to dispose of their lands, except they could make a feoffment, or levy a fine, or suffer a recovery, which lack of time would not permit; and for men to do it by these means, when they could not undo it again, was hard: besides, even to the last hour of death, men's minds might alter upon further proofs of their children or kindred, or increase of children or debt, or defect of servants, or friends, to be altered.

The not disposing of lands by will was thought to be a defect at the common law.

For which cause it was reason that the law should permit him to reserve to the last instant the disposing of his lands, and to give him means to dispose it, which seeing it did not fitly serve, men used this device.

They conveyed their full estates of their lands, in their good health, to friends in trust, properly called feoffees in trust, and then they would, by their wills, declare how their friends should dispose of their lands; and if those friends would not perform it, the Court of Chancery was to compel them, by reason of the trust; and this trust was called the use of the land, so as the feoffees had the land, and the party himself had the use; which use was in equity, to take the profits for himself, and that the feoffees should make such an estate as he should appoint them; and if he appointed none, then the use should go to the heir, as the estate itself of the land should have done; for the use was to the estate like a shadow following the body.

The court that was invented before the stat. of 32 H. 8. first gave power to devise lands by will, which was a conveyance of lands to feoffees in trust, to such persons as they should declare in their will.

By this course of putting lands into use, there were many inconveniences (as this use which grew first for a reasonable cause), viz. to give men power and liberty to dispose of their own, was turned to deceive many of their just and reasonable rights; as, namely, a man that had cause to sue for his land, knew not against whom to bring

The inconveniences of putting land into use.

his action, nor who was owner of it. The wife was defrauded of her thirds; the husband of being tenant by courtesy; the lord of his wardship, relief, heriot, and escheat; the creditor of his extent for debt; the poor tenant of his lease, for these rights and duties were given by law from him that was owner of the land, and none other, which was now the feoffee of trust, and so the old owner, which we call the feoffor, should take the profits, and leave the power to dispose of the land at his discretion to the feoffee, and yet he was not such a tenant as to be seised of the land, so as his wife could have dower, or the lands be extended for his debts, or that he could forfeit it for felony or treason, or that his heir could be ward for it, or any duty of tenure fall to the lord by his death, or that he could make any leases of it.

The frauds of conveyances to use by degrees of time, as they increased, were remedied by the statutes 1 H. 6. 4 H. 8. 1 R. 3. 4 H. 7. 16 H. 8.

Which frauds, by degrees of time, as they increased, were remedied by divers statutes; as, namely, by a statute of 1 H. VI. and 4 H. VIII. it was appointed that the action may be tried against him which taketh the profits, which was then *cestuy que use* by a statute made 1 R. III. Leases and estates made by *cestuy que use* are made good, and statutes by him acknowledged. 4 H. VII. the heir of *cestuy que use* is to be in ward. 16 H. VIII. the lord is to have relief upon the death of any *cestuy que use.*

27 H. 8. taking away all uses reduceth the law to the ancient form of conveyances of land by feoffment, fine, and recovery.

Which frauds nevertheless multiplying daily, in the end 27 H. VIII. the parliament, purposing to take away all those uses, and reducing the law to the ancient form of conveying of lands by public livery of seisin, fine, and recovery, did ordain, that where lands were put in trust or use, there the possession and estate should be presently carried out of the friends in trust, and settled and invested on him that had the uses, for such term and time as he had the use.

In what manner the stat. of 32 H. 8. giveth power to dispose of lands by will.

By this statute of 27 H. VIII. the power of disposing land by will is clearly taken away amongst those frauds; whereupon 32 H. VIII. another statute was made, to give men power to give lands by will in this sort. First, it must be by will in writing. Secondly, he must be seised of an estate in fee-simple; for tenant for another man's life, or term in tail, cannot give land by will, by that statute, 32 H. VIII. he must be solely seised, and not jointly with another; and then being thus seised, for all the land he holdeth in soccage tenure, he may give it by will, except he hold any piece of land in capite, by knight's service of the king; and then, laying all his lacks together, he can give but two parts by will, for the third part of the whole,

If a man be seised of capite lands and soccage, he cannot devise but two parts of the whole.

as well in soccage as in capite, must descend to the heir, to answer wardship, livery, and primer seisin to the crown.

The third part must descend to the heir to answer guardship, livery, and seisin to the crown.

And so if he hold lands by knight's service of a subject, he can devise of the land but two parts, and the third the lord by wardship, and the heir by descent, is to hold.

And if a man that hath three acres of land holden in capite, by knight's service, do make a jointure to his wife of one, and convey another to any of his children, or to friends, to take the profits and to pay his debts, or legacies, or daughters' portions, then the third acre, or any part thereof, he cannot give by will, but must suffer it to descend to the heir, and that must satisfy wardship.

A conveyance by devise of capite lands to the wife for her jointure, or to his children for their good, or to pay debts is void for a third part, by 32 H. 8.

Yet a man, having three acres as before, may convey all to his wife or children, by conveyance, in his life time, as by feoffment, fine, recovery, bargain, and sale, or covenant to stand seised to uses, and to disinherit the heir. But if the heir be within age when his father dieth, the king or other lord shall have that heir in ward, and shall have one of the three acres during the wardship, and to sue livery and seisin. But at full age the heir shall have no part of it, but it shall go according to the conveyance made by the father.

But a conveyance by act executed in the life time of the party of such lands to such uses is not void, but a third part; but if the heir be within age, he shall have one of the acres to be in ward.

It hath been debated how the thirds shall be set forth. For it is the use that all lands which the father leaveth to descend to the heir, being fee-simple, or in tail, must be part of the thirds; and if it be a full third, then the king, nor heir, nor lord, can intermeddle with the rest; if it be not a full third yet they must take it so much as it is, and have a supply out of the rest.

Entailed lands part of the thirds.

The king nor lord cannot intermeddle if a full third part be left to descend to the heir.

This supply is to be taken thus; if it be the king's ward, then by a commission out of the court of wards, whereupon a jury by oath must set forth so much as shall make up the thirds, except the officers of the court of wards can otherwise agree with the parties. If there be no wardship due to the king, then the other lord is to have this supply by a commission out of the chancery, and jury thereupon.

The manner of making supply when the part of the heir is not a full third.

But in all those cases the statutes do give power to him that maketh the will to set forth, and appoint of himself, which lands shall go for thirds, and neither king nor lord can refuse it. And if it be not enough, yet they must take that in part, and only have a supply in manner as before is mentioned out of the rest.

The statutes give power to the testator to set out the third himself, and if it be not a third part, yet the king or lord must take that in part, and have a supply out of the rent.

Property in goods.

Of the several ways whereby a man may get property in goods or chattels.

1. By gift.
2. By sale.
3. By stealing.
4. By waving.
5. By straying.
6. By shipwreck.
7. By forfeiture.
8. By executorship.
9. By administration.
10. By legacy.

I. *Property by gift.*

A deed of gift of goods to deceive his creditors is void against them, but good against the executors, administrators, or vender of the party himself.

By gift the property of goods may be passed by word or writing; but if there be a general deed of gift made of all his goods, this is suspicious to be done upon fraud, to deceive the creditors.

And if a man who is in debt make a deed of gift of all his goods to protract the taking of them in execution for his debt, this deed of gift is void, as against those to whom he stood indebted; but as against himself, his own executors or administrators, or any man to whom afterwards he shall sell or convey them, it is good.

II. *By sale.*

What is a sale *bona fide* and what not, when there is a private reservation of trust between the parties.

Property in goods by sale. By sale any man may convey his own goods to another: and although he may fear execution for debts, yet he may sell them outright for money at any time before the execution served, so that there be no reservation of trust between them; paying the money, he shall have the goods again; for that trust, in such case, doth prove plainly a fraud to prevent the creditors from taking the goods in execution.

III. *By theft, or taking in jest.*

How a sale in market shall be a bar to the owner.

Property of goods by theft, or taking in jest. If any man steal my goods or chattels, or take them from me in jest, or borrow them of me, or as a trespasser or felon carry them to the market or fair, and sell them, this sale doth bar me of the property of my goods, saving that if he be a horse he must be ridden two hours in the market or fair, between ten and five o'clock, and tolled for in the toll book, and the seller must bring one to avouch his sale, known to the toll book keeper, or else the sale bindeth me not. And for any other goods, where the sale in a market or fair shall bar the owner, being not the seller of his property, it must be sale in a market or fair where usually things of that nature are sold. As for example: if a man steal a horse, and sell him in Smithfield, the true owner is barred by this sale; but if he sell the horse in Cheapside, Newgate, or Westminster Market, the true owner is not barred by this sale, because these markets are usual for flesh, fish, &c. and not for horses.

Of markets, and what markets such a sale ought to be made in.

So, whereas, by the custom of London, in every shop there is a market all the days of the week, saving Sundays and holidays. Yet if a piece of plate or jewel that is lost, or chain of gold or pearl that is stolen or borrowed, be sold in a draper's or scrivener's shop, or any others but a goldsmith, this sale barreth not the true owner, *et sic in similibus.*

Yet by stealing alone of goods the thief getteth not such property, but that the owner may seize them again wheresoever he findeth them; except they were sold in fair or market, after they were stolen, and that *bona fide* without fraud.

The owner may seize his oods after theyg are stolen.

But if the thief be condemned of the felony, or outlawed for the same, or outlawed in any personal action, or have committed a forfeiture of goods to the crown, then the true owner is without remedy.

Nevertheless, if fresh after the goods were stolen, the true owner maketh pursuit after the thief and goods, and taketh the goods with the thief, he may take them again. And if he make no fresh pursuit, yet if he prosecute the felon so far as justice requireth, that is, to have him arraigned, indicted, and found guilty (though he be not hanged, nor have judgment of death), or have him outlawed upon the indictment; in all these cases he shall have his goods again, by a writ of restitution to the party in whose hands they are.

If the thief be condemned for felony, or outlawed, or forfeit the stolen goods to the crown, the owner is without remedy. But if he make fresh pursuit he may take his goods from the thief. Or if he prosecuted the law against the thief, and convict him of the same felony, he shall have his goods again by a writ of restitution.

IV. *By waving of goods.*

By waving of goods a property is gotten thus. A thief having stolen goods, being pursued, flieth away and leaveth the goods. This leaving is called waving, and the property is in the king; except the lord of the manor have right to it by custom or charter.

But if the felon be indicted, adjudged, or found guilty, or outlawed at the suit of the owner of these goods, he shall have restitution of these goods as before.

V. *By straying.*

By straying property in live cattle is thus gotten. When they come into other men's grounds, straying from the owners, then the party or lord into whose grounds or manors they come causeth them to be seized, and a withe put about their necks, and to be cried in three markets adjoining, showing the marks of the cattle; which done, if the true owner claimeth them not within a year and a day, then the property of them is in the lord of the manor whereunto they did stray, if he have all strays by custom or charter, else to the king.

VI. *Wreck, and when it shall be said to be.*

By shipwreck property of goods is thus gotten. When a ship laden is cast away upon the coasts, so that no living creature that was in it when it began to sink escapeth to land with life, then all those goods are said to be wrecked, and they belong to the crown if they be found; except the lord of the soil adjoining can entitle himself unto them by custom, or by the king's charter.

VII. *Forfeitures.*

By forfeitures goods and chattels are thus gotten. If the owner be outlawed, if he be indicted of felony or treason, or either confess it, or be found guilty of it, or refuse to be tried by peers or jury, or be attainted by judgment, or fly for felony, although he be not guilty, or suffer the exigent to go forth against him, although he be not outlawed, or that he go over the seas without license, all the goods he had at the judgment he forfeiteth to the crown, except some lord by charter can claim them. For in those cases prescripts will not serve, except it be so ancient, that it hath had allowance before the justices in eyre in their circuits, or in the King's Bench in ancient time.

VIII. *By executorship.*

By executorship goods are gotten. When a man possessed of goods maketh his last will and testament in writing, or by word, and maketh one or more executors thereof, these executors have by the will and death of the parties all the property of their goods, chattels, leases for years, wardships, and extents, and all right concerning those things.

Those executors may meddle with the goods, and dispose them before they prove the will, but they cannot bring an action for any debt or duty before they have proved the will.

Executors may, before probate, dispose of the goods, but not bring an action for any debt.

The proving of the will is thus. They are to exhibit the will into the bishop's court, and there they are to bring the witnesses, and there they are to be sworn, and the bishop's officers are to keep the will original, and certify the copy thereof in parchment under the bishop's seal of office, which parchment, so sealed, is called the will proved.

What probate of the will is, and in what manner it is made.

IX. *By letters of administration.*

By letters of administration property in goods is thus gotten. When a man possessed of goods dieth without any will, there such goods as the executors should have had if he had made a will were by ancient law to come to the bishop of the diocess, to dispose for the good of his soul that died, he first paying his funerals and debts, and giving the rest, *ad pios usus.*

Pii usus.

This is now altered by statute laws, so as the bishops are to grant letters of administration of the goods at this day to the wife if she require it, or children, or next of kin; if they refuse it, as often they do, because the debts are greater than the estate will bear, then some creditor, or some other, will take it as the bishop's officers shall think meet. It groweth often in question what bishop shall have the right of proving wills, and granting administration of goods.

In which controversy the rule is thus:. That if the party dead had, at the time of his death, *bona notabilia* in divers diocesses of some reasonable value, then the archbishop of the province where he died is to have the probate of his will, and to grant the administration of his goods as the case falleth out; otherwise, the bishop of the diocess where he died is to do it.

Where the intestate had *bona notabilia* in divers diocesses, then the archbishop of that province where he died is to commit the administration.

If there be but one executor made, yet he may refuse the executorship coming before the bishop, so that he hath not intermeddled with any of the goods before, or with receiving debts, or paying legacies.

Executor may refuse before the bishop, if he have not intermeddled the goods.

And if there be more executors than one, so many as list may refuse; and if any one take it upon him, the rest that

Executor ought

to pay, 1. Judgments. 2. Stat. recogn. 3. Debts by bonds and bills sealed. 4. Rent unpaid. 5. Servants' wages. 6. Head workmen. 7. Shop-book, and contracts by word.

did once refuse may when they will take it upon them, and no executor shall be further charged with debts or legacies than the value of the goods come to his hands. So that he foresee that he pay debts upon record, first debts to the king, then upon judgments, statutes, recognizances, then debts by bond and bill sealed, rent unpaid, servants' wages, payment to head workmen, and, lastly, shop-books, and contracts by word. For if an executor, or administrator pay debts to others before to the king, or debts due by bond before those due by record, or debts by shop-books and contracts before those by bond, arrearages of rent, and servants', or workmen's wages, he shall pay the same over again to those others in the said degrees.

Debts due in equal degree of record, the executor may pay which of them he please before suit commenced.

But yet the law giveth them choice, that where divers have debts due in equal degree of record or specialty, he may pay which of them he will, before any suit brought against him; but if suit be brought he must pay them that get judgment against him.

Any one executor may do as much as all together, but if a debt be released, and assets wanting, he shall only be discharged.

Any one executor may convey the goods, or release debts without his companion, and any one by himself may do as much as all together; but one man's releasing of debts or selling of goods, shall not charge the other to pay so much of the goods, if there be not enough to pay debts; but it shall charge the party himself that did so release or convey.

Otherwise of administrators.

But it is not so with administrators, for they have but one authority given them by the bishop over the goods, which authority being given to many, is to be executed by all of them joined together.

Executor dieth making his executor, the second executor shall be executor to the first testator.

And if an executor die making an executor, the second executor is executor to the first testator.

But otherwise, if the administrator die making his executor, or if administration be committed of his goods. In both cases the ordinary shall commit administration of the goods of the first intestate.

But if an administrator die intestate, then his administrator shall not be executor or administrator to the first. But in that case the bishop, whom we call the ordinary, is to commit the administration of the first testator's goods to his wife, or next of kin, as if he had died intestate. Always provided, that that which the executor did in his lifetime is to be allowed for good. And so if an administrator die, and make his executor, the executor of the administrator shall not be executor to the first intestate; but the ordinary must new commit the administration of the goods of the first intestate again.

Executors or administrators may retain.

If the executor or administrator pay debts, or funerals, or legacies of his own money, he may retain so much of the goods in kind, of the testator or intestate, and shall have property of it in kind.

X. *Property by legacy.*

Property by legacy is where a man maketh a will and executors, and giveth legacies, he or they to whom the legacies are given must have the assent of the executors, or one of them, to have his legacy, and the property of that lease, or other goods bequeathed unto him, is said to be in him; but he may not enter nor take his legacy without the assent of the executors, or one of them, because the executors are charged to pay debts before legacies. And if one of them assent to pay legacies, he shall pay the value thereof of his own purse if there be not otherwise sufficient to pay debts.

Executors or administrators may retain; because the executors are charged to pay some debts before legacies.

But this is to be understood by debts of record to the king, or by bill and bond sealed, or arrearages of rent, or servants' or workmen's wages; and not debts of shop-books, or bills unsealed, or contract by word; for before them legacies are to be paid.

Legacies are to be paid before debts by shop-books, bills unsealed, or contracts by word.

And if the executors doubt that they shall not have enough to pay every legacy, they may pay which they list first; but they may not sell any special legacy which they will to pay debts, or a lease of goods to pay a money-legacy. But they may sell any legacy which they will to pay debts, if they have not enough besides.

Executor may pay which legacy he will first.

If the executors do want they may sell any legacy to pay debts.

If a man make a will, and make no executors, or if the executors refuse, the ordinary is to commit administration *cum testamento annexo*, and take bonds of the administrators to perform the will, and he is to do it in such sort as the executor should have done, if he had been named.

When a will is made, and no executor named, administration is to be committed *cum testamento annexo.*

THE

ARGUMENTS IN LAW

OF

SIR FRANCIS BACON, KNIGHT,

THE KING'S SOLICITOR GENERAL

IN CERTAIN GREAT AND DIFFICULT CASES.

TO MY

LOVING FRIENDS AND FELLOWS,

THE

READERS, ANCIENTS, UTTER-BARRISTERS, AND STUDENTS OF GRAY'S INN.

I do not hold the law of England in so mean an account, but that which other laws are held worthy of should be due likewise to our laws, as no less worthy for our state. Therefore, when I found that, not only in the ancient times, but now at this day, in France, Italy, and other nations, the speeches, and, as they term them, pleadings, which have been made in judicial cases, where the cases were mighty and famous, have been set down by those that made them, and published; so that not only a Cicero, a Demosthenes, or an Æschines hath set forth his orations, as well in the judicial as deliberative, but a Marrian and a Pavier have done the like by their pleadings; I know no reason why the same should not be brought in use by the professors of our law, for their arguments in principal cases. And this I think the more necessary, because the compendious form of reporting resolutions, with the substance of the reasons lately used by Sir Edward Coke, Lord Chief Justice of the King's Bench, doth not delineate or trace out to the young practisers of law a method and form of argument for them to imitate. It is true, I could have wished some abler person had begun; but it is a kind of order sometimes to begin with the meanest. Nevertheless, thus much I may say with modesty, that these arguments which I have set forth, most of them are upon subjects not vulgar; and therewithal, in regard of the commixture, which the course of my life hath made of law with other studies, they may have the more variety, and perhaps the more depth of reason: for the reasons of municipal laws, severed from the grounds of nature, manners, and policy, are like wall flowers, which, though they grow high upon the crests of states, yet they have no deep root: besides, in all public services I ever valued my reputation more than my pains; and, therefore, in weighty causes I always used extraordinary diligence; in all which respects I persuade myself the reading of them will not be unprofitable. This work I knew not to whom to dedicate rather than to the Society of GRAY'S INN, the place whence my father was called to the highest place of justice, and where myself have lived and had my procedure so far as, by his majesty's rare, if not singular grace, to be of both his councils; and therefore few men so bound to their societies by obligation, both ancestral and personal, as I am to yours, which I would gladly acknowledge, not only in having your name joined with mine own in a book, but in any other good office and effect which the active part of my life and place may enable me unto toward the Society, or any of you in particular. And so I bid you right heartily farewell.

Your assured loving Friend and Fellow,

FRANCIS BACON.

THE

CASE OF IMPEACHMENT OF WASTE.

ARGUED

BEFORE ALL THE JUDGES IN THE EXCHEQUER CHAMBER.

THE case needs neither repeating nor opening. The point is, in substance, but one, familiar to be put, but difficult to be resolved; that is, Whether, upon a lease without impeachment of waste, the property of the timber trees, after severance, be not in him that is owner of the inheritance?

The case is of great weight, and the question of great difficulty: weighty it must needs be, for that it doth concern, or may concern, all the lands in England; and difficult it must be, because this question sails *in confluentiis aquarum*, in the meeting or strife of two great tides. For there is a strong current of practice and opinion on the one side, and there is a more strong current, as I conceive, of authorities, both ancient and late, on the other side. And, therefore, according to the reverend custom of the realm, it is brought now to this assembly; and it is high time the question receive an end, the law a rule, and men's conveyances a direction.

This doubt ariseth and resteth upon two things to be considered; first, to consider of the interest and property of a timber tree, to whom it belongeth: and, secondly, to consider of the construction and operation of these words or clause, *absque impetitione vasti:* for within these two branches will aptly fall whatsoever can be pertinently spoken in this question, without obscuring the question by any other curious division.

For the first of these considerations, which is the interest or property of a timber tree, I will maintain and prove to your lordships three things.

First, That a timber tree, while it groweth, is merely parcel of the inheritance, as well as the soil itself.

And, secondly, I will prove, that when either nature, or accident, or the hand of man hath made it transitory, and cut it off from the earth, it cannot change the owner, but the property of it goes where the inheritance was before. And thus much by the rules of the common law.

And, thirdly, I will show that the statute of Gloucester doth rather corroborate and confirm the property in the lessor than alter it, or transfer it to the lessee.

And for the second consideration, which is the force of that clause, *absque impetitione vasti,* I will also uphold and make good three other assertions.

First, That if that clause should be taken in the sense which the other side would force upon it, that it were a clause repugnant to the estate and void.

Secondly, That the sense which we conceive and give is natural in respect of the words; and for the matter agreeable to reason and the rules of law.

And, lastly, That if the interpretation seem ambiguous and doubtful, yet the very mischief itself, and consideration of the commonwealth, ought rather to incline your lordships' judgment to our construction.

My first assertion therefore is, that a timber tree is a solid parcel of the inheritance; which may seem a point admitted, and not worth the labouring. But there is such a chain in this case, as that which seemeth most plain, if it is sharply looked into, doth invincibly draw on that which is most doubtful. For if the tree be parcel of the inheritance unsevered, inherent in the reversion, severance will not alien it, nor the clause will not divest it.

To open, therefore, the nature of an inheritance: sense teacheth there be, of the soil and earth, parts that are raised and eminent, as timber trees, rocks, houses. There be parts that are sunk and depressed, as mines, which are called by some *arbores subterraneæ,* because that as trees have great branches and smaller boughs and twigs, so have they in their region greater and smaller veins; so if we had in England beds of porcelain, such as they have in China, which porcelain is a kind of a plaster buried in the earth, and by length of time congealed and glazed into that fine substance, this were as an artificial mine, and no doubt part of the inheritance. Then are the ordinary parts, which make the mass of the earth, as stone, gravel, loam, clay, and the like.

Now as I make all these much in one degree, so there is none of them, not timber trees, not quarries, not minerals nor fossils, but hath a double nature; inheritable and real while it is contained within the mass of the earth, and transitory and personal when it is once severed. For even gold and precious stone, which is more durable out of earth than any tree is upon the earth, yet the law doth not hold of that dignity as to be matter of inheritance if it be once severed. And this is not because it becometh moveable, for there be moveable inheritances, as villains in gross, and dignities which are judged hereditaments; but because by their severance they lose their nature of perpetuity, which is of the essence of an inheritance.

Nevil's case proving there are inheritances which are not local.

The consent of the law with philosophy in distinguishing between perpetual and transitory.

And herein I do not a little admire the wisdom of the laws of England, and the consent which they have with the wisdom of philosophy and nature itself: for it is a maxim in philosophy, that *in regione elementari nihil est æternum, nisi per propagationem speciei, aut per successionem partium.*

And it is most evident that the elements themselves, and their products, have a perpetuity not *in individuo*, but by supply and succession of parts. For example, the vestal fire that was nourished by the virgins at Rome was not the same fire still, but was in perpetual waste, and in perpetual renovation. So it is of the sea and waters, it is not the same water individually, for that exhales by the sun, and is fed again by showers. And so of the earth itself, and mines, quarries, and whatsoever it containeth, they are corruptible individually, and maintained only by succession of parts, and that lasteth no longer than they continue fixed to the main and mother globe of the earth, and is destroyed by their separation.

According to this I find the wisdom of the law, by imitation of the course of nature, to judge of inheritances and things transitory; for it alloweth no portions of the earth, no stone, no gold, no mineral, no tree, no mould to be longer inheritance than they adhere to the mass, and so are capable of supply in their parts; for by their continuance of body stands their continuance of time.

Neither is this matter of discourse, except the deep and profound reasons of law, which ought chiefly to be searched, shall be accounted discourse, as the slighter sort of wits, *Scioli*, may esteem them.

And, therefore, now that we have opened the nature of inheritable and transitory, let us see, upon a division of estates, and before severance, what kind of interests the law allotteth to the owner of inheritance, and what to the particular tenant, for they be competitors in this case.

The consent of the law with the civil law in the distinguishing between inheritance and particular estates, which hath relation to their division of *dominium* and *usus-fructus*. Owner in the stat. 4 H. 7.

First, In general the law doth assign to the lessor those parts of the soil conjoined, which have obtained the reputation to be durable, and of continuance, and such as being destroyed are not but by long time renewed; and to the terminors it assigneth such interests as are tender and feeble against the force of time, but have an annual or seasonable return or revenue. And herein it consents again with the wisdom of the civil law; for our inheritance and particular estate is in effect their *dominium* and *usus-fructus;* for so it was conceived upon the ancient statute of depopulations, 4 Hen. VII. which was penned, " that the owner of the land should reedify the houses of husbandry," that the word owner, which answereth to *dominus,* was he that had the immediate inheritance; and so ran the later statutes. Let us see therefore what judgment the law maketh of a timber tree; and whether the law doth not place it within the lot of him that hath the inheritance as parcel thereof.

The writ of waste supposeth the felling timber to be *ad exhæredationem.*

First, It appeareth by the register out of the words of the writ of waste, that the waste is laid to be *ad exhæredationem,* which presupposeth *hæreditatem:* for there cannot be a disinherison by the cutting down of the tree, except there was an inheritance in the tree, *quia privatio præsupponit actum.*

The statute of Gloucester, *quod recuperet rem vastatam,* not *locum vastatum.*

Again it appeareth out of the words of the statute of Gloucester, well observed, that the tree and the soil are one entire thing, for the words are *quod recuperet rem vastatam;* and yet the books speak, and the very judgment in waste is *quod recuperet locum vastatum,* which shows, that *res* and *locus* are in exposition of law taken indifferently; for the lessor shall not recover only the stem of the tree, but he shall recover the very soil, whereunto the stem continues. And therefore it is notably ruled in 22 H. VI. f. 13, that if the terminor do first cut down the tree, and then destroy the stem, the lessor shall declare upon two several wastes, and recover treble damages for them severally. But, says the book, he must bring but one writ, for he can recover the place wasted but once. 22 H. 6. f. 13.

And farther proof may be fitly alleged out of Mullin's case in the commentaries, where it is said, that for timber trees tithes shall not be paid. And the reason of the book is well to be observed; " for that tithes are to be paid for Mullin's case.

the revenue of the inheritance, and not for the inheritance itself."

Nay, my lords, it is notable to consider what a reputation the law gives to the trees, even after they are severed by grant, as may be plainly inferred out of Herlackenden's case, L. Coke, p. 4. f. 62. I mean the principal case; where it is resolved, that if the trees being excepted out of a lease granted to the lessee, or if the grantee of trees accept a lease of the land, the property of the trees drown not, as a term should drown in a freehold, but subsist as a chattel divided; which shows plainly, though they be made transitory, yet they still to some purpose savour of the inheritance: for if you go a little farther, and put the case of a state tail, which is a state of inheritance, then I think clearly they are reannexed. But, on the other side, if a man buy corn standing upon the ground, and take a lease of the same ground, where the corn stands, I say plainly it is reaffixed, for *paria copulantur cum paribus.*

Co. p. 4. f. 62.

And it is no less worthy the note, what an operation the inheritance leaveth behind it in matter of waste, even when it is gone, as appeareth in the case of tenant after possibility, who shall not be punished; for though the new reason be, because his estate was not within the statute of Gloucester; yet I will not go from my old master Littleton's reason, which speaketh out of the depth of the common law, he shall not be punished "for the inheritance sake which was once in him."

But this will receive a great deal of illustration, by considering the terminor's estate, and the nature thereof, which was well defined by Mr. Heath, who spake excellent well to the case, that it is such as he ought to yield up the inheritance in as good plight as he received it; and therefore the word *firmarius,* which is the word of the statute of Marlebridge, cometh, as I conceive, *a firmando;* because he makes the profit of the inheritance, which otherwise should be upon account, and uncertain, firm and certain; and accordingly *feodi firma,* fee-farm, is a perpetuity certain. Therefore the nature and limit of a particular tenant is to make the inheritance certain, and not to make it worse.

The derivation and force of the word *firmarius.*

1. Therefore he cannot break the soil otherwise than with his ploughshare, to turn up perhaps a stone that lieth aloft; his interest is in *superficie,* not in *profundo,* he hath but *tunicam terræ,* little more than the vesture.

If we had fir timber here, as they have in Muscovy, he

could not pierce the tree to make the pitch come forth, no more than he may break the earth.

So we see the evidence, which is *propugnaculum hæreditatis*, the fortress and defence of the land belongeth not to the lessee, but to the owner of the inheritance.

The evidence *propugnaculum hæreditatis*.

So the lessee's estate is not accounted of that dignity, that it can do homage, because it is a badge of continuance in the blood of lord and tenant. Neither for my own opinion can a particular tenant of a manor have aid *pour file marier, ou pour faire fitz chevalier;* because it is given by law upon an intendment of continuance of blood and privity between lord and tenant.

Homage importeth continuance in the blood. Particular tenants of seigniories shall not have aid.

And for the tree, which is now in question, do but consider in what a revolution the law moves, and as it were in an orb: for when the tree is young and tender, *germen terræ*, a sprout of the earth, the law giveth it to the lessee, as having a nature not permanent, and yet easily restored; when it comes to be a timber-tree, and hath a nature solid and durable, the law carrieth it to the lessor. But after again if it become a sear and a dotard, and its solid parts grow putrified, and as the poet saith, *non jam mater alit tellus viresque ministrat*, then the law returns it back to the lessee. This is true justice, this is *suum cuique tribuere;* the law guiding all things with line of measure and proportion.

And therefore that interest of the lessee in the tree, which the books call a special property, is scarce worth that name. He shall have the shade, so shall he have the shade of a rock; but he shall not have a crystal or Bristol diamond growing upon the rock. He shall have the pannage; why? that is the fruit of the inheritance of a tree, as herb or grass is of the soil. He shall have seasonable loppings; why? so he shall have seasonable diggings of an open mine. So all these things are rather profits of the tree, than any special property in the tree. But about words we will not differ.

The phrase that the lessee hath a special property in the tree, very improper; for he hath but the profits of the tree.

So as I conclude this part, that the reason and wisdom of law doth match things, as they consort, ascribing to permanent states permanent interest, and to transitory states transitory interest; and you cannot alter this order of law by fancies of clauses and liberties, as I will tell you in the proper place. And therefore the tree standing belongs clearly to the owner of the inheritance.

Now come I to my second assertion, that by the severance the ownership or property cannot be altered; but that he that had the trees as part of the inheritance before, must have it as a chattel transitory after. This is pregnant and followeth of itself, for it is the same tree still, and, as the Scripture saith, *uti arbor cadet, ita jacet.*

The owner of the whole must needs own the parts; he that owneth the cloth owneth the thread, and he that owneth an engine when it is intire, owneth the parts when it is broken; breaking cannot alter property.

Herlackenden's case.

And therefore the book in Herlackenden's case doth not stick to give it somewhat plain terms; and to say that it were an absurd thing, that the lessee which hath a particular interest in the land, should have an absolute property in that which is part of the inheritance: you would have the shadow draw the body, and the twigs draw the trunk. These are truly called absurdities. And therefore in a conclusion so plain, it shall be sufficient to vouch the authorities without enforcing the reasons.

And although the division be good, that was made by Mr. Heath, that there be four manners of severances, that is, when the lessee fells the tree, or when the lessor fells it, or when a stranger fells it, or when the act of God, a tempest, fells it; yet this division tendeth rather to explanation than to proof, and I need it not, because I do maintain that in all these cases the property is in the lessor.

Three arguments of property, damages, seisure, and power to grant.

And therefore I will use a distribution which rather presseth the proof. The question is of property. There be three arguments of property; damages, seisure, and grant: and according to these I will examine the property of the trees by the authority of books.

And first for damages.

For damages, look into the books of the law, and you shall not find the lessee shall ever recover damages, not as they are a badge of property; for the damages, which he recovereth, are of two natures, either for the special property, as they call it, or as he is chargeable over. And for this, to avoid length, I will select three books, one where the lessee shall recover treble damages, another where he shall recover but for his special property, and the third where he shall recover for the body of the tree, which is a special case, and standeth merely upon a special reason.

44 E. 3. f. 27.

The first is the book of 44 E. III. f. 27. where it is agreed, that if tenant for life be, and a disseisor commit waste, the lessee shall recover in trespass as he shall answer in waste; but that this is a kind of recovery of damages, though *per accidens*, may appear plainly.

For if the lessor die, whereby his action is gone, then the disseisor is likewise discharged, otherwise than for the special property.

The second book is 9 E. IV. f. 35. where it is admitted, that if the lessor himself cut down the tree, the lessee shall recover but for his special profit of shade, pannage, loppings, because he is not charged over. 9 E. 4. f. 35.

The third is 44 E. III. f. 44. where it is said, that if the lessee fell trees to repair the barn, which is not ruinous in his own default, and the lessor come and take them away, he shall have trespass, and in that case he shall recover for the very body of the tree, for he hath an absolute property in them for that intent. 44 E. 3. f. 44.

And that it is only for that intent appeareth notably by the book 38 *Ass.* f. 1. If the lessee after he hath cut down the tree employ it not to reparations, but employ other trees of better value, yet it is waste; which showeth plainly the property is respective to the employment. 38 Ass. f. 1.

Nay, 5 E. IV. f. 100. goeth farther and showeth, that the special property which the lessee had was of the living tree, and determines, as Herlackenden's case saith, by severance; for then *magis dignum trahit ad se minus dignum:* for it saith, that the lessee cannot pay the workmen's wages with those parts of the tree which are not timber. And so I leave the first demonstration of property, which is by damages; except you will add the case of 27 H. VIII. f. 13. where it is said, that if tenant for life, and he in the reversion join in a lease for years, and lessee for years fell timber trees, they shall join in an action of waste; but he in the reversion shall recover the whole damages: and great reason, for the special property was in the lessee for years, the general in him in the reversion, so the tenant for life meane had neither the one nor the other. 5 E. 4. f. 100. 27 H. 8. f. 13.

Now for the seisure, you may not look for plentiful authority in that: for the lessor, which had the more beneficial remedy by action for treble damages, had little reason to resort to the weaker remedy by seisure, and leases without impeachment were then rare, as I will tell you anon. And therefore the question of the seisure came chiefly in experience upon the case of the windfalls, which could not be punished by action of waste.

First, therefore, the case of 40 E. III. pl. 22. is express, where at the King's suit, in the behalf of the heir of Darcy, who was in ward, the King's lessee was questioned in waste, and justified the taking of the trees, because they 40 E. 3 pl. 22.

were overthrown by winds, and taken away by a stranger. But Knevet saith, although one be guardian, yet the trees, when by their fall they are severed from the freehold, he hath no property of the chattels, but they appertain to the heir, and the heir shall have trespass of them against a stranger, and not the guardian, no more than the bailiff of a manor. So that that book rules the interest of the tree to be in the heir, and goes to a point farther, that he shall have trespass for them; but of seisure there had been no question.

2 H. 7. f. 14. So again in 2 H. VII. the words of Brian are, that for the timber-trees the lessor may take them; for they are his; and seemeth to take some difference between them and the gravel.

34 E. 3. f. 5. The like reason is of the timber of an house, as appears 34 E. III. f. 5. abridged by Brook, tit. *waste*, pl. 34. when it is said, it was doubted who should have the timber of a house which fell by tempest; and saith the book, it seems it doth appertain to the lessor; and good reason, for it is no waste, and the lessee is not bound to reedify it: and therefore it is reason the lessor have it; but Herlackenden's case goes farther, where it is said that the lessee may help himself with the timber, if he will reedify it; but clearly he hath no interest but towards a special employment.

Now you have had a case of the timber-tree, and of the timber of the house, now take a case of the mine, where 9 E. 4. f. 35. that of the trees is likewise put, and that is 9 E. IV. f. 35. where it is said by Needham, that if a lease be made of land wherein there is tin, or iron, or lead, or coals, or quarry, and the lessor enter and take the tin or other materials, the lessee shall punish him for coming upon his land, but not for taking of the substances. And so of great trees; but Danby goes farther, and saith, the law that gives him the thing, doth likewise give him means to come by it; but they both agree that the interest is in the lessor. And thus much for the seisure.

For the grant; it is not so certain a badge of property as the other two; for a man may have a property, and yet not grantable, because it is turned into a right, or otherwise suspended. And therefore it is true, that by the book in 21 H. VI. that if the lessor grant the trees, the grantee shall not take them, no not after the lease expired; because this property is but *de futuro*, expectant; but it is as plain on the other side that the lessee cannot grant them, as was resolved in two notable cases, namely, the case of Marwood and Sanders, 41 El. *in communi banco;* where it was ruled, that the tenant of the inheritance may make a feoffment with exception of timber trees: but that if lessee for life or years set over his estate with an exception of the trees, the exception is utterly void; and the like resolution was in the case between Foster and Mills plaintiff, and Spencer and Boord defendant, 28 Eliz. rot. 820. Marwood and Sanders. C. Foster and Spencer's case.

Now come we to the authorities, which have an appearance to be against, us, which are not many, and they be easily answered, not by distinguishing subtilly, but by marking the books advisedly.

1. There be two books that seem to cross the authorities touching the interest of the windfalls, 7 H. VI. and 44 E. III. f. 44, where, upon waste brought and assigned in the succision of trees, the justification is, that they were overthrown by wind, and so the lessee took them for fuel, and allowed for a good plea; but these books are reconciled two ways: first, look into both the justifications, and you shall find that the plea did not rely only in that they were windfalls, but couples it with this, that they were first sear, and then overthrown by wind; and that makes an end of it, for sear trees belong to the lessee, standing or felled, and you have a special replication in the book of 44 E. III. that the wind did but rend them, and buckle them, and that they bore fruit two years after. And secondly, you have ill luck with your windfalls, for they be still apple-trees, which are but wastes *per accidens*, as willows or thorns are in the sight of a house; but when they are once felled they are clearly matter of fuel. 7 H. 6. 44 E. 3. f. 44.

Another kind of authorities, that make show against us, are those that say that the lessee shall punish the lessor in trespass for taking the trees, which are 5 H. IV. f. 29. and 1 Mar. *Dier*. f. 90, Mervin's case; and you might add if you will 9 E. IV. the case vouched before: unto which the answer is, that trespass must be understood for the special property, and not for the body of the tree; for those two books speak not a word what he shall recover, nor that it shall be to the value. And, therefore, 9 E. IV. is a good expositor, for that distinguisheth where the other two books speak indefinitely; yea, but 5 H. IV. goes farther, and saith, that the writ shall purport *arbores suas*, which is true in respect of the special property; neither are writs to be varied according to special cases, but are framed to the general case, as upon lands recovered in value in tail, the writ shall suppose *donum*, a gift. 5 H. 4. f. 29. 1 Ma. f. 90.

And the third kind of authority is some books, as 13 13 H. 7. f. 9

H. VII. f. 9, that say, that trespass lies not by the lessor against the lessee for cutting down trees, but only waste; but that it is to be understood of trespass *vi et armis*, and would have come fitly in question if there had been no seisure in this case.

Upon all which I conclude, that the whole current of authorities proveth the properties of the trees upon severance to be in the lessor by the rules of the common law; and that although the common law would not so far protect the folly of the lessor, as to give him remedy by action, where the state was created by his own act, yet the law never took from him his property; so that, as to the property, before the statute and since, the law was ever one.

Now come I to the third assertion, that the statute of Gloucester hath not transferred the property of the lessee upon an intendment of recompense to the lessor; which needs no long speech: it is grounded upon a probable reason, and upon one special book.

The reason is, that damages are a recompense for property; and, therefore, that the statute of Gloucester giving damages should exclude property. The authority seems
12 E. 4. f. 8. to be 12 E. IV. f. 8, where Catesbey, affirming that the lessee at will shall have the great trees, as well as lessee for years or life; Fairfax and Jennings correct it with a difference, that the lessor may take them in the case of tenant at will, because he hath no remedy by the statute, but not in case of the termors.

This conceit may be reasonable thus far, that the lessee shall not both seise and bring waste; but if he seise, he shall not have his action; if he recover by action, he shall not seise: for a man shall not have both the thing and recompense; it is a bar to the highest inheritance, the kingdom of heaven, *receperunt mercedem suam.* But at the first, it is at his election whether remedy he will use, like as in the case of trespass: where if a man once recover in damages, it hath concluded and turned the property. Nay, I invert the argument upon the force of the statute of Gloucester thus: that if there had been no property at common law, yet the statute of Gloucester, by restraining the waste, and giving an action, doth imply a property: whereto a better case cannot be put than the case upon the statute *de donis conditionalibus*, where there are no words to give any reversion or remainder; and yet the statute giving a *formedon*, where it lay not before, being but an action, implies an actual reversion and remainder.

A statute giving Thus have I passed over the first main part, which I have insisted upon the longer, because I shall have use of it for the clearing of the second. an action implieth an interest.

Now to come to the force of the clause *absque impetitione vasti*. This clause must of necessity work in one of these degrees, either by way of grant of property, or by way of power and liberty knit to the state, or by way of discharge of action; whereof the first two I reject, the last I receive.

Therefore I think the other side will not affirm that this clause amounts to a grant of trees; for then, according to the resolution in Herlackenden's case, they should go to the executors, and the lessee might grant them over, and they might be taken after the state determined. Now it is plain that this liberty is created with the estate, passeth with the estate, and determines with the estate. No grant of property.

That appears by 5 Hen. V. where it is said, that if lessee for years without impeachment of waste accept a confirmation for life, the privilege is gone. 5 H. 5.

And so are the books in 3 E. III. and 28 H. VIII. that if a lease be made without impeachment of waste *pour autre vie*, the remainder to the lessee for life, the privilege is gone, because he is in of another estate; so then plainly it amounts to no grant of property, neither can it any ways touch the property, nor enlarge the special property of the lessee: for will any man say, that if you put Marwood and Sanders's case of a lease without impeachment of waste, that he may grant the land with the exception of the trees any more than an ordinary lessee? Or shall the windfalls be more his in this case than in the other? for he was not impeachable of waste for windfalls no more than where he hath the clause. Or will any man say, that if a stranger commit waste, such a lessee may seise? These things, I suppose, no man will affirm. Again, why should not a liberty or privilege in law be as strong as a privilege in fact? as in the case of tenant after possibility: or where there is a lessee for life the remainder for life? for in these cases they are privileged from waste, and yet that trenches not the property. 3 E. 3. 28 H. 8.

Now, therefore, to take the second course, that it should be as a real power annexed to the state; neither can that be, for it is the law that mouldeth estates, and not men's fancies. And therefore if men by clauses, like voluntaries in music, run not upon the grounds of law, and do restrain an estate more than the law restrains it, or enable an estate more than the law enables it, or guide an estate otherwise than the law guides it, they be mere repugnancies and vanities. And therefore, if I make a feoffment in fee, provided the feoffee shall not fell timber, the clause of condition is void. And so on the other side, if I make a lease with a power that he shall fell timber, it is void.

So if I make a lease with a power that he may make feoffment, or that he may make leases for forty years, or that if he make default I shall not be received, or that the lessee may do homage; these are plainly void, as against law, and repugnant to the state. No, this cannot be done by way of use, except the words be apt, as in Mildmay's case: neither is this clause, in the sense that they take it, any better.

Therefore, laying aside these two constructions, whereof the one is not maintained to be, the other cannot be: let us come to the true sense of this clause, which is by way of discharge of the action, and no more: wherein I will speak first of the words, then of the reason, then of the authorities which prove our sense, then of the practice, which is pretended to prove theirs; and, lastly, I will weigh the mischief how it stands for our construction or theirs.

It is an ignorant mistaking of any man to take impeachment for *impedimentum*, and not for *impetitio;* for it is true that *impedimentum* doth extend to all hindrances, or disturbances, or interruptions, as well in *pais* as judicial. But *impetitio* is merely a judicial claim or interruption by suit in law, and upon the matter all one with *implacitatio*. Wherein first we may take light of the derivation of *impetitio*, which is a compound of the preposition *in* and the verb *peto*, whereof the verb *peto* itself doth signify a demand, but yet properly such a demand as is not *extrajudicial:* for the words *petit judicium petit auditum brevis*, &c. are words of acts judicial; as for the demand in *pais*, it is rather *requisitio* than *petitio*, as *licet sæpius requisitus;* so much for the verb *peto*. But the preposition *in* enforceth it more, which signifies against: as *Cicero in Verrem, in Catilinam;* and so in composition, to inveigh, is to speak against; so it is such a demand only where there is a party raised to demand against, that is an adversary, which must be in a suit in law; and so it is used in records of law.

As Coke, lib. 1. f. 17, Porter's case, it was pleaded in bar, that *dicta domina regina nunc ipsos Johannem et Henricum Porter petere seu occasionare non debet*, that is, *implacitare.*

So likewise Coke l. 1. f. 27, case of Alton Woods, *quod dicta domina regina nunc ipsum proinde aliqualiter impetere seu occasionare non debet.*

So in the book of entries, f. I. *lit.* D. 15 H. VII. rot. 2, *inter placita regis, et super hoc venit W. B. commonachus abbatis W. loci illius ordinarii, gerensque vices ipsius abbatis, ad quoscunque clericos de quolibet crimine coram domino rege impetitos sive irritatos calumniand'.* So much *ex vi et usu termini.*

For reason: first, it ought to be considered that the punishment of waste is strict and severe, because the penalty is great, treble damages, and the place wasted: and again, because the lessee must undertake for the acts of strangers; whereupon I infer, that the reason which brought this clause in use, *ab initio*, was caution to save, and to free men from the extremity of the penalty, and not any intention to countermand the property.

Add to this, that the law doth assign in most cases double remedy, by matter of suit, and matter in pais; for disseisins, actions and entries; for trespasses, action and seisure; for nuisances, action and abatement: and, as Littleton doth instruct us, one of these remedies may be released without touching the other. If the disseisee release all actions, saith Littleton, yet my entry remains; but if I release all demands or remedies, or the like words of a general nature, it doth release the right itself. And, therefore, I may be of opinion, that if there be a clause of grant in my lease expressed, that if my lessee or his assigns cut down and take away any timber-trees, that I and my heirs will not charge them by action, claim, seisure, or other interruption, either this shall inure by way of covenant only, or if you take it to inure by way of absolute discharge, it amounts to a grant of property in the trees, like as the case of 31 *Assis.* I grant, that if I pay not you ten pounds per annum at such feasts, you shall distrain for it in my manor of Dale, though this sound executory in power, yet it amounts to a present grant of a rent. So as I conclude that the discharge of action the law knows, grant of the property the law knows, but this same mathematical power being a power amounting to a property, and yet no property, and knit to a state that cannot bear it, the law knoweth not, *tertium penitus ignoramus.*

31 *Assis.* A clause that sounds to a power amounts to a property, if the state bear it.

For the authorities, they are of three kinds, two by inference, and the third direct.

The first I do collect upon the books of 42 Edw. III. fol. 23 and 24, by the difference taken by Mowbray, and agreed by the court, that the law doth intend the clause of disimpeachment of waste to be a discharge special, and not general or absolute; for there the principal case was, that there was a clause in the lease, that the lessor should not demand any right, claim, or challenge in the lands during

42 E. 3. f. 23, 24.

the life of the lessee. It is resolved by the book, that it is no bar in waste; but that if the clause had been, that the lessee should not have been impeached for waste, clearly a good bar; which demonstrates plainly, that general words, be they never so loud and strong, bear no more than the state will bear, and to any other purpose are idle. But special words that inure by way of discharge of action, are good and allowed by law.

4 E. 2. Fitzh. tit. waste 15. 17 E. 3. f. 7. Fitzh. tit. waste 101.

The same reason is of the books 4 Ed. II. Fitzh. tit. waste 15, and 17 E. III. f. 7. Fitzh. tit. waste 101, where there was a clause, *Quod liceat facere commodum suum meliori modo quo poterit.* Yet, saith Skipwith, doth this amount, that he shall, for the making of his own profit, disinherit the lessor? *Nego consequentiam;* so that still the law allows not of the general discharge, but of the special that goeth to the action.

9 H. 6. f. 35. Fitzh. tit. waste 39. 32 H. 8. Dyer, f. 47.

The second authority by inference is out of 9 H. VI. fol. 35. Fitzh. tit. waste 39, and 32 H. VIII. Dyer, fol. 47, where the learning is taken, that notwithstanding this clause be inserted into a lease, yet a man may reserve unto himself remedy by entry: but say I, if this clause should have that sense, which they on the other side would give it, namely, that it should amount to an absolute privilege and power of disposing, then were the proviso flat repugnant, all one as if it were *absque impetitione vasti, proviso quod non faciet vastum;* which are contradictories: and note well that in the book of 9 H. VI. the proviso is *quod non faceat vastum voluntarium in domibus;* which indeed doth but abridge in one kind, and therefore may stand without repugnancy: but in the latter book it is general, that is to say, *absque impetitione vasti, et si contigerit ipsum facere vastum tunc licebit reintrare.* And there Shelley making the objection, that the condition was repugnant, it is salved thus, *sed aliqui tenuerunt,* that this word *impetitione vasti* is to be understood that he shall not be impleaded by waste, or punished by action; and so indeed it ought: those *aliqui recte tenuerunt.*

27 H. 6. Fitzh. tit. waste 8.

For the authorities direct, they are two, the one 27 H. VI. Fitzh. tit. waste 8, where a lease was made without impeachment of waste, and a stranger committed waste, and the rule is, that the lessee shall recover in trespass only for the crop of the tree, and not for the body of the tree. It is true it comes by a *dicitur,* but it is now a *legitur;* and a query there is, and reason, or else this long speech were time ill spent.

And the last authority is the case of Sir Moyle Finch,

and his mother, referred to my Lord Wrey and Sir Roger Manwood, resolved upon conference with other of the judges vouched by Wrey in Herlackenden's case, and reported to my Lord Chief Justice here present, as a resolution of law, being our very case.

And for the cases to the contrary, I know not one in all the law direct; they press the statute of Marlebridge, which hath an exception in the prohibition, *firmarii non facient vastum, etc. nisi specialem inde habuerint concessionem per scriptum conventionis, mentionem faciens, quod hoc facere possint.* This presseth not the question; for no man doubteth, but it will excuse in an action of waste; and again, *nisi habeant specialem concessionem* may be meant of an absolute grant of the trees themselves; and otherwise the clause *absque impetitione vasti* taketh away the force of the statute, and looseth what the statute bindeth; but it toucheth not the property at common law. Statute, &c. Marlebridge.

For Littleton's case, in his title Of Conditions, where it is said, that if a feoffment in fee be made upon condition, that the feoffee shall infeoff the husband and wife, and the heirs of their two bodies; and that the husband die, that now the feoffee ought to make a lease without impeachment of waste to the wife, the remainder to the right heirs of the body of her husband and her begotten; whereby it would be inferred, that such a lessee should have equal privilege with tenant in tail: the answer appears in Littleton's own words, which is, that the feoffee ought to go as near the condition, and as near the intent of the condition as he may. But to come near is not to reach, neither doth Littleton undertake for that. Littleton.

As for Culpepper's case, it is obscurely put, and concluded in division of opinion; but yet so as it rather makes for us. The case is 2 Eliz. Dyer, fol. 184, and is in effect this: a man makes a lease for years, excepting timber-trees, and afterwards makes a lease without impeachment of waste to John a Style, and then granteth the land and trees to John a Down, and binds himself to warrant and save harmless John a Down against John a Style; John a Style cutteth down the trees; the question was, whether the bond were forfeited? and that question resorteth to the other question: whether John a Style, by virtue of such lease, could fell the trees? and held by Weston and Brown that he could not: which proves plainly for us, that he had no property by that clause in the tree; though it is true that in that case the exception of the trees turneth the case, and so in effect it proveth neither way. Culpepper's case. 2 Eliz. Dyer, f. 184.

Practice. For the practice, if it were so ancient and common, as is conceived; yet since the authorities have not approved, but condemned it, it is no better than a popular error: it is but *pedum visa est via,* not *recta visa est via.* But I conceive it to be neither ancient nor common. It is true I find it first in 19 E. II. I mean such a clause, but it is one thing to say that the clause is ancient; and it is another thing to say, that this exposition, which they would now introduce, is ancient. And therefore you must note that a practice doth then expound the law, when the act, which is practised, were merely tortuous or void, if the law should not approve it; but that is not the case here, for we agree the clause to be lawful; nay, we say that it is in no sort inutile, but there is use of it, to avoid this severe penalty of treble damages. But to speak plainly, I will tell you how this clause came in from 13 of E. I. till about 12 of E. IV. The state tail, though it had the qualities of an inheritance, yet it was without power to alien; but as soon as that was set at liberty, by common recoveries, then there must be found some other device, that a man might be an absolute owner of the land for the time, and yet not enabled to alien, and for that purpose was this clause found out; for you shall not find in one amongst a hundred, that farmers had it in their leases; but those that were once owners of the inheritance, and had put it over to their sons or next heirs, reserved such a beneficial state to themselves. And therefore the truth is, that the flood of this usage came in with perpetuities, save that the perpetuity was to make an inheritance like a stem for life, and this was to make a stem for life like an inheritance; both concurring in this, that they presume to create phantastical estates, contrary to the ground of law.

And, therefore, it is no matter though it went out with the perpetuities, as it came in, to the end that men that have not the inheritance should not have power to abuse the inheritance.

And for the mischief, and consideration of *bonum publicum,* certainly this clause with this opposition tendeth but to make houses ruinous, and to leave no timber upon the ground to build them up again; and therefore let men, in God's name, when they establish their states, and plant their sons or kinsmen in the inheritance of some portions of their lands, with reservation of the freehold to themselves, use it, and enjoy it in such sort, as may tend *ad ædificationem,* and not *ad destructionem;* for that it is good for posterity, and for the state in general.

And for the timber of this realm, it is *vivus thesaurus regni;* and it is the matter of our walls, walls not only of our houses, but of our island; so as it is a general disinherison to the kingdom to favour that exposition, which tends to the decay of it, being so great already; and to favour waste when the times themselves are set upon waste and spoil. Therefore since the reason and authorities of law, and the policy of estate do meet, and that those that have, or shall have such conveyances, may enjoy the benefit of that clause to protect them in a moderate manner, that is, from the penalty of the action; it is both good law and good policy for the kingdom, and not injurious or inconvenient for particulars, to take this clause strictly, and therein to affirm the last report. And so I pray judgment for the plaintiff.

THE

ARGUMENT

IN

LOW'S CASE OF TENURES

IN THE KING'S BENCH.

THE manor of Alderwasley, parcel of the duchy, and lying out of the county palatine, was, before the duchy came to the crown, held of the king by knight's service in capite. The land in question was held of the said manor in soccage. The duchy and this manor parcel thereof descended to King Henry IV. King Henry VIII. by letters patent the 19th of his reign, granted this manor to Anthony Low, grandfather of the ward, and then tenant of the land in question, reserving twenty-six pounds ten shillings rent and fealty, *tantum pro omnibus servitiis,* and this patent is under the duchy-seal only. The question is, how this tenancy is held, whether in capite or in soccage.

The case resteth upon a point, unto which all the questions arising are to be reduced.

The first is, whether this tenancy, being by the grant of the king of the manor to the tenant grown to a unity of possession with the manor, be held as the manor is held, which is expressed in the patent to be in soccage.

The second, whether the manor itself be held in soccage according to the last reservation, or in capite by revivor of the ancient seigniory, which was in capite before the duchy came to the crown.

Therefore my first proposition is, that this tenancy, which without all colour is no parcel of the manor, cannot be comprehended within the tenure reserved upon the manor, but that the law createth a several and distinct tenure thereupon, and that not guided according to the express tenure of the manor, but merely *secundum normam legis*, by the intendment and rule of law, which must be a tenure by knight's service in capite.

The king's tenures may take more hurt by a resolution in law, than by many suppressions or concealments.

And my second proposition is, that admitting that the tenure of the tenancy should ensue the tenure of the manor, yet, nevertheless, the manor itself, which was first held of the crown in capite, the tenure suspended by the conquest of the duchy to the crown, being now conveyed out of the crown under the duchy-seal only, which hath no power to touch or carry any interest, whereof the king was vested in right of the crown, is now so severed and disjoined from the ancient seigniory, which was in capite, as the same ancient seigniory is revived, and so the new reservation void; because the manor cannot be charged with two tenures.

This case concerneth one of the greatest and fairest flowers of the crown, which is the king's tenures, and that in their creation; which is more than their preservation: for if the rules and maxims of law in the first raising of tenures in capite be weakened, this nips the flower in the bud, and may do more hurt by a resolution in law, than the losses which the king's tenures do daily receive by oblivion or suppression, or the neglect of officers, or the iniquity of jurors, or other like blasts, whereby they are continually shaken: and therefore it behoveth us of the king's council to have a special care of this case, as much as in us is, to give satisfaction to the court. Therefore, before I come to argue these two points particularly, I will speak something of the favour of law towards tenures in capite, as that which will give a force and edge to all that I shall speak afterwards.

No land in the

The constitution of this kingdom appeareth to be a free

monarchy in nothing better than in this: that as there is no land of the subject that is charged to the crown by way of tribute, or tax, or talliage, except it be set by parliament: so on the other side there is no land of the subject but is charged to the crown by tenure, mediate or immediate, and that by the grounds of the common law. This is the excellent temper and commixture of this estate, bearing marks of the sovereignty of the king, and of the freedom of the subject from tax, whose possessions are *feodalia*, not *tributaria*.

kingdom of England charged by way of tribute, and all land charged by way of tenure.

Tenures, according to the most general division, are of two natures, the one containing matter of protection, and the other matter of profit; that of protection is likewise double, divine protection and military. The divine protection is chiefly procured by the prayers of holy and devout men; and great pity it is that it was depraved and corrupted with superstition: This begot the tenure in frankalmoigne, which though in burden it is less than in soccage, yet in virtue it is more than knight's service. For we read how, during the while Moses in the mount held up his hands, the Hebrews prevailed in battle; as well as when Elias prayed, rain came after drought, which made the plough go; so that I hold the tenure in frankalmoigne in the first institution indifferent to knight's service and soccage. Setting apart this tenure, there remain the other two, that of knight's service, and that of soccage; the one tending chiefly to defence and protection, the other to profit and maintenance of life. They are all three comprehended in the ancient verse, *Tu semper ora, tu protege, tuque labora.* But between these two services, knight's service and soccage, the law of England makes a great difference: for this kingdom, my lords, is a state neither effeminate nor merchantlike; but the laws give the honour unto arms and military service, like the laws of a nation before whom Julius Cæsar turned his back, as their own prophet says; *Territa quæsitis ostendit terga Britannis.* And therefore howsoever men, upon husbandlike considerations of profit, esteem of soccage tenures; yet the law, that looketh to the greatness of the kingdom, and proceedeth upon considerations of estate, giveth the preeminence altogether to knight's service.

We see that the ward, who is ward for knight's service land, is accounted in law disparaged, if he be tendered a marriage of the burghers parentage: and we see that the knight's fees were by the ancient laws the materials of all nobility; for that it appears by divers records how many knight's fees should by computation go to a barony, and so to an earldom. Nay, we see that, in the very summons of parliament, the knights of the shire are required to be chosen *milites gladio cincti;* so as the very call though it were to council bears a mark of arms and habiliments of war. To conclude, the whole composition of this warlike nation, and the favours of law, tend to the advancement of military virtue and service.

But now farther, amongst the tenures by knight's service, that of the king in capite is the most high and worthy; and the reason is double; partly because it is held of the king's crown and person, and partly because the law createth such a privity between the line of the crown and the inheritors of such tenancies, as there cannot be an alienation without the king's license, the penalty of which alienation was by the common law the forfeiture of the state itself, and by the statute of E. III. is reduced to fine and seisure. And although this also has been unworthily termed by the vulgar, not capite, captivity and thraldom; yet that which they count bondage, the law counteth honour, like to the case of tenants in tail of the king's advancement, which is a great restraint by the statute of 34 H. VIII. but yet by that statute it is imputed for an honour. This favour of law to the tenure by knight's service in capite produceth this effect, that wheresoever there is no express service effectually limited, or wheresoever that, which was once limited, faileth, the law evermore supplieth a tenure by knight's service in capite; if it be a blank once—that the law must fill it up, the law ever with her own hand writes, tenure by knight's service in capite. And therefore the resolution

44 E. 3. f. 45. was notable by the judges of both benches, that where the king confirmed to his farmers' tenants for life, *tenend' per servitia debita,* this was a tenure in capite; for other services are *servitia requisita,* required by the words of patents or grants; but that only is *servitium debitum,* by the rules of law.

The course, therefore, that I will hold in the proof of the first main point, shall be this. First, I will show, maintain, and fortify my former grounds, that wheresoever the law createth the tenure of the king, the law hath no variety, but always raises a tenure in capite.

Secondly, that in the case present, there is not any such tenure expressed, as can take place, and exclude the tenure in law, but that there is as it were a lapse to the law.

And, lastly, I will show in what cases the former general rule receiveth some show of exception; and will show the difference between them and our case; wherein I shall include an answer to all that hath been said on the other side.

For my first proposition I will divide into four branches; first, I say, where there is no tenure reserved, the law createth a tenure in capite; secondly, where the tenure is uncertain; thirdly, where the tenure reserved is impossible or repugnant to law; and, lastly, where a tenure once created is afterwards extinct.

For the first, if the king give lands and say nothing of the tenure, this is a tenure in capite; nay, if the king give whiteacre and blackacre, and reserves a tenure only of whiteacre, and that a tenure expressed to be in soccage; yet you shall not for fellowship-sake, because they are in one patent, intend the like tenure of blackacre; but that shall be held in capite. *Per Prisot in fine*, 33 H. 6. f. 7. 8 H. 7. f. 3. b.

So if the king grant land, held as of a manor, with warranty, and a special clause of recompense, and the tenant be impleaded, and recover in value, this land shall be held in capite, and not of the manor.

So if the king exchange the manor of Dale for the manor of Sale, which is held in soccage, although it be by the word *excambium*, yet that goeth to equality of the state, not of the tenure, and the manor of Dale, if no tenure be expressed, shall be held in capite. So much for silence of tenure.

For the second branch, which is incertainty of tenure; first, where an *ignoramus* is found by office, this, by the common law, is a tenure in capite, which is most for the king's benefit; and the presumption of law is so strong, that it amounts to a direct finding or affirmative, and the party shall have a negative or traverse, which is somewhat strange to a thing indefinite. 5 Mar. Dyer, 14. Eliz. Dyer, 306.

So if in ancient time one held of the king, as of a manor by knight's service, and the land return to the king by attainder, and then the king granteth it *tenend' per fidelitatem tantum*, and it returneth the second time to the king, and the king granteth it *per servitia antehac consueta*; now because of the incertainty neither service shall take place, and the tenure shall be in capite, as was the opinion of you, my lord chief justice, where you were commissioner to find an office after Austin's death. Austin's office.

So if the king grant land *tenend' de manerio de* East Greenwich *vel de honore de* Hampton, this is void for the non-certainty, and shall be held of the king in capite.

33 H. 6. f. 7. For the third branch, if the king limit land to be discharged of tenure, as *absque aliquo inde reddendo*, this is a tenure in capite; and yet if one should go to the next, *ad proximum*, it should be a soccage, for the least is next to none at all; but you may not take the king's grant by argument; but where they cannot take place effectually and punctually, as they are expressed, there you shall resort wholly to the judgment of the law.

14 H. 6. f. 12. So if the king grant land *tenend' si frankment come il en son corone*, this is a tenure in capite.

Merefeild's case. If land be given to be held of a lordship not capable, as of Salisbury Plain, or a corporation not in esse, or of the manor of a subject, this is a tenure in capite.

So if land be given to hold by impossible service, as by performing the office of the sheriff of Yorkshire, which no man can do but the sheriff, and fealty for all service, this is a tenure in capite.

For the fourth branch, which cometh nearest to our case; let us see where a seigniory was once, and is after extinguished; this may be in two manners, by release in fact, or by unity of profession, which is a release or discharge in law.

Vide 30 H. 8. Dyer 8. H. 7. f. 13. And therefore let the case be, that the king releaseth to his tenant that holds of him in soccage; this release is good, and the tenant shall now hold in capite, for the former tenure being discharged, the tenure in law ariseth.

1 E. 3. f. 4. fine accept. So the case, which is in 1 E. III. a fine is levied to J. S. in tail, the remainder ouster to the king, the state tail shall be held in capite, and the first tenancy, if it were in soccage, by the unity of the tenancy, shall be discharged, and a new raised thereupon: and therefore the opinion, or rather the *query* in Dyer no law.

4 et. 5. P. M. Thus much for my major proposition: now for the minor, or the assumption, it is this: first, that the land in question is discharged of tenure by the purchase of the manor; then that the reservation of the service upon the manor cannot possibly inure to the tenancy; and then if a corruption be of the first tenure, and no generation of the new, then cometh in the tenure *per norman legis*, which is in capite.

And the course of my proof shall be *ab enumeratione partium*, which is one of the clearest and most forcible kinds of argument.

If this parcel of land be held by fealty and rent *tantum*, either it is the old fealty before the purchase of the manor, or it is the new fealty reserved and expressed upon the grant of the manor, or it is a new fealty raised by intendment of law in conformity and congruity of the fealty reserved upon the manor; but none of these, *ergo*, &c.

That it should be the old fealty, is void of sense; for it is not *ad eosdem terminos.* The first fealty was between the tenancy and the manor, that tenure is by the unity extinct. Secondly, that was a tenure of a manor, this is a tenure in gross. Thirdly, the rent of twenty-six pounds ten shillings must needs be new, and will you have a new rent with an old fealty? These things are *portenta in lege;* nay, I demand if the tenure of the tenancy, Low's tenure, had been by knight's service, would you have said that had remained? No, but that it was altered by the new reservation; *ergo*, no colour of the old fealty.

That it cannot be the new fealty is also manifest; for the new reservation is upon the manor, and this is no part of the manor: for if it had escheated to the king in an ordinary escheat, or come to him upon a mortmain, in these cases it had come in lieu of the seigniory, and been parcel of the manor, and so within the reservation, but clearly not upon a purchase in fact.

Again, the reservation cannot inure, but upon that which is granted; and this tenancy was never granted, but was in the tenant before; and therefore no colour it should come under the reservation. But if it be said, that nevertheless the seigniory of that tenancy was parcel of the manor, and is also granted; and although it be extinct in substance, yet it may be in esse as to the king's service: this deserveth answer: for this assertion may be colourably inferred out of Carr's case. 9 Eliz. Coke, Lib. 3. f. 30.

King Edward VI. grants a manor, rendering ninety-four pounds rent in fee farm *tenendum de* East Greenwich in soccage; and after, Queen Mary granteth these rents amongst other things *tenendum in capite*, and the grantee released to the heir of the tenant; yet the rent shall be in esse, as to the king, but the land, saith the book, shall be deviseable by the statute for the whole, as not held in capite.

And so the case of the honour of Pickeringe, where the king granted the bailywick rendering rent; and after granted the honour, and the bailywick became forfeited, and the grantee took forfeiture thereof, whereby it was extinct; yet the rent remaineth as to the king out of the bailywick extinct. 25 Ass. pl. 60.

These two cases partly make not against us, and partly

make for us: there be two differences that avoid them. First, there the tenures or rents are in esse in those cases for the king's benefit, and here they should be in esse to the king's prejudice, who should otherwise have a more beneficial tenure. Again, in these cases the first reservation was of a thing in esse at the time of the reservation; and then there is no reason the act subsequent of the king's tenant should prejudice the king's interest once vested and settled: but here the reservation was never good, because it is out of a thing extinct in the instant.

But the plain reason which turneth Carr's case mainly for us is: for that where the tenure is of a rent or seigniory, which is afterwards drowned or extinct in the land, yet the law judgeth the same rent or seigniory to be in esse, as to support the tenure: but of what? only of the said rent or seigniory, and never of the land itself; for the land shall be held by the same tenure it was before. And so is the rule of Carr's case, where it is adjudged, that though the rent be held in capite, yet the land was nevertheless deviseable for the whole, as no ways charged with that tenure.

Why then, in our case, let the fealty be reserved out of the seigniory extinct, yet that toucheth not at all the land: and then of necessity the land must be also held; and therefore you must seek out a new tenure for the land, and that must be in capite.

And let this be noted once for all, that our case is not like the common cases of a menalty extinct, where the tenant shall hold of the lord, as the mean held before; as where the menalty is granted to the tenant, or where the tenancy is granted to the mean, or where the menalty descendeth to the tenant, or where the menalty is forejudged. In all these cases the tenancy, I grant, is held as the menalty was held before, and the difference is because there was an old seigniory in being; which remaineth untouched and unaltered, save that it is drawn a degree nearer to the land, so as there is no question in the world of a new tenure; but in our case there was no lord paramount, for the manor itself was in the crown, and not held at all, nor no seigniory of the manor in esse; so as the question is wholly upon the creation of a new seigniory, and not upon the continuance of an old.

For the third course, that the law should create a new distinct tenure by fealty of this parcel, guided by the express tenure upon the manor; it is the probablest course of the three: but yet, if the former authorities I have alleged be well understood and marked, they show the law plainly, that it cannot be; for you shall ever take the king's grant *ad idem*, and not *ad simile*, or *ad proximum*, no more than in the case of the *absque aliquo reddendo*, or as free as the crown; who would not say that in those cases it should amount to a soccage tenure? for *minimum est nihilo proximum:* and yet they are tenures by knight's service in capite. So if the king by one patent pass two acres, and a fealty reserved but upon the one of them, you shall not resort to this *ut expressum servitium regat, vel declaret tacitum.* No more shall you in our case imply that the express tenure reserved upon the manor shall govern, or declare the tenure of the tenancy, or control the intendment of law concerning the same.

Now will I answer the cases, which give some shadow on the contrary side, and show they have their particular reasons, and do not impugn our case.

First, if the king have land by attainder of treason, and grant the land to be held of himself, and of other lords, this is no new tenure *per normam legis communis;* but the old tenure *per normam statuti*, which taketh away the intendment of the common law; for the statute directeth it so, and otherwise the king shall do a wrong.

So if the king grant land parcel of the demesne of a manor *tenendum de nobis*, or reserving no tenure at all, this is a tenure of the manor or of the honour, and not in capite: for here the more vehement presumption controlleth the less; for the law doth presume the king hath no intent to dismember it from the manor, and so to lose his court and the perquisites.

So if the king grant land *tenendum* by a rose *pro omnibus servitiis*, this is not like the cases of the *absque aliquo inde reddendo*, or as free as the crown: for *pro omnibus servitiis* shall be intended for all express service: whereas fealty is incident, and passeth tacit, and so it is no impossible or repugnant reservation. 25 H. 6. f. 56. 9.

The case of the frankalmoigne, I mean the case where the king grants lands of the Templers to J. S. to hold as the Templers did, which cannot be frankalmoigne; and yet hath been ruled to be no tenure by knight's service in capite, but only a soccage tenure, is easily answered; for that the frankalmoigne is but a species of a tenure in soccage with a privilege, so the privilege ceaseth, and the tenure remains. This is no frankalmoigne. Wood's case.

To conclude, therefore, I sum up my arguments thus: My major is, where *calamus legis* doth write the tenure, it is knight's service in capite. My minor is, this tenure is left to the law; *ergo*, this tenure is in capite.

For the second point, I will first speak of it according to the rules of the common law, and then upon the statutes of the duchy.

First I do grant, that where a seigniory and a tenancy, or a rent and land, or trees and land, or the like primitive and secondary interest are conjoined in one person, yea, though it be in *autre droit;* yet if it be of like perdurable estate, they are so extinct, as by act in law they may be revived, but by grant they cannot.

For if a man have a seigniory in his own right, and the land descend to his wife, and his wife dieth without issue, the seigniory is revived; but if he will make a feoffment in fee, saving his rent, he cannot do it. But there is a great difference, and let it be well observed, between *autre capacitie* and *autre droit;* for in case of *autre capacitie* the interests are *contigua*, and not *continua*, conjoined, but not confounded. And, therefore, if the master of an hospital have a seigniory, and the mayor and commonalty of St. Albans have a tenancy, and the master of the hospital be made mayor, and the mayor grant away the tenancy under the seal of the mayor and commonalty, the seigniory of the hospital is revived.

So between natural capacity and politic, if a man have a seigniory to him and his heirs, and a bishop is tenant, and the lord is made bishop, and the bishop, before the statute, grants away the land under the chapter's seal, the seigniory is revived.

The same reason is between the capacity of the crown and the capacity of the duchy, which is in the king's natural capacity, though illustrated with some privileges of the crown; if the king have the seigniory in the right of his crown, and the tenancy in the right of the duchy, as our case is, and make a feoffment of the tenancy, the tenure must be revived; and this is by the ground of the common law. But the case is the more strong by reason of the statute of 1 H. IV. 3 H. V. and 1 H. VII. of the duchy, by which the duchy-seal is enabled to pass lands of the duchy, but no ways to touch the crown: and whether the king be in actual possession of the thing that should pass, or have only a right, or a condition, or a thing in suspense, as our case is, all is one; for that seal will not extinguish so much as a spark of that which is in the right of the crown; and so a plain revivor.

And if it be said that a mischief will follow, for that upon every duchy patent men shall not know how to hold, because men must go back to the ancient tenure, and not rest on the tenure limited; for this mischief there grows an easy remedy, which, likewise, is now in use, which is to take both seals, and then all is safe.

Secondly, as the king cannot under the duchy-seal grant away his ancient seigniory in the right of his crown, so he cannot make any new reservation by that seal, and so, of necessity, it falleth to the law to make the tenure; for every reservation must be of the nature of that that passeth, as a dean and chapter cannot grant land of the chapter, and reserve a rent to the dean and his heirs, nor *e converso:* nor no more can the king grant land of the duchy under that seal, and reserve a tenure to the crown: and therefore it is warily put in the end of the case of the duchy in the commentaries, where it is said, if the king make a feoffment of the duchy land, the feoffee shall hold in capite; but not a word of that it should be by way of express reservation, but upon a feoffment simply, the law shall work it and supply it.

To conclude, there is direct authority in the point, but that it is *via versa;* and it was the Bishop of Salisbury's case: the king had in the right of the duchy a rent issuing out of land, which was monastery land, which he had in the right of the crown, and granted away the land under the great seal to the bishop; and yet, nevertheless, the rent continued to the duchy, and so upon great and grave advice it was in the duchy decreed: so, as your lordship seeth, whether you take the tenure of the tenancy, or the tenure of the manor, this land must be held in capite. And therefore, &c.

THE

CASE OF REVOCATION OF USES

IN THE KING'S BENCH.

The Case shortly put, without names or dates more than of necessity, is this.

Sir John Stanhope conveys the manor of Burrough-ash to his lady for part of her jointure, and intending, as is manifest, not to restrain himself, nor his son, from disposing some proportion of that land according to their occasions, so as my lady were at no loss by the exchange, inserteth into the conveyance a power of revocation and alteration in this manner; provided that it shall be lawful for himself and his son successively to alter and make void the uses, and to limit and appoint new uses, so it exceed not the value of twenty pounds, to be computed after the rents then answered: and that immediately after such declaration, or making void, the feoffees shall stand seised to such new uses; *ita quod*, he or his son, within six months after such declaration, or making void shall assure, within the same town, *tantum terrarum et tenementorum, et similis valoris*, as were so revoked, to the uses expressed in the first conveyance.

Sir John Stanhope, his son, revokes the land in Burrough-ash, and other parcels not exceeding the value of twenty pounds, and within six months assures to my lady and to the former uses Burton-joice and other lands; and the jury have found that the lands revoked contain twice so much in number of acres, and twice so much in yearly value, as the new lands, but yet that the new lands are rented at twenty-one pounds, and find the lands of Burrough-ash now out of lease formerly made: and that no notice of this new assurance was given before the ejectment, but only that Sir John Stanhope had, by word, told his mother that such an assurance was made, not showing or delivering the deed.

The question is, Whether Burrough-ash be well revoked? Which question divides itself into three points.

First, whether the *ita quod* be a void and idle clause? for if so, then there needs no new assurance, but the revocation is absolute *per se.*

The next is, if it be an effectual clause, whether it be pursued or no? wherein the question will rest, whether the value of the reassured lands shall be only computed by rents?

And the third is, if in other points it should be well pursued, yet whether the revocation can work until a sufficient notice of the new assurance?

And I shall prove plainly, that *ita quod* stands well with the power of revocation; and if it should fall to the ground, it draws all the rest of the clause with it, and makes the whole void, and cannot be void alone by itself.

I shall prove likewise that the value must needs be accounted not a tale value, or an arithmetical value by the rent, but a true value in quantity and quality.

And lastly, that a notice is of necessity, as this case is.

I will not deny, but it is a great power of wit to make clear things doubtful; but it is the true use of wit to make doubtful things clear, or at least to maintain things that are clear to be clear, as they are. And in that kind I conceive my labour will be in this case, which I hold to be a case rather of novelty than difficulty, and therefore may require argument, but will not endure much argument, but to speak plainly to my understanding, as the case hath no equity in it, I might say piety, so it hath no great doubt in law.

First, therefore, this it is, that I affirm that the clause so that, *ita quod,* containing the recompense, governs the clause precedent of the power, and that it makes it wait and expect otherwise than as by way of inception, but the effect and operation is suspended, till that part also be performed; and if otherwise, then I say plainly, you shall not construe by fractions; but the whole clause and power is void, not *in tanto,* but *in toto.* Of the first of them I will give four reasons.

The first reason is, that the wisdom of the law useth to transpose words according to the sense; and not so much to respect how the words do take place, but how the acts, which are guided by those words, may take place.

Hill and Graunger's case comment. 171. A man in August makes a lease, rendering ten pounds rent yearly to Hill and Graunger's case, com. f. 171.

be paid at the feasts of Annunciation and Michaelmas; these words shall be inverted by law, as if they had been set thus, at Michaelmas and the Annunciation: for else he cannot have a rent yearly; for there will be fourteen months to the first year.

Fitzwilliams's case, 2 Jac. Co. p. 6. f. 33.

Fitzwilliams's case, 2 Jac. Co. p. 6. f. 33. it was contained in an indenture of uses, that Sir William Fitzwilliams should have power to alter, and change, revoke, determine, and make void the uses limited: the words are placed disorderly; for it is in nature first to determine the uses, and after to change them by limitation of new. But the chief question being in the book, whether it might be done by the same deed; it is admitted and thought not worth the speaking to, that the law shall marshal the acts against the order of the words, that is, first to make void, then to limit.

So if I convey land and covenant with you to make farther assurance, so that you require it of me, there, though the request be placed last, yet it must be acted first.

So if I let land to you for a term, and say, farther, it shall be lawful for you to take twenty timber trees to erect a new tenement upon the land, so that my bailiff do assign you where you shall take them, here the assignment, though last placed, must precede. And therefore the grammarians do infer well upon the word period, which is a full and complete clause or sentence, that it is *complexus orationis circularis:* for as in a circle there is not *prius* nor *posterius,* so in one sentence you shall not respect the placing of words; but though the words lie in length, yet the sense is round, so as *prima erunt novissima et novissima prima.* For though you cannot speak all at once so, yet you must construe and judge upon all at once.

To apply this; I say these words, so that, though *loco et textu posteriora,* yet they be *potestate et sensu priora:* as if they had been penned thus, that it shall be lawful for Sir Thomas Stanhope, so that he assure lands, &c. to revoke; and what difference between, so that he assure, he may revoke; or, he may revoke, so that he assure; for you must either make the so that to be precedent or void, as I shall tell you anon. And therefore the law will rather invert the words than pervert the sense.

But it will be said, that in the cases I put it is left indefinite, when the act last limited shall be performed; and so the law may marshal it as it may stand with possibility; and so if it had been in this case no more but, so that Sir Thomas or John should assure new lands, and no time spoken of, the law might have intended it precedent. But in this case it is precisely put to be at any time within six months after the declaration, and therefore you cannot vary in the times.

To this I answer, that the new assurance must be in deed in time after the instrument or deed of the declaration; but, on the other side, it must be time precedent to the operation of the law, by determining the uses thereupon; so as it is not to be applied so much to the declaration itself, but to the warrant of the declaration. It shall be lawful, so that, &c. And this will appear more plainly by my second reason, to which now I come; for as for the cavillation upon the word immediately, I will speak to it after.

My second reason therefore is out of the use and signification of this conjunction or bond of speech, so that: for no man will make any great doubt of it, if the words had been *si*, if Sir Thomas shall within six months of such declaration convey; but that it must have been intended precedent; yet if you mark it well, these words *ita quod* and *si*, howsoever in propriety the *ita quod* may seem subsequent, and the *si* precedent, yet they both bow to the sense.

So we see in 4 Edw. VI. Colthurst's case, a man leaseth to J. S. a house, *si ipse vellet habitare et residens esse;* there the word *si* amounts to a condition subsequent; for he could not be resident before he took the state; and so *via versa* may *ita quod* be precedent, for else it must be idle or void. But I go farther, for I say *ita quod*, though it be good words of condition, yet more properly it is neither condition, precedent, nor subsequent, but rather a qualification, or form, or adherent to the acts, whereto it is joined, and made part of their essence, which will appear evidently by other cases. For allow it had been thus, so that the deed of declaration be inrolled within six months, this is all one, as by deed inrolled within six months, as it is said in Digg's case, 42 Eliz. f. 173, that by deed indented to be inrolled is all one with deed indented and inrolled. It is but a *modus faciendi*, a description, and of the same nature is the *ita quod:* so if it had been thus, it shall be lawful for Sir Thomas to declare, so that the declaration be with the consent of my lord chief justice, is it not all one with the more compendious form of penning, that Sir Thomas shall declare with the consent of my lord chief justice? And if it had been thus, so that Sir John within six months after such declaration shall obtain the consent of my lord chief justice, should not the uses have expected? But these

4 E. 6. Pl. Com. Colthurst's case.

Digg's case, 42 Eliz. Co. P. l. f. 173.

you will say are forms and circumstances annexed to the conveyance required: why surely any collateral matter coupled by the *ita quod* is as strong? If the *ita quod* had been, that Sir John Stanhope within six months should have paid my lady one thousand pounds, or entered into bond never more to disturb her, or the like, all these make but one entire idea or notion, how that his power should not be categorical, or simple at pleasure, but hypothetical, and qualified, and restrained, that is to say, not the one without the other, and they are parts incorporated into the nature and essence of the authority itself.

The third reason is, the justice of the law in taking words so, as no material part of the parties' intent perish; for, as one saith, *præstat torquere verba quam homines,* better wrest words out of place than my Lady Stanhope out of her jointure, that was meant to her. And therefore it is elegantly said in Fitzwilliams's case, which I vouched before, though words be contradictory, and, to use the phrase of the book, *pugnant tanquam ex diametro;* yet the law delighteth to make atonement, as well between words as between parties, and will reconcile them so as they may stand, and abhorreth a *vacuum,* as well as nature abhorreth it; and as nature, to avoid a *vacuum,* will draw substances contrary to their propriety, so will the law draw words. Therefore, saith Littleton, if I make a feoffment *reddendo* rent to a stranger, this is a condition to the feoffor, rather than it shall be void, which is quite cross; it sounds a rent, it works a condition, it is limited to a third person, it inureth to the feoffor; and yet the law favoureth not conditions, but to avoid a *vacuum.*

45 E. 3. So in the case of 45 E. III. a man gives land in frank-marriage, the remainder in fee. The frank-marriage is first put, and that can be but by tenure of the donor; yet rather than the remainder should be void, though it be last placed, the frank-marriage, being but a privilege of estate, shall be destroyed.

So 33 H. VI. Tressham's case; the king granteth a ward-ship, before it fall; good, because it cannot inure by covenant, and if it should not be good by plea, as the book terms it, it were void; so that, no, not in the king's case, the law will not admit words to be void.

So then the intent appears most plainly, that this act of Sir John should be *actus geminus,* a kind of twine to take back, and to give back, and to make an exchange, and not a resumption; and therefore upon a conceit of repugnancy, to take the one part, which is the privation of my lady's jointure, and not the other, which is the restitution or compensation, were a thing utterly injurious in matter, and absurd in construction.

The fourth reason is out of the nature of the conveyance, which is by way of use, and therefore ought to be construed more favourably according to the intent, and not literally or strictly; for although it be said in Frene and Dillon's case, and in Fitzwilliams's case, that it is safe so to construe the statute of 27 H. VIII. as that uses may be made subject to the rules of the common law, which the professors of the law do know, and not leave them to be extravagant and irregular; yet if the late authorities be well marked, and the reason of them, you shall find this difference, that uses in point of operation are reduced to a kind of conformity with the rules of the common law, but that in point of exposition of words they retain somewhat of their ancient nature, and are expounded more liberally according to the intent; for with that part the statute of 27 doth not meddle. And therefore if the question be, whether a bargain and sale upon condition be good to reduce the state back without an entry? or whether, if a man make a feoffment in fee to the use of John a Style for years, the remainder to the right heirs of John a Downe, this remainder be good or no? these cases will follow the grounds of the common law for possessions, in point of operation; but so will it not be in point of exposition.

For if I have the manor of Dale and the manor of Sale lying both in Vale, and I make a lease for life of them both, the remainder of the manor of Dale, and all other my lands in Vale to John a Style, the remainder of the manor of Sale to John a Downe, this latter remainder is void, because it comes too late, the general words having carried it before to John a Style. But put it by way of use a man makes a feoffment in fee of both manors, and limits the use of the manor of Dale, and all the other lands in Vale to the use of himself, and his wife for her jointure, and of the manor of Sale to the use of himself alone. Now his wife shall have no jointure in the manor of Sale, and so was it judged in the case of the manor of Odiam. The case of the manor of Odiam.

And therefore our case is more strong, being by way of use, and you may well construe the latter part to controul and qualify the first, and to make it attend and expect: nay, it is not amiss to see the case of Peryman, 41 Eliz. Coke, p. 5. f. 84. where by a custom a livery may expect; 41 Eliz. Co. p. 5. f. 84.

for the case was, that in the manor of Portchester the custom was, that a feoffment of land should not be good, except it were presented within a year in the court of the manor, and there ruled that it was but *actus inchoatus*, till it was presented; now if it be not merely against reason of law, that so solemn a conveyance as livery, which keeps state, I tell you, and will not wait, should expect a farther perfection, *a fortiori*, may a conveyance in use or declaration of use receive a consummation by degrees, and several acts. And thus much for the main point.

Now for the objection of the word immediate, it is but light and a kind of sophistry. They say that the words are, that the uses shall rise immediately after the declaration, and we would have an interposition of an act between, namely, that there should be a declaration first, then a new assurance within the six months; and lastly, the uses to rise: whereunto the answer is easy; for we have showed before that the declaration and the new assurance are in the intent of him that made the conveyance, and likewise in eye of law, but as one compounded act. So as immediately after the declaration must be understood of a perfect and effectual declaration, with the adjuncts and accouplements expressed.

49. E. 3. f. 11. So we see in 49 E. III. f. 11. if a man be attainted of felony, that holds lands of a common person, the king shall have his year, day, and waste; but when? Not before an office found; and yet the words of the statute of *prærogativa regis* are, *rex habebit catalla felonum, et si ipsi habent liberum tenementum, statim capiatur in manus domini, et rex habebit annum, diem et vastum:* and here the word *statim* is understood of the effectual and lawful time, that is, after office found.

2 H. 4. f. 17. So in 2 H. IV. f. 17. it appears that by the statute of Acton Burnell, if the debt be acknowledged, and the day past that the goods of the debtors shall be sold *statim*, in French *maintenant;* yet, nevertheless, this *statim* shall not be understood before the process of law requisite passed, that is, the day comprised in the extent.

27 H. 8. f. 19. So it is said 27 H. VIII. f. 19. by Audley the Chancellor, that the present tense shall be taken for the future; *a fortiori*, say I, the immediate future tense may be taken for a distant future tense; as if I be bound that my son, being of the age of twenty-one years, shall marry your daughter, and that he be now of twelve years; yet this shall be understood, when he shall be of the age of twenty-one years.

And so in our case immediately after the declaration is intended when all things shall be performed, that are coupled with the said declaration.

But in this I doubt I labour too much; for no man will be of opinion, that it was intended that the Lady Stanhope should be six whole months without either the old jointure or the new; but that the old should expect until the new were settled without any interim. And so I conclude this course of atonements, as Fitzwilliams's case calls it, whereby I have proved, that all the words, by a true marshaling of the acts, may stand according to the intent of the parties.

I may add *tanquam ex abundanti*, that if both clauses do not live together, they must both die together; for the law loves neither fractions of estates nor fractions of constructions; and therefore in Jermin and Askew's case, 37 Eliz. a man did devise lands in tail with proviso, that if the devisee did attempt to alien, his estate should cease, as if he were naturally dead. Is it said there that the words, as if he were naturally dead, shall be void, and the words, that his estate shall cease, good? No, but the whole clause shall be void. And it is all one reason of a so that, as of an as if, for they both suspend the sentence.

Jermin and Askew's case.

So if I make a lease for life, upon condition he shall not alien, nor take the profits, shall this be good for the first part, and void for the second? No, but it shall be void for both.

So if the power of declaration of uses had been thus penned, that Sir John Stanhope might by his deed indented declare new uses, so that the deed were inrolled before the mayor of St. Albans, who hath no power to take inrolments; or so that the deed were made in such sort, as might not be made void by parliament: in all these and the like cases the impossibility of the last part doth strike upwards, and infect, and destroy the whole clause. And therefore, that all the words may stand, is the first and true course; that all the words be void, is the second and probable; but that the revoking part should be good, and the assuring part void, hath neither truth nor probability.

Now come I to the second point, how this value should be measured, wherein methinks you are as ill a measurer of values as you are an expounder of words; which point I will divide, first considering what the law doth generally intend by the word value; and secondly to see what special words may be in these clauses, either to draw it to a value of a present arrentation, or to understand it of a just and true value.

The word value is a word well known to the law, and therefore cannot be, except it be willingly, misunderstood. By the common law there is upon a warranty a recovery in value. I put the case therefore that I make a feoffment in fee with warranty of the manor of Dale, being worth twenty pounds per annum, and then in lease for twenty shillings. The lease expires, for that is our case, though I hold it not needful, the question is, whether, upon an eviction, there shall not be recovered from me land to the value of twenty pounds.

So if a man give land in frank-marriage then rented at forty pounds and no more worth, there descendeth other lands, let perhaps for a year or two for twenty pounds, but worth eighty pounds, shall not the donee be at liberty to put this land in hotchpotch?

So if two parceners be in tail, and they make partition of lands equal in rent, but far unequal in value, shall this bind their issues? By no means; for there is no calendar so false to judge of values as the rent, being sometimes improved, sometimes ancient, sometimes where great fines have been taken, sometimes where no fines; so as in point of recompense you were as good put false weights into the hands of the law, as to bring in this interpretation of value by a present arrentation. But this is not worth the speaking to in general; that which giveth colour is the special words in the clause of revocation, that the twenty pounds' value should be according to the rents then answered; and therefore that there should be a correspondence in the computation likewise of the recompense. But this is so far from countenancing that exposition, as, well noted, it crosseth it; for *opposita juxta se posita magis elucescunt:* first, it may be the intent of Sir Thomas, in the first clause, was double, partly to exclude any land in demesne, partly knowing the land was double, and as some say quadruple, better than the rent, he would have the more scope of revocation under his twenty pounds' value.

But what is this to the clause of recompense? first, are there any words *secundum computationem prædictam?* There are none. Secondly, doth the clause rest upon the words *similis valoris?* No, but joineth *tantum et similis valoris:* confound not predicaments; for they are the mere-stones of reason. Here is both quantity and quality; nay he saith farther, within the same towns. Why, marry, it is somewhat to have men's possessions lie about them, and not dispersed. So it must be as much, as good, as near; so plainly doth the intent appear, that my lady should not be a loser.

[For the point of the notice, it was discharged by the court.]

THE

JURISDICTION OF THE MARCHES.

The effect of the first argument of the king's solicitor-general, in maintaining the jurisdiction of the council of the marches over the four shires.

THE question for the present is only upon the statute of 32 H. VIII. and though it be a great question, yet it is contracted into small room; for it is but a true construction of a monosyllable, the word march.

The exposition of all words resteth upon three proofs, the propriety of the word, and the matter precedent, and subsequent.

Matter precedent concerning the intent of those that speak the words, and matter subsequent touching the conceit and understanding of those that construe and receive them.

First, therefore, as to *vis termini*, the force and propriety of the word; this word marches signifieth no more but limits, or confines, or borders, in Latin *limites*, or *confinia*, or *contermina;* and thereof was derived at the first *marchio*, a marquis, which was *comes limitaneus*.

Now these limits cannot be *linea imaginaria*, but it must have some contents and dimension, and that can be no other but the counties adjacent; and for this construction we need not wander out of our own state, for we see the counties of Northumberland, Cumberland, and Westmoreland lately the borders upon Scotland. Now the middle shires were commonly called the east, west, and middle marches.

To proceed, therefore, to the intention of those that made the statute, in the use of this word; I shall prove that the parliament took it in this sense by three several arguments.

The first is, that otherwise the word should be idle; and it is a rule, *verba sunt accipienda, ut sortientur effectum:* for this word marches, as is confessed on the other side, must be either for the counties' marches, which is our sense, or the lordships' marchers, which is theirs; that is, such lordships, as by reason of the incursions and infestation of the Welsh, in ancient time, were not under the constant possession of either dominion, but like the bateable ground where the war played. Now if this latter sense be destroyed, then all equivocation ceaseth.

That it is destroyed appears manifestly by the statute of 27 H. VIII. made seven years before the statute of which we dispute; for by that statute all the lordships' marchers are made shire ground, being either annexed to the ancient counties of Wales, or to the ancient counties of England, or erected into new counties, and made parcel of the dominion of Wales, and so no more marches after the statute of 27: so as there were no marches in that sense at the time of the making of the statute of 34.

The second argument is from the comparing of the place of the statute, whereupon our doubt riseth, namely, that there shall be and remain a lord president and council in the dominion of Wales and the marches of the same, &c. with another place of the same statute, where the word marches is left out; for the rule is, *opposita juxta se posita magis elucescunt.* There is a clause in the statute which gives power and authority to the king to make and alter laws for the weal of his subjects of his dominion of Wales; there the word marches is omitted, because it was not thought reasonable to invest the king with a power to alter the laws, which is the subjects' birthright, in any part of the realm of England; and therefore, by the omission of the word marches in that place, you may manifestly collect the signification of the word in the other, that is to be meant of the four counties of England.

The third argument which we will use is this: the council of the marches was not erected by the act of parliament, but confirmed; for there was a president and council long before in E. IV. his time, by matter yet appearing; and it is evident upon the statute itself, that in the very clause which we now handle it referreth twice to the usage, as heretofore hath been used.

This then I infer, that whatsoever was the king's intention in the first erection of this court, was, likewise, the intention of the parliament in the establishing thereof, because the parliament builded upon an old foundation.

The king's intention appeareth to have had three branches, whereof every of them doth manifestly comprehend the four shires.

The first was the better to bridle the subject of Wales, which at that time was not reclaimed: and therefore it was necessary for the president and council there to have jurisdiction and command over the English shires; because that by the aid of them, which were undoubted good subjects, they might the better govern and suppress those that were doubtful subjects.

And if it be said, that it is true, that the four shires were comprehended in the commission of oyer and terminer, for the suppression of riots and misdemeanors, but not for the jurisdiction of a court of equity; to that I answer, that their commission of oyer and terminer was but *gladius in vagina*, for it was not put in practice amongst them; for even in punishment of riots and misdemeanors, they proceed not by their commission of oyer and terminer by way of jury, but as a council by way of examination. And again it was necessary to strengthen that court for their better countenance with both jurisdictions, as well civil as criminal, for *gladius gladium juvat.*

The second branch of the king's intention was to make a better equality of commerce and intercourse in contracts and dealings between the subjects of Wales and the subjects of England; and this of necessity must comprehend the four shires; for otherwise, if the subject of England had been wronged by the Welsh on the sides of Wales, he might take his remedy nearer hand. But if the subject of Wales, for whose weal and benefit the statute was chiefly made, had been wronged by the English in any of the shires, he might have sought his remedy at Westminster.

The third branch of the king's intent was to make a convenient dignity and state of the mansion and resiance of his eldest son, when he should be created Prince of Wales, which likewise must plainly include the four shires; for otherwise to have sent *primogenitum regis* to a government, which without the mixture of the four shires, as things then were, had more pearl than honour or command; or to have granted him only a power of lieutenancy in those shires, where he was to keep his state, not adorned with some authority civil, had not been convenient.

So that here I conclude the second part of that I am to say touching the intention of the parliament precedent.

Now touching the construction subsequent, the rule is good, *optimus legum interpres consuetudo*; for our labour is not to maintain a usage against a statute, but by a usage to expound a statute; for no man will say but the word marches will bear the sense that we give it.

This usage or custom is fortified by four notable circumstances; first, that it is ancient, and not late or recent; secondly, it is authorised, and not popular or vulgar; thirdly, that it hath been admitted and quiet, and not litigious or interrupted; and fourthly, when it was brought in question, which was but once, it hath been affirmed, *judicio controverso*.

For the first, there is record of a president and council, that hath exercised and practised jurisdiction in these shires, as well sixty years before the statute, namely, since 18 E. IV. as the like number of years since; so that it is *Janus bifrons*, it hath a face backward from the statute, as well as forwards.

For the second, it hath received these allowances by the practice of that court, by suits originally commenced there, by remanding from the courts of Westminster, when causes within those shires have been commenced here above; sometimes in chancery, sometimes in the star-chamber, by the admittance of divers great learned men and great judges, that have been of that council, and exercised that jurisdiction; as at one time Bromley, Morgan, and Brook, being the two chief justices, and chief baron, and divers others; by the king's learned council, which always were called to the penning of the king's instructions; and, lastly, by the king's instructions themselves, which though they be not always extant, yet it is manifest that since 17 H. VIII. when Princess Mary went down, that the four shires were ever comprehended in the instructions, either by name, or by that that amounts to so much. So as it appears that this usage or practice hath not been an obscure custom practised by the multitude, which is many times erroneous, but authorised by the judgment and consent of the state: for as it is *vera vox* to say, *maximus erroris populus magister;* so it is *dura vox* to say, *maximus erroris princeps magister.*

For the third, it was never brought in question till 16 Eliz. in the case of one Wynde.

And for the fourth, the controversy being moved in that case, it was referred to Gerrard, attorney, and Bromley, solicitor, who was afterwards chancellor of England, and had his whole state of living in Shropshire and Worcester, and by them reported to the lords of the council in the star-chamber, and upon their report decreed, and the jurisdiction affirmed.

Lastly, I will conclude with two manifest badges and tokens, though but external yet violent in demonstration, that these four shires were understood by the word marches; the one the denomination of that council, which was ever in common appellation termed and styled the council of the marches, or in the marches, rather than the council of Wales, or in Wales, and *denominatio est a digniore.* If it had been intended of lordships' marches, it had been as if one should have called my lord mayor my lord mayor of the suburbs. But it was plainly intended of the four English shires, which indeed were the more worthy.

And the other is of the perpetual resiance and mansion of the council, which was evermore in the shires; and to imagine that a court should not have jurisdiction where it sitteth, is a thing utterly improbable, for they should be *tanquam piscis in arido.*

So as upon the whole matter, I conclude that the word marches in that place by the natural sense, and true intent of the statute, is meant the four shires.

The effect of that that was spoken by Serjeant Hutton and Serjeant Harris, in answer of the former argument, and for the excluding of the jurisdiction of the marches in the four shires.

That which they both did deliver was reduced to three heads:

The first to prove the use of the word marches for lordships' marchers.

The second to prove the continuance of that use of the word, after the statute of 27, that made the lordships' marchers shire-grounds; whereupon it was inferred, that though the marches were destroyed in nature, yet they remained in name.

The third was some collections they made upon the statute of 34; whereby they inferred, that that statute intended that word in that signification.

For the first, they did allege divers statutes before 27 H. VIII. and divers book-cases of law in print, and divers offices and records, wherein the word marches of Wales was understood of the lordships' marchers.

They said farther, and concluded, that whereas we show our sense of the word but rare, they show theirs common and frequent; and whereas we show it but in a vulgar use and acceptation, they show theirs in a legal use in statutes, authorities of books, and ancient records.

They said farther, that the example we brought of marches upon Scotland was not like, but rather contrary; for they were never called marches of Scotland, but the marches of England: whereas the statute of 34 doth not speak of the marches of England, but of the marches of Wales.

They said farther, that the county of Worcester did in no place or point touch upon Wales, and therefore that county could not be termed marches.

To the second they produced three proofs; first, some words in the statute of 32 H. VIII. where the statute, providing for a form of trial for treason committed in Wales, and the marches thereof, doth use that word, which was in time after the statute of 27; whereby they prove the use of the word continued.

The second proof was out of two places of the statute, whereupon we dispute, where the word marches is used for the lordships' marchers.

The third proof was the stile and form of the commission of oyer and terminer even to this day, which run to give power and authority to the president and council there, *infra principalitat. Walliæ*, and *infra* the four counties by name, with this clause farther, *et marchias Walliæ eisdem comitatibus adjacent'*: whereby they infer two things strongly, the one that the marches of Wales must needs be a distinct thing from the four counties; the other that the word marches was used for the lordships' marchers long after both statutes.

They said farther, that otherwise the proceeding, which had been in the four new erected counties of Wales by the commission of oyer and terminer, by force whereof many had been proceeded with both for life and other ways, should be called in question, as *coram non judice*, insomuch as they neither were part of the principality of Wales, nor part of the four shires; and therefore must be contained by the word marches, or not at all.

For the third head, they did insist upon the statute of 34, and upon the preamble of the same statute.

The title being an act for certain ordinances in the king's majesty's dominion and principality of Wales; and the preamble being for the tender zeal and affection that the king bears to his subjects of Wales; and again, at the humble suit and petition of his subjects of Wales: whereby they infer that the statute had no purpose to extend or intermeddle with any part of the king's dominions or subjects, but only within Wales.

And for usage and practice, they said, it was nothing against an act of parliament.

And for the instructions, they pressed to see the instructions immediately after the statute made.

And for the certificate and opinions of Gerrard and Bromley, they said they doubted not, but that if it were now referred to the attorney and solicitor, they would certify as they did.

And, lastly, they relied, as upon their principal strength, upon the precedent of that, which was done of the exempting of Cheshire from the late jurisdiction of the said council; for they said, that from 34 of H. VIII. until 11 of Queen Eliz. the court of the marches did usurp jurisdiction upon that county, being likewise adjacent to Wales, as the other four are; but that in the eleventh year of Queen Elizabeth aforesaid, the same, being questioned at the suit of one Radforde, was referred to the Lord Dyer, and three other judges, who, by their certificate at large remaining of record in the chancery, did pronounce the said shire to be exempted, and that in the conclusion of their certificate they gave this reason, because it was no part of the principality or marches of Wales. By which reason, they say, it should appear their opinion was, that the word marches could not extend to counties adjacent. This was the substance of their defence.

The reply of the king's solicitor to the arguments of the two serjeants.

Having divided the substance of their arguments, *ut supra*, he did pursue the same division in his reply, observing nevertheless both a great redundancy and a great defect in that which was spoken. For, touching the use of the word marches, great labour had been taken, which was not denied: but touching the intent of the parliament, and the reasons to demonstrate the same, which were the life of the question, little or nothing had been spoken.

And, therefore, as to the first head, that the word marches had been often applied to the lordships' marchers, he said it was the sophism which is called *sciomachia*, fighting with their shadows; and that the sound of so many statutes, so many printed book-cases, so many records, were *nomina magna*, but they did not press the question; for we grant that the word marches had significations, sometimes for the counties, sometimes for the lordships' marchers, like as Northampton and Warwick are sometimes taken for the towns of Northampton and Warwick, and sometimes for the counties of Northampton and Warwick. And Dale and Sale are sometimes taken for the villages or hamlets of Dale and Sale, and sometimes taken for the parishes of Dale and Sale: and therefore that the most part of that they had said went not to the point.

To that answer, which was given to the example of the middle shires upon Scotland, it was said, it was not *ad idem;* for we used it to prove that the word marches may and doth refer to whole counties; and so much it doth manifestly prove; neither can they deny it. But then they pinch upon the addition, because the English counties adjacent upon Scotland are called the marches of England, and the English counties adjacent upon Wales are called the marches of Wales; which is but a difference in phrase: for sometimes limits and borders have their names of the inward country, and sometimes of the outward country; for the distinction of *exclusivè* and *inclusivè* is a distinction both in time and place; as we see that that which we call this day fortnight, excluding the day, the French and the law-phrase calls this day fifteen days, or *quindena*, including the day. And if they had been called the marches upon Wales or the marches against Wales, then it had been clear and plain; and what difference between the banks of the sea and the banks against the sea? So that he took this to be but a toy or cavillation, for that phrases of speech are *ad placitum, et recipiunt casum.*

As to the reason of the map, that the county of Worcester doth no way touch upon Wales, it is true; and I do find when the lordships' marchers were annexed, some were laid to every other of the three shires, but none to Worcester. And no doubt but this emboldened Wynde to make the claim to Worcester, which he durst not have thought on for any of the other three. But it falls out well that that which is the weakest in probability, is strongest in proof; for there is a case ruled in that more than in the rest. But the true reason is, that usage must overrule propriety of speech; and therefore if all commissions, and instructions, and practices, have coupled these four shires, it is not the map that will sever them.

To the second head he gave this answer. First he observed in general that they had not showed one statute, or one book-case, or one record, the commissions of oyer and terminer only excepted, wherein the word marches was used for lordships' marchers since the statute of 34. So that it is evident, that as they granted the nature of those marches was destroyed and extinct by 27, so the name was discontinued soon after, and did but remain a very small while, like the sound of a bell, after it hath been rung; and as indeed it is usual when names are altered, that the old name, which is expired, will continue for a small time.

Secondly, he said, that whereas they had made the comparison, that our acceptation of the word was popular, and theirs was legal, because it was extant in book-cases, and statutes, and records, they must needs confess that they are beaten from that hold; for the name ceased to be legal clearly by the law of 27, which made the alteration in the thing itself, whereof the name is but a shadow; and if the name did remain afterwards, then it was neither legal, nor so much as vulgar, but it was only by abuse, and by a trope or *catachresis*.

Thirdly, he showed the impossibility how that signification should continue, and be intended by the statute of 34. For if it did, it must be in one of these two senses, either that it was meant of the lordships' marchers made part of Wales, or of the lordships' marchers annexed to the four shires of England.

For the first of these, it is plainly impugned by the statute itself; for the first clause of the statute doth set forth that the principality and dominion of Wales shall consist of twelve shires: wherein the four new erected counties, which were formerly lordships' marchers, and whatsoever else was lordships' marchers annexed to the ancient counties of Wales, is comprehended; so that of necessity all that territory or border must be Wales; then followeth the clause immediately, whereupon we now differ, namely, that there shall be and remain a president and council in the principality of Wales, and the marches of the same; so that the parliament could not forget so soon what they had said in the clause next before: and therefore by the marches they meant somewhat else besides that which was Wales. Then if they fly to the second signification, and say that it was meant by the lordships' marchers annexed to the four English shires, that device is merely *nuper nata oratio*, a mere fiction and invention of wit, crossed by the whole stream and current of practice; for if that were so, the jurisdiction of the council should be over part of those shires, and in part not; and then in the suits commenced against any of the inhabitants of the four shires, it ought to have been laid or showed that they dwelt within the ancient lordships' marchers, whereof there is no shadow that can be showed.

Then he proceeded to the three particulars. And for the statute of 32, for trial of treason, he said it was necessary that the word marches should be added to Wales, for which he gave this reason, that the statute did not only extend to the trial of treasons, which should be committed after the statute, but did also look back to treasons committed before: and, therefore, this statute being made but five years after the statute of 27, that extinguished the lordships' marchers, and looking back, as was said, was fit to be penned with words that might include the preterperfect tense as well as the present tense; for if it had rested only upon the word Wales, then a treason committed before the lordships' marchers were made part of Wales might have escaped the law.

To this also another answer was given, which was, that the word marches as used in that statute, could not be referred to the four shires, because of the words following, wherewith it is coupled, namely, in Wales, and the marches of the same, where the king's writ runs not.

To the two places of the statute of 34 itself, wherein the word marches is used for lordships' marchers; if they be diligently marked, it is merely sophistry to allege them; for both of them do speak by way of recital of the time past before the statute of 27, as the words themselves being read over will show without any other enforcement; so that this is still to use the almanack of the old year with the new.

To the commissions of oyer and terminer, which seemeth to be the best evidence they show for the continuance of the name in that tropical or abused sense, it might move somewhat, if this form of penning those commissions had been begun since the statute of 27. But we show forth the commission in 17 H. VIII. when the Princess Mary went down, running in the same manner *verbatim*, and in that time it was proper, and coûld not otherwise be. So that it appeareth that it was but merely a facsimile, and that notwithstanding the case was altered, yet the clerk of the crown pursued the former precedent; hurt it did none, for the word marches is there superfluous.

And whereas it was said, that the words in those commissions were effectual, because else the proceeding in the four new erected shires of Wales should be *coram non judice*, that objection carrieth no colour at all; for it is plain, they have authority by the word principality of Wales, without adding the word marches; and that is proved by a number of places in the statute of 34, where if the word Wales should not comprehend those shires, they should be excluded in effect of the whole benefit of that statute; for the word marches is never added in any of these places.

To the third head touching the true intent of the statute, he first noted how naked their proof was in that kind, which was the life of the question, for all the rest was but *in litera et in cortice*.

He observed also that all the strength of our proof, that concerned that point, they had passed over in silence, as belike not able to answer: for they had said nothing to the first intentions of the erections of the court, whereupon the parliament built: nothing to the diversity of penning, which was observed in the statute of 34, leaving out the word marches, and resting upon the word Wales alone: nothing to the resiance, nothing to the denomination, nothing to the continual practice before the statute and after, nothing to the king's instructions, &c.

As for that, that they gather out of the title and preamble, that the statute was made for Wales, and for the weal and government of Wales, and at the petition of the subjects of Wales, it was little to the purpose; for no man will affirm on our part the four English shires were brought under the jurisdiction of that council, either first by the king, or after by the parliament, for their own sakes, being in parts no farther remote; but it was for congruity's sake, and for the good of Wales, that that commixture was requisite: and *turpis est pars, quæ non congruit cum toto*. And therefore there was no reason that the statute should be made at their petition, considering they were not *primi in intentione*, but came *ex consequenti*.

And whereas they say that usage is nothing against an act of parliament, it seems they do voluntarily mistake, when they cannot answer; for we do not bring usage to cross an act of parliament, where it is clear, but to expound an act of parliament, where it is doubtful, and evermore *contemporanea interpretatio*, whether it be of statute or

Scripture, or author whatsoever, is of greatest credit: for to come now, above sixty years after, by subtilty of wit to expound a statute otherwise than the ages immediately succeeding did conceive it, is *expositio contentiosa*, and not *naturalis*. And whereas they extenuate the opinion of the attorney and solicitor, it is not so easy to do; for first they were famous men, and one of them had his patrimony in the shires; secondly, it was of such weight, as a decree of the council was grounded upon it; and, thirdly, it was not unlike, but that they had conferred with the judges, as the attorney and solicitor do often use in like cases.

Lastly, for the exemption of Cheshire he gave this answer. First, that the certificate in the whole body of it, till within three or four of the last lines, doth rely wholly upon that reason, because it was a county palatine: and to speak truth, it stood not with any great sense or proportion, that that place which was privileged and exempted from the jurisdiction of the courts of Westminster, should be meant by the parliament to be subjected to the jurisdiction of that council.

Secondly, he said that those reasons, which we do much insist upon for the four shires, hold not for Cheshire, for we say it is fit the subject of Wales be not forced to sue at Westminster, but have his justice near hand; so may he have in Cheshire, because there is both a justice for common law and a chancery; we say it is convenient for the prince, if it please the king to send him down, to have some jurisdiction civil as well as for the peace; so may he have in Cheshire, as earl of Chester. And therefore those grave men had great reason to conceive that the parliament did not intend to include Cheshire.

And whereas they pinch upon the last words in the certificate, namely, that Cheshire was no part of the dominion, nor of the marches, they must supply it with this sense, not within the meaning of the statute; for otherwise the judges could not have discerned of it; for they were not to try the fact, but to expound the statute; and that they did upon those reasons, which were special to Cheshire, and have no affinity with the four shires.

And, therefore, if it be well weighed, that certificate makes against them; for as *exceptio firmat legem in casibus non exceptis*, so the excepting of that shire by itself doth fortify, that the rest of the shires were included in the very point of difference.

After this he showed a statute in 18 Eliz. by which provision is made for the repair of a bridge called Chepstowbridge, between Monmouth and Gloucester, and the charge lay in part upon Gloucestershire; in which statute there is a clause, that if the justices of peace do not their duty in levying of the money, they shall forfeit five pounds to be recovered by information before the council of the marches; whereby he inferred that the parliament would never have assigned the suit to that court, but that it conceived Gloucestershire to be within the jurisdiction thereof. And therefore he concluded that here is in the nature of a judgment by parliament, that the shires are within the jurisdiction.

The third and last argument of the king's solicitor in the case of the marches, in reply to Serjeant Harris.

This case groweth now to some ripeness, and I am glad we have put the other side into the right way; for in former arguments they laboured little upon the intent of the statute of 34 H. VIII. and busied themselves in effect altogether about the force and use of the word marches; but now finding that *litera mortua non prodest,* they offer at the true state of the question, which is the intent: I am determined therefore to reply to them in their own order, *ut manifestum sit,* as he saith, *me nihil aut subterfugere voluisse reticendo, aut obscurare dicendo.*

All which hath been spoken on their part consisteth upon three proofs.

The first was by certain inferences to prove the intent of the statute.

The second was to prove the use of the word marches in their sense long after both statutes; both that of 27, which extinguished the lordships' marchers, and that of 34, whereupon our question ariseth.

The third was to prove an interruption of that practice and use of jurisdiction, upon which we mainly insist, as the best exposition of the statute.

For the first of these, concerning the intention, they brought five reasons.

The first was that this statute of 34 was grounded upon a platform, or preparative of certain ordinances made by the king two years before, namely, 32; in which ordinances there is the very clause, whereupon we dispute, namely, That there should be and remain in the dominion and principality of Wales a president and a council: in which clause nevertheless the word marches is left out, whereby they collect that it came into the statute of 34 but as a slip, without any farther reach or meaning.

The second was, that the mischief before the statute, which the statute means to remedy, was, that Wales was not governed according to similitude or conformity with the laws of England. And therefore, that it was a cross and perverse construction, when the statute laboured to draw Wales to the laws of England, to construe it, that it should abridge the ancient subjects of England of their own laws.

The third was, that in a case of so great importance it is not like that if the statute had meant to include the four shires, it would have carried it in a dark general word, as it were *noctanter*, but would have named the shires to be comprehended.

The fourth was, the more to fortify the third reason, they observed that the four shires are remembered and named in several places of the statute, three in number; and therefore it is not like that they would have been forgotten in the principal place, if they had been meant.

The fifth and last was, that there is no clause of attendance, that the sheriffs of the four shires should attend the lord president and the council; wherein there was urged the example of the acts of parliament, which erected courts; as the court of augmentations, the court of wards, the court of survey; in all which there are clauses of attendance; whereupon they inferred that evermore, where a statute gives a court jurisdiction, it strengtheneth it with a clause of attendance; and therefore no such clause being in this statute, it is like there was no jurisdiction meant. Nay, farther they noted, that in this very statute for the justices of Wales there is a clause of attendance from the sheriffs of Wales.

In answer to their first reason, they do very well, in my opinion, to consider Mr. Attorney's business and mine, and therefore to find out for us evidence and proofs, which we have no time to search; for certainly nothing can make more for us than these ordinances, which they produce; for the diversity of penning of that clause in the ordinances, where the word marches is omitted, and that clause in the statute where the word marches is added, is a clear and perfect direction what was meant by that word. The ordinances were made by force and in pursuance of authority given to the king by the statute of 27; to what did the statute extend? Only to Wales. And therefore the word marches in the ordinances is left out; but the statute of 34 respected not only Wales, but the commixed government, and therefore the word marches was put in. They might have remembered that we built an argument upon the difference of penning of that statute of 34 itself in the several clauses of the same; for that in all other clauses, which concern only Wales, the word marches is ever omitted; and in that clause alone that concerneth the jurisdiction of the president and council, it is inserted. And this our argument is notably fortified by that they now show of the ordinances, wherein the very selfsame clause touching the president and council, because the king had no authority to meddle but with Wales, the word marches is omitted. So that it is most plain that this word comes not in by chance or slip, but with judgment and purpose, as an effectual word; for, as it was formerly said, *opposita juxta se posita magis elucescunt;* and therefore I may likewise urge another place in the statute which is left out in the ordinance; for I find there is a clause that the town of Bewdley, which is confessed to be no lordships' marcher, but to lie within the county of Worcester; yet because it was an exempted jurisdiction, is by the statute annexed unto the body of the said county. First, this shows that the statute of 34 is not confined to Wales, and the lordships' marchers, but that it intermeddles with Worcestershire. Next, do you find any such clause in the ordinance of 32? No. Why? Because they were appropriated to Wales. So that in my opinion nothing could inforce our exposition better than the collating of the ordinance of 32 with the statute of 34.

In answer to the second reason, the course that I see often taken in this cause makes me think of the phrase of the psalm, "starting aside like a broken bow:" so when they find their reasons broken, they start aside to things not in question. For now they speak, as if he went about to make the four shires Wales, or to take from them the benefit of the laws of England, or their being accounted amongst the ancient counties of England: doth any man say that those shires are not within the circuits of England, but subject to the justices of Wales? or that they should send but one knight to the parliament, as the shires of Wales do? or that they may not sue at Westminster, in chancery, or at common law, or the like? No man affirms any such things; we take nothing from them, only we give them a court of summary justice in certain causes at their own doors.

And this is *nova doctrina* to make such an opposition

between law and equity, and between formal justice and summary justice. For there is no law under heaven which is not supplied with equity; for *summum jus, summa injuria*, or, as some have it, *summa lex, summa crux*. And therefore all nations have equity; but some have law and equity mixed in the same court, which is the worse; and some have it distinguished in several courts, which is the better. Look into any counties palatine, which are small models of the great government of kingdoms, and you shall never find any but had a chancery.

Lastly, it is strange that all other places do require courts of summary justice, and esteem them to be privileges and graces; and in this cause only they are thought to be servitudes and loss of birthright. The universities have a court of summary justice, and yet I never heard that scholars complain their birthright was taken from them. The stannaries have them, and you have lately affirmed the jurisdiction; and yet you have taken away no man's birthright. The court at York, whosoever looks into it, was erected at the petition of the people, and yet the people did not mean to cast away their birthright. The court of wards is mixed with discretion and equity; and yet I never heard that infants and innocents were deprived of their birthright. London, which is the seat of the kingdom, hath a court of equity, and holdeth it for a grace and favour; how then cometh this case to be singular? And therefore these be new phrases and conceits, proceeding of error or worse; and it makes me think that a few do make their own desires the desires of the country, and that this court is desired by the greater number, though not by the greater stomachs.

In answer to the third reason, if men be conversant in the statutes of this kingdom, it will appear to be no new thing to carry great matters in general words without other particular expressing. Consider but of the statute of 26 H. VIII. which hath carried estates tails under the general words of estates of inheritance. Consider of the statute of 16 R. II. of *præmunire*, and see what great matters are thought to be carried under the word *alibi*. And, therefore, it is an ignorant assertion to say that the statute would have named the shires, if it had meant them.

Secondly, the statute had more reason to pass it over in general words, because it did not ordain a new matter, but referreth to usage; and though the statute speaks generally, yet usage speaks plainly and particularly, which is the strongest kind of utterance or expressing. *Quid verba audiam cum facta videam.*

And, thirdly, this argument of theirs may be strongly retorted against them, for as they infer that the shires were not meant, because they were not included by name, so we infer that they are meant, because they are not excepted by name, as is usual by way of proviso in like cases: and our inference hath far greater reason than theirs, because at the time of the making of the statute they were known to be under the jurisdiction: and, therefore, that ought to be most plainly expressed, which should work a change, and not that which should continue things as they were.

In answer to their fourth reason, it makes likewise plainly against them; for there be three places where the shires be named, the one for the extinguishing of the custom of gavelkind; the second for the abolishing of certain forms of assurance which were too light to carry inheritance and freehold; the third for the restraining of certain franchises to that state they were in by a former statute. In these three places the words of the statute are, The lordships' marchers annexed unto the counties of Hereford, Salop, &c.

Now mark, if the statute conceived the word marches to signify lordships' marchers, what needeth this long circumlocution? It had been easier to have said, within the marches. But because it was conceived that the word marches would have comprehended the whole counties, and the statute meant but of the lordships' marchers annexed; therefore they were enforced to use that periphrasis or length of speech.

In answer to the fifth reason I give two several answers; the one, that the clause of attendance is supplied by the word incidents; for the clause of establishment of the court hath that word, " with all incidents to the same as heretofore hath been used:" for execution is ever incident to justice or jurisdiction. The other because it is a court, that standeth not by the act of parliament alone, but by the king's instructions, whereto the act refers. Now no man will doubt but the king may supply the clause of attendance; for if the king grant forth a commission of oyer and terminer, he may command what sheriff he will to attend it; and therefore there is a plain diversity between this case and the cases they vouch of the court of wards, survey, and augmentations: for they were courts erected *de novo* by parliament, and had no manner of reference either to usage or instructions; and therefore it was necessary that the whole frame of those courts, and their authority both for judicature and execution, should be described and expressed by parliament. So was it of the authority of the justices of Wales in the statute of 34 mentioned, because there are many ordinances *de novo* concerning them; so that it was a new erection, and not a confirmation of them.

Thus have I, in confutation of their reasons, greatly, as I conceive, confirmed our own, as it were with new matter; for most of that they have said made for us. But as I am willing to clear your judgments, in taking away the objections, so I must farther pray in aid of your memory for those things which we have said, whereunto they have offered no manner of answer; for unto all our proofs which we made touching the intent of the statute, which they grant to be the spirit and life of this question, they said nothing: as not a word to this; That otherwise the word marches in the statute should be idle or superfluous: not a word to this; That the statute doth always omit the word marches in things that concern only Wales: not a word to this; That the statute did not mean to innovate, but to ratify, and therefore if the shires were in before, they are in still: not a word to the reason of the commixed government, as that it was necessary for the reclaiming of Wales to have them conjoined with the shires; that it was necessary for commerce and contracts, and properly for the ease of the subjects of Wales against the inhabitants of the shires; that it was not probable that the parliament meant the prince should have no jurisdiction civil in that place, where he kept his house. To all these things, which we esteem the weightiest, there is *altum silentium,* after the manner of children that skip over where they cannot spell.

Now to pass from the intent to the word; first, I will examine the proofs they have brought that the word was used in their sense after the statute 27 and 34; then I will consider what is gained, if they should prove so much: and, lastly, I will briefly state our own proofs, touching the use of the word.

For the first, it hath been said, that whereas I called the use of the word marches, after the statute of 27, but a little chime at most of an old word, which soon after vanished, they will now ring us a peal of statutes to prove it; but if it be a peal, I am sure it is a peal of bells, and not a peal of shot: for it clatters, but it doth not strike: for of all the catalogue of statutes I find scarcely one, save those that were answered in my former argument; but we may with as good reason affirm in every of them the word marches to be meant of the counties' marches, as they can of the lordships' marchers: for to begin upwards:

The statute 39 Eliz. for the repair of Wilton Bridge, no doubt doth mean the word marches for the counties; for the bridge itself is in Herefordshire, and the statute imposeth the charge of reparation upon Herefordshire by compulsory means, and permitteth benevolence to be taken in Wales, and the marches; who doubts, but this meant of the other three shires, which have far greater use of the bridge than the remote counties of Wales?

For the statute 5 Eliz. concerning perjury, it hath a proviso, that it shall not be prejudicial to the council of the marches for punishing of perjury; who can doubt but that here marches is meant of the shires, considering the perjuries committed in them have been punished in that court as well as in Wales?

For 2 E. VI. and the clause therein for restraining tithes of marriage portions in Wales and the marches, why should it not be meant of counties? For if any such customs had crept and encroached into the body of the shires out of the lordships' marchers, no doubt the statute meant to restrain them as well there as in the other places.

And so for the statute of 32 H. VIII. which ordains that the benefit of that statute for distress to be had by executors, should not extend to any lordship in Wales, or the marches of the same where *mises* are paid, because that imports a general release; what absurdity is there, if there the marches be meant for the whole shires? for if any such custom had spread so far, the reason of the statute is alike.

As for the statutes of 37 H. VIII. and 4 E. IV. for the making and appointing of the *custos rotulorum*, there the word marches must needs be taken for limits, according to the etymology and derivation; for the words refer not to Wales, but are thus, within England and Wales, and other the king's dominions, marches, and territories, that is, limits and territories; so as I see no reason but I may truly maintain my former assertion, that after the lordships' marchers were extinct by the statute of 27, the name also of marches was discontinued, and rarely if ever used in that sense.

But if it should be granted that it was now and then used in that sense, it helps them little; for first it is clear that the legal use of it is gone, when the thing was extinct, for *nomen est rei nomen;* so it remains but *abusivè*, as if one should call Guletta Carthage, because it was once Carthage; and next, if the word should have both senses, and that we admit an equivocation, yet we so overweigh them upon the intent, as the balance is soon cast.

Yet one thing I will note more, and that is, that there is a certain confusion of tongues on the other side, and that they cannot well tell themselves what they would have to be meant by the word marches; for one while they say it is meant for the lordships' marchers generally, another while they say that it is meant for the inward marches on Wales' side only; and now at last they are driven to a poor shift, that there should be left some little lordship marcher in the dark, as *casus omissus*, not annexed at all to any county; but if they would have the statute satisfied upon that only, I say no more to them, but *aquila non capit muscas*.

Now I will briefly remember unto you the state of our proofs of the word.

First, according to the laws of speech we prove it by the etymology or derivation, because march is the Saxon word for limit, and *marchio* is *comes limitaneus;* this is the opinion of Camden and others.

Next, we prove the use of the word in the like case to be for counties, by the example of the marches of Scotland: for as it is prettily said in Walker's case by Gawdy, if a case have no cousin, it is a sign it is a bastard, and not legitimate; therefore we have showed you a cousin, or rather a brother, here within our own island of the like use of the word. And whereas a great matter was made that the now middle shires were never called the marches of Scotland, but the marches of England against Scotland, or upon Scotland, it was first answered that that made no difference; because sometimes the marches take their name of the inward country, and sometimes of the out country; so that it is but *inclusivè* and *exclusivè:* as for example, that which we call in vulgar speech this day fortnight, excluding the day, that the law calls *quindena*, including the day; and so likewise, who will make a difference between the banks of the sea, and the banks against the sea, or upon the sea? But now to remove all scruple, we show them Littleton in his chapter Of Grand Serjeanty, where he saith, there is a tenure by cornage in the marches of Scotland; and we show them likewise the statute of 25 E. III.

Of Labourers, where they are also called the marches of Scotland.

Then we show some number of bills exhibited to the council there before the statute, where the plaintiffs have the addition of place confessed within the bodies of the shires, and no lordships' marchers, and yet are laid to be in the marches.

Then we show divers accounts of auditors in the duchy from H. IV. downwards, where the indorsement is in *marchiis Walliæ*, and the contents are possessions only of Hereford and Gloucestershire (for in Shropshire and Worcestershire the duchy hath no lands); and whereas they would put it off with a *cuique in sua arte credendum*, they would believe them, if it were in matter of accounts; we do not allege them as auditors, but as those that speak English to prove the common use of the word, *loquendum ut vulgus*.

We show likewise an ancient record of a patent to Herbert in 15 E. IV. where Kilpeck is laid to be in *com.* Hereford in *marchiis Walliæ;* and, lastly, we show again the statute of 27 E. III. where provision is made, that men shall labour in the summer where they dwell in the winter; and there is an exception of the people of the counties of Stafford and Lancashire, &c. and of the marches of Wales and Scotland; where it is most plain, that the marches of Wales are meant for counties, because they are coupled both with Stafford and Lancashire, which are counties, and with the marches of Scotland, which are likewise counties; and as it is informed, the labourers of those four shires do come forth of their shires, and are known by the name of Cokers to this day.

To this we add two things, which are worthy consideration; the one, that there is no reason to put us to the proof of the use of this word marches sixty years ago, considering that usage speaks for us; the other, that there ought not to be required of us to show so frequent a use of the word marches of ancient time in our sense, as they showed in theirs, because there was not the like occasion: for when a lordship marcher was mentioned it was of necessity to lay it in the marches, because they were out of all counties; but when land is mentioned in any of these counties, it is superfluous to add, in the marches; so as there was no occasion to use the word marches, but either for a more brief and compendious speech to avoid the naming of the four shires, as it is in the statute of 25 E. III. and in the indorsement of accounts; or to give a court cognizance and jurisdiction, as in the bills of complaint; or *ex abundanti*, as in the record of Kilpeck.

There resteth the third main part, whereby they endeavour to weaken and extenuate the proofs which we offer touching practice and possession, wherein they allege five things.

First, that Bristol was in until 7 Eliz. and then exempted.

Secondly, that Cheshire was in until 11 Eliz. and then went out.

Thirdly, they allege certain words in the instructions to Cholmley, vice-president, in 11 Eliz. at which time the shires were first comprehended in the instructions by name, and in these words, annexed by our commission: whereupon they would infer that they were not brought in the statute, but only came in by instructions, and do imagine that when Cheshire went out they came in.

Fourthly, they say, that the intermeddling with those four shires before the statute was but a usurpation and toleration, rather than any lawful and settled jurisdiction; and it was compared to that, which is done by the judges in their circuits, who end many causes upon petitions.

Fifthly, they allege Sir John Mullen's case, where it is said, *consuetudo non prœjudicat veritati.*

There was moved also, though it were not by the council, but from the judges themselves, as an extenuation, or at least an obscuring of the proofs of the usage and practice, in that we show forth no instructions from 17 H. VIII. to 1 Mariæ.

To these six points I will give answer, and, as I conceive, with satisfaction.

For Bristol, I say it teacheth them the right way, if they can follow it; for Bristol was not exempt by any opinion of law, but was left out of the instructions upon supplication made to the queen.

For Cheshire, we have answered it before, that the reason was, because it was not probable that the statute meant to make that shire subject to the jurisdiction of that council, considering it was not subject to the high courts at Westminster, in regard it was a county palatine. And whereas they said, that so was Flintshire too, it matcheth not, because Flintshire is named in the statute for one of the twelve shires of Wales.

We showed you likewise effectual differences between Cheshire and these other shires: for that Cheshire hath a chancery in itself, and over Cheshire the princes claim jurisdiction, as Earl of Chester; to all which you reply nothing.

Therefore I will add this only, that Cheshire went out *secundo flumine*, with the good will of the state; and this is sought to be evicted *adverso flumine*, cross the state; and as they have opinion of four judges for the excluding of Cheshire, so we have the opinion of two great learned men, Gerrard and Bromley, for the including of Worcester; whose opinions, considering it was but matter of opinion, and came not judicially in question, are not inferior to any two of the other; but we say that there is no opposition or repugnancy between them, but both may stand.

For Cholmley's instructions, the words may well stand, that those shires are annexed by commission; for the king's commission or instructions, for those words are commonly confounded, must cooperate with the statute, or else they cannot be annexed. But for that conceit that they should come in but in 11, when Cheshire went out, no man that is in his wits can be of that opinion, if he mark it: for we see that the town of Glocester, &c. is named in the instructions of 1 Mar. and no man, I am sure, will think that Glocester town should be in, and Glocestershire out.

For the conceit, that they had it but *jurisdictionem precariam*, the precedents show plainly the contrary; for they had coercion, and they did fine and imprison, which the judges do not upon petitions; and besides, they must remember that many of our precedents, which we did show forth, were not of suits originally commenced there, but of suits remanded from hence out of the king's courts as to their proper jurisdiction.

For Sir John Mullen's case, the rule is plain and sound, that where the law appears contrary, usage cannot control law; which doth not at all infringe the rule of *optima legum interpres consuetudo;* for usage may expound law, though it cannot overrule law.

But of the other side I could show you many cases, where statutes have been expounded directly against their express letter to uphold precedents and usage, as 2 and 3 Phil. et Mar. upon the statute of Westminster, that ordained that the judges *coram quibus formatum erit appellum* shall inquire of the damages, and yet the law ruled that it shall be inquired before the judges of Nisi Prius. And the great reverence given to precedents appeareth in 39 H. VI. 3 E. IV. and a number of other books; and the difference is exceedingly well taken in Slade's case, Coke's

Reports, 4. that is, where the usage runs but amongst clerks, and where it is in the eye and notice of the judge; for there it shall be presumed, saith the book, that if the law were otherwise than the usage hath gone, that either the council or the parties would have excepted to it, or the judges *ex officio* would have discerned of it, and found it; and we have ready for you a calendar of judges more than sit at this table, that have exercised jurisdiction over the shires in that county.

As for exception, touching the want of certain instructions, I could wish we had them; but the want of them, in my understanding, obscureth the case little. For let me observe unto you, that we have three forms of instructions concerning these shires extant; the first names them not expressly, but by reference it doth, namely, that they shall hear and determine, &c. within any of the places or counties within any of their commissions; and we have one of the commissions, wherein they were named; so as upon the matter they are named. And of this form are the ancient instructions before the statute 17 H. VIII. when the Princess Mary went down.

The second form of instructions go farther, for they have the towns, and exempted places within the counties named, with *tanquam* as well within the city of Glocester, the liberties of the duchy of Lancaster, &c. as within any of the counties of any of their commissions; which clearly admits the counties to be in before. And of this form are the instructions 1 Mariæ, and so long until 11 Eliz.

And the third form, which hath been continued ever since, hath the shires comprehended by name. Now it is not to be thought, but the instructions which are wanting, are according to one of these three forms which are extant. Take even your choice, for any of them will serve to prove that the practice there was ever authorized by the instructions here. And so upon the whole matter, I pray report to be made to his majesty, that the president and the council hath jurisdiction, according to his instructions, over the four shires, by the true construction of the statute of 34 H. VIII.

THE

LEARNED READING

OF

MR. FRANCIS BACON,

ONE OF HER MAJESTY'S COUNCIL AT LAW,

UPON

THE STATUTE OF USES.

BEING

HIS DOUBLE READING TO THE HONOURABLE SOCIETY OF GRAY'S INN. 42. ELIZ.

The introduction.

I HAVE chosen to read upon the Statute of Uses, made 27 H. VIII. ch. 10, a law whereupon the inheritances of this realm are tossed at this day, like a ship upon the sea, in such sort, that it is hard to say which bark will sink, and which will get to the haven; that is to say, what assurances will stand good, and what will not. Neither is this any lack or default in the pilots, the grave and learned judges; but the tides and currents of received error, and unwarranted and abusive experience have been so strong, as they were not able to keep a right course according to the law, so as this statute is in great part as a law made in the parliament, held 35 Reginæ; for, in 37 Reginæ, by the notable judgment given upon solemn arguments of all the judges assembled in the exchequer chamber, in the famous case between Dillon and Freine, concerning an assurance made by Chudleigh, this law began to be reduced to a true and sound exposition, and the false and perverted exposition, which had continued for so many years, but never countenanced by any rule or authority of weight, but only entertained in a popular conceit, and put in practice at adventure, grew to be controled; since which time (as it cometh to pass always upon the first reforming of inveterate errors) many doubts and perplexed questions have risen, which are not yet resolved, nor the law thereupon settled: the consi-

Reason of writing this treatise.

Chudleigh's case, 1 Rep. 121. Poph. 71. 1 And. 314.

deration whereof moved me to take the occasion of performing this particular duty to the house, to see if I could, by my travel, bring the exposition thereof to a more general good of the commonwealth.

Herein, though I could not be ignorant either of the difficulty of the matter, which he that taketh in hand shall soon find, or much less of my own unableness, which I had continual sense and feeling of; yet, because I had more means of absolution than the younger sort, and more leisure than the greater sort, I did think it not impossible to work some profitable effect; the rather because where an inferior wit is bent and constant upon one subject, he shall many times, with patience and meditation, dissolve and undo many of the knots, which a greater wit, distracted with many matters, would rather cut in two than unknit: and, at the least, if my invention or judgment be too barren or too weak, yet, by the benefit of other arts, I did hope to dispose or digest the authorities and opinions which are in cases of uses in such order and method, as they should take light one from another, though they took no light from me. And like to the matter of my reading shall my manner be, for my meaning is to revive and recontinue the ancient form of reading, which you may see in Mr. Frowicke's upon the prerogative, and all other readings of ancient time, being of less ostentation, and more fruit than the manner lately accustomed: for the use then was, substantially to expound the statutes by grounds and diversities; as you shall find the readings still to run upon cases of like law and contrary law; whereof the one includes the learning of a ground, the other the learning of a difference; and not to stir conceits and subtle doubts, or to contrive a multitude of tedious and intricate cases, whereof all, saving one, are buried, and the greater part of that one case which is taken, is commonly nothing to the matter in hand; but my labour shall be in the ancient course, to open the law upon doubts, and not to open doubts upon the law.

EXPOSITIO STATUTI.

The order of it. THE exposition of this statute consists upon matter without the statute, and matter within the statute.

3 Rep. 7. Heydon's case. There be three things concerning this statute, and all other statutes, which are helps and inducements to the right understanding of any statute, and yet are no part of the statute itself.

1. The consideration of the case at the common law.

2. The consideration of the mischief which the statute intendeth to redress, as also any other mischief, which an exposition of the statute this way or that way may breed.

3. Certain maxims of the common law, touching exposition of statutes.

Having therefore framed six divisions, according to the number of readings upon the statute itself, I have likewise divided the matter without the statute into six introductions or discourses, so that for every day's reading I have made a triple provision.

1. A preface or introduction.

2. A division upon the law itself.

3. A few brief cases for exercise and argument.

The last of which I would have forborn; and, according to the ancient manner, you should have taken some of my points upon my divisions, one, two, or more, as you should have thought good; save that I had this regard, that the younger sort of the bar were not so conversant in matters upon the statutes; and for that cause I have interlaced some matters at the common law, that are more familiar within the books.

1. The first matter I will discourse unto you is the nature and definition of a use, and its inception and progression before the statute.

2. The second discourse shall be of the second spring of this tree of uses since the statute.

3. The third discourse shall be of the estate of the assurances of this realm at this day upon uses, and what kind of them is convenient and reasonable, and not fit to be touched, as far as the sense of law and a natural construction of the statute will give leave; and what kind of them is inconvenient and meet to be suppressed.

4. The fourth discourse shall be of certain rules and expositions of laws applied to this present purpose.

5. The fifth discourse shall be of the best course to remedy the same inconveniences now a foot, by construction of the statute, without offering either violence to the letter or sense.

6. The sixth and last discourse shall be of the best course to remedy the same inconveniences, and to declare the law by act of parliament; which last I think good to reserve, and not to publish.

The nature of a use is best discerned by considering, first, what it is not, and then what it is; for it is the na- Of the nature of uses before the statute.

ture of all human science and knowledge to proceed most safely, by negative and exclusion, to what is affirmative and inclusive.

First, negatively what it is not. 1 Rep. 121. Chudleigh's case.

First, a use is no right, title, or interest in law; and therefore, master attorney, Coke, who read upon this statute, said well, that there are but two rights.

Jus in re: Jus ad rem.

The one is an estate, which is *Jus in re:* the other a demand, which is *Jus ad rem:* but a use is neither: so that in 24 H. VIII. it is said that the saving of the statute of 1 R. III. which saveth any right or interest of intails, must be understood of intails of the possession, and not of the part of the use, because a use is no right nor interest. So again, you see that Littleton's conceit, is that a use should amount to a tenancy at will, whereupon a release might well inure, because of privity, is controlled by 4 and 15 H. VII. and divers other books, which say that *cestuy que use* is punishable in an action of trespass towards the feoffees; only 5 H. V. seemeth to be at some discord with other books, where it is admitted for law, that if there be *cestuy que use* of an advowson, and he be outlawed in a personal action, the king should have the presentment; which case Master Ewens, in the argument of Chudleigh's case, did seek to reconcile thus: where *cestuy que use*, being outlawed, had presented in his own name, there the king should remove his incumbent; but no such thing can be collected upon the book: and, therefore, I conceive the error grew upon this, that because it was generally thought, that a use was but a pernancy of profits; and then again, because the law is, that, upon outlaw in a personal action, the king shall have the pernancy of the profits, they took that to be one and the selfsame thing *cestuy que use* had, and which the king was intitled unto; which was not so; for the king had remedy in law for his pernancy of the profits, but *cestuy que use* had none. The books go further, and say, that a use is nothing, as in 2 H. VII. *det* was brought and counted *sur leas* for years rendering rent, &c. The defendant pleaded in bar, that the plaintiff *nihil habuit tempore dimissionis*: the plaintiff made a special replication, and showed that he had a use, and issue joined upon that; wherefore it appeareth, that if he had taken issue upon the defendant's plea, it should have been found against him. So again in 4 Reginæ, in the case of the Lord Sandys, the truth of the cause was, a fine was levied by *cestuy que use*

Bro. Feoffm. to uses, pl. 40.
5 H. 7. 5.
15 H. 7. 2.
5 H. 5. 3.
Br. Forfeiture, 14.
5 H. 5. 3.
Dyer, 12.
2 H. 7. 4.
7 H. 7. 11, 12.
Dyer, 215. 6,

before the statute, and this coming in question since the statute upon an averment by the plaintiff *quod partes finis nihil habuerunt,* it is said that the defendant may show the special matter of the use, and it shall be no departure from the first pleading of the fine; and it is said farther, that the form of averment given in 4 H. VII. *quod partes finis nihil habuerunt, nec in possessione, nec in usu,* was ousted by this statute of 27 H. VIII. and was no more now to be accepted; but yet it appears, that if issue had been taken upon the general averment, without the special matter showed, it should have been found for him that took the averment, because a use is nothing. But these books are not to be taken generally or grossly; for we see in the same books, that when a use is specially alleged, the law taketh knowledge of it; but the sense of it is, that a use is nothing for which remedy is given by the course of the common law, so as the law knoweth it, but protects it not; and, therefore, when the question cometh, whether it hath any being in nature or in conscience, the law accepteth of it; and therefore Littleton's case is good law, that he that had but forty shillings freehold in use, shall be sworn of an inquest, for that is ruled *secundum dominium naturale,* and not *secundum dominiam legitimum, nam natura dominus est, qui fructum ex re percipit.* And so, no doubt, upon subsidies and taxes *cestuy que use* should have been valued as an owner; so, likewise, if *cestuy que use* had released his use unto the feoffee for six pounds, or contracted with a stranger for the like sum, there was no doubt but it was a good condition or contract whereon to ground an action upon the case for the money: for a release of a suit in the chancery is a good *quid pro quo;* therefore, to conclude, though a use be nothing in law to yield remedy by course of law, yet it is somewhat in reputation of law and in conscience; for that may be something in conscience which is nothing in law, like as that may be something in law which is nothing in conscience; as, if the feoffees had made a feoffment over in fee, *bona fide,* upon good consideration, and, upon a *subpœna* brought against them, had pleaded this matter in chancery, this had been nothing in conscience, not as to discharge them of damages.

Co. Lit. 272. 15 H. 7. 13. per Cl. J. 21 H. 7. 6.

A second negative fit to be understood is, that a use is no covin, nor it is no collusion, as the word is now used; for it is to be noted, that where a man doth remove the estate and possession of lands or goods, out of himself unto another upon trust, it is either a special trust, or a general trust.

The special trust is either lawful or unlawful.

The special trust unlawful is, according to the cases provided for by ancient statutes of fermours of the profits; as where it is to defraud creditors, or to get men to maintain suits, or to defeat the tenancy to the *præcipe*, or the statute of mortmain, or the lords of their wardships, or the like; and those are termed frauds, covins, or collusions.

The special trust lawful is, as when I infeoff some of my friends, because I am to go beyond the seas, or because I would exempt the land from some general statute, or bond, which I am to enter into, or upon intent to be reinfeoffed, or intent to be vouched, and so to suffer a common recovery, or upon intent that the feoffees shall infeoff over a stranger, and infinite the like intents and purposes, which fall out in men's dealings and occasions; and this we call confidence, and the books do call them intents; but where the trust is not special, nor transitory, but general and permanent, there it is a use; and therefore these three are to be distinguished, and not confounded; the covin, the confidence, and the use.

Secondly, affirmatively. 1 Rep. 121. Chudleigh's case, Poph. 71, 72. Delamer's case, Plow. 343, 352. Dyer, 186.

So as now we are come by negatives to the affirmative, what a use is, agreeable to the definition in Plowden, 352. In Barnard and Delamer's case, where it is said:—that

Use is a trust reposed in any person by the terre-tenant, that he may suffer him to take the profits, and that he will perform his intent.

But it is a shorter speech to say, that

Usus est dominium fiduciarium: Use is an owner's life in trust.

So that *usus et status, sive possessio, potius differunt secundum rationem fori, quam secundum naturam rei*, for that one is in course of law, the other is in course of conscience; and for a trust, which is the way to a use, it is exceedingly well defined by Azo, a civilian of great understanding:

Fides est obligatio conscientiæ unius ad intentionem alterius.

And they have a good division likewise of rights when they say there is

Jus precarium: Jus fiduciarium: Jus legitimum.

1. A right in courtesy, for the which there is no remedy at all

2. A right in trust, for which there is a remedy, but only in conscience.

3. A right in law.

And so much of the nature and definition of a use.

It followeth to consider the parts and properties of a use: wherein it appeareth by the consent of all books, and it was distinctly delivered by Justice Walmsley in 36 of Elizabeth: That a trust consisteth upon three parts. The parts and properties of a use.

The first, that the feoffee will suffer the feoffor to take the profits. The parts.

The second, that the feoffee upon request of the feoffor, or notice of his will, will execute the estates to the feoffor, or his heirs, or any other at his direction.

The third, that if the feoffee be disseised, and so the feoffor disturbed, the feoffee will reenter, or bring an action to recontinue the possession; for that those three, pernancy of profits, execution of estates, and defence of the land, are the three points of the trust.

For the properties of a use, they are exceedingly well set forth by Fenner, justice, in the same case; and they be three: The properties.

1. Uses, saith he, are created by confidence:

2. Preserved by privity, which is nothing else but a continuance of the confidence, without interruption: and

3. Ordered and guided by conscience: either by the private conscience of the feoffee, or the general conscience of the realm, which is chancery.

The two former of which, because they be matters more thoroughly beaten, and we shall have occasion hereafter to handle them, we will not now dilate upon:

But the third we will speak somewhat of; both because it is a key to open many of the true reasons and learnings of uses, and because it tendeth to decide our great and principal doubts at this day,

Coke, solicitor, entering into his argument of Chudleigh's case, said sharply and fitly: "I will put never a case but it shall be of a use, for a use in law hath no fellow;" meaning, that the learning of uses is not to be matched with other learnings. And Anderson, chief justice, in the argument of the same case, did truly and profoundly control the vulgar opinion collected upon 5 E. IV. that there might be *possessio fratris* of a use; for he said, that it was no more but that the chancellor would consult with the rules of law, where the intention of the parties did not specially appear; and therefore the private conceit, which Glanvile, justice, cited in the 42 Reginæ, in the case of Corbet and Corbet, in the Common Pleas, of one of Lincoln's Inn, whom he 5 E. 4. 7. 1 Rep. 88.

named not, but seemed well to allow of the opinion, is not sound; which was, that a use was but a limitation, and did ensue the nature of a possession.

27 H. 8. 9, 10. This very conceit was set on foot in 27 H. VIII. in the lord Darcie's case, in which time they began to heave at uses: for thereafter the realm had many ages together put in action the passing of uses by will, they began to argue that a use was not devisable, but that it did ensue the nature of the land: and the same year after this statute was made; so that this opinion seemeth ever to be a prelude and forerunner to an act of parliament touching uses; and if it be so meant now, I like it well: but in the meantime the opinion itself is to be rejected; and because, in the same case

1 Rep. 88. of Corbet and Corbet, three reverend judges of the court of Common Pleas did deliver and publish their opinion, though not directly upon the point adjudged, yet *obiter* as one of the reasons of their judgment, that a use of inheritance could not be limited to cease; and again, that the limitation of a new use could not be to a stranger; ruling uses merely according to the ground of possession; it is worth the labour to examine that learning. By 3 H. VII. you may collect, that if the feoffees had been disseised by the common law, and an ancestor collateral of *cestuy que use* had released unto the disseisor, and his warranty had attached upon *cestuy que use*, yet the chancellor, upon this matter showed, would have no respect unto it, to compel the feoffees to execute the estate unto the disseisor: for there the case being, that *cestuy que use* in tail having made an assurance by fine and recovery, and by warranty which descended upon his issue, two of the judges held, that the use is not extinct; and Bryan and Hussey, that held the contrary, said, that the common law is altered by the new statute; whereby they admit, that by the common law that warranty will not bind and extinct a right of a use, as it will do a right of possession; and the reason is, because the law of collateral warranty is a hard law, and not to be considered

5 E. 4. 7. in a court of conscience. In 5 E. IV. it is said, that if *cestuy que use* be attainted, *query*, who shall have the land, for the lord shall not have the land; so as there the use doth not imitate the possession; and the reason is, because the lord hath a tenant in by title; for that is nothing to the *subpœna*, because the feoffor's intent was never to advance the lord, but only his own blood; and therefore the *query* of the book ariseth, what the trust and confidence of the feoffee did tie him to do, as whether he should not sell the

land to the use of the feoffee's will, or *in pios usus?* So favourably they took the intent in those days, like as you may find in 37 H. VI. that if a man had appointed his use to one for life, the remainder in fee to another, and *cestuy que use* for life had refused, because the intent appeared not to advance the heir at all, nor him in reversion, presently the feoffee should make the estate for life of him that refused, some ways to the behoof of the feoffor. But to proceed in some better order towards the disproof of this opinion of imitation, there be four points wherein we will examine the nature of uses.

37 H. 6. 36.
Sug. Gilb. 247. n. Coup.

1. The raising of them.
2. The preserving of them.
3. The transferring of them.
4. The extinguishing of them.

1. In all these four you shall see apparently that uses stand upon their own reasons, utterly differing from cases of possession. I would have one case showed by men learned in the law, where there is a deed; and yet there needs a consideration; as for parole, the law adjudgeth it too light to give a use without consideration; but a deed ever in law imports a consideration, because of the deliberation and ceremony in the confection of it: and therefore in 8 Reginæ it is solemnly argued, that a deed should raise a use without any other consideration. In the queen's case a false consideration, if it be of record, will hurt the patent, but want of consideration doth never hurt it; and yet they say that a use is but a nimble and light thing; and now, contrariwise, it seemeth to be weightier than any thing else: for you cannot weigh it up to raise it, neither by deed, nor deed inrolled, without the weight of a consideration; but you shall never find a reason of this to the world's end, in the law: but it is a reason of chancery, and it is this:

That no court of conscience will inforce *donum gratuitum*, though the intent appear never so clearly, where it is not executed, or sufficiently passed by law; but if money had been paid, and so a person damnified, or that it was for the establishment of his house, then it is a good matter in the chancery. So again I would see in all the law, a case where a man shall take by conveyance, be it by deed, livery, or word, that is not party to the grant: I do not say that the delivery must be to him that takes by the deed, for a deed may be delivery to one man to the use of another. Neither do I say that he must be party to the livery or deed, for he in the remainder may take though he be

2 Roll. Abr. 785. Plow. 303. Dy. 160. 337. 7 Rep. 40. 2 Vern. 239.

party to neither; but he must be party to the words of the grant; here again the case of the use goeth single, and the reason is, because a conveyance in use is nothing but a publication of the trust; and therefore, so as the party trusted be declared, it is not material to whom the publication be. So much for the raising of uses. Now as to the preserving of them.

2. There is no case in the common law wherein notice simply and nakedly is material to make a coven, or *particeps criminis;* and therefore if the heir, which is in by descent, infeoff one which had notice of the disseisin, if he
33 H. 6. 5. were not a *disseisor de facto,* it is nothing: so in 33 H. VI. if a feoffment be made upon collusion, and that feoffee make a feoffment over upon good consideration, the collusion is discharged, and it is not material whether the second feoffee had notice or no. So as it is put in 14 H. VIII. if a sale be made in a market overt upon good consideration, although it be to one that hath notice that they are stolen goods, yet the property of a stranger is bound; though in the book before remembered, 35 H. VI. there be some opinion to the contrary, which is clearly no law; so in 31 E. III. if assets descend to the heir, and he alien it upon good consideration, although it be to one that had notice of the debt, or of the warranty, yet it is good enough. So 25 Ass. p. 1, if a man enter of purpose into my lands, to the end that a stranger which hath right, should bring his *præcipe* and evict the land, I may enter notwithstanding any such recovery: but if he enter, having notice that the stranger hath right, and the stranger likewise having notice of his entry, yet if it were not upon confederacy or collusion between them, it is nothing; and the reason of these cases is, because the common law looketh no farther than to see whether the act were merely *actus fictus in fraudem legis;* and therefore wheresoever it findeth consideration given, it dischargeth the coven.

Dy. 12. But come now to the case of the use, and there it is otherwise, as it is in 14 H. VIII. and 28 H. VIII. and divers other books; which prove that if the feoffee sell the land for good consideration to one that hath notice, the
3 Rep. 81. purchaser shall stand seised to the ancient use; and the
1 Roll. Abr. 779. reason is, because the chancery looketh farther than the common law, namely, to the corrupt conscience of him that will deal with the land, knowing it in equity to be another's; and therefore if there were *radix amaritudinis,* the consideration purgeth it not, but it is at the peril of him that

giveth it: so that a consideration, or no consideration, is an issue at the common law; but notice, or no notice, is an issue in the chancery. And so much for the preserving of uses.

3. For the transferring of uses there is no case in law whereby an action may be transferred, but the *subpœna* we see in case of use was always assignable; nay, farther, you find twice 27 H. VIII. fol. 20, pla. 9; and again, fol. 30, and pla. 21, that a right of use may be transferred; for in the former case Montague maketh an objection, and saith, that a right of use cannot be given by fine, but to him that hath the possession; Fitzherbert answereth, Yes, well enough; *query* the reason, saith the book. The transfering of uses.

And in the latter case, where *cestuy que use* was infeoffed by the disseisor of the feoffee, and made a feoffment over, Englefield doubted whether the second feoffee should have the use. Fitzherbert said, "I marvel you will make a doubt of it, for there is no doubt but the use passeth by the feoffment to the stranger, and therefore this question needeth not to have been made." So the great difficulty in 10 Reginæ, Delamer's case, where the case was in effect, there being tenant in tail of a use, the remainder in fee, tenant in tail made a feoffment in fee, by the statute of 1 R. III. and that feoffee infeoffed him in the remainder of the use, who made a feoffment over; and there question being made, whether the second feoffee should have the use in remainder, it is well said, that the second feoffee must needs have the best right in conscience; because the first feoffee claimeth nothing but in trust, and the *cestuy que use* cannot claim it against his sale; but the reason is apparent, as is touched before, that a use in *esse* was but a thing in action, or in suit to be brought in court of conscience; and whether the *subpœna* was to be brought against the feoffee in possession to execute the estate, or against the feoffee out of possession to recontinue the estate, always the *subpœna* might be transferred; for still the action at the common law was not stirred, but remained in the feoffee; and so no mischief of maintainance or transferring rights.

And if any use being but in right may be assigned, and passed over to a stranger, *a multo fortiori*, it may be limited to a stranger upon the privity of the first conveyance, as shall be handled in another place; and whereas Glanvile, justice, said, that he could never find, neither in book, nor evidences of any antiquity, a contingent use limited over Gilb. v.

to a stranger; I answer, first, it is no marvel that you find no case before E. IV. his time, of contingent uses, where there be not six of uses in all; and the reason, no doubt, was, because men did choose well whom they trusted, and trust was well observed; and at this day, in Ireland, where uses are in practice, cases of uses come seldom in question, except it be sometimes upon the alienations of tenants in tail by fine, that the feoffees will not be brought to execute estates to the disinheritance of ancient blood. But for experience of contingent uses, there was nothing more usual in obits than to will the use of the land to certain persons and their heirs, so long as they shall pay the chantry priests their wages, and in default of payment, then to limit the use over to other persons and their heirs; and so, in case of forfeiture, through many degrees; and such conveyances are as ancient as R. II. his time.

1 Rep.121.129.

The extinguishment of uses.

14 H. 8. 4.

4. Now for determining and extinguishing of uses, we put the case of collateral warranty before; add to that, the notable case of 14 H. VIII. Halfpenny's case, where this very point is in the principal case; for a right out of land, and the land itself, in case of possession, cannot stand together, but the rent shall be extinct; but there the case is, that the use of the land and the use of the rent may stand well enough together; for a rent charge was granted by the feoffee to one that had notice of the use, and ruled, that the rent was to the ancient use, and both uses were *in esse simul et semel;* and though Brudenell, chief justice, urged the ground of possession to be otherwise, yet he was overruled by other three justices; and Brooke said unto him, he thought he argued much for his pleasure. And to conclude, we see that things may be avoided and determined by the ceremonies and acts, like unto those by which they are created and raised: that which passeth by livery ought to be avoided by entry; that which passeth by grant, by claim; that which passeth by way of charge, determineth by way of discharge; and so a use which is raised but by a declaration or limitation may cease by words of declaration or limitation, as the civil law saith, *in his magis consentaneum est, quam ut iisdem modis res dissolvantur quibus constituantur.*

Co. Lit. 237. Digges's case, 1 Rep. 174.

The inception and progress of uses.

For the inception and progression of uses, I have, for a precedent in them, searched other laws, because states and commonwealths have common accidents; and I find, in the civil law, that that which cometh nearest in name to the use is nothing like in matter, which is *usus fructus;*

for *usus fructus et dominium* is, with them, as with us, particular tenancy and inheritance. But that which resembleth the use most is, *fidei commisseo*, and therefore you shall find, in Justinian, lib. 2, that they had a form in testaments, to give inheritance to one to the use of another, *Hæredem constituo Caium; rogo autem te, Caie, ut hæreditatem restituas Scio.* And the text of the civilians saith, that for a great time, if the heir did not as he was required, *cestuy que use* had no remedy at all, until, about the time of Augustus Cæsar, there grew in custom a flattering form of trust, for they penned it thus: *Rogò te per salutem Augusti*, or, *per fortunam Augusti*, &c. Whereupon Augustus took the breach of trust to sound in derogation of himself, and made a rescript to the *prætor* to give remedy in such cases; whereupon, within the space of a hundred years, these trusts did spring and speed so fast, as they were forced to have a particular chancellor only for uses, who was called *prætor fidei-commissarius;* and not long after, the inconvenience of them being found, they resorted unto a remedy much like unto this statute; for, by two decrees of senate, called *senatus consultum Trebellianum et Pegasianum*, they made *cestuy que use* to be heir in substance. I have sought, likewise, whether there be any thing which maketh with them in our law, and I find that Periam, chief baron, in the argument of Chudleigh's case, compareth them to copyholders, and aptly for many respects.

First, in the civil law. Contra Sigon. de Judiciis, lib. 1. cap. 5. Inst. 1, 2. Tit. 2. Domat, tom. 3. lib. 5. tit. 3.

Second, in our law.

First, because, as a use seemeth to be an hereditament in the court of chancery, so the copyhold seemeth to be an hereditament in the lord's court.

Secondly, this conceit of limitation hath been troublesome in copyholders, as well as in uses; for it hath been of late days questioned, whether there should be dowers, tenancies by the courtesy, intails, discontinuances, and recoveries of copyholds, in the nature of inheritances, at the common law; and still the judgments have weighed, that you must have particular customs in copyholds, as well as particular reasons of conscience in use, and the limitation rejected.

And thirdly, because they both grew to strength and credit by degrees; for the copyholder first had no remedy at all against the lord, and were as tenancy at will. Afterwards it grew to have remedy in chancery, and afterwards against their lords by trespass at the common law; and now, lastly, the law is taken by some, that they have remedy by *ejectione firmæ;* without a special custom of leasing. So no doubt in uses: at the first the chancery made question to give remedy, until uses grew more general, and the chancery more eminent; and then they grew to have remedy in conscience: but they could never maintain any manner of remedy at the common law, neither against the feoffee, nor against strangers; but the remedy against the feoffee was but by the *subpœna;* and the remedy against strangers to the feoffee by *subpœna.*

The causes of them.

Now for the causes whereupon uses were put in practice: Master Coke, in his reading, doth say well, that they were produced sometimes for fear, and many times for fraud. But I hold that neither of these cases were so much the reasons of uses, as another reason in the beginning, which was, that the lands by the common law of England were not testamentary or devisable; and of late years, since the statute, the case of the conveyance for sparing of purchases and execution of estates; and now, last of all, an express liberty of will in men's minds, affecting to have assurances of their estates and possessions to be revocable in their own times, and irrevocable after their own times.

Their commencement and progress. First, in course of common law. 27 H. 8. 9, 10. Ld. Dacre's case.

Now for the commencement and proceeding of them, I have considered what it hath been in course of common law, and what it hath been in course of statute. For the common law, the conceit of Shelley, in 24 H. VIII. and of Pollard, in 27 H. VIII. seemeth to me to be without ground, which was, that the use succeeded the tenure: for that the statute of *Quia emptores terrarum,* which was made 18 E. I. had taken away the tenure between the feoffor and the feoffee, and left it to the lord paramount; they said that the feoffment, being then merely without consideration, should therefore intend a use to the feoffor, which cannot be; for, by that reason, if the feoffment before the statute had been made *tenendum de capitalibus dominis,* as it might be, there should have been a use unto the feoffor before that statute. And again, if a grant had been of such things as consist in tenure, as advowsons, rents, villains, and the like, there should have been a use of them, wherein the law was quite contrary; for after the time that uses grew common, yet it was, nevertheless, a great doubt whether things that did lie in grant, did not carry a consideration in themselves because of the deed.

7 E. 4. 16. Shortridge v. Lamplugh. Salk. 678.

And therefore I do judge that the intendment of a use to the feoffor, where the feoffment was without consideration, grew long after, when uses waxed general; and for this reason, because when feoffments were made, and that it rested doubtful whether it were in use or in purchase, because purchases were things notorious, and trusts were things secret, the chancellor thought it more convenient to put the purchaser to prove his confidence, than the feoffor and his heirs to prove the use; and so made the intendment towards the use, and put the proof upon the purchaser.

And therefore as uses do carry at the common law in no reason, for whatsoever is not by statute, nor against law, may be said to be at the common law; and both the general trust and the special were things not prohibited by law, though they were not remedied by law; so the experience and practice of uses were not ancient; and my reasons why I think so are these four: 37 H. 8. 9, 10. Montague. Doctor & Stud. part 2. c. 22.

First, I cannot find in any evidence before King R. II. his time, the clause *ad opus et usum*, and the very Latin of it savoureth of that time; for in ancient time, about E. I. and before, when lawyers were part civilians, the Latin phrase was much purer, as you may see partly by Bracton's writing, and by ancient patents and deeds, and chiefly by the register of writs, which is good Latin; whereas the phrase *ad opus et usum*, as to the words *ad opus*, is a barbarous phrase, and like enough to be in the penning of some chaplain that was not much past his grammar, when he found *opus et usus* coupled together, and (preceding) that they govern an ablative case; as they do indeed since this statute, for they take away the land and so put them into a conveyance.

Secondly, I find in no private act of attainder, in the clause of forfeiture of lands, the words, "which he hath in possession or in use," until about E. IV.'s reign.

Thirdly, I find the word "use" in no statute until 7 R. II. cap. 12. Of Provisors, and in 13 R. Of Mortuaries.

Fourthly, I collect out of Choke's speech in 8 E. IV. where he saith, that by the advice of all the judges it was thought that the *subpœna* did not lie against the heir of the feoffee which was in by law, but that the *cestuy que use* was driven to bill in parliament, so that uses at that time were but in their infancy; for no doubt at the first the chancery made difficulty to give any remedy at all, but to leave to the particular conscience of the feoffee: but after the chancery grew absolute, as may appear by the statute made in H. VI. that complainants in chancery should enter into bond to prove their suggestions, which showeth that the chancery at 8 E. 4. 5.

that time began to embrace too far, and was used for vexation; yet, nevertheless, it made scruple to give remedy against the heir, being in by act in law, though he were privy; so that it cannot be that uses had been in any great continuance when they made that question; as for the case of *matrimonii prælocuti,* it hath no affinity with uses; for wheresoever there was remedy at the common law by action, it cannot be intended to be of the nature of a use.

And for the book commonly vouched of 8 Ass. where Earl calleth the possession of a conuzee upon a fine levied by consent and entry in *autre droit,* and 44 of E. III. where there is mention of the feoffors that sued by petition to the king, they be but implications of no moment. So as it appeareth the first practice of uses was about R. II. his time; and the great multiplying and overspreading of them was partly during the wars in France, which drew most of the nobility to be absent from their possessions; and partly during the time of the trouble and civil wars between the two houses about the title of the crown.

Second course of statutes.

Now to conclude the progression of uses in courts of statutes, I do note three special points.

1. That a use had never any force at all at the common law, but by statute law.

2. That there was never any statute made directly for the benefit of *cestuy que use,* as that the descent of a use should toll an entry, or that a release should be good to the pernor of the profits, or the like; but always for the benefit of strangers, and third persons against *cestuy que use,* and his feoffees: for though by the statute of R. III. he might alter his feoffee, yet that was not the scope of the statute, but to make good his assurance to third persons, and the other came in but *ex obliquo.*

3. That the special intent unlawful and covinous was the original of uses, though after it induced to the lawful intent general and special: so 50 E. III. is the first statute I find wherein mention is made of the taking of profits by one, where the estate in law is in another.

50 E. 3. c. 6.

For as for the opinion in 27 H. VIII. that in case of the statute of Marlebridge, the feoffor took the profits, it is but a conceit: for the law is at this day, that if a man infeoff his eldest son, within age, and without consideration, although the profits be taken to the use of the son, yet it is a feoffment within the statute. And for the statute *De religiosis* 7 E. 1. which prohibits generally that religious persons should not purchase *arte vel ingenio,* yet it maketh no mention of a use, but it saith *colore donationis, termini, vel alicujus tituli,* reciting there three forms of conveyances, the gift, the long lease, and feigned recovery; which gift cannot be understood of a gift to a stranger to their use, for that same to be holpen by 15 R. II. long after. 15 R. 2. c. 5.

But to proceed, in 50 E. III. a statute was made for the relief of creditors against such as made covinous gifts of their lands and goods, and conveyed their bodies into sanctuaries, there living high upon other men's goods; and therefore that statute made their lands and goods liable to their creditors' executions in that particular case, if they took the profits. 50 E. 3. c. 6.

In 1 R. II. c. 9, a statute was made for relief of those as had right of action, against such as had removed the tenancy of the *præcipe* from them sometimes by infeoffing great persons, for maintenance; and sometimes by feoffments to other persons, whereof the defendants could have no notice; and therefore the statute maketh the recovery good in all actions against the first feoffors, so as they took the profits, and so as the defendants bring their actions within a year of their expulsions. In 2 R. II. cap. 3, an imperfection in the statute of 50 E. III. was holpen; for whereas the statute took no place, but where the defendant appeared, and so was frustrated, the statute giveth upon proclamation made at the gate of the place privileged, that the land should be liable without appearance.

In 7 R. II. cap. 12, a statute was made for the restraint of aliens, to take any benefices, or dignities ecclesiastical, or farms, or administration of them, without the king's special license, upon pain of the statute of provisors; which being remedied by a former statute, where the alien took it to his own use; it is by that statute remedied, where the alien took it to the use of another, as it is printed in the book; though I guess that if the record were searched, it should be, if any other purchased it to the use of an alien, and that the words, "or to the use of another," should be, "or any other to his use." In 15 R. II. cap. 5, a statute was made for the relief of lords against mortmain, were feoffments were made to the use of corporations; and an ordinance made that for feoffments past the feoffees should, before a day, either purchase license to amortise them, or alien them to some other use, and for feoffments to come, or they should be within the statute of mortmain. In 4 H. VIII. cap. 7, the statute of 1 R. II. 5 is enlarged in the limitation of time; whereas that statute did limit the action to be brought within the year of the feoffment, this statute in case of a disseisin extends the time to the life of the disseisor; and in all other actions, leaves it to the year from time to time of the action grown. In 11 H. VI. cap. 3, the statute of 4 H. IV. is declared, because that conceit was upon that statute, that in case of disseisin the limitation of the life of the disseisor went only to the assize of novel disseisin, and to no other action; and, therefore, that statute declareth the former law to extend to all other actions, grounded upon novel disseisin. In 11 H. IV. cap. 5, a statute was made for relief of him in remainder against particular tenants, for lives, or years, that assigned over their estates, and took the profits, and then committed waste; and therefore this statute giveth an action of waste against them, being pernors of profits. In all this course of statutes no relief is given to purchasers, that come in by the party, but to such as come in by law, as defendants in *præcipes*, whether they be creditors, disseisors, or lessors, and lands, and that only in case of mortmain: and note also, that they be all in cases of special covinous intents, as to defeat executions, tenancy to the *præcipe*, and the statute of mortmain, or provisors. From 11 H. VI. to 1 R. III. being a space of some fifty years, a great silence of uses in the statute book, which was this time no question, they were favoured most. In 1 R. III. cap. 1, cometh that great statute for the relief of those that come in by the party, and at that time a use appeareth in his likeness; for there is not a word spoken of any taking of the profits, to describe a use by, but of claiming to a use; and this statute ordained, that all feoffments, gifts, grants, &c. shall be good against the feoffors, donors, and grantors, and all other persons claiming only to their use; so as here the purchaser was fully relieved, and *cestuy que use* was *obiter* enabled to change his feoffees; because there were no words in the statute of feoffments, grants, &c. upon good consideration, but generally. In H. VII.'s time new statutes were made for further help and remedy to those that came in by act in law; as I H. VII. cap. 1, a *formedon* is given without limitation of time against *cestuy que use;* and *obiter*, because they make him tenant, they give him the advantage of a tenant, with age and a voucher over: *query* 4 H. VII. cap. 17, the wardship is given to the lord of the heir of *cestuy que use*, dying, and no will declared, as if he had died seised in demesne, and *triprice* the action of waste given to the heir against the guardian, and damages, if the lord were barred in his writ of ward; and relief is likewise given unto the lord, if he, holding by knight service, be of full age.

In 19 H. VII. cap. 15, there is relief again in three cases, first to the creditors upon matter of record, as upon recognisance, statute, or judgment, whereof the two former were not aided at all by any statute: and the last was aided by a statute of 50 E. III. and 2 R. II. only in cases of sanctuary men. Secondly, to the lords in soccage for the reliefs, and herriots upon death, which was omitted in the 4 H. VII. and lastly to the lords of villains, upon the purchase of their villains in use.

In 23 H. VIII. cap. 10, a further remedy was given in a case like unto the case of mortmain; for in the statute of 15 R. II. remedy was given where the use came *ad manum mortuam*, which was when it came to some corporation: now when uses were limited to a thing, apt or worthy, and not to a person or body, as to corporation of a church or chaplain, or obiit, but not incorporate as to priests or to such guilds or fraternities as are only in reputation, and not incorporate, the case was omitted, which by the statute was remedied, but not by way of giving entry unto the lord, but by way of making the use utterly void; neither doth the statutes express to whose benefit the use shall be void, either the feoffor or feoffee, but leaveth it to law, and addeth a *proviso*, that such uses may be limited from the gift, and no longer.

This is the whole course of the statute law, before this statute. Thus have I set forth unto you the nature and definition of a use, the differences and trusts of a use, the parts of a use, the qualities of it; and by what rules and learnings uses shall be guided and ordered: a precedent of them in other laws, the causes of the springing and proceeding of them, the continuance of uses, and the proceeding that they have had both in common and statute law; whereby it may appear, that a use is no more but a general trust when a man will trust the conscience of another better than his own estate and possession, which is an accident or event of him and society, which hath been, and will be in all laws, and therefore was at the common law; for as Fitzherbert saith in the 14 H. VIII. common reason is common law, and not conscience; but common reason doth define that uses should be remedied in conscience, and not in courts of law, and ordered by rules in conscience, and not by straight cases of law; for the common law hath a kind of rule on the chancery, to determine what belongs unto the chancery. And therefore we may truly conclude, that the force and strength of the use had or hath in con-

14 H. 8. 4.

science, is by common law; and therefore that it had or hath in law, is only by statute.

Of uses since the statute.

Now followeth in course both of time and matter, the consideration of this statute, our principal labour; and whereunto this former consideration which we have handled serve but for introduction.

This statute, as it is the statute which of all others hath the greatest power and operation over the inheritance of the realm, so howsoever it hath been by the humour of the time perverted in exposition, yet itself is the most perfect and exactly conceived and penned of any law in the book. It is induced with the most declaring and understanding preamble, consisting and standing upon the wisest and fittest ordinances, and qualified with the most foreseeing and circumspect savings and provisoes: and lastly, the best pondered of all the words and clauses of it of any statute that I find. But before I come to the statute itself, I will note unto you three matters of circumstance.

Of the circumstances attending the statute.

1. The time of the statute. 2. The title of it. 3. The precedent or pattern of it.

1. The time of the statute.

For the time it was made in 27 H. VIII. when the kingdom was in full peace, and in a wealthy and in a flourishing time, in which nature of time men are most careful of the assurance of their possessions; as well because purchasers are most stirring, as again, because the purchaser, when he is full, is no less careful of his assurance to his children, and of disposing that which he hath gotten, than he was of his bargain and compassing thereof.

About that time the realm began to be enfranchised from the tributes to Rome, and the possessions that had been in mortmain began to stir abroad; for this year was the suppression of the smaller houses, all tending to plenty, and purchasing: and this statute came in consort with divers excellent statutes, made for the kingdom in the same parliament; as the reduction of Wales to a more civil government, the reedifying of divers cities and towns, the suppressing of depopulation and inclosures, all badges of a time that did extraordinarily flourish.

2. The title.

For the title, it hath one title in the roll, and another in course of pleading. The title in the roll is no solemn title, but an apt title, viz. An act expressing an order for uses and wills; it was time, for they were out of order. The title in course of pleading is, *Statutum de usibus in possessionem transferendis:* wherein Walmsly, justice, noted well, 40 Reginæ, that if a man look to the working of the statute, he would think that it should be turned the other way, *de possessionibus ad usus transferendis:* for that is the course that the statute holdeth, to bring possession to the use. But the title is framed not according to the working of the statute, but according to the scope and intention of the statute, *nam quod primum est intentione ultimum est opere.* And the intention of the statute was by carrying the possession to the use, to turn the use into a possession; for the words are not *de possessionibus ad usus sed in usus transferendis;* and as the grammarian saith, *præpositio, ad, denotat motum actionis, sed præpositio,* in, *cum accusativo denotat motum alterationis:* And therefore Kingsmill, justice, in the same case said, that the meaning of the statute was to make a transubstantiation of the use into a possession.

But it is to be noted, that titles of acts of parliament severally came in H. VIII. for before that time there was but one title to all the acts made in one parliament; and that was no title neither, but a general preface of the good intent of the king, but now it is parcel of the record.

For the precedent of this statute upon which it is drawn, I do find it by the first R. III. c. 5, whereupon you may see the very mould whereon this statute was made, where the said king having been infeoffed (before he usurped) to uses, it was ordained that the land whereof he was jointly infeoffed with others should be in his other cofeoffees as if he had not been named; and where he was solely infeoffed, it should be in *cestuy que use,* in estate, as he had the use.

The precedent upon which it is drawn.

Now to come to the statute itself, the statute consisteth, as other laws do, upon a preamble, the body of the law, and certain savings, and provisoes. The preamble setteth forth the inconvenience, the body of the law giveth the remedy. For new laws are like the apothecaries' drugs, though they remedy the disease, yet they trouble the body; and therefore they use to correct with spices: and so it is not possible to find a remedy for any mischief in the commonwealth, but it will beget some new mischief; and therefore they spice their laws with provisoes to correct and qualify them.

The preamble of this law was justly commended by Popham, chief justice, in 36 Eliz. where he saith, that there is little need to search and collect out of cases, before this statute, what the mischief was which the scope of the statute was to redress; because there is a shorter way offered us, by the sufficiency and fulness of the preamble, and because it is indeed the very level which doth direct the very ordi-

The preamble. In Chudleigh's case, 1 Rep. 123.

nance of the statute, and because all the mischief hath grown by expounding of this statute, as if they had cut off the body of this statute from the preamble; it is good to consider it and ponder it thoroughly.

Its parts.

The preamble hath three prats.

First, a recital of our principal inconvenience, which is the root of all the rest.

Secondly, an enumeration of divers particular inconveniences, as branches of the former.

Thirdly, a taste or brief note of the remedy that the statute meaneth to apply.

1. The principal inconvenience.

The principal inconvenience, which is *radix omnium malorum*, is the digressing from the grounds and principles of the common law, by inventing a mean to transfer lands and hereditaments without any solemnity or act notorious; so as the whole statute is to be expounded strongly towards the extinguishment of all conveyances, whereby the freehold or inheritance may pass without any new confections of deeds, executions of estate or entries, except it be where the estate is of privity and dependence one towards the other; in which cases, *mutatis mutandis*, they might pass by the rules of the common law.

2. The particular inconvenience.

The particular inconveniences by the law rehearsed may be reduced into four heads.

1. First, that these conveyances in use are weak for consideration.

2. Secondly, that they are obscure and doubtful for trial.

3. Thirdly, that they are dangerous for lack of notice and publication.

4. Fourthly, that they are exempted from all such titles as the law subjecteth possessions unto.

The first inconvenience lighteth upon heirs.

The second upon jurors and witnesses.

The third upon purchasers.

The fourth upon such as come in by gift in law.

All which are persons that the law doth principally respect and favour.

1. They are weak in consideration.

For the first of these are there three impediments to the judgment of man, in disposing wisely and advisedly of his estate.

First, nonability of mind.

Secondly, want of time.

Thirdly, of wise and faithful counsel about him.

I. And all these three the statute did find to be in the disposition of a use by will, whereof followed the unjust disinherison of many. Now the favour of the law unto heirs appeareth in many parts of the law; of descent which privilegeth the possession of the heir against the entry of him that hath right by the law; that a man shall not warrant against his heir, except he warrant against himself, and divers other cases too long to stand upon; and we see the ancient law in Glanvill's time was, that the ancestor could not disinherit his heir by grant, or other act executed not in time of sickness; neither could he alien land which had descended unto him, except it were for consideration of money or service; but not to advance any younger brother without the consent of the heir. Glanb. b. 7. ch. 1. fo. 44.

2. For trials, no law ever took a stricter course that evidence should not be perplexed, nor juries inveigled, than the common law of England; as on the other side, never law took a stricter or more precise course with juries, that they should give a direct verdict. For whereas in a manner all laws do give the triers, or jurors (which in other laws are called judges *de facto*) leave to give a *non liquet*, that is, no verdict at all, and so the cause to stand abated; our law enforceth them to a direct verdict, general or special; and whereas other laws accept of plurality of voices to make a verdict, our law enforceth them all to agree in one; and whereas other laws leave them to their own time and ease, and to part, and to meet again; our law doth duress and imprison them in the hardest manner, without food, light, or other comfort, until they be agreed. In consideration of which strictness and coercion, it is consonant, that the law do require in all matters brought to issue, that there be full proof and evidence; and therefore if the matter of itself be in the nature of simple contracts, which are made by parole without writing. They are both obscure and doubtful for trial.

In issue upon the mere right, which is a thing hard to discern, it alloweth the wager of battail to spare jurors. If time have wore the marks and badges of truth: from time to time there have been statutes of limitation, where you shall find this mischief of perjuries often recited; and lastly, which is the matter in hand, all inheritances could not pass but by acts overt and notorious, as by deed, livery, and record.

3. For purchasers, *bonâ fide*, it may appear that they were ever favoured in our law, as first by the great favour of warranties which were ever for the indemnity of purchasers: as where we see that by the law in E. III.'s time, the disseisee could not enter upon the feoffee in regard of 3. The use dangerous for want of notice.

the warranty. So again the collateral garranty, which otherwise is a hard law, grew no doubt only upon favour of purchasers; so likewise that the law doth take strictly rent charge, conditions, extent, was merely in favour of purchasers; so was the binding of fines at the common law, the invention and practice of recoveries, to defeat the statute of entails, and many more grounds and learnings of law are to be found, respect the quiet possession of purchasers. And therefore, though the statute of 1 R. III. had provided for the purchaser in some sort, by enabling the acts and conveyances of *cestuy que use*, yet, nevertheless, the statute did not at all disable the acts or charges of the feoffees: and so as Walmsly justice said, 42 Eliz. they played at double hand, for *cestuy que use* might sell, and the feoffee might sell, which was a very great uncertainty to the purchaser.

4. They are exempt from all titles in law.

4. For the fourth point of inconvenience towards those that come in by law; conveyances in uses were like privileged places or liberties: for as there the law doth not run, so upon such conveyances the law could take no hold, but they were exempted from all titles in law. No man is so absolute owner in his own possessions, but that the wisdom of the law doth reserve certain titles unto others; and such persons come not in by the pleasure and disposition of the party, but by the justice and consideration of law, and therefore of all others they are most favoured: and they are principally three.

1. The king and lords, who lost the benefit of attainders, fines for alienations, escheats, aids, herriots, reliefs, &c.

2. The demandents in *præcipes* either real or personal, for debt and damages, who lost the benefit of their recoveries and executions.

3. Tenants in dower, and by the courtesy, who lost their estates and titles.

1. First for the king: no law doth endow the king or sovereign with more prerogatives than one: for it preserveth and exempteth his person from suits and actions, his possessions from interruption or disturbance, his right from limitation of time, his patents from all deceits and false suggestions. Next the king is the lord, whose duties and rights the law doth much favour, because the law supposeth the land did originally come from him; for until the statute of *quia emptores terrarum*, the lord was not forced to distract or dismember his signiory or service. So until 15 H. VII. the law was taken, that the lord, upon his

title of wardship, should oust a reconuzee of a statute, or a termor: So again we see, that the statute of mortmain was made to preserve the lord's escheats and wardships. The tenant in dower is so much favoured, as that it is the common saying and bye-word in the law, that the law favoureth three things.

1. Life. 2. Liberty. 3. Dower.

So in case of voucher, the feme shall not be delayed, but shall recover against the heir maintenant: So likewise for the tenant by courtesy, as it is called, and by the law of England, and therefore specially favoured, as a proper conceit and invention of our law. So, again, they principally favour such as have ancient rights, and therefore Lett telleth us that it is commonly said that a right cannot die: and that ground of law, that a freehold cannot be in suspense, showeth it well, insomuch that the law will rather give the land to the first comer, which we call an occupant, than want a tenant to a stranger's action.

And again, the other ancient ground of law of *remitter*, showeth that where the tenant faileth without folly in the demandant, the law executeth the ancient right. To conclude, therefore, this part, when this practice of feoffments in use did prejudice and damnify all those persons that the ancient common law favoured, and did absolutely cross the wisdom of the law, which was to have conveyances considerate and notorious, and to have trial thereupon clear and not inveigled, it is no marvel that the statute concludeth, that the subtle imaginations and abuses tended to the utter subversion of the ancient common laws of this realm.

The third part giveth a touch of the remedy which the statute intendeth to minister, consisting in two parts. 3. A touch of the remedy.

First, the extirpation of feoffments.

Secondly, the taking away of the hurt, damage, and deceit of uses; out of which have been gathered two extremities of opinions.

The first opinion is, that the intention of the statute was to discontinue and banish all conveyances in use; grounding themselves both upon the words, that the statute doth not speak of the extinguishment or extirpation of the use, namely, by a unity of possession, but of an extinguishment or extirpation of the feoffment, &c. which is the conveyance itself.

Secondly, out of the words abuse and errors, heretofore used and accustomed, as if uses had not been at the common law, but had been only an erroneous device or practice. To both which I answer.

To the former, that the extirpation which the statute meant was plain, to be of the feoffee's estate, and not of the form of conveyances.

To the latter I say, that for the word abuse, that may be an abuse of the law, which is not against law, as the taking of long leases of lands at this day in capite to defraud wardships is an abuse of law, but yet it is according to law, and for the word (errors) the statute meant by it, not a mistaking of the law, but a wandering or going astray, or digressing from the ancient practice of the law, into a bye-course: as when we say, *erravimus cum patribus nostris*, it is not meant of ignorance, but of perversity. But to prove that the statute meant not to suppress the form of conveyances, there be three reasons which are not answerable.

The first is, that the statute in every branch thereof hath words *de futuro*, that are seised, or hereafter shall be seised; and whereas it may be said that these words were put in, in regard of uses suspended by discontinuance, and so no present seisin to the use, until a regress of the feoffees; that intendment is very particular, for commonly such cases special are brought in by provisos, or special branches, and not intermixed in the body of a statute; and it had been easy for the statute to have, "or hereafter shall be seised upon every feoffment, &c. heretofore had or made."

My second reason is upon the words of the statute of inrolment, which saith, that (no hereditaments shall pass, &c. or any use thereof, &c.) whereby it is manifest, that the statute meant to leave the form of conveyance with the addition of a farther ceremony.

The third reason I make is out of the words of the first proviso, where it is said, that no primer seisin, livery, fine, nor alienation, &c. shall be taken for any estate executed
27 H. 8. by force of the statute, before the first of May, 1536, but that they shall be paid for uses made and executed in possession for the time after; where the word made directly goeth to conveyances in use made after the statute, and can have no other understanding; for the words, executed in possession, would have served for the case of regress: and, lastly, which is more than all, if they have had any such intent, the case being so general and so plain, they would have had words express, that every limitation of use made after the statute should have been void; and this was the exposition, as tradition goeth, that a reader of Gray's Inn, that read soon after the statute, was in trouble for, and worthily, which, I suppose, was Boiser, whose

reading I could never see; but I do now insist upon it, because now again some, in an immoderate invective against uses, do relapse to the same opinion.

The second opinion, which I call a contrary extremity, is that the statute meant only to remedy the mischiefs in the preamble, recited as they grew by reason of divided uses; although the like mischief may grow upon the contingent uses, yet the statute had no foresight of them at that time, and so it was merely a new case not comprised. Whereunto I answer, that I grant the work of the statute is to execute the divided use; and, therefore, to make any use void by this statute which was good before, though it doth participate of the mischief recited in the statute, were to make a law upon a preamble without a purview, which were grossly absurd. But upon the question what uses are executed, and what not; and whether out of the possessions of a disseisin, or other possessions out of privity or not, there you shall guide your exposition according to the preamble; as shall be handled in my next day's discourse, and so much touching the preamble of this law. Opinion.

For the body of the law, I would wish all readers that expound statutes to do as scholars are willed to do: that is, first, to seek out the principal verb; that is, to note and single out the material words whereupon this statute is framed; for there are, in every statute, certain words, which are veins where the life and blood of the statute cometh, and where all doubts do arise and issue forth, and all the rest of the words are but *literæ mortuæ*, fulfilling words. Cap. 2. The body of the law.

The body of the statute consisteth upon two parts.

First, a supposition, or case put, as Anderson, 36 Eliz. called it.

Secondly, a purview, or ordinance thereupon.

The cases of the statute are three, and every one hath his purview: the general case; the case of feoffees to the use of some of them; and the general case of feoffees to the use or pernors of rents or profits. The cases of the statute.

The general case is built upon eight material words: four on the part of the feoffees; three on the part of *cestuy que use;* and one common to them both. 2. The general case.

The first material word on the part of the feoffees is the word person. This excludes all abeyance; for there can be no confidence reposed but in a person certain. It excludes again all corporations: for they are enabled to a use certain; for note on the part of the feoffor over the statute insists upon the word person; and on the part of *cestuy que use*, it ever addeth, body politic.

Dy. 49. Cramlington's case, 2 Ventr. 310.

The second word material is the word seised. This excludes chattels. The reason they meant to remit the common law, and not to alter that chattels might ever pass by testament or by parole; therefore the use did not pervert them. It excludes again rights, for it was against the rules of the common law to grant or transfer rights; therefore the statute would execute them. Thirdly, it excludes contingent uses, because the seisin can be but to a fee-simple of a use; and when that is limited, the seisin of the feoffee is spent; for Littleton tells us, that there are but two seisins; one, *in dominio ut de feodo;* the other, *ut de feodo;* and the feoffee by the common law could execute but the fee-simple to uses present, and no post uses; and therefore the statute meant not to execute them.

The third material word is the word hereafter: that bringeth in conveyances made after the statute. It brings in again conveyances made before and disturbed by disseisin and recontinued after; for it is not said, infeoffed to use, but hereafter seised.

The fourth word is hereditament, which is to be understood of those things whereof an inheritance may be, and not of those things whereof an inheritance is in esse; for if I grant a rent charge *de novo* for life to a use, this is good enough; and yet there is no inheritance in being of this rent. This word likewise excludes annuities and uses themselves, so that a use cannot be to a use.

The first words on the part of *cestuy que use* are the words, use, trust, or confidence; whereby it is plain that the statute meant not to make use *vocabulatum artis*, but it meant to remedy matter, and not word; and in all the clauses it still carrieth the words.

Broughton v. Langley. Salk. 679. 1 Lutw. 823. Contr. Burchett v. Durdant. 2 Ventr. 312.

The second word is the word person, again, which excludeth all abeyance; it excludeth also dead uses, which are not to bodies lively and natural, as the building of a church, the making of a bridge; but here, as was noted before, is ever coupled with body politic.

The third word is the word other: The statute meant not to cross the common law. Now at this time uses were grown into such familiarity, as men could not think of a possession, but in course of use; and so every man was said to be seised to his own use, as well as to the use of others; therefore, because the statute would not stir nor turmoil possessions settled at common law, it putteth in precisely this word, other; meaning the divided use, and not the conjoined use; and this word causeth the clause in joint feoffees to follow in a branch by itself; for else that case had been doubtful upon this word, other.

The words that are common to both are words expressing the conveyance whereby the use ariseth, of which words those that breed any question are, agreement, will, otherwise, whereby some have inferred that uses might be raised by agreement parole, so there were a consideration of money or other matter valuable; for it is expressed in the words before, bargain, sale, and contract, but of blood, or kindred; the error of which collection appeareth in the word immediately following, namely, will, whereby they might as well include, that a man seised of land might raise a use by will, especially to any of his sons or kindred, where there is a real consideration; and by that reason, mean, betwixt this statute and by the statute of 32 of wills, lands were devisable, especially to any man's kindred, which was clearly otherwise; and therefore those words were put in, but in regard of uses formerly transferred by those conveyances; for it is clear that a use in esse by simple agreement, with consideration, or without, or likewise by will, might be transferred; and there was a person seised to a use, by force of that agreement or will, namely, to the use of the assignee; and for the word otherwise, it should by the generality of the word include a disseisin to a use. But the whole scope of the statute crosseth that which was to execute such uses, as were confidences and trust, which could not be in case of disseisin; for if there were a commandment precedent, then the land was vested in *cestuy que use* upon the entry; and if the disseisin were of the disseisor's own head, then no trust. And thus much for the case of exposition of this statute: here follow the ordinance and purview thereupon.

Collard v. Call. 2 R. Abr. 788. How v. Dixe. 1 Sid. 26.

The purview hath two parts: the first *operatio statuti*, the effect that the statute worketh; and there is *modus operandi*, a fiction, or explanation how the statute doth work that effect. The effect is, that *cestuy que use* shall be in possession of like estate as he hath in the use; the fiction *quomodo* is, that the statute will have the possession of *cestuy que use*, as a new body compounded of matter and form; and that the feoffees shall give matter and substance, and the use shall give form and quality. The material words in the first part of the purview are four.

Purview or ordinance thereupon.

Coltemar v. Senhouse. Pollexf. 525. 586. Lisle v. Gray. 1 Rep. 10. 28. 138. Chudleigh's case.

The first words are, remainder and reverter, the statute having spoken before of uses in fee-simple, in tail, for life, or years, addeth, or otherwise in remainder or reverter;

Cooper v. Franklyn. 1 Ro. Abr. 780. Cro. Jac. 401.

whereby it is manifest, that the first words are to be understood of uses in possession. For there are two substantial and essential differences of estates; the one limiting the times, for all estates are but times of their continuances; the former maketh like difference of fee-simple, fee-tail, for life or years; and the other maketh difference of possession as remainder; all other differences of estate are but accidents, as shall be said hereafter. These two the statute meant to take hold of, and at the words, remainder and reverter, it stops: it adds not words, right, title, or possibility, nor it hath not general words, or otherwise; whereby it is most plain, that the statute meant to execute no inferior uses to remainder or reverter: that is to say, no possibility or contingencies, but estates, only such as the feoffees might have executed by conscience made. Note also, that the very letter of the statute doth take notice of a difference between a use in remainder and a use in reverter; which though it cannot be properly, because it doth not depend upon particular estates, as remainders do, neither did then before the statute draw any tenures as reversions do; yet the statute intends there is a difference when the particular use, and the use limited upon the particular use, are both new uses, in which case it is a use in remainder; and where the particular use is a new use, and the remnant of the use is the old use, in which case it is a use in reverter.

The next material words are, from henceforth, which doth exclude all conceit of relation that *cestuy que use* shall not come in: as from the time of the first feoffments to use, as Brudnell's conceit was in 14 H. VIII. That is, the feoffee had granted a rent charge, and *cestuy que use* had made a feoffment in fee, by the statute of 1 R. III. the feoffee should have held it discharged, because the act of *cestuy que use* shall put the feoffee in, as if *cestuy que use* had been seised in from the time of the first use limited; and therefore the statute doth take away all such ambiguities, and expresseth that *cestuy que use* shall be in possession from henceforth; that is, from the time of the parliament for uses then in being, and from the time of the execution for uses limited after the parliament.

The third material words are, lawful seisin, state, and possession, not a possession in law only, but a seisin in fact; not a title to enter into the land, but an actual estate.

The fourth words are, of and in such estates as they had in the use; that is to say, like estates, fee-simple, fee-tail, for life, for years at will, in possession, and reversion, which are the substantial differences of estates, as was expounded by the branch of the fiction of the statute which follows.

This branch of fiction hath three material words or clauses: the first material clause is, that the estate, right, title, and possession that was in such person, &c. shall be in *cestuy que use;* for that the matter and substance of the estate of *cestuy que use* is the estate of the feoffee, and more he cannot have; so as if the use were limited to *cestuy que use* and his heirs, and the estate out of which it was limited was but an estate for life, *cestuy que use* can have no inheritance: so if when the statute came, the heir of the feoffee had not entered after the death of his ancestor, but had only a possession in law, *cestuy que use* in that case should not bring an assize before entry, because the heir of the feoffee could not; so that the matter whereupon the use might work is the feoffee's estate. But note here: whereas before, when the statute speaks of the uses, it spake only of uses in possession, remainder and reverter, and not in title or right: now when the statute speaks what shall be taken from the feoffee, it speaks of title and right: so that the statute takes more from the feoffee than it executes presently, in cases where there are uses in contingence which are but titles.

The second word is clearly, which seems properly and directly to meet with the conceit of *scintilla juris*, as well as the words in the preamble of extirpating and extinguishing such feoffments, so as their estate is clearly extinct.

Dy. 340. Haly v. Ryley. Pollexf. 385. 1And.331,332. Barker v. Neale, 2 Mod. 251. Shortridge v. Lamplugh. Salk. 678.

The third material clause is, after such quality, manners, form, and condition as they had in the use, so as now as the feoffee's estate gives matter, so the use gives form: and as in the first clause the use was endowed with the possession in points of estate, so there it is endowed with the possession in all accidents and circumstances of estate. Wherein first note, that it is gross and absurd to expound the form of the use any whit to destroy the substance of the estate; as to make a doubt, because the use gave no dower or tenancy by the courtesy, that therefore the possession when it is transferred would do so likewise: no, but the statute meant such quality, manner, form, and condition, as it is not repugnant to the corporal presence and possession of the estate.

Next for the word condition, I do not hold it to be put in for uses upon condition, though it be also comprised within the general words; but because I would have things stood upon learnedly, and according to the true sense, I hold it but for an explaining, or word of the effect; as it is

26 Hen. 8. 13. in the statute of 26 of treasons, where it is said, that the offenders shall be attainted of the overt fact by men of their condition, in this place, that is to say, of their degree and sort: and so the word condition in this place is no more, but in like quality, manner, form and degree, or sort; so as all these words amount but to *modo et forma*. Hence therefore all circumstances of estate are comprehended as sole seisin, or jointly seisin, by intierties, or by moieties, a circumstance of estate to have age as coming in by descent, or not age as purchaser; a circumstance of estate descendable to the heir of the part of the father, or of the part of the mother; a circumstance of estate conditional or absolute, remitted or not remitted, with a condition of intermarriage or without. All these are accidents and circumstances of estate, in all which the possession shall ensue the nature and quality of the use: and thus much of the first case, which is the general case.

The second case. The second case of the joint feoffees needs no exposition; for it pursueth the penning of the general case: only this I will note, that although it had been omitted, yet the law upon the first case would have been taken as the case provided: so that it is rather an explanation than an addition; for turn that case the other way, that one were infeoffed to the use of himself, and others as that case is, that divers were infeoffed to the use of one of them, I hold the law to be, that in the former case they shall be seised jointly; and so in the latter case *cestuy que use* shall be seised solely; for the word other, it shall be qualified by construction of cases, as shall appear when I come to my division. But because this case of cofeoffees to the use of one of them was a general case in the realm, therefore they foresaw it, and passed over the case *e converso*, which was but an especial case: and they were loth to bring in this case, by inserting the word only into the first case, to have penned it to the use only of other persons: for they had experience what doubt the word only bred upon the statute of 1 R. III. after this third case: and before the third case of rents comes in the second saving; and the reason of it is worth the noting, why the savings are interlaced before the third case; the reason of it is, because the third case needeth no saving, and the first two cases did need savings; and that is the reason of that again.

It is a general ground, that where an act of parliament is donor, if it be penned with an *ac si*, it is not a saving, for it is a special gift, and not a general gift, which includes all rights; and therefore in 11 H. VII. where upon the alienation of women, the statute entitles the heir of him in remainder to enter, you find never a stranger, because the statute gives entry not *simpliciter*, but within an *ac si;* as if no alienation had been made, or if the feme had been naturally dead. Strangers that had right might have entered; and therefore no saving needs. So in the statute of 32 of leases, the statute enacts, that the leases shall be good and effectual in law, as if the lessor had been seised of a good and perfect estate in fee-simple; and therefore you find no saving in the statute; and so likewise of diverse other statutes, where the statute doth make a gift or title good specially against certain persons, there needs no saving, except it be to exempt some of those persons, as in the statute of 1 R. III. Now to apply this to the case of rents, which is penned with an *ac si,* namely, as if a sufficient grant or other lawful conveyance had been made, or executed by such as were seised; why if such a grant of a rent had been made, one that had an ancient right might have entered and have avoided the charge; and therefore no saving needeth: but the second and first cases are not penned with an *ac si,* but absolute, that *cestuy que use* shall be adjudged in estate and possession, which is a judgment of parliament stronger than any fine, to bind all rights; nay, it hath farther words, namely, in lawful estate and possession, which maketh that the stronger than any in the first clause. For if the words only had stood upon the second clause, namely, that the estate of the feoffee should be in *cestuy que use,* then perhaps the gift should have been special, and so the saving superfluous: and this note is very material in regard of the great question, whether the feoffees may make any regress; which opinion, I mean, that no regress is left unto them, is principally to be argued out of the saving; as shall be now declared: for the savings are two in number: the first saveth all stranger's rights, with an exception of the feoffee's; the second is a saving out of the exception of the first saving, namely, of the feoffees' in case where they claim to their own proper use: it had been easy in the first saving out of the statute, other than such persons as are seised, or hereafter should be seised to any use, to have added to these words, executed by this statute; or in the second saving to have added unto the words, claiming to their proper use, these words, or to the use of any other, and executed by this statute: but the regress of the feoffee is shut out between the two savings; for it is the right of a person claiming to a use, and not unto his own proper use: but it is to be added, that the first saving is not to be understood as the letter implieth, that feoffees to use shall be barred of their regress, in case that it be of another feoffment than that whereupon the statute hath wrought, but upon the same feoffment; as if the feoffee before the statute had been disseised, and the disseised had made a feoffment in fee to I. D. his use, and then the statute came; this executeth the use of the second feoffment; but yet the first feoffees may make a regress, and they yet claim to a use, but not by that feoffment upon which the statute hath wrought.

The third case. Boscawen & al. v. Cooke. 1 Mod. 223.

Now followeth the third case of the statute, touching execution of rents; wherein the material words are four:

First, whereas diverse persons are seised, which hath bred a doubt that it should only go to rents in use at the time of the statute; but it is explained in the clause following, namely, as if a grant had been made to them by such as are or shall be seised.

The second word is profit; for in the putting of the case, the statute speaketh of a rent; but after in the purview is added these words, or profit.

The third word is, *ac si, scilicet,* that they shall have the rent as if a sufficient grant or other lawful conveyance had been made and executed unto them.

The fourth words are, the words of liberty or remedies attending upon such rent, *scilicet,* that he shall distrain, &c. and have such suits, entries, and remedies, relying again with an *ac si*, as if the grant had been made with such collateral penalties and advantages.

Now for the provisos; the makers of this law did so abound with policy and discerning, as they did not only foresee such mischiefs as were incident to this new law immediately, but likewise such as were consequent in a remote degree; and, therefore, besides the express provisos, they did add three new provisos, which are in themselves subtractive laws: for, foreseeing that by the execution of uses, wills formerly made should be overthrown; they made an ordinance for wills. Foreseeing, likewise, that by execution of uses women should be doubly advanced; they made an ordinance for dowers and jointures. Foreseeing, again, that the execution of uses would make frank-tenement pass by contracts parole, they made an ordinance for enrolments of bargains and sales. The two former they inserted into this law, and the third they distinguished into a law apart, but

2 Inst. 672. Beny v. Bowes. 1 Ventr. 361.

without any preamble as may appear, being but a proviso to this statute. Besides all these provisional laws; and besides five provisos, whereof three attend upon the law of jointure, and two born in Wales, which are not material to the purpose in hand; there are six provisos, which ar natural and true members and limbs of the statute, whereof four concern the part of *cestuy que use*, and two concern the part of the feoffees. . The four which concern the part of *cestuy que use*, tend all to save him from prejudice by the execution of the estate.

The first saveth him from the extinguishment of any statute or recognisance, as if a man had an extent of a hundred acres, and a use of the inheritance of one; now the statute executing the possession to that one, would have extinguished his extent being intire in all the rest; or as if the conuzee of a statute having ten acres liable to the statute, had made a feoffment in fee to a stranger of two, and after had made a feoffment in fee to the use of the conuzee and his heirs. And upon this proviso there arise three questions:

First, whether this proviso were not superfluous, in regard that *cestuy que use* was comprehended in the general saving, though the feoffees be excluded?

Secondly, whether this proviso doth save statutes or executions, with an apportionment, or intire?

Thirdly, because it is penned indefinitely in point of time, whether it shall go to uses limited after the statute, as well as to those that were in being at the time of the statute; which doubt is rather enforced by this reason, because there was for* uses at the time of the statute; for that the execution of the statute might be waved; but both possession and use, since the statute, may be waved.

The second proviso saveth *cestuy que use* from the charge of *primer seisin, liveries, ouster les maines*, and such other duties to the king, with an express limitation of time, that he shall be discharged from the time past, and charged for the time to come to the king, namely, May 1536, to be *communis terminus*.

The third proviso doth the like for fines, reliefs, and herriots, discharging them from the time past, and speaking nothing of the time to come.

The fourth proviso giveth to *cestuy que use* all collateral

---

* The text here is manifestly corrupted, nor does any probable conjecture occur for its amendment.

benefits of vouchers, aid-priers, actions of waste, trespass, conditions broken, and which the feoffees might have had; and this is expressly limited for estates executed before May 1, 1536. And this proviso giveth occasion to intend that none of these benefits would have been carried to *cestuy que use*, by the general words in the body of the law, *scilicet*, that the feoffee's estate, right, title, and possession, &c.

For the two provisos on the part of the tertenant, they both concern the saving of strangers from prejudice, &c.

Cheney's case. Moor, 196.

The first saves actions depending against the feoffees, that they shall not abate.

The second saves wardships, liveries, and *ouster les maines*, whereof title was vested in regard of the heir of the feoffee, and this in case of the king only.

What persons may be seised to a use, and what not.
What persons may be cestuy que use, *and what not.*
What persons may declare a use, and what not.

Of the estate of the assurance of this realm at this day upon uses. First, the raising of uses.

Though I have opened the statute in order of words, yet I will make my division in order of matter, namely,

1. The raising of uses.
2. The interruption of uses.
3. The executing of uses.

Again, the raising of uses doth easily divide itself into three parts. 1. The persons that are actors to the conveyance to use. 2. The use itself. 3. The form of the conveyance.

Then it is first to be seen what persons may be seised to a use, and what not; and what persons may be *cestuy que use*, and what not; and what persons may declare a use, and what not.

1. What persons may be seised to a use.

The king cannot be seised to a use; no, not where he taketh in his natural body, and to some purpose as a common person; and, therefore, if land be given to the king and I. D. *pour terme de leur vies*, this use is void for a moiety.

Like law is, if the king be seised of land in the right of his duchy of Lancaster, and covenanteth by his letters patents under the duchy seal to stand seised to the use of his son, nothing passeth.

Like law, if King R. III. who was feoffor to diverse uses before he took upon him the crown, had, after he was king, by his letters patents granted the land over, the uses had not been renewed.

The queen, not speaking of an imperial queen by marriage, cannot be seised to a use, though she be a body enabled to grant and purchase without the king; yet in regard of the government and interest the king hath in her possession, she cannot be seised to a use.

A corporation cannot be seised to a use, because their capacity is to a use certain; again, because they cannot execute an estate without doing wrong to their corporation or founder; but chiefly because of the letter of this statute, which, in any clause when it speaketh of the feoffee, resteth only upon the word person, but when it speaketh of *cestuy que use*, it addeth person or body politic.

If a bishop bargain and sell lands whereof he is seised in the right of his see, this is good during his life; otherwise it is where a bishop is infeoffed to him and his successors, to the use of I. D. and his heirs, that is not good, no not for the bishop's life, but the use is merely void.

Contrary law of tenant in tail; for if I give land in tail by deed since the statute to A., to the use of B. and his heirs; B. hath a fee-simple determinable upon the death of A. without issue. And like law, though doubtful before the statute, was; for the chief reason which bred the doubt before the statute was because tenant in tail could not execute an estate without wrong; but that since the statute is quite taken away, because the statute saveth no right of intail, as the statute of 1 R. III. did; and that reason likewise might have been answered before the statute, in regard of the common recovery.

Vide contra. Cooper v. Franklyn. Cro. Jac. 401.

A feme covert and an infant, though under years of discretion, may be seised to a use; for as well as land might descend to them from a feoffee to use, so may they originally be infeoffed to a use; yet if it be before the statute, and they had, upon a *subpœna* brought, executed their estate during the coverture or infancy, they might have defeated the same; and then they should have been seised again to the use, and not to their own use; but since the statute no right is saved unto them.

If a feme covert or an infant be infeoffed to a use present since the statute, the infant or baron come too late to discharge or root up the feoffment; but if an infant be infeoffed to the use of himself and his heirs, and I. D. pay such a sum of money to the use of I. G. and his heirs, the infant may disagree and overthrow the contingent use.

Contrary law, if an infant be infeoffed to the use of himself for life, the remainder to the use of I. S. and his heirs, he may disagree to the feoffment as to his own estate, but not to divest the remainder, but it shall remain to the benefit of him in remainder.

And yet if an attainted person be infeoffed to a use, the king's title, after office found, shall prevent the use, and relate above it; but until office the *cestuy que use* is seised of the land.

Like law of an alien; for if land be given to an alien to a use, the use is not void *ab initio:* yet neither alien or attainted person can maintain an action to defend the land.

The king's villain if he be infeoffed to a use, the king's title shall relate above the use; otherwise in case of a common person.

But if the lord be infeoffed to the use of his villain, the use neither riseth, but the lord is in by the common law, and not by the statute discharged of the use.

But if the husband be infeoffed to the use of his wife for years, if he die the wife shall have the term, and it shall not inure by way of discharge, although the husband may dispose of the wife's term.

So if the lord of whom the land is held be infeoffed to the use of a person attainted, the lord shall not hold by way of discharge of the use, because of the king's title, *annum, diem et vastum.*

A person uncertain is not within the statute, nor any estate *in nubibus* or suspense executed; as if I give land to I. S. the remainder to the right heirs of I. D. to the use of I. N. and his heirs, I. N. is not seised of the fee-simple of an estate *pour vie* of I. S. till I. D. be dead, and then in fee-simple.

Like law, if before the statute I give land to I. S. *pour autre vie* to a use, and I. S. dieth, living *cestuy que use,* whereby the freehold is in suspense, the statute cometh, and no occupant entereth: the use is not executed out of the freehold in suspense for the occupant, the disseisor, the lord by escheat. The feoffee upon consideration, not having notice, and all other persons which shall be seised to use, not in regard of their persons but of their title; I refer them to my division touching disturbance and interruption of uses.

2. What person may be a *cestuy que use.*

It followeth now to see what person may be a *cestuy que use.* The king may be *cestuy que use;* but it behoveth both the declaration of the use, and the conveyance itself, to be matter of record, because the king's title is compounded of both; I say, not appearing of record, but by conveyance of record. And therefore if I covenant with I. S. to levy a fine to him to the king's use, which I do accordingly; and this deed of covenant be not inrolled, and the deed be found by office, the use vesteth not. *E converso*, if inrolled. If I covenant with I. S. to infeoff him to the king's use, and the deed be inrolled, and the feoffment also be found by office, the use vesteth.

But if I levy a fine, or suffer a recovery to the king's use, and declare the use by deed of covenant inrolled, though the king be not party, yet it is good enough.

A corporation may take a use, and yet it is not material whether the feoffment or the declaration be by deed; but I may infeoff I. S. to the use of a corporation, and this use may be averred.

A use to a person uncertain is not void in the first limitation, but executeth not till the person be in esse; so that this is positive, that a use shall never be in abeyance as a remainder may be, but ever in a person certain upon the words of the statute, and the estate of the feoffees shall be in him or them which have the use. The reason is, because no confidence can be reposed in a person unknown and uncertain; and therefore, if I make a feoffment to the use of I. S. for life, and then to the use of the right heirs of I. D. the remainder is not in abeyance, but the reversion is in the feoffor, *quousque*. So that upon the matter all persons uncertain in use are like conditions or limitations precedent. Of a use to a person uncertain.

Like law, if I infeoff one to the use of I. S. for years, the remainder to the right heirs of I. D. this is not executed in abeyance, and therefore not void.

Like law, if I make a feoffment to the use of my wife that shall be, or to such persons as I shall maintain, though I limit no particular estate at all; yet the use is good, and shall in the interim return to the feoffor.

Contrary law, if I once limit the whole fee-simple of the use out of me, and part thereof to a person uncertain, it shall never return to the feoffor by way of fraction of the use; but look how it should have gone unto the feoffor; if I begin with a contingent use, so it shall go to the remainder; if I intail a contingent use, both estates are alike subject to the contingent use when it falleth; as when I make a feoffment in fee to the use of my wife for life, the remainder to my first begotten son; I having no son at that time, the remainder to my brother and his heirs: if my wife die before I have any son, the use shall not be in me, but in my brother. And yet if I marry again, and have a son, Purefoy v Rogers. 2 Saund. 386. Q. Chudleigh's case. 1 Rep. 129. 138. 2 Sid. 64. 129. 157. Heyne's v. Villiers. Bidford's case. 2 Ro. Abr. 791. Mo. 720. Badger v. Lloyd. Salk. 224. ib. 232. Scattergood v. Edge, ib. 229. Goodright v. Hornish, ib. 226. Davis v. Speed. ib. 675. Sir Ed. Lloyd v. Carew. Prec. in Chan. 74. Mo. 506. Ld. Buckhurst's case. Yelv. 37. Machell v. Clerk, Salk. 619. 7 Rep. 14.

it shall divest from my brother, and be in my son, which is the skipping they talk so much of.

So if I limit a use jointly to two persons, not in esse, and the one cometh to be in esse, he shall take the entire use; and yet if the other afterward come in esse, he shall take jointly with the former; as if I make a feoffment to the use of my wife that shall be, and my first begotten son for their lives, and I marry; my wife taketh the whole use, and if I afterwards have a son, he taketh jointly with my wife.

But yet where words of abeyance work to an estate executed in course of possession, it shall do the like in uses; as if I infeoff A. to the use of B. for life, the remainder to C. for life, the remainder to the right heirs of B. this is a good remainder executed.

So if I infeoff A. to the use of his right heirs, A. is in the fee-simple, not by the statute, but by the common law.

Now are we to examine a special point of the disability of persons as take by the statute: and that upon the words of the statute, where divers persons are seised to the use of other persons; so that by the letter of the statute, no use is contained: but where the feoffor is one, and *cestuy que use* is another.

Therefore it is to be seen in what cases the same persons shall be both seised to the use and *cestuy que use,* and yet in by the statute; and in what cases they shall be diverse persons, and yet in by the common law; wherein I observe unto you three things: First, that the letter is full in the point. Secondly, that it is strongly urged by the clause of joint estates following. Thirdly, that the whole scope of the statute was to remit the common law, and never to intermeddle where the common law executed an estate; therefore the statute ought to be expounded, that where the party seised to the use, and the *cestuy que use* is one person, he never taketh by the statute, except there be a direct impossibility or impertinency for the use, to take effect by the common law.

As if I give land to I. S. to the use of himself and his heirs, and if I. D. pay a sum of money, then to the use of I. D. and his heirs, I. S. is in by the common law, and not by the statutes.

Like law is, if I give lands to I. S. and his heirs, to the use of himself for life or for years, and then to the use of I. D. and his heirs, I. S. is in of an estate for life, or for years, by way of abridgment of estate in course of possession, and I. D. in of the fee-simple by the statute.

So if I bargain and sell my land after seven years, the inheritance of the use only passeth; and there remains an estate for years by a kind of subtraction of the inheritance or reoccupier of my estate, but merely at the common law.

3. Contr. the fee-simple remaius, per Ld. C. J. Hale, in Weale v. Lower, Poll. 65, 66. and Gilb. v. infra. 2 Raym. 855.

But if I infeoff I. S. to the use of himself in tail, and then to the use of I. D. in fee, or covenant to stand seised to the use of myself in tail, and then to the use of my wife in fee; in both these cases the estate tail is executed by this statute: because an estate tail cannot be reoccupied out of a fee-simple, being a new estate, and not like a particular estate for life or years, which are but portions of the absolute fee; and, therefore, if I bargain and sell my land to I. S. after my death without issue, it doth not leave an estate tail in me, nor vesteth any present fee in the bargain, but is a use expectant.

See Mr. Sugden's remarks in Gilb. V. & T. ed. Sugd. 162. Ans. 17.

1 And. 328.

So if I infeoff I. S. to the use of I. D. for life, and then to the use of himself and his heirs, he is in of the fee-simple merely in course of possession, and as of a reversion, and not of a remainder.

Contrary law, if I infeoff I. S. to the use of I. D. for life, then to the use of himself for life, the remainder to the use of I. N. in fee: now the law will not admit fraction of estates; but I. S. is in with the rest by the statute.

So if I infeoff I. S. to the use of himself and a stranger, they shall be both in by the statute, because they could not take jointly, taking by several titles.

Gilb. Us. 70. ed. Sugd. 132.

Like law, if I infeoff a bishop and his heirs to the use of himself and his successors, he is in by the statute in the right of his see.

And as I cannot raise a present use to one out of his own seisin; so if I limit a contingent or future use to one being at the time of limitation not seised, but after become seised at the time of the execution of the contingent use, there is the same reason and the same law, and upon the same difference which I have put before.

As if I covenant with my son, that, after his marriage, I will stand seised of land to the use of himself and his heirs; and, before marriage, I infeoff him to the use of himself and his heirs, and then he marrieth; he is in by the common law, and not by the statute; like law of a bargain and sale.

But if I had let to him for life only, then he should have been in for life only by the common law, and of the fee-simple by the statute. Now let me advise you of this, that it is only a matter of subtilty or conceit to take the law right, when a man cometh in by the law in course of possession, and where he cometh in by the statute in course of possession; but it is natural for the deciding of many causes and questions, as for warranties, actions, conditions, waivers, suspensions, and divers other provisos.

This learning material for deciding many questions.

For example; a man's farmer committed waste: after he in reversion covenanteth to stand seised to the use of his wife for life, and after to the use of himself and his heirs; his wife dies; if he be in of his fee untouched, he shall punish the waste; if he be in by the statute, he shall not punish it.

So if I be infeoffed with warranty, and I covenant with my son to stand seised to the use of myself for life, and after to him and his heirs; if I be in by the statute, it is clear my warranty is gone; but if I be in by the common law, it is doubtful.

So if I have an eigne right, and be infeoffed to the use of I. S. for life, then to the use of myself for life, then to the use of I. D. in fee, I. S. dieth. If I be in by the common law, I cannot waive my estate, having agreed to the feoffment; but if I am in by the statute, yet I am not remitted, because I come in by my own act: but I may waive my use, and bring an action presently; for my right is saved unto me by one of the savings in the statute.

Where there is a seisin to the use of another, and yet it is out of the statute.

Now on the other side it is to be seen, where is a seisin to the use of another person; and yet it is out of the statute which is in special cases upon the ground, wheresoever *cestuy que use* had remedy for the possession by course of common law, there the statute never worketh; and therefore if a disseisin were committed to a use, it is in him by the common law upon agreement. So if one enter as occupant to the use of another, it is in him till disagreement.

So if a feme infeoff a man, *causa matrimonii prælocuti*, she hath remedy for the land again by course of the law; and, therefore, in those special cases the statute worketh not; and yet the words of the statute are general, where any person stands seised by force of any fine, recovery, feoffment, bargain and sale, agreement or otherwise; but yet the feme is to be restrained for the reason aforesaid.

What persons may limit and declare a use.

It remaineth to show what persons may limit and declare a use: wherein we must distinguish; for there are two kinds of declarations of uses, the one of a present use upon the first conveyance, the other upon a power of revocation or new declaration; the latter of which I refer to the division of revocation: now for the former.

The king upon his letters patent may declare a use, though the patent itself implieth a use, if none be declared.

If the king gives lands by his letters patent to I. S. and his heirs, to the use of I. S. for life, the king hath the inheritance of the use by implication of the patent, and no office needeth; for implication out of matter of record amounteth ever to matter of record.

If the queen give land to I. S. and his heirs to the use of the churchwardens of the church of Dale, the patentee is seised to his own use, upon that confidence or intent; but if a common person had given land in that manner, the use had been void by the statute of 23 H. VIII. and the use had returned to the feoffor and his heirs. A corporation may take a use without deed, as hath been said before; but can limit no use without deed.

An infant may limit a use upon a feoffment, fine, or recovery, and he cannot countermand or avoid the use, except he avoid the conveyance: contrary, if an infant covenant in consideration of blood or marriage to stand seised to a use, the use is merely void.

If an infant bargain and sell his land for money, for commons or teaching, it is good with averment; if for money, otherwise; if it be proved it is avoidable; for money recited and not paid, it is void; and yet in the case of a man of full age the recital sufficeth.

If baron and feme be seised in the right of the feme, or by joint purchase during the coverture, and they join in a fine, the baron cannot declare the use for longer time than the coverture, and the feme cannot declare alone; but the use goeth, according to the limitation of law, unto the feme and her heirs; but they may both join in declaration of the use in fee; and if they sever, then it is good for so much of the inheritance as they concurred in; for the law accounteth all one, as if they joined; as if the baron and feme declare a use to I. S. and his heirs, and the feme another to I. D. for life, and then to I. S. and his heirs, the use is good to I. S. in fee.

Vid. A. Beckwith's case, de cest. matter, fo. 57.

See Gilb. Us. ed. Sugd. 448, 449.

And if upon examination the feme will declare the use to the judge, and her husband agree not to it, it is void, and the baron's use is only good; the rest of the use goeth according to the limitation of law.

THE

OFFICE OF CONSTABLES,

ORIGINAL AND USE OF

COURTS LEET, SHERIFF'S TURN, ETC.

WITH

THE ANSWERS TO THE QUESTIONS PROPOUNDED BY SIR ALEXANDER HAY, KNT. TOUCHING THE OFFICE OF CONSTABLES. A. D. 1608.

---

1. *Question.* WHAT is the original of constables?

Answer. To the first question of the original of constables it may be said, *caput inter nubila condit;* for the authority was granted upon the ancient laws and customs of this kingdom practised long before the conquest, and intended and executed for conservation of peace, and repression of all manner of disturbance and hurt of the people, and that as well by way of prevention as punishment; but yet so, as they have no judicial power, to hear and determine any cause, but only a ministerial power, as in the answer to the seventh article is demonstrated.

As for the office of high or head constable, the original of that is yet more obscure; for though the high constable's authority hath the more ample circuit, he being over the hundred, and the petty constable over the village; yet I do not find that the petty constable is subordinate to the high constable, or to be ordered or commanded by him; and therefore, I doubt, the high constable was not *ab origine;* but that when the business of the county increased, the authority of justices of peace was enlarged by divers statutes, and then, for conveniency sake, the office of high constable grew in use for the receiving of the commandments and prescripts from the justices of peace, and distributing them to the petty constables: and in token of this, the election of high constable in most parts of the kingdom is by the appointment of the justices of the peace, whereas, the election of the petty constable is by the people.

But there are two things unto which the office of constables hath special reference, and which, of necessity, or at least a kind of congruity, must precede the jurisdiction of that office; either the things themselves, or something that hath a similitude or analogy towards them.

1. The division of the territory, or gross of the shires, into hundreds, villages, and towns; for the high constable is officer over the hundred, and the petty constable is over the town or village.

2. The court-leet, unto which the constable is attendant and minister; for there the constables are chosen by the jury, there sworn, and there that part of their office which concerneth information is principally to be performed: for the jury being to present offences and offenders, are chiefly to take light from the constable of all matters of disturbance and nuisance of the people: which they, in respect of their office, are presumed to have best and most particular knowledge of.

The jurisdiction of the court-leet is to three ends.

1. To take the ancient oath of allegiance of all males above twelve years.

2. To inquire of all offences against the peace; and for those that are against the crown and peace of both, to inquire of only, and certify to the justices of gaol delivery; but those that are against the peace simply, they are to inquire of and punish.

3. To inquire of, punish, and remove all public nuisances and grievances concerning infection of air, corruption of victuals, ease of chaffer, and contract of all other things that may hurt or grieve the people in general, in their health, quiet, and welfare.

And to these three ends, as matters of policy subordinate, the court-leet hath power to call upon the pledges that are to be taken of the good behaviour of the resiants that are not tenants, and to inquire of all defaults of officers, as constables, ale-tasters, and the like: and likewise for the choice of constables, as was said.

The jurisdiction of these leets is either remaining in the king, and in that case exercised by the sheriff in his turn, which is the grand leet, or granted over to subjects; but yet it is still the king's court.

2. *Question.* Concerning the election of constables?

Answer. The election of the petty constable, as was said, is at the court-leet by the inquest that make the presentments; and election of head constables is by the justices of the peace at their quarter sessions.

3. *Question.* How long is their office?

Answer. The office of constable is annual, except they be removed.

4. *Question.* Of what rank or order of men are they?

Answer. They be men, as it is now used, of inferior, yea, of base condition, which is a mere abuse or degenerating from the first institution; for the petty constables in towns ought to be of the better sort of resiants in the same; save that they be not aged or sickly, but of able bodies in respect of keeping watch and toil of their place; nor must they be in any man's livery. The high constables ought to be of the ablest freeholders, and substantialest sort of yeomen, next to the degree of gentlemen; but should not be incumbered with any other office, as mayor of a town, under-sheriff, bailiff, &c.

5. *Question.* What allowance have the constables?

Answer. They have no allowance, but are bound by duty to perform their office gratis; which may the rather be endured because it is but annual, and they are not tied to keep or maintain any servants or under-ministers, for that every one of the king's people within their limits are bound to assist them.

6. *Question.* What if they refuse to do their office?

Answer. Upon complaint made of their refusal to any one justice of peace, the said justice may bind them over to the sessions, where, if they cannot excuse themselves by some allegation that is just, they may be fined and imprisoned for their contempt.

7. *Question.* What is their authority or power?

Answer. The authority of the constable, as it is substantive, and of itself, or substituted, and astricted to the warrants and commands of the justices of the peace; so again it is original, or additional: for either it was given them by the common law, or else annexed by divers statutes. And as for subordinate power, wherein the constable is only to execute the commands of the justices of peace, likewise the additional power which is given by divers statutes, it is hard to comprehend in any brevity; for that they do correspond to the office and authority of justices of peace, which is very large, and are created by the branches of several statutes: but for the original and substantive power of constables, it may be reduced to three heads; namely,

1. For matter of peace only.
2. For peace and the crown.
3. For matter of nuisance, disturbance, and disorder, although they be not accompanied with violence and breach of the peace.

First, for pacifying of quarrel begun, the constable may, upon hot words given, or likelihood of breach of the peace to ensue, command them in the king's name to keep peace, and depart, and forbear: and so he may, where an affray is made, part the same, and keep the parties asunder, and arrest and commit the breakers of the peace, if they will not obey; and call power to assist him for that purpose.

For punishment of breach of peace past, the law is very sparing in giving any authority to constables, because they have not power judicial, and the use of his office is rather for preventing or staying of mischief, than for punishment of offences; for in that part he is rather to execute the warrants of the justices; or, when sudden matter ariseth upon his view, or notorious circumstances, to apprehend offenders, and to carry them before the justices of peace, and generally to imprison in like cases of necessity, where the case will not endure the present carrying of the party before the justices. And so much for peace.

Secondly, For matters of the crown, the office of the constable consisteth chiefly in these four parts:
1. To arrest.
2. To make hue and cry.
3. To search.
4. To seize goods.

All which the constable may perform of his own authority, without any warrant from the justices of the peace.

1. For, first, if any man will lay murder or felony to another's charge, or do suspect him of murder or felony, he may declare it to the constable, and the constable ought, upon such declaration or complaint, to carry him before a justice of peace; and if by common voice or fame any man be suspected, the constable of duty ought to arrest him, and bring him before a justice of peace, though there be no other accusation or declaration.

2. If any house be suspected for receiving or harbouring of any felon, the constable, upon complaint or common fame, may search.

3. If any fly upon the felony, the constable ought to raise hue and cry.

4. And the constable ought to seize his goods, and keep

them safe without impairing, and inventary them in presence of honest neighbours.

Thirdly, for matters of common nuisance and grievances, they are of very variable nature, according to the several comforts which man's life and society requireth, and the contraries which infest the same.

In all which, be it matter of corrupting air, water, or victuals, stopping, straitening, or endangering of passages, or general deceits in weights, measures, sizes, or counterfeiting wares, and things vendible; the office of constable is to give, as much as in him lies, information of them, and of the offenders, in leets, that they may be presented; but because leets are kept but twice in the year, and many of those things require present and speedy remedy, the constable, in things notorious and of vulgar nature, ought to forbid and repress them in the mean time: if not, they are for their contempt to be fined and imprisoned, or both, by the justices in their sessions.

8. *Question.* What is their oath?

Answer. The manner of the oath they take is as followeth:

"You shall swear that you shall well and truly serve the king, and the lord of this law-day; and you shall cause the peace of our sovereign lord the king well and truly to be kept to your power: and you shall arrest all those that you see committing riots, debates, and affrays in breach of peace: and you shall well and truly endeavour yourself to your best knowledge, that the statute of Winchester for watching, hue and cry, and the statutes made for the punishment of sturdy beggars, vagabonds, rogues, and other idle persons coming within your office be truly executed, and the offenders be punished: and you shall endeavour, upon complaint made, to apprehend barreters and riotous persons making affrays, and likewise to apprehend felons; and if any of them make resistance with force, and multitude of misdemeanors, you shall make outcry, and pursue them till they be taken; and shall look unto such persons as use unlawful games; and you shall have regard unto the maintenance of artillery; and you shall well and truly execute all process and precepts sent unto you from the justices of the peace of the county; and you shall make good and faithful presentments of all bloodsheds, outcries, affrays, and rescues made within your office: and you shall well and truly, according to your own power and knowledge, do that which belongeth to your office of constable to do, for this year to come. So help," &c.

9. *Question.* What difference is there betwixt the high constables and petty constables?

Answer. Their authority is the same in substance, differing only in the extent; the petty constable serving only for one town, parish, or borough; the head constable for the whole hundred: nor is the petty constable subordinate to the head constable for any commandment that proceeds from his own authority; but it is used, that the precepts of the justices be delivered unto the high constables, who, being few in number, may better attend the justices, and then the head constables, by virtue thereof, make their precepts over to the petty constables.

10. *Question.* Whether a constable may appoint a deputy?

Answer. In case of necessity a constable may appoint a deputy, or in default thereof, the steward of the court-leet may; which deputy ought to be sworn before the said steward.

The constable's office consists in three things:

1. Conservation of the peace.
2. Serving precepts and warrants.
3. Attendance for the execution of statutes.

Of the Jurisdiction of Justices itinerant in the Principality of Wales.

1. They have power to hear and determine all criminal causes, which are called, in the laws of England, pleas of the crown; and herein they have the same jurisdiction that the justices have in the court of the King's Bench.

2. They have power to hear and determine all civil causes, which in the laws of England are called common pleas, and to take knowledge of all fines levied of lands or hereditaments, without suing any *dedimus potestatem;* and herein they have the same jurisdiction that the justices of the Common Pleas do execute at Westminster.

3. They have power also to hear and determine all assizes upon disseisin of lands or hereditaments, wherein they equal the jurisdiction of the justices of assize.

4. Justices of oyer and terminer therein may hear all notable violences and outrages perpetrated within their several precincts in the said principality of Wales.

The prothonotary's office is to draw all pleadings, and entereth and engrosseth all the records and judgments in all trivial causes. These offices are in the king's gift.

The clerk of the crown, his office is to draw and engross

all proceedings, arraignments, and judgments in criminal causes.

These offices are in the judges' disposition.

The marshal's office is to attend the persons of the judges at their coming, sitting, and going from their sessions or court.

The crier is, *tanquam publicus præco*, to call for such persons whose appearances are necessary, and to impose silence to the people.

The Office of Justice of Peace.

The office of justice of peace.

There is a commission under the great seal of England to certain gentlemen, giving them power to preserve the peace, and to resist and punish all turbulent persons, whose misdemeanors may tend to the disquiet of the people; and these be called justices of the peace, and every of them may well and truly be called *eirenarcha*.

The chief of them is called *custos rotulorum*, in whose custody all the records of their proceedings are resident.

Justice of peace appointed by the lord keeper.

Others there are of that number called justices of peace and *quorum*, because in their commission they have power to sit and determine causes concerning breach of peace and misbehaviour. The words of their commission are conceived thus, *quorum* such and such, *unum vel duos*, &c. *esse volumus;* and without some one or more of the *quorum*, no sessions can be holden; and for the avoiding of a superfluous number of such justices (for through the ambition of many it is counted a credit to be burthened with that authority), the statute of 38 H. VIII. hath expressly prohibited that there shall be but eight justices of the peace in every county. These justices hold their sessions quarterly.

In every shire where the commission of the peace is established, there is a clerk of the peace for the entering and engrossing of all proceedings before the said justices. And this officer is appointed by the *custos rotulorum.*

The Office of Sheriffs.

Every shire hath a sheriff, which word, being of the Saxon English, is as much as to say shire-reeve, or minister of the county: his function or office is twofold, namely,

1. Ministerial.
2. Judicial.

34 H. 8. c. 16.

1. He is the minister and executioner of all the process and precepts of the courts of law, and therefore ought to make return and certificate.

2. The sheriff hath authority to hold two several courts of distinct natures: 1. The turn, because he keepeth his turn and circuit about the shire, holdeth the same court in several places, wherein he doth inquire of all offences perpetrated against the common law, and not forbidden by any statute or act of parliament; and the jurisdiction of this court is derived from justice distributive, and is for criminal offences, and held twice every year.

The county court, wherein he doth determine all petty and small causes civil under the value of forty shillings, arising within the said county, and therefore it is called the county court.

The jurisdiction of this court is derived from justice commutative, and held every month. The office of the sheriff is annual, and in the king's gift, whereof he is to have a patent.

The Office of Escheator.

Every shire hath an officer called an escheator, which is to attend the king's revenue, and to seize into his majesty's hands all lands escheated, and goods or lands forfeited, and therefore is called escheator; and he is to inquire by good inquest of the death of the king's tenant, and to whom the lands are descended, and to seize their bodies and lands for ward, if they be within age, and is accountable for the same; he is named or appointed by the lord treasurer of England.

The Office of Coroner.

Two other officers there are in every county called coroners; and by their office they are to inquest in what manner, and by whom every person, dying of a violent death, came so to their death; and to enter the same of record; which is matter criminal, and a plea of the crown: and therefore they are called coroners, or crowners, as one hath written, because their inquiry ought to be in *corona populi.*

These officers are chosen by the freeholders of the shire, by virtue of a writ out of the chancery *de coronatore eligendo:* and of them I need not to write more, because these officers are in use every where.

General Observations touching Constables, Gaolers, and Bailiffs.

Forasmuch as every shire is divided into hundreds, there are also by the statute of 34 H. VIII. cap. 26, ordered and appointed, that two sufficient gentlemen or yeomen shall be appointed constables of every hundred.

Also there is in every shire a gaol or prison appointed for the restraint of liberty of such persons as for their offences are thereunto committed, until they shall be delivered by course of law.

In every hundred of every shire the sheriff thereof shall nominate sufficient persons to be bailiffs of that hundred, and under-ministers of the sheriffs: and they are to attend upon the justices in every of their courts and sessions.

Note. Archbishop Sancroft notes on this last chapter, written, say some, by Sir John Dodderidge, one of the justices of the King's Bench, 1608.

AN

ACCOUNT OF THE LATELY ERECTED SERVICE,

CALLED,

THE OFFICE OF COMPOSITIONS

FOR

ALIENATIONS.

WRITTEN [ABOUT THE CLOSE OF 1598] BY MR. FRANCIS BACON,

AND PUBLISHED FROM A MS. IN THE INNER-TEMPLE LIBRARY.

The sundry sorts of the royal revenue.

ALL the finances or revenues of the imperial crown of this realm of England be either extraordinary or ordinary.

Those extraordinary be fifteenths and tenths, subsidies, loans, benevolences, aids, and such others of that kind, that have been or shall be invented for supportation of the charges of war; the which, as it is entertained by diet, so can it not be long maintained by the ordinary fiscal and receipt.

Of these that be ordinary, some are certain and standing, as the yearly rents of the demesne or lands; being either of the ancient possessions of the crown, or of the later augmentations of the same.

Likewise the fee-farms reserved upon charters granted to cities and towns corporate, and the blanch rents and lath silver answered by the sheriffs. The residue of these ordinary finances be casual, or uncertain, as be the escheats and forfeitures, the customs, butlerage, and impost, the advantages coming by the jurisdiction of the courts of record and clerks of the market, the temporalities of vacant bishoprics, the profits that grow by the tenures of lands, and such like, if there any be.

And albeit that both the one sort and other of these be at the last brought unto that office of her majesty's exchequer, which we, by a metapor, do call the pipe, as the civilians do by a like translation mame it *fiscus*, a basket or bag, because the whole receipt is finally conveyed into it by the means of divers small pipes or quills, as it were water into a great head or cistern; yet nevertheless some of the same be first and immediately left in other several places and courts, from whence they are afterwards carried by silver streams, to make up that great lake, or sea, of money. The pipe.

As for example, the profits of wards and their lands be answered into that court which is proper for them; and the fines for all original writs, and for causes that pass the great seal, were wont to be immediately paid into the hanaper of the chancery; howbeit now of late years, all the sums which are due, either for any writ of covenant, or of other sort, whereupon a final concord is to be levied in the common bench, or for any writ of entry, whereupon a common recovery is to be suffered there; as also all sums demandable, either for license of alienation to be made of lands holden in chief, or for the pardon of any such alienation, already made without license, together with the mean profits that be forfeited for that offence and trespass, have been stayed in the way to the hanaper, and been let to farm, upon assurance of three hundred pounds of yearly standing profit, to be increased over and above that casual commodity, that was found to be answered in the hanaper for them, in the ten years, one with another, next before the making of the same lease. The hanaper. This office is derived out of the hanaper.

And yet so as that yearly rent of increase is now still paid into the hanaper by four gross portions, not altogether equal, in the four usual open terms of St. Michael, and St. Hilary, of Easter, and the Holy Trinity, even as the former casualty itself was wont to be, in parcel meal, brought in and answered there.

The name of the office.

And now forasmuch as the only matter and subject about which this farmer or his deputies are employed, is to rate or compound the sums of money payable to her majesty, for the alienation of lands that are either made without license, or to be made by license, if they be holden in chief, or to pass for common recovery, or by final concord to be levied, though they be not so holden, their service may therefore very aptly and agreeably be termed the office of compositions for alienations. Whether the advancement of her majesty's commodity in this part of her prerogative, or the respect of private lucre, or both, were the first motives thus to dissever this member, and thereby as it were to mayhem the chancery, it is neither my part nor purpose to dispute.

The scope of the discourse, and the parts thereof.

But for a full institution of the service as it now standeth, howsoever some men have not spared to speak hardly thereof, I hold worthy my labour to set down as followeth:

First, that these fines, exacted for such alienations, be not only of the greatest antiquity, but are also good and reasonable in themselves; secondly, that the modern and present exercise of this office is more commendable than was the former usage; and lastly, that as her majesty hath received great profit thereby, so may she, by a moderate hand, from time to time reap the like, and that without just grief to any of her subjects.

The first part of this treatise.

As the lands that are to be aliened, be either immediately holden in chief, or not so holden of the queen, so be these fines or sums respectively of two sundry sorts; for upon each alienation of lands, immediately held of her majesty in chief, the fine is rated here, either upon the license, before the alienation is made, or else upon the pardon when it is made without license. But generally, for every final concord of lands to be levied upon a writ of covenant, *warrantia chartæ*, or other writ, upon which it may be orderly levied, the sum is rated here upon the original writ, whether the lands be held of the queen, or of any other person; if at the least the lands be of such value, as they may yield the due fine. And likewise for every writ of entry, whereupon a common recovery is to be suffered, the queen's fine is to be rated there upon the writ original, if the lands comprised therein be held of her by the tenure of her prerogative, that is to say, in chief, or of her royal person.

The king's tenant in chief

So that I am hereby enforced, for avoiding of confusion,

to speak severally, first of the fines for alienation of lands held in chief, and then of the fines upon the suing forth of writs original. That the king's tenant in chief could not in ancient time alien his tenancy without the king's license it appeareth by the statute, 1 E. III. cap. 12, where it is thus written: "Whereas divers do complain that the lands holden of the king in chief, and aliened without license, have been seized into the king's hands for such alienation, and holden as forfeit: the king shall not hold them as forfeit in such a case, but granteth that, upon such alienations, there shall be reasonable fines taken in the chancery by due process."

could never alien without license.

1 E. III. c. 12.

So that it is hereby proved, that before this statute, the offence of such alienation, without license, was taken to be so great, that the tenant did forfeit the land thereby; and consequently, that he found great favour there by this statute, to be reasonably fined for his trespass.

And although we read an opinion 20 lib. *Assis. parl.* 17, *et* 26, *Assis. parl.* 37, which also is repeated by Hankf. 14 H. IV. fol. 3, in which year Magna Charta was confirmed by him, the king's tenant in chief might as freely alien his lands without license, as might the tenant of any other lord; yet forasmuch as it appeareth not by what statute the law was then changed, I had rather believe, with old judge Thorpe and late justice Stanford, that even at the common law, which is as much as to say, as from the beginning of our tenures, or from the beginning of the English monarchy, it was accounted an offence in the king's tenant in chief, to alien without the royal and express license.

And I am sure, that not only upon the entering, or recording, of such a fine for alienation, it is wont to be said *pro transgressione in hac parte facta;* but that you may also read amongst the records in the Tower, Fines 6 Hen. Reg. 3, Memb. 4, a precedent of a *capias in manum regis terras alienatas sine licentia regis,* and that, namely, of the manor of Coselescombe in Kent, whereof Robert Cesterton was then the king's tenant in chief. But were it that, as they say, this began first 20 H. III. yet it is above three hundred and sixty years old, and of equal, if not more antiquity than Magna Charta itself, and the rest of our most ancient laws; the which never found assurance by parliament until the time of King Edward I. who may be therefore worthily called, our English Solon or Lycurgus.

The fine for alienation is moderate.

Now therefore, to proceed to the reason and equity of exacting these fines for such alienations, it standeth thus: when the king, whom our law understandeth to have been at the first both the supreme lord of all the persons, and sole owner of all the lands within his dominions, did give lands to any subject to hold them of himself, as of his crown and royal diadem, he vouchsafed that favour upon a chosen and selected man, not minding that any other should, without his privity and good liking, be made owner of the same; and therefore his gift has this secret intention inclosed within it, that if his tenant and patentee shall dispose of the same without his kingly assent first obtained, the lands shall revert to the king, or to his successors, that first gave them. And that also was the very cause, as I take it, why they were anciently seized into the king's hands, as forfeited by such alienation, until the making of the said statute, 1 E. III. which did qualify that rigour of the former law.

Neither ought this to seem strange in the case of the king, when every common subject, being lord of lands which another holdeth of him, ought not only to have notice given unto him upon every alienation of his tenant, but shall, by the like implied intention, re-have the lands of his tenants dying without heirs, though they were given out never so many years agone, and have passed through the hands of howsoever many and strange possessors.

Not without good warrant, therefore, said Mr. Fitzherbert, in his Nat. Brev. fol. 147, that the justices ought not wittingly to suffer any fine to be levied of lands holden in chief, without the king's license. And as this reason is good and forcible, so is the equity and moderation of the fine itself most open and apparent; for how easy a thing is it to redeem a forfeiture of the whole lands for ever with the profits of one year, by the purchase of a pardon? Or otherwise, how tolerable is it to prevent the charge of that pardon, with the only cost of a third part thereof, timely and beforehand bestowed upon a license?

The antiquity and moderation of fines upon writs original.

Touching the king's fines accustomably paid for the purchasing of writs original, I find no certain beginning of them, and do therefore think that they also grew up with the chancery, which is the shop wherein they be forged; or, if you will, with the first ordinary jurisdiction and delivery of justice itself.

For when as the king had erected his courts of ordinary resort, for the help of his subjects in suit one against another, and was at the charge not only to wage justices and their ministers, but also to appoint places and officers for safe custody of the records that concerned not himself; by which means each man might boldly both crave and have law for the present, and find memorials also to maintain his right and recovery, for ever after, to the singular benefit of himself and all his posterity; it was consonant to good reason, that the benefited subject should render some small portion of his gain, as well towards the maintenance of this his own so great commodity, as for the supportation of the king's expense, and the reward of the labour of them that were wholly employed for his profit.

And therefore it was well said by Littleton, 34 H. VI. fol. 38, that the chancellor of England is not bound to make writs, without his due fee for the writing and seal of them. And that, in this part also, you may have assurance of good antiquity, it is extant among the records in the Tower, 2 H. III. Memb. 6, that Simon Hales and others gave unto him their king, *unum palfredum pro summonendo Richardo filio et hærede Willielmi de Hanred, quod teneat finem factum coram justiciariis apud Northampton inter dictum Willielmum et patrem dicti Arnoldi de feodo in Barton.* And besides that, *in oblatis de Ann.* I, 2, and 7, *regis Johannis*, fines were diversely paid to the king, upon the purchasing writs of mort d'auncestor, dower, pone, to remove pleas, for inquisitions, trial by juries, writs of sundry summons, and other more. Litt. 34 H. 6 fol. 38.

Hereof then it is, that upon every writ procured for debt or damage, amounting to forty pounds or more, a noble, that is, six shillings and eight pence, is, and usually hath been paid to fine; and so for every hundred marks more a noble; and likewise upon every writ called a *præcipe* of lands, exceeding the yearly value of forty shillings, a noble is given to a fine; and for every other five marks by year, moreover another noble, as is set forth 20 R. II. abridged 20 Rich. II. both by justice Fitzherbert and justice Brooke; and may also appear in the old *Natura Brevium*, and the Register, which have a proper writ of deceipt, formed upon the case, where a man did, in the name of another, purchase such a writ in the chancery without his knowledge and consent.

And herein the writ of right is excepted, and passeth freely, not for fear of the words in Magna Charta, *Nulli vendemus justitiam vel rectum*, as some do phantasy, but rather because it is rarely brought; and then also bought dearly enough without such a fine, for that the trial may be by battle, to the great hazard of the champion.

The like exemption hath the writ to inquire of a man's death, which also, by the twenty-sixth chapter of that Magna Charta, must be granted freely, and without giving any thing for it; which last I do rather note, because it may be well gathered thereby, that even then all those other writs did lawfully answer their due fines; for otherwise the like prohibition would have been published against them, as was in this case of the inquisition itself.

I see no need to maintain the mediocrity and easiness of this last sort of fine, which in lands exceedeth not the tenth part of one year's value, and in goods the two hundredth part of the thing that is demanded by the writ.

Neither has this office of ours* originally to meddle with the fines of any other original writs, than of such only as whereupon a fine or concord may be had and levied; which is commonly the writ of covenant, and rarely any other. For we deal not with the fine of the writ of entry of lands holden in chief, as due upon the original writ itself; but only as payable in the nature of a license for the alienation, for which the third part of the yearly rent is answered; as the statute 32 H. VIII. cap. 1. hath specified, giving the direction for it; albeit now lately the writs of entry be made parcel of the parcel ferm also; and therefore I will here close up the first part, and unfold the second.

* Right, or some word of the like import, seems to be omitted here.

The second part of this treatise.

Before the institution of this ferm and office no writ of covenant for the levying any final concord, no writ of entry for the suffering of any common recovery of lands holden in chief, no doquet for license to alien, nor warrant for pardon of alienation made, could be purchased and gotten without an oath called an affidavit, therein first taken either before some justices of assize, or master of the chancery, for the true discovery of the yearly value of the lands comprised in every of the same; in which doing, if a man shall consider on the one side the care and severity of the law, that would not be satisfied without an oath; and, on the other side, the assurance of the truth to be had by so religious an affirmation as an oath is, he will easily believe that nothing could be added unto that order, either for the ready dispatch of the subject, or for the uttermost advancement of the king's profit. But *quid verba audiam, cum facta videam?* Much peril to the swearer, and little good to our sovereign hath ensued thereof. For, on the one side, the justices of assize were many times abused by their clerks,

All fines upon oath.

that preferred the recognitions of final concords taken in their circuit; and the masters of the chancery were often overtaken by the fraud of solicitors and attorneys, that followed their clients' causes here at Westminster; and, on the other side, light and lewd persons, especially, that the exactor of the oath did neither use exhortation, nor examining of them for taking thereof, were as easily suborned to make an affidavit for money, as post-horses and hackneys are taken to hire in Canterbury and Dover way; insomuch that it was usual for him that dwelt in Southwark, Shoreditch, or Tothill Street, to depose the yearly rent or valuation of lands lying in the north, the west, or other remote part of the realm, where either he never was at all, or whence he came so young, that little could he tell what the matter meaned. And thus *consuetudinem peccandi fecit multitudo peccantium.* For the removing of which corruption, and of some others whereof I have long since particularly heard, it was thought good that the justice of assize should be entreated to have a more vigilant eye upon their clerks writing; and that one special master of the chancery should be appointed to reside in this office, and to take the oaths concerning the matters that come hither; who might not only reject such as for just causes were unmeet to be sworn, but might also instruct and admonish in the weight of an oath, those others that are fit to pass and perform it; and forasmuch as thereby it must needs fall out very often, that either there was no man ready and at hand that could, with knowledge and good conscience, undertake the oath, or else, that such honest persons as were present, and did right well know the yearly value of the lands, would rather choose and agree to pay a reasonable fine without any oath, than to adventure the uttermost, which, by the taking of their oath, must come to light and discovery. It was also provided, that the fermour, and the deputies, should have power to treat, compound, and agree with such, and so not exact any oath at all of them.

How much this sort of finance hath been increased by this new device, I will reserve, as I have already plotted it, for the last part of this discourse: but in the mean while I am to note first, that the fear of common perjury, growing by a daily and over-usual acquaintance with an oath, by little and little raiseth out that most reverend and religious opinion thereof, which ought to be planted in our hearts, is hereby for a great part cut off and clean removed: then that the subject yieldeth little or nothing more now than he did before, considering that the money, which was wont to be saved by the former corrupt swearing, was not saved unto him, but lost to her majesty and him, and found only in the purse of the clerk, attorney, solicitor, or other follower of the suit; and, lastly, that the client, besides the benefit of retaining a good conscience in the passage of this his business, hath also this good assurance, that he is always a gainer, and by no means can be at any loss, as seeing well enough, that if the composition be over-hard and heavy for him, he may then, at his pleasure, relieve himself by recourse to his oath; which also is no more than the ancient law and custom of the realm hath required at his hands. And the selfsame thing is moreover, that I may shortly deliver it by the way, not only a singular comfort to the executioners of this office, a pleasant seasoning of all the sour of their labour and pains, when they shall consider that they cannot be guilty of the doing of any oppression or wrong; but it is also a most necessary instruction and document for them, that even as her majesty hath made them dispensators of this her royal favour towards her people, so it behoveth them to show themselves *peregrinatores*, even and equal distributors of the same; and, as that most honourable lord and reverend sage counsellor, the late Lord Burleigh,* late lord treasurer, said to myself, to deal it out with wisdom and good dexterity towards all the sorts of her loving subjects.

* This passage ascertains the date of this writing.

The part of each officer.

But now that it may yet more particularly appear what is the sum of this new building, and by what joints and sinews the same is raised and knit together, I must let you know, that besides the fermour's deputies, which, at this day, be three in number, and besides the doctor of whom I spake, there is also a receiver, who alone handleth the moneys, and three clerks, that be employed severally, as anon you shall perceive; and by these persons the whole proceeding in this charge is thus performed.

Proceeding upon fines.

If the recognition or acknowledgment of a final concord upon any writ of covenant finable, for so we call that which containeth lands above the yearly value of forty shillings, and all others we term unfinable, be taken by justice of assize, or by the chief justice of the Common Pleas, and the yearly value of those lands be also declared by affidavit made before the same justice; then is the recognition and value, signed with the handwriting of that justice, carried by the cursitor in chancery for that shire where those lands do lie, and by him is a writ of covenant thereupon drawn and ingrossed in parchment; which, having the same value indorsed on the backside thereof, is brought, together with the said paper that doth warrant it, into this office; and there first the doctor, conferring together the paper and writ, indorseth his name upon that writ, close underneath the value thereof; then forasmuch as the valuation thereof is already made, that writ is delivered to the receiver, who taketh the sum of money that is due, after the rate of that yearly value, and indorseth the payment thereof upon the same writ accordingly: this done, the same writ is brought to the second clerk, who entereth it into a several book, kept only for final writs of covenant, together with the yearly value, and the rate of the money paid, with the name of the party that made the affidavit, and of the justice that took it: and at the foot of that writ maketh a secret mark of his said entry: lastly, that writ is delivered to the deputies, who seeing that all the premises be orderly performed, do also indorse their own names upon the same writ for testimony of the money received. Thus passeth it from this office to the *custos brevium*, from him to the queen's silver, then to the chirographer to be ingrossed, and so to be proclaimed in the court. But if no affidavit be already made touching the value, then is the writ of covenant brought first to the deputies ready drawn and ingrossed; and then is the value made either by composition had with them without any oath, or else by oath taken before the doctor; if by composition, then one of the deputies setteth down the yearly value, so agreed upon, at the foot of the backside of the writ; which value the doctor causeth one of the clerks to write on the top of the backside of the writ, as the cursitor did in the former, and after that the doctor indorseth his own name underneath it, and so passeth it through the hands of the receiver, of the clerk that maketh the entry, and of the deputies, as the former writ did. But if the valuation be made by oath taken before the doctor, then causeth he the clerk to indorse that value accordingly, and then also subscribeth he his name as before; and so the writ taketh the same course through the office that the others had.

Proceeding upon writs of entry.

And this is the order for writs of covenant that be finable: the like whereof was at the first observed, in the passing of writs of entry of lands holden in chief; saving that they be entered into another book, especially appointed for them, and for licenses and pardons of alienations; and the like is now severally done with the writs of entry of lands not so holden: which writs of covenant or entry not finable, thus it is done: an affidavit is made either before some such justice, or before the said doctor, that the lands, comprised in the writ, be not worth above forty shillings by the year, to be taken. And albeit now here can be no composition, since the queen is to have no fine at all for unfinable writs, yet doth the doctor indorse his name, and cause the youngest, or third clerk, both to make entry of the writ into a third book, purposely kept for those only writs, and also to indorse it thus, *finis nullus.* That done, it receiveth the names of the deputies, indorsed as before, and so passeth hence to the *custos brevium* as the rest. Upon every doquet for license of alienation, or warrant for pardon of alienation, the party is likewise at liberty either to compound with the deputies, or to make affidavit touching the yearly value; which being known once and set down, the doctor subscribeth his name, the receiver taketh the money after the due rate and proportion; the second clerk entereth the doquet or warrant into the book that is proper for them, and for the writs of entry, with a notice also, whether it passeth by oath or by composition; then do the deputies sign it with their hands, and so it is conveyed to the deputy of Mr. Bacon, clerk of the licenses, whose charge it is to procure the hand of the lord chancellor, and consequently the great seal for every such license or pardon.

Proceeding upon forfeiture of mean profits.

There yet remaineth untouched the order that is for the mean profits; for which also there is an agreement made here when it is discovered that any alienation hath been made of lands holden in chief, without the queen's license; and albeit that in the other cases, one whole year's profit be commonly payable upon such a pardon, yet where the alienation is made by devise in a last will only, the third part of these profits is there demandable, by special provi-
34 H. 8. c. 5. sion thereof made in the statute of 34 H. VIII. c. 5. but yet every way the yearly profits of the lands so aliened without license, and lost even from the time of the writ of *scire facias*, or inquisition thereupon returned into the Exchequer, until the time that the party shall come hither to sue forth his charter of pardon for that offence.

In which part the subject hath in time gained double ease of two weighty burdens, that in former ages did grievously press him; the one before the institution of this office, and the other sithence; for in ancient time, and of right, as it is adjudged 46 E. III. Fitzh. *forfait* 18. the mean profits were precisely answered after the rate and proportion *per diem*, even from the time of the alienation made. . Again, whereas before the receipt of them in this office, they were assessed by the affidavit from the time of the inquisition found, or *scire facias* returned, now not so much at any time as the one half, and many times not the sixth part of them, is exacted. Here, therefore, above the rest, is great necessity to show favour and merciful dealing; because it many times happeneth, that either through the remote dwelling of the party from the lands, or by the negligence or evil practice of under-sheriffs and their bailiffs, the owner hath incurred the forfeiture of eight or ten years whole profits of his lands, before he cometh to the knowledge of the process that runneth against him; other times an alienation made without license is discovered when the present owner of the lands is altogether ignorant that his lands be holded in chief at all: other times also some man concludeth himself to have such a tenure by his own suing forth of a special writ of livery, or by causeless procuring a license, or pardon, for his alienation, when in truth the lands be not either holden at all of her majesty, or not holden in chief, but by a mean tenure in soccage, or by knight's service at the most. In which cases, and the like, if the extremity should be rigorously urged and taken, especially where the years be many, the party should be driven to his utter overthrow, to make half a purchase, or more, of his own proper land and living.

The chief clerk.

About the discovery of the tenure in chief, following of process for such alienation made, as also about the calling upon sheriffs for their accounts, and the bringing in of the parties by seisure of their lands, therefore the first and principal clerk in this office, of whom I had not before any cause to speak, is chiefly and in a manner wholly occupied and set on work. Now if it do at any time happen, as, notwithstanding the best endeavour, it may and doth happen, that the process, howsoever colourably awarded, hath not hit the very mark whereat it was directed, but haply calleth upon some man who is not of right to be charged with the tenure in chief, that is objected against; then is he, upon oath and other good evidence, to receive his discharge under the hands of the deputies, but with a *quousque*, and with *salvo jure dominæ*. Usage and deceivable manner of awarding process cannot be avoided, especially where a man, having in some one place both lands holden in chief, and other lands not so holden, alieneth the laws not holden: seeing that it cannot appear by record nor otherwise, without the

The discharge of him that holdeth not in chief when he is sued erroneously.

express declaration and evidences of the party himself, whether they be the same lands that be holden, or others. And therefore albeit the party grieved thereby may have some reason to complain of an untrue charge, yet may he not well call it an unjust vexation; but ought rather to look upon that ease, which in this kind of proceeding he hath found, where, besides his labour, he is not to expend above two and twenty shillings in the whole charge, in comparison of that toil, cost, and care, which he in the case was wont to sustain by the writ of *certiorari* in the exchequer; wherein, besides all his labour, it did cost him fifty shillings at the least, and sometimes twice so much, before he could find the means to be delivered.

Policy for avoiding corruption.

Thus have I run through the whole order of this practice, in the open time of the term; and that the more particularly and at full, to the end that thereby these things ensuing might the more fully appear, and plainly bewray themselves: first, that this present manner of exercising of this office hath so many testimonies, interchangeable warrants, and counter-rolments, whereof each, running through the hands and resting in the power of so many several persons, is sufficient to argue and convince all manner of falsehood; so as with a general conspiracy of all those offices together, it is almost impossible to contrive any deceit therein: a right ancient, and sound policy, whereupon both the order of the accounts in the exchequer, and of the affairs of her majesty's own household, are so grounded and built, that the infection of an evil mind in some one or twain cannot do any great harm, unless the rest of the company be also poisoned by their contagion. And, surely, as Cicero said, *Nullum est tam desperatum collegium, in quo non unus e multis sit sana mente prædítus.* Secondly, that here is great use both of discretion, learning, and integrity; of discretion, I say, for examining the degrees of favour, which ought to be imparted diversely, and for discerning the valuations of lands, not in one place or shire, but in each county and corner of the realm; and that not of one sort or quality, but of every kind, nature, and degree: for a taste whereof, and to the end that all due quality of rates be not suddenly charged with infidelity, and condemned for corruption; it is note-worthy, that favour is here sometimes right worthily bestowed, not only in a general regard of the person, by which every man ought to have a good pennyworth of his own, but more especially also and with much distinction: for a peer of the realm, a counsellor of state, a judge of the

Inequality of rates justifiable.

The person.

land, an officer that laboureth in furtherance of the tenure, or a poor person, are not, as I think, to be measured by the common yard, but by the pole of special grace and dispensation. Such as served in the wars have been permitted, by many statutes, to alien their lands of this tenure, without suing out of any license. All those of the chancery have claimed and taken the privilege to pass their writs without fine; and yet, therefore, do still look to be easily fined: yea the favourites in court, and as many as serve the queen in ordinary, take it unkindly if they have not more than market measure.

Again, the consideration of the place or county where the lands do lie, may justly cause the rate or valuation to be the more or less; for as the writs too commonly report the land by numbers of acres, and as it is allowable, for the eschewing of some dangers, that those numbers do exceed the very content and true quantity of the lands themselves; so in some counties they are not much acquainted with admeasurement by acre; and thereby, for the most part, the writs of those shires and counties do contain twice or thrice so many acres more than the land hath. In some places the lands do lie open in common fields, and be not so valuable as if they were inclosed; and not only in one and the same shire, but also within the selfsame lordship, parish, or hamlet, lands have their divers degrees of value, through the diversity of their fertility or barrenness: wherein how great odds and variety there is, he shall soonest find, that will examine it by his own skill in whatsoever place that he knoweth best. The place.

Moreover some lands be more chargeable than others are, respecting either the tenure, as knight's service, and the tenure in chief, or in regard of defence against the sea and great rivers; as for their lying near to the borders of the realm, or because of great and continual purveyances that are made upon them, or such like.

And in some counties, as namely, westward, their yearly rents, by which most commonly their value to her majesty is accounted, are not to this day improved at all, the landlords making no less gain by fines and incomes, than there is raised in other places by inhancement of rents.

The manner and sorts of the conveyance of the land itself is likewise variable, and therefore deserveth a diverse consideration and value: for in a pardon one whole year's value, together with the mean rates thereof, is due to be paid; which ought therefore to be more favourably assessed, The manner of that assurance.

than where but a third part of one year's rent, as in a license or writ of entry, or where only a tenth part, as in a writ of covenant, is to be demanded.

A license also and a pardon are to pass the charges of the great seal, to the which the bargain and sale, the fine and recovery are not subject. Sometimes upon one only alienation and change, the purchaser is to pass both license, fine, and recovery, and is for this multiplicity of payments more to be favoured, than he which bringeth but one single pay for all his assurance.

Moreover, it is very often seen that the same land suffereth sundry transmutations of owners within one term, or other small compass of time; by which return much profit cometh to her majesty, though the party feel of some favour in that doing.

The end of conveyances.

Neither is it of small moment in this part, to behold to what end the conveyances of land be delivered; seeing that sometimes it is only to establish the lands in the hands of the owner and his posterity, without any alienation and change of possession to be made: sometimes a fine is levied only to make good a lease for years, or to pass an estate for life, upon which no yearly rent is reserved; or to grant a reversion, or remainder, expectant upon a lease, or estate, that yieldeth no rent. Sometimes the land is given in mortgage only, with full intention to be redeemed within one year, six months, or a lesser time. Many assurances do also pass to godly and charitable uses alone; and it happeneth not seldom, that, to avoid the yearly oath, for averment of the continuance of some estate for life, which is eigne, and not subject to forfeiture, for the alienation that cometh after it, the party will offer to sue a pardon uncompelled before the time; in all which some mitigation of the uttermost value may well and worthily be offered, the rather for that the statute, 1 E. III. c. 12, willeth, that in this service generally a reasonable fine shall be taken.

1 E. 3. c. 12.

Error and mistaking.

Lastly, error, misclaim, and forgetfulness do now and then become suitors for some remission of extreme rigour: for I have sundry times observed, that an assurance, being passed through for a competent fine, hath come back again by reason of some oversight, and the party hath voluntarily repassed it within a while after. Sometimes the attorney, or follower of the cause, unskilfully thrusteth into the writ, both the uttermost quantity, or more, of the land, and the full rent also that is given for it; or else setteth down an entierty, where but a moiety, a third or fourth part only was to be passed; or causeth a bargain and sale to be inrolled, when nothing passed thereby, because a fine had transferred the land before; or else inrolleth it within the six months; whereas, before the end of those months, the land was brought home to the first owner, by repayment of the money for which it was engaged. In which and many other like cases, the client will rather choose to give a moderate fine for the alienation so recharged, than to undertake a costly plea in the exchequer, for reformation of that which was done amiss. I take it for a venial fault also to vouchsafe a pardon, after the rate and proportion of a license, to him that without fraud or evil mind hath slipped a term or two months, by forgetting to purchase his license.

Much more could I say concerning this unblamable inequality of fines and rates: but as I meant only to give an essay thereof, so not doubting but that this may stand, both for the satisfaction of such as be indifferent, and for the discharge of us that be put in trust with the service, wherein no doubt a good discretion and dexterity ought to be used, I resort to the place where I left, affirming that there is in this employment of ours great use of good learning also, as well to distinguish the manifold sorts of tenures and estates; to make construction of grants, conveyances, and wills, and to sound the validity of inquisitions, liveries, licenses, and pardons; as also to decipher the manifold slights and subtleties that are daily offered to defraud her majesty in this her most ancient and due prerogative, and finally to handle many other matters, which this purpose will not permit me to recount at large.

Lastly, here is need, as I said, of integrity throughout the whole labour and practice, as without the which both the former learning and discretion are no better than *armata nequitia,* and nothing else but detestable craft and double villany.

And now as you have seen that these clerks want not their full task of labour during the time of the open term, so is there for them whereupon to be occupied in the vacation also.

For whereas alienations of lands, holden by the tenure of prerogative, be continually made, and that by many and divers ways, whereof all are not, at the first, to be found of record; and yet for the most part do come to be recorded in the end: the clerks of this office do, in the time of the vacation, repair to the rolls and records, as well of the Chancery and King's Bench, as of the Common Pleas and

Exchequer, whence they extract notes not only of inquisitions, common recoveries, and indentures of bargains and sales, that cannot but be of record, but also of such feoffments, exchanges, gifts by will, and indentures of covenants to raise uses of lands holden in chief, as are first made in the country without matter of record, and come at the length to be found by office or inquisition, that is of record; all which are digested into apt books, and are then sent to the remembrancer of the lord treasurer in the Exchequer, to the end that he may make and send out processes upon them, as he doth upon the extracts of the final concords of such lands, which the clerk of the fines doth convey unto him.

Thus it is plain, that this new order by many degrees excelleth the former usage; as also for the present advancement of her majesty's commodity, and for the future profit which must ensue by such discovery of tenures as were concealed before, by awaking of such as had taken a long sleep, and by reviving a great many that were more than half dead.

The fees or allowances, that are termly given to these deputies, receiver, and clerks, for recompense of these their pains, I do purposely pretermit; because they be not certain, but arbitrary, at the good pleasure of those honourable persons that have the dispensation of the same: howbeit hitherto each deputy and the receiver hath received twenty pounds for his travel in each term, only the doctor hath not allowance of any sum in gross, but is altogether paid in petty fees, by the party or suitor; and the clerks are partly rewarded by that mean also, for their entries, discharges, and some other writings, besides that termly fee which they are allowed.

Note. But if the deputies take one penny besides their known allowance, they buy it at the dearest price that may be; I mean the shipwreck of conscience, and with the irrecoverable loss of their honesty and credit; and, therefore, since it appeareth which way each of these hath his reward, let us also examine that increase of benefit and gain, which is brought to her majesty by the invention of this office.

At the end of Hilary term, 1589, being the last open term of the lease of these profits granted to the late Earl of Leicester, which also was to expire at the feast of the Annunciation of the blessed Virgin Mary, 1590, then shortly to ensue; the officers above remembered thought it, for good causes, their duties to exhibit to the said right honourable the lord treasurer a special declaration of the yearly profits of these finances, paid into the hanaper during every of the six years before the beginning of the demise thereof made to that earl, conferred with the profits thereof that had been yearly taken during the last six years before the determination of the lease. By which it plainly appeared, that in all those first six years, next before the demise, there had been raised only 12,798*l.* 15*s.* 7*d.* ob. and in these last six years of the demise the full sum of 32,160*l.* 4*s.* 10*d.* qu. and so in all 19,362*l.* 2*s.* 2*d.* ob. qu. more in these last, than in those former six years. But because it may be said, that all this increase redounded to the gain of the fermor only, I must add, that during all the time of the demise, he answered 300*l.* rent, of yearly increase, above all that profit of 2,133*l.* 2*s.* 7*d.* qu. which had been yearly and casually made in the sixteen years one with another next before: the which, in the time of fourteen years, for so long these profits have been demised by three several leases, did bring 4,200*l.* to her majesty's coffers. I say yearly; which may seem strange, that a casual and thereby uncertain profit should yearly be all one; but indeed such was the wonderous handling thereof, that the profit was yearly neither more nor less to her majesty, howsoever it might casually be more or less to him that did receive it. For the writs of covenant answered year by year 1,152*l.* 16*s.* 8*d.* the licenses and pardons 934*l.* 3*s.* 11*d.* qu. and the mean rates 46*l.* 2*s.* in all 2,133*l.* 2*s.* 7*d,* qu. without increase or diminution.

Moreover, whereas her majesty did, after the death of the earl, buy of the countess, being his executrix, the remanent of the last term of three years in those profits, whereof there were only then six terms, that is, about one year and a half, to come, paying for it the sum of 3,000*l.* her majesty did clearly gain by that bargain the sum of 1,173*l.* 15*s.* 8*d.* ob. above the said 3,000*l.* above the rent of 3,649*l.* 13*s.* 10*d.* ob. qu. proportionably due for that time, and above all fees and other reprises. Neither hath the benefit of this increase to her majesty been contained within the bounds of this small office, but hath swelled over the banks thereof, and displayed itself apparently, as well in the hanaper, by the fees of the great seal, which yielding 20*s.* 4*d.* towards her majesty for every license and pardon, was estimated to advantage her bigness during those fourteen years, the sum of 3,721*l.* 6*s.* ob. qu. more than without that demise she was like to have found. As also in the court of wards and liveries, and in the Exchequer itself:

where, by reason of the tenures in chief revived through the only labours of these officers, both the sums for respect of homage be increased, and the profits of wardships, primer seisins, ouster le maine, and liveries, cannot but be much advanced. And so her majesty's self hath, in this particular, gained the full sum of 8,736*l.* 5*s.* 5*d.* ob. qu. not comprising those profits in the Exchequer and court of wards, the very certainty whereof lieth not in the knowledge of these officers, nor accounting any part of that great benefit which the earl and his executrix have made by the demises: which one year with another, during all the thirteen years and a half, I suppose to have been 2,263*l.* or thereabouts; and so in all about 27,158*l.* above all his costs and expenses. The which albeit I do here report only for the justification of the service in this place; yet who cannot but see withal, how much the royal revenues might be advanced, if but the like good endeavours were showed for her majesty in the rest of her finances, as have been found in this office for the commodity of this one subject?

The views of all which matter being presented to the most wise and princely consideration of her majesty, she was pleased to demise these profits and fines for other five years, to begin at the feast of the Annunciation, 1590, in the thirty-second year of her reign, for the yearly rent formerly reserved upon the leases of the earl; within the compass of which five years, expired at the Annunciation, 1595, there was advanced to her majesty's benefit, by this service, the whole sum of 13,013*l.* 14*s.* 1*d.* qu. beyond the ancient yearly revenues, which, before any lease, were usually made of these finances. To which, if there be added 5,700*l.* for the gain given to her majesty by the yearly receipt of 300*l.* in rent, from the first demise to the earl, until the time of his death, together with the sum of 1,173*l.* 15*s.* 8*d.* ob. clearly won in those six terms bought of the countess; then the whole commodity, from the first institution of this office, till the end of these last five years expired at the Annunciation, 1595, shall appear to be 19,887*l.* 9*s.* 9*d.* ob. qu. To the which sum also if 28,550*l.* 15*s.* 6*d.* ob. qu. which the earl and the countess levied hereby, be likewise adjoined, then the whole profit taken in these nineteen years, that is, from the first lease, to the end of the last, for her majesty, the earl, and the countess, will amount unto 48,438*l.* 5*s.* 4*d.* This labour hitherto thus luckily succeeding, the deputies in this office finding by daily proof, that it was wearisome to the subject to travel to divers places, and through sundry hands, for the pursuing of common recoveries, either not holden of her majesty at all, or but partly holden in chief; and not doubting to improve her majesty's revenue therein, and that without loss to any, either private person or public officer, if the same might be managed by them jointly with the rest whereof they had the charge; they found, by search in the hanaper, that the fruits of those writs of entry had not, one year with another, in the ten years next before, exceeded 400*l.* by the year. Whereupon they took hold of the occasion then present, for the renewing of the lease of the former profits; and moved the lord treasurer, and Sir John Fortescue, under treasurer and chancellor of the Exchequer, to join the same in one and the same demise, and to yield unto her majesty 500*l.* by year therefore; which is 100*l.* yearly of increase. The which desire being by them recommended to her majesty, it liked her forthwith to include the same, and all the former demised profits, within one intire lease, for seven years, to begin at the said feast of the Annunciation, 1597, under the yearly rent of 2,933*l.* 2*s.* 7*d.* qu. Since which time hitherto, I mean to the end of Michaelmas term, 1598, not only the proportion of the said increased 100*l.* but almost of one other 100*l.* also, hath been answered to her majesty's coffers, for those recoveries so drawn into the demise now continuing.

Thus I have opened both the first plotting, the especial practice, and the consequent profit arising by these officers; and now if I should be demanded, whether this increase of profit were likely to stand without fall, or to be yet amended or made more? I would answer, that if some few things were provided, and some others prevented, it is probable enough in mine own opinion, that the profit should rather receive accession than decay.

The things that I wish to be provided are these: first, that by the diligence of these officers, assisted with such other as can bring good help thereunto, a general and careful collection be made of all the tenures in chief; and that the same be digested by way of alphabet into apt volumes, for every part, or shire, of the realm. Then that every office, or inquisition, that findeth any tenure in chief, shall express the true quantities of the lands so holden, even as in ancient time it was wont to be done by way of admeasurement, after the manner of a perfect extent or survey; whereby all the parts of the tenancy in chief may be wholly brought to light, howsoever in process of time it hath been, or shall be torn and dismembered. For prevention, I wish likewise, first, that some good means were devised for the restraint of making these inordinate and covenous leases of lands, holden in chief, for hundreds or thousands of years, now grown so bold, that they dare show themselves in fines, levied upon the open stage of the Common Pleas; by which one man taketh the full profit, and another beareth the empty name of tenancy, to the infinite deceit of her majesty in this part of her prerogative. Then, that no alienation of lands holden in chief should be available, touching the freehold or inheritance thereof, but only where it were made by matter of record, to be found in some of her majesty's treasuries; and, lastly, that a continual and watchful eye be had, as well upon these new founden traverses of tenure, which are not now tried *per patriam*, as the old manner was; as also upon all such pleas whereunto the confession of her majesty's said attorney general is expected: so as the tenure of the prerogative be not prejudiced, either by the fraud of counsellors at the law, many of which do bend their wits to the overthrow thereof; or by the greediness of clerks and attorneys, that, to serve their own gain, do both impair the tenure, and therewithal grow more heavy to the client, in so costly pleading for discharge, than the very confession of the matter itself would prove unto him. I may yet hereunto add another thing, very meet not only to be prevented with all speed, but also to be punished with great severity: I mean that collusion set on foot lately, between some of her majesty's tenants in chief, and certain others that have had to do in her highness's grants of concealed lands: where, under a feigned concealment of the land itself, nothing else is sought but only to make a change of the tenure, which is reserved upon the grant of those concealments, into that tenure in chief: in which practice there is no less abuse of her majesty's great bounty, than loss and hinderance of her royal right. These things thus settled, the tenure in chief should be kept alive and nourished; the which, as it is the very root that doth maintain this silver stem, that by many rich and fruitful branches spreadeth itself into the Chancery, Exchequer, and court of wards; so, if it be suffered to starve, by want of ablaqueation, and other good husbandry, not only this yearly fruit will much decrease from time to time, but also the whole body and boughs of that precious tree itself will fall into danger of decay and dying.

And now, to conclude therewith, I cannot see how it may

justly be misliked, that her majesty should, in a reasonable and moderate manner, demand and take this sort of finance; which is not newly out and imposed, but is given and grown up with the first law itself, and which is evermore accompanied with some special benefit to the giver of the same: seeing that lightly no alienation is made, but either upon recompense in money, or land, or for marriage, or other good and profitable consideration that doth move it: yea rather all good subjects and citizens ought not only to yield that gladly of themselves, but also to further it with other men; as knowing that the better this and such like ancient and settled revenues shall be answered and paid, the less need her majesty shall have to ask subsidies, fifteens, loans, and whatsoever extraordinary helps, that otherwise must of necessity be levied upon them. And for proof that it shall be more profitable to her majesty, to have every of the same to be managed by men of fidelity, that shall be waged by her own pay, than either to be letten out to the fermours benefits, or to be left at large to the booty and spoil of ravenous ministers, that have not their reward; let the experiment and success be in this one office, and persuade for all the rest.

Laus Deo.

DRAUGHT OF AN ACT

AGAINST A USURIOUS SHIFT OF GAIN, IN DELIVERING COMMODITIES INSTEAD OF MONEY.

Whereas it is a usual practice, to the undoing and overthrowing many young gentlemen and others, that when men are in necessity, and desire to borrow money, they are answered, that money cannot be had, but that they may have commodities sold unto them upon credit, whereof they may make money as they can: in which course it ever comes to pass, not only that such commodities are bought at extreme high rates, and sold again far under foot to a double loss;

but also that the party which is to borrow is wrapt in bonds and counter-bonds; so that upon a little money which he receiveth, he is subject to penalties and suits of great value.

Be it therefore enacted, by the authority of this present parliament, that if any man, after forty days from the end of this present session of parliament to be accounted, shall sell in gross sale any quantity of wares or commodities unto such a one as is no retailer, chapman, or known broker of the same commodities, and knowing that it is bought to be sold again, to help and furnish any person, that tradeth not in the same commodity, with money, he shall be without all remedy by law, or custom, or decree, or otherwise, to recover or demand any satisfaction for the said wares or commodities, what assurance soever he shall have by bond, surety, pawn, or promise of the party, or any other in his behalf. And that all bonds and assurances whatsoever, made for that purpose directly or indirectly, shall be utterly void.

And be it further enacted, by the authority aforesaid, that every person, which shall after the time aforesaid be used or employed as a broker, mean, or procurer, for the taking up of such commodities, shall forfeit for every such offence the sum of one hundred pounds, the same to be and shall be farther punished by six months imprisonment, without bail or mainprise, and by the pillory.

A PROPOSITION FOR THE REPRESSING OF SINGULAR COMBATS OR DUELS, IN THE HAND-WRITING OF SIR FRANCIS BACON.*

FIRST, for the ordinance which his majesty may establish herein, I wish it may not look back to any offence pas , for that strikes before it warns. I wish also it may be declared to be temporary, until a parliament; for that will be very acceptable to the parliament; and it is good to teach a parliament to work upon an edict or proclamation precedent.

For the manner, I should think fit there be published a grave and severe proclamation, induced by the overflow of the present mischief.

For the ordinance itself: first, I consider that offence hath vogue only amongst noble persons, or persons of quality. I consider also that the greatest honour for subjects of quality in a lawful monarchy, is to have access and approach to their sovereign's sight and person, which is the fountain of

* On occasion of this letter, in which is mentioned Sir Francis Bacon's speech against duels, it may not be improper to insert here this curious paper from Sir David Dalrymple's Memorials and Letters, p. 51.

honour: and though this be a comfort all persons of quality do not use; yet there is no good spirit but will think himself in darkness, if he be debarred of it. Therefore I do propound, that the principal part of the punishment be, that the offender, in the cases hereafter set down, be banished perpetually from approach to the courts of the king, queen, or prince.

Secondly, That the same offender receive a strict prosecution by the king's attorney, *ore tenus*, in the Star-chamber; for the fact being notorious, will always be confessed, and so made fit for an *ore tenus*. And that this prosecution be without respect of persons, be the offender never so great; and that the fine set be irremissible.

Lastly, For the causes, that they be these following:

1. Where any singular combat, upon what quarrel soever, is acted and performed, though death do not ensue.
2. Where any person passeth beyond the seas, with purpose to perform any singular combat, though it be never acted.
3. Where any person sendeth a challenge.
4. Where any person accepteth a challenge.
5. Where any person carrieth or delivereth a challenge.
6. Where any person appointeth the field, directly or indirectly, although it be not upon any cartel or challenge in writing.
7. Where any person accepteth to be a second in any quarrel.

ADVICE TO THE KING FOR REVIVING THE COMMISSION OF SUITS.

THAT which for the present I would have spoken with his majesty about, was a matter wherein time may be precious, being upon the tenderest point of all others. For though the particular occasion may be despised (and yet nothing ought to be despised in this kind), yet the counsel thereupon I conceive to be most sound and necessary, to avoid future perils.

There is an examination taken within these few days by Mr. Attorney, concerning one Bayntan, or Baynham (for his name is not yet certain), attested by two witnesses, that the said Bayntan, without any apparent show of being overcome with drink, otherwise than so as might make him less wary to keep secrets, said that he had been lately with the king, to petition him for reward of service; which was denied him. Whereupon it was twice in his mind to have killed his majesty. The man is not yet apprehended, and said by some to be mad, or half mad; which, in my opinion, is not the less dangerous; for such men commonly do most mischief; and the manner of his speaking imported no distraction. But the counsel I would out of my care ground hereupon, is, that his majesty would revive the commission for suits, which hath been now for these three years or more laid down. For it may prevent any the like wicked cogitations, which the devil may put into the mind of a roarer or swaggerer upon a denial: and, besides, it will free his majesty from much importunity, and save his coffers also. For I am sure when I was a commissioner, in three whole years space there passed scarce ten suits that were allowed. And I doubt now, upon his majesty's coming home from this journey, he will be much troubled with petitions and suits, which maketh me think this remedy more seasonable. It is not meant, that suits generally should pass that way, but only such suits as his majesty would be rid on.

Indorsed—*September* 21, 1617—*To revive the commission of suits. For the King.*

REASONS WHY THE NEW COMPANY IS NOT TO BE TRUSTED AND CONTINUED WITH THE TRADE OF CLOTHES.

FIRST, The company consists of a number of young men and shopkeepers, which not being bred in the trade, are fearful to meddle with any of the dear and fine clothes, but only meddle with the coarse clothes, which is every man's skill; and, besides, having other trades to live upon, they come in the sunshine so long as things go well, and as soon as they meet with any storm or cloud, they leave trade, and go back to shopkeeping. Whereas the old company were beaten traders, and having no other means of living but that trade, were fain to ride out all accidents and difficulties (which being men of great ability), they were well able to do.

Secondly, These young men being the major part, and having a kind of dependance upon Alderman Cockaine, they carry things by plurality of voices. And yet those few of the old company which are amongst them do drive almost three parts of the trade; and it is impossible things should go well, where one part gives the vote, and the other doth the work; so that the execution of all things lies chiefly upon them that never consented, which is merely *motus violentus,* and cannot last.

Thirdly, The new company make continually such new springing demands, as the state can never be secure nor trust to them, neither doth it seem that they do much trust themselves.

Fourthly, The present stand of cloth at Blackwell-hall (which is that that presseth the state most, and is provided for but a temporary and weak remedy) is supposed would be presently at an end, upon the revivor of the old; in respect that they are able men and united amongst themselves.

Fifthly, In these cases, *opinio est veritate major,* and the very voice and expectation of revivor of the old company will comfort the clothiers, and encourage them not to lay down their looms.

Sixthly, the very Flemings themselves (in regard of the pique they have against the new company) are like to be more pliant and tractable towards his majesty's ends and desires.

Seventhly, Considering the business hath not gone on well; his majesty must either lay the fault upon the matter itself, or upon the persons that have managed it; wherein the king shall best acquit his honour, to lay it where it is indeed; that is, upon the carriage and proceedings of the new company, which have been full of uncertainty and abuse.

- Lastly, The subjects of this kingdom generally have an ill taste and conceit of the new company, and therefore the putting of them down will discharge the state of a great deal of envy.

INDEX TO THE ENGLISH WORKS.

h

INDEX TO THE LATIN WORKS.

END OF THE THIRTEENTH VOLUME.

C. Whittingham, Tooks Court, Chancery Lane.